The Log of the "Cutty Sark"

"CUTTY SARK" in Sydney Harbour.   Awaiting the wool clip

THE LOG OF
THE "CUTTY SARK"

BY

BASIL LUBBOCK

WITH ILLUSTRATIONS AND PLANS

GLASGOW
BROWN, SON & FERGUSON, Ltd., NAUTICAL PUBLISHERS
4-10 DARNLEY STREET

First Edition   1924
Reprinted - 1974
Reprinted - 1994

ISBN 0 85174 115 0

©1994—BROWN, SON & FERGUSON, LTD., GLASGOW, G41 2SD
Printed and Made in Great Britain

Dedication

Dedicated to all who served aboard the "Cutty Sark."

PREFACE

NEXT to the *Victory* the most interesting survivor of the days of sail is undoubtedly the famous tea and wool clipper, *Cutty Sark*.

She represents the last word in composite clipper ship designing, being launched at a time when the iron sailing ship was just beginning to supplant the wood and composite. Thus her design is of special interest to all who would follow the gradual development of ship architecture from wood to composite, composite to iron and iron to steel.

For the material of this book I am indebted not only to those who served on the *Cutty Sark*, but to many other seafarers, who had first hand aquaintance with her rivals in the tea and wool trade.

I have been fortunate in being able to obtain most of her abstract logs and also a great many of those belonging to her rivals.

I have had to compress a great deal of material into a very small space, and this must be my excuse for the number of passage tables, which were necessary in order that a complete record might be preserved.

Many of the photographs reproduced in this book were taken by Captain Woodget, the *Cutty Sark's* best known and most successful commander.

Others are of special value, as being the only known portraits of the ships they represent. I have been specially lucky in being able to find two photographs of *Thermopylae* after years of search; whilst that of *Taeping*, lying at the Pagoda Anchorage in the Min River, is surely unique, being at least 50 years old.

For the beautiful drawings of *Cutty Sark's* lines I am indebted to Mr. Charles H. Jordan, M.I.N.A., late Lloyd's surveyor and the author of that well-known standard work, *Jordan's Tabulated Weights of Iron and Steel.*

In this book I have given further details about the tea and wool races, for which room could not be found in my *China Clippers* and *Colonial Clippers*. It therefore forms a sequel to those two books.

The lives of some ships are as humdrum as those of some men, but certain vessels have adventures which are more romantic and exciting than any invented by the sea novelist, and of these the *Cutty Sark* is assuredly a most conspicuous example.

CONTENTS

ILLUSTRATIONS

PLANS

THE LOG OF THE "CUTTY SARK."

CHAPTER I.

"WEEL DONE, CUTTY SARK!"

HISTORY, for the most part, consists of deeds either fair or foul, glorious or despicable, which have certain names for their centre of energy, just as the sun is the centre of energy in the Solar System. Without these names the most important events would lack colour, would lose focus; and the history of this planet would be reduced to a string of dates, a catalogue of emotions and a column of statistics.

All action, indeed, pivots round a name. Sometimes it is the name of a man or a woman, of a warrior or a queen, a traitor or a country maid; and at once we are intrigued.

But the human element is far from being all sufficing, the names of ancient towns, of hard-fought battles, of besieged castles, of lonely islands, rushing rivers, sentinel capes and mountain peaks all bring a gush of memory and, often, a quicker beat to the heart. And beyond all these in their effect upon our pulses are the romantic names of ships, which stand out like jewels on the most glorious pages of our Empire's history.

As one turns over a British history book, one's eye is caught by certain words, which are usually printed in italics or between inverted commas. These words, whether picturesque, romantic or commonplace, at once focus our attention; they are the names of ships, usually of fighting ships, but sometimes of those which were manned by the merchant adventurers, the lion-hearted circum-navigators or the ever-enduring Arctic explorers: and, as we spell them out, the subject matter becomes, as it were, vitalized, **our** blood quickens and our imagination takes fire. Eagerly we picture Britain's battle-line at handgrips with the foe, the blood-red flags of "close action" streaming out above the smoke of the double-shotted broadsides; or we watch the lone adventurer pitching into the sixty-foot greybeards, as he lies a-trie in a Cape Horn snorter; or we listen for the scrunch as the searcher for the North-West Passage breasts his way through the grim fields of pack ice.

For all Britishers the story of the sea begins in the age of good Queen Bess. How nobly these Elizabethans rose to their great occasions! The very names of their ships spell out the great adventure of the Spanish Main and the glorious victory of the Armada. What could be more inspiriting to a crew than to fare forth in a *Dreadnought* or a *Warspite* in order to singe the King of Spain's beard? What name could nerve one's sword-arm better than *Victory* or *Defiance*, *Repulse* or *Swiftsure*?*

What more fitting for the keel of a punctilious, gentlemanly pirate than *Bonaventure* or *The Goulden Vanitee*? And what more suitable for the great ship with its wealth of gilded carving, its crimson cloths and flying pendants than *Ark Royal* or *Harry-Grace-a-Dieu*, *Sovereign of the Seas* or *Nonpareil*?

In the naming of their fast "frigots", the Tudors and the Stuarts turned to the beasts and birds of prey, such as *Lion's Whelp*, *Leopard*, *Wolf*, *Gyrfalcon* and *Eagle*.

No age used the English language with more imagery than Shakespeare's, and thus we find this naming of ships carried to almost fantastic lengths. Fancy hailing a ship which rejoiced in such a name as *Katherin Pleasaunce*, or *Cloud in the Sun*, or *Falcon in the Fetterlock*. No doubt the mariners of the *Happy Entrance* were jovial souls, far different from the hard-bitten rogues aboard the *Scourge of Malice* or the dressed-up gallants aboard the *Popinjay*.

Yet this imagery, this riot in nomenclature, if I may so call it, has only just been extinguished along with masts and yards, sails and figure-heads; for during the height of the clipper ship era it was never more rampant; witness the names of some of the British tea clippers: *Lord of the Isles*, *Crest of the Wave*, *Spirit of the Age*,

---

* The *Repulse* was originally the *Dieu Repulse*, whilst the old spelling of *Swiftsure* was "Swift-suer," meaning "Swift-pursuer."

Fiery Cross, Flying Spur, Belted Will, Forward-Ho, and *Coral Nymph.**

Then there were the Yankee clippers:—*Flying Cloud, Glory of the Seas, Herald of the Morning, Eagle Wing, Neptune's Car, Westward-Ho, Winged Racer, Seaman's Bride* and *Dashing Wave.*

Also the Australian emigrant ships:—*Red Jacket, Champion of the Seas, Queen of the Colonies, Chariot of Fame, Fiery Star* and *Dawn of Hope*—to mention but a few out of dozens of romantic names.

Old John Willis, however, beat the most original of the Elizabethans and the most inventive of the Yankees when he took the *Cutty Sark* or short chemise of Burns's witch, Nannie, and carved it on the name-boards of his new tea clipper.

One would have thought that such a name would have covered the new ship with ridicule; that the crews of neighbouring vessels would have shouted taunts across the water anent "her cutty sark o' Paisley harn"; and that in every saloon the *Cutty Sark's* crowd would have been met by a quotation from "Tam o' Shanter", and more especially with the last four lines:—

> When'er to drink you are inclined,
> Or Cutty Sarks run in your mind,
> Think, you may buy the joys ower dear,
> Remember Tam o' Shanter's mare.

The Portuguese, indeed, when they bought the famous little clipper, took care to rename her *Ferreira*, though they always spoke of her as the *Pequina Camisola.*

But of those old seamen who knew the *Cutty Sark* in her prime, there was, perhaps, but one in a hundred who, if asked the meaning of her name, could give it. The usual answer of one of these old timers would probably run on these lines:—"*Cutty Sark?* Oh, ay, I mind her; a beggar to go, she were! strewth! how she could sail! Name? what j'ou mean? why 'Cutty Sark', that's all. I never heard tell of it meaning anything—just the *Cutty Sark.* What

---

* The *Coral Nymph* was a very fast Sunderland-built ship, launched in 1864. She made a very fine passage out to Hong Kong on her maiden voyage, beating the *Whiteadder* by 13 days; she came up with the *Taeping* off the cape, and ran her out of sight in 6 hours. Unfortunately she was lost on her homeward passage, or she would have made a great name in the China trade.

else would you be callin' her but her own name, wot is known from Shanghai to the London River, from Sydney to the East India Docks"?

This would be the reply, in spite of the fact that the *Cutty Sark* carried a gilded shirt on her maintruck, that the story of Tam o' Shanter was most skilfully carved upon her bow and counter and Nannie, with flying locks and scanty chemise, formed a most artistic and beautiful figure-head. A ship, however, has to make her name. It will not give her fame or even good repute unless deserved. A name, be it ever so romantic, ever so original, ever so catching to the eye, will soon be forgotten—or worse, remembered with curses, unless it be worthily carried. The *Cutty Sark* has made her name so well known throughout the seven seas, that it is more than probable that most Britishers, at its mention, will remember the ship before the classic poem.

This is a world where man is not always fair in his judgment of his fellows; but, where ships are concerned, the sailor man is rarely at fault in his criticisms. No true tarpaulin has ever libelled a ship. Thus it is that when you hear a ship spoken of you can always take the character given as correct, except in one respect— that vexed one of speed, for though the men of the sea have the most acute memories regarding their ships, in the matter of speed they are as prone to exaggeration as a fisherman when giving the weight of his fish.

This is because speed has become the most prized of all sea-going qualities; as long as a ship had speed in the clipper ship era it did not much matter whether she worked easily or required an extra hand on every rope; whether she was handy in a seaway or as uncertain and contrary as a buck jumper; whether she was dry as a bone or wet as a half-tide rock, or whether she would run within half a point with a boy steering or needed a lee-wheel as soon as the royals came in.

Speed has not always been one of the most important factors in life. Not much more than a hundred years ago, the greater number of the world's inhabitants were as indifferent in the matter of time and its wastage as the present day Indian coolie. But the struggle for life in the more developed parts of our planet gradually set more and more weight upon the shoulders of Father Time, and it was slowly realised that the only way to lessen the burden on those shoulders was to speed up the leisurely way in which most people went about their business.

In those early days the desire for speed of transit centred itself upon that universal carrier, the horse. And because there was money in it, the brainiest of that brainy tribe, the horsey world set about improving the breed, a move which our sporting noblemen still further encouraged by wagering vast sums upon their Arabians and Barbs.

There were four methods of making a journey by land at this date (I am referring to the early eighteenth century). These were —Shank's mare, the country ox-wagon, the riding horse and the stage-coach. For a time the badness of the roads delayed any improvements in land travel, but as soon as this was rectified the proprietors of the stage-coaches began to develop pace in their teams and to shorten the times of their stages, until, at the heyday of the coaching age, galloping stages were advertised upon most routes. Then came the railways, against which the lovers of the stage-coach fought every bit as strenuously as the sailing ship owners did against the paddle-wheel and screw.

The records of the galloping stages were broken every day. About the fastest 4-mile stage ever covered behind four horses was, I believe, that between Wincanton and Last Gate, which was once driven by an amateur coachman in 15 minutes, a rate of 20 miles an hour. One of the fastest drivers was that celebrated Duke of Beaufort, whose coach was called the "Quicksilver." On this vehicle was painted the motto:—

Nemo me impune lacessit.

which the Duke translated as:—

Nobody ever gives me the go-by.

Such a coachman was on a par with the captain who padlocked his sheets.

The ballads of "the road" were in their day as widely sung and well known as the sea songs and chanties during the age of sail.

> Here's to the arm that holds them when gone
>   Still to a gallop inclined, sir,
> Heads to the front with no bearing reins on,
>   Tails with no cruppers behind, sir,

And here is a contemptuous allusion to steam, which would have pleased the sailor's heart.

> Let the steam-pot
> Hiss till it's hot,
> Give me the speed
> Of the Tantivy trot.

In less than a hundred years the necessity for quicker transit on land has increased the stamina and speed of the horse to such a pitch that our grandfathers and great-grandfathers would have been thunderstruck could they have seen the present-day thoroughbred.

Speed on land was sought after some fifty years before it was thought of much importance at sea. Even the slavers were slow to perceive the need of getting their perishable cargoes of black ivory from the steamy West African rivers to the sugar plantations of the Indies with as little loss of time as possible.

It was the British frigate which made the slaver hurry up and gave cause for the Baltimore clipper. During the eighteenth and first quarter of the nineteenth century, the man of affairs, before making a voyage, which nowadays would be accomplished in three weeks or less, calmly made his will, bought his cabin furniture and prepared for six months of sunshine and storm, of peril and boredom, and of complete divorcement, not only from his business and his pleasures, but from all he held dear in the world. But scarcely was Napoleon safely shut up in St. Helena before the Admiralty began to concern themselves about ship designing from a speed point of view, the result being the experimental squadron and the Symondites.

About the same date the tall clipper ships of America with their beautifully cut cotton sails and streamline hulls began to force themselves more and more into the great trades of the world. And it was their successful venture into the Chinese tea trade which led to the building of the first British ship, designed purely for speed, the Aberdeen clipper.

Yet so quick is man to improve whatever he takes in hand, that barely twenty years after the launch of the first Aberdeen clipper, the fastest ship that ever left the ways took to water, namely the *Cutty Sark*. She was the supreme development of the sailing merchantman, whose chief object was speed. She was the final effort of the builder of composite ships, before he had to bow his head to iron plates on the one hand and the thrash of the screw on the other.

After what I have said about the manner in which seamen glorify the speed of their ships, my readers would no doubt like me to show good reason for such a statement as "the fastest ship that ever left the ways." I can but give the evidence of the men who knew and sailed her, supplement it with her records, and allow the reader to judge for himself.

The following letter from an old seaman should be sufficiently conclusive, when we note that he served not only on *Cutty Sark's* chief rivals in the tea trade, but upon the *James Baines* and *Lightning*, Black Ballers celebrated for the largest days' runs ever recorded, and also on what was probably the fastest four-mast barque ever launched, the *Loch Torridon*.

He writes:—"I served on board the *Thermopylae* on her maiden voyage, 1868-9, when she made the quickest passage ever made between London and Melbourne, 60 days from pilot to pilot, and 61 port to port.

"I also served on board the *Ariel, Cutty Sark, James Baines, Lightning, Serica, Taeping* and *Loch Torridon* and haven't the slightest hesitation in saying that the *Cutty Sark* was the swiftest of the lot. No vessel, either steamer or sail, ever passed us all the time I was on her. Having come in contact with a good few, who, like myself, have sailed on what were considered the crack clippers, both in the Australian and Chinese trade, I never knew one who for a moment ever had the least doubt but that the *Cutty Sark* was the swiftest ship built or likely to be built."

Here is another from a seaman, who now commands a large steamship.—

"During the voyage she never lost steerage way, as the flap of her sails put her through the water. Taking her all round she was a marvel, either on or off the wind and a credit to her builders. During the whole time I never saw anything pass her, steam or sail."

Another master mariner, who served his apprenticeship in the *Cutty Sark*, in the middle eighties, when she was commanded by Captain Woodget, wrote of her as follows:—

"It was thrilling on the old 'Cutty' at the wheel with the wind on the quarter, the fore and mizen upper topsails off and mainsail stowed—the ship, as steady as a rock, cutting her 15 to 16 knots out with a furious sea running. I really believe there was not a ship that could come within 'cooey' of her in a heavy quartering wind and sea. She sailed like the witch that she really was then."

Her first master, Captain Moodie, gave her the following testimonial:—

"I never sailed a finer ship. At 10 or 12 knots an hour she did not disturb the water at all. She was the fastest ship of her day, a grand ship, and a ship that will last for ever."

When the "Cutty" was going close-hauled through the trades, the second of the two Moores, who commanded her, used to call his apprentices up and tell them impressively that they would never see another ship showing anything near her speed under such conditions.

Captain Woodget himself, the most famous of all her commanders, wrote the following letter to the *Australian Star* in 1893, on his arrival in Sydney, after beating the *Cromdale* and two of the Loch liners by six weeks from the Channel:—

"Captains do not like to admit that the *Cutty Sark* can sail, and yet not one of them can show that she has ever been beaten by any sailing vessel that has left London or Sydney about the same time. I have been in company and sailed with some of the fastest vessels that trade here (Sydney) and Melbourne; viz., *Samuel Plimsoll, Aristides, Salamis, Thermopylae, Cimba, Rodney, Patriarch* and the *West Lothian*, and have always managed to reach port before them by some days."

Mr. W. G. Deuchar, the well-known Sydney agent, in writing some reminiscences of the wool clippers with which he had to deal, remarks,—

"*Cutty Sark* was absolutely the fastest ship I have ever had to do with in my 35 or 40 years' experience."

Let us now see what her captains and officers have to say about her actual speed through the water, as recorded by sights and log.

Some years ago Captain Moodie, who commanded her for the first three years of her existence, wrote to me:—

"I have measured the *Cutty Sark*, both by patent log and common log, going 17 and 17½ knots an hour; but the highest distance for the 24 hours on several occasions was 363 knots."

The following letter from another master mariner refers to her passage out to Sydney in 1875-6, when on her seventh voyage:—

"Running the easting down *Cutty Sark* did 2163 miles in six days, an average of 15 knots, at times doing over 17 knots. She must have done 370 some of the days, as some of the watches when the log was hove, it being marked to 15½ knots, she took it all out easily and it got to be quite a common saying then:—'Fifteen knots and two apprentices,' as it took the two to hold the reel."

And here is another interesting letter recording one of the little clipper's phenomenal bursts of speed before the westerlies:—

"And now for a yarn about a great run in a storm at sea, 11th, 12th, and 13th July, 1880, from latitude 42° 30′ S., longitude 23° 00′ E. A little east of the longitude of the Cape we were favoured by a great fair wind blow, that tested all the resources of ship and crew. At the first spurt, heavy squalls came up from S. W., that threatened to take toll of our masts, but later it steadied down to a hurricane straight from the west.

"Captain Wallace was sure in his element now. It was 'Stand by!' the whole time, not knowing whether the sticks would go, but the splendid rigging and equipment of sails in the *Cutty Sark* stood the strain. We lost two brand new topgallant sails and one lower fore topsail.

"A tremendous sea was running and needs must we carry on or be pooped. The partial becalming of the lower sails by the stern seas was a great danger, as they filled again with a bang that threatened to bust them into tatters, It was some trick rebending sails. I had a time on the fore topsail yard for two hours. The ship took a green sea over the stern, and it appeared as if there were just three sticks set in the ocean, as it swept the length of the deck.

"The morning of the second day we took three test heaves of the log when she was doing her best and wind steady, 17½, 17 and 17½ were recorded.

"The special feature of the blow was its steadiness, no variation of blow or speed; 15½ and 16 knots were often recorded.

"The captain told Kirby and myself, who were at dinner on the following Sunday, that she had made 1050 miles in the three days, and that it was the best record the ship had ever done."

A few years later one of *Cutty Sark's* officers wrote to *Fairplay*, and he may possibly be referring to the above:—

"In your last issue are some remarks on the record breaking of Captain Willis's famous *Cutty Sark*. Permit me to give my quota of evidence as to this ship's extraordinary performances. At an earlier period of her career she made 362 and 363 knots in 24 hours on two consecutive days."

Captain Woodget wrote a number of letters to Australian papers about his records in the *Cutty Sark*. I will quote from the the last of them, written in 1894:—

"On the 27th, 28th and 29th September (1893) *Cutty Sark* covered the distance of 974 miles. From the 14th to 20th October (1893) she ran 2180 knots, the 15th was the best day ever done under my command, namely 353 knots. The best eleven days during the passage (Antwerp to Sydney) was 3457 miles.

"I might also mention that the *Cutty Sark* once registered 80 miles in five hours by patent log. When bound to China (1886) drawing 21 feet loaded with scrap iron, in three days she covered the distance of 1017 knots.

"These are a few days' work that I have taken from my log books—330, 336, 340, 342, 350 and 360 knots, and I can give a little more distance still, also I can give all the necessary data for working those distances. *Cutty Sark* once covered the distance of 182 knots in 12 hours and I think I can about double that in the 24 hours."

These records quoted by Captain Woodget, we must remember, were all made after she was cut down and had discarded her stunsails.

Many old sailors are very sceptical about 24 hour runs, as they argue that it is so easy to screw up a few more miles on the sextant and cook ones' reckoning. But the *Cutty Sark* made many records between coastal points which there is no getting away from; whilst the number of full-powered steamers which she overtook and passed was very large.

In the last days of sail, the despised windjammer had had one supreme delight and satisfaction, and that is when she has been able to give the go-by to the smoke stack. There were not many steamers in the seventies which could keep alongside a sailing ship in a slashing breeze, but the *Cutty Sark* constantly passed mail steamers and even outran them for days on end, and this not only in the seventies but in the nineties.

Let me give a few examples of these mail steamer scalps captured by the wonderful little ship. Here is a mail boat officer's account:—

"In September, 1873, on a homeward bound voyage from Callao in the Pacific Navigation Company's ss. *Garonne*, we converged, in the vicinity of Cape Verde, on the course of the homeward bound vessels from the east. On our starboard hand, out of line of some 15 fine vessels, one immediately arrested our attention and admiration. This was a beautiful full-rigged ship, canvas (possibly cotton) as white as snow, with everything drawing from courses to skysail.

"This beautiful yacht-like vessel, the famous *Cutty Sark*—then four years old and at her best—with a good S.W. breeze on the port quarter, soon ran ahead of the line of sailors, and ignominiously left the mail steamer astern. We were completely doing 11 knots—a fair speed at that time—whilst the speed of the *Cutty Sark* was judged to be 15. As our commander (Captain Hume) said, we might well have transferred our mails, as the sailer would reach home long before us."

In December, 1875, when outward bound, the *Cutty Sark* overtook the Cape Mail boat; and the incident is thus described by one of her crew:—

"Between Madeira and Teneriffe we passed one of the Castle Line steamers bound South; rose her in the morning and left her hull down at dark. We were then doing 14 to 15 knots with fresh trades, varying main royal."

The most famous scalp, however, in the *Cutty Sark's* locker was that of the new P. & O. mail steamer *Britannia*, in 1889.

Captain Woodget relates:—"We were rounding Gabo Island to signal, when the P. & O. *Britannia* came inside of us, but we beat her into Sydney. The *Cutty Sark* ran from Cape Otway in 40 hours or at the rate of 14½ knots per hour."

A Sydney newspaper gives the following account:—"The *Cutty Sark* passed Green Cape at 3.40 p.m. on Thursday and yesterday before 9 o'clock entered Port Jackson, having thus covered the distance, some 220 miles, in the very short time of 17 hours. Some idea of the pace at which the vessel travelled up the coast may be inferred from the fact that she overtook and passed the R.M.S. *Britannia*, entering the Heads, fully half-an-hour before her. The *Britannia* made Sydney Heads some time after daylight and entered the port shortly before 10 o'clock. She left Melbourne at 1.30 p.m. on 24th. On the run round the steaming rate was 16 knots."

I have two accounts from officers aboard the *Britannia*. Mr. F. H. Mascall writes:—

"Two voyages after this the P. & O. *Britannia*, then cock of the walk from London to Sydney, left Melbourne for Sydney, and the afternoon following passed the *Cutty Sark* running before a strong southerly breeze under her main topgallant sail. She signalled to be reported. During the night it blew strongly from the south'ard. At 10 a.m. the *Britannia* brought to off Sydney Heads and almost rolled her keel out with the sea abeam—the vessel was light and it was blowing hard.

"When we got inside there was the *Cutty Sark* lying at anchor with all her sails fast. She was lying inside the South Head. The *Cutty Sark* looked as if she had been at anchor for a week. She must have cracked on during the night and have got in before it was light almost.

"She was lying with us at Circular Quay the Sunday after and entertained the greater number of visitors that day."

The other officer of the *Britannia* was Robert Olivey, her second officer. It happened to be his watch when the *Cutty Sark* actually passed the *Britannia*. When he saw the sailing ship's lights steadily overhauling the crack ship of the P. & O. Company, he was so struck with the fact that he went down and called the skipper and made the following entry in the ship's log:—"Sailing ship overhauled and passed us." Neither the captain of the *Britannia* nor his second officer imagined for one instant that the passing ship could possibly be the *Cutty Sark*, which they had signalled on the previous afternoon at 1.30 p.m.

Walter Naylor, second mate of the *Cutty Sark*, gave me the following account:—

"After getting through the Bass Strait, we experienced a strong southerly buster and 36 hours afterwards, at 6 a.m., we were off Sydney taking our pilot and tug. During the run we sighted ahead, overhauled, passed and left out of sight the P. & O. mail steamer *Britannia*, then nearly a new ship. We passed her at about a mile, and as we did so her crew and passengers cheered us. We were then under mizen topsails, all sail on the main including royal, except mainsail which was furled, and all sail on the fore except the royal.

"As far as I remember it was admitted by the *Britannia* in a letter to one of the Sydney daily papers that she was steaming at 15 knots at the time and that our land bearings showed us to be making something in the region of 17 knots per hour.

"When the *Britannia* arrived and proceeded to her moorings in Sydney Harbour she passed fairly close to us, then at anchor with all sails furled except the mainsail. Her crew and passengers again cheered us and we answered from the mainyard, where all hands were putting a harbour stow on the mainsail under my direction."

Curiously enough in the following year the *Cutty Sark* also beat the mail boat in the run from Cape Otway to Sydney Heads, which she made in 1 day 22 hours or an average of $14\frac{1}{2}$ knots.

Even in 1894, on her last voyage under the Red Ensign, I find an example of the "Cutty" outrunning a steamer in Captain Woodget's abstracts.:

Aug. 18.—Lat. 40° 03′ S., long. 27° 21′ E., S. 89° E. 200 miles. Moderate N.W. wind and fine. 8 a.m., a steamer steering the same as ourselves on port quarter, gradually falling astern. 5 p.m., could just see steamer's sails west. Midnight wind falling light; steamer passed close to south of us, yellow funnel and black top.

As regards the *Cutty Sark* passing other sailing ships, the records are so monotonously the same that I have searched rather to find an example of another ship passing Willis's clipper.

Captain Woodget could only give me two instances. On the first occasion he was bound to Shanghai, but the *Cutty Sark* was loaded very deep with scrap iron. One of Smith's smart little Cities, flying light, passed her in the light airs of the Java Sea.

The second case occurred on her last homeward bound passage, also in a very light wind. Her log records:—

March 13.—29° 47′ N., 42° 49′ W. Course N. 30° E. Distance 111 miles. Gentle south breeze. Noon, spoke the ship *Torridon* from Sydney. She was at least 6 miles ahead at 6 p.m. Our metal hanging all in rags.

As the *Torridon* was nothing like as fast as the *Cutty Sark* in any wind, it is evident that the badness of the *Cutty Sark's* copper must have been the cause of this feat of the *Torridon's*.

The following are specimens of the way in which the *Cutty Sark* generally treated ships going the same way:—

"One day we sighted a vessel, a mere speck on the horizon, astern of us, and the way she came into view it was evident she was travelling much faster than ourselves. 'Bringing the wind up with her' was remarked on board, and that seemed the only feasible conclusion to arrive at and account for the manner in which she overhauled us. In a few hours she was alongside us, and proved to be the famous British clipper *Cutty Sark*, one of the fastest ships afloat. She was now going two feet to our one, and in a short time was hull down ahead of us."

This encounter took place in January 1879, when the *Cutty Sark* was bound from Shanghai to Sydney under Captain Wallace. The other ship was a fast wool clipper.

The second case which I have picked as an example was related by Thos. S. Sinclair:

"I remember my father, the late Captain A. W. Sinclair, relating an incident in his career—he was master of a St. John (N.B.) vessel, herself no 'slouch' at sailing—of the *Cutty Sark* overhauling his vessel in the South Atlantic, and with a fair wind, stunsails all set and drawing well, passing him as though his vessel were at anchor."

The third instance comes from one of the *Cutty Sark's* crew, and took place in the nineties:—

"On the passage home we sighted a big barque, laden with nitrate, going the same way; but the race was too unequal—the *Cutty Sark* sailed up to leeward within hailing distance, and although blanketed by the barque still forged ahead with spanker hauled in.

"There followed the usual conversation, then out spanker, ensign dipped, and we shot away across her bows up to windward."

After reading the above evidence, I do not think that anyone will dispute the following dictum by the late John Rennie, the designer of the *Cutty Sark's* sail plan:—

"So far as available printed records go to show, at the time she was built there was no ocean going vessel afloat, steam or sail, either in the Mercantile or Naval services, which could keep abreast of her in a good, strong, steady breeze of wind."

If her wonderful speed is the *Cutty Sark's* chief claim to fame, she had many other characteristics, which we must not neglect; for a sailing ship has a character, which is just as complex as that of a human being, and it is this that gives a peculiar fascination and everlasting interest to those who have the handling of her. She has her moods, her days of sweet reasonableness and her days of bad temper and sulks. Again she has her likes and dislikes, being responsive to every action of one man, whilst to another she will prove as obstinate as a jibbing horse.

There was a ship once that would never stay. In vain captain after captain tried his hand. Everything was done that seamanship could devise. Experiments were made in her trim, in her ballasting, in her sails; it was no use, man after man had to give it up and wear her round. Then a day came when a young apprentice, just out of his time, acting as third mate, had a try in the middle watch at a sudden shift of wind in the tropics. The watch below were not even called, yet she came round without the least hesitation. The skipper declared that it was a fluke and that a drain of current must have helped the lad; but the latter stoutly declared that he had got the hang of her, and he was soon able to prove his words. From that date he was always called to put her round, for she remained as balky as ever with everyone else.

Some men lack courage in the handling of ships. One or two of the *Cutty Sark's* skippers were afraid of her—afraid to let her go in hard winds; and the little clipper seemed to know it as she snatched at every opportunity to run away with them, just as if she had a sense of humour.

But those two fearless drivers, Wallace and Woodget, both realised the extraordinary capacity which she possessed to stand hard driving and boldly took every advantage of it. Woodget, indeed, never hove her to in all his ten years of command. He fitted wire braces and sheets and rove double sets of buntlines; went aloft himself and having satisfied himself as to the state of her gear, was ready to drive her through anything. On more than one occasion, when he had been carrying on hard and had at last decided that the royals must come in, the sails, even new ones, were cut through whilst being hauled up owing to the pressure of the wind.

Such a man could do anything with a willing vessel like the *Cutty Sark*. A spoke or two steered her; a boy could keep her straight on her course even when running in a big following sea.

"The *Cutty Sark* was a wonderful runner: she was never pooped and kept wonderfully dry aft. I never hove her to and always ran everything out," declared Captain Woodget.

The Steele-designed tea clippers with their bird-tail counters did not always lift to the seas when running in heavy weather, and used to scoop up the heads of the waves over their raised quarter-decks, making it dangerous work carrying on in easting weather, but the *Cutty Sark* with her well-modelled stern lifted over everything, so that even in the roaring forties Captain Woodget was accustomed to go about in carpet slippers and rarely got wet feet.

The *Cutty Sark* was no man-killer, nor did she drown the hands on her jibboom footropes. In 1893 two seamen were washed off her jibboom and drowned, but it was not the ship's fault. Captain Woodget thus describes the incident. "No sooner had the man Lewis got to the wheel than he ran the ship off to E. by S. $\frac{1}{2}$ S., wind almost abeam, which, of course, increased her speed about from 7 to 11 knots, and then brought her up to E. $\frac{1}{2}$ N. and almost head to sea. I told him that he would wash someone from the

"THERMOPYLAE"

Photo by W. Williamson, Hobart, Tas.

[See Page

"CUTTY SARK," "BRILLIANT" AND "YALLAROI" LOADING WOOL AT CIRCULAR QUAY

(*Cutty Sark* outside)

[*See Page* 13]

foc's'le head: no sooner had I spoken than she gave a plunge and put the jibboom under.

"During the seven years that I had commanded the *Cutty Sark*, I never saw her put the boom under before."

Some ships are very hard on their gear and for ever carrying away things.

The *Cutty Sark* was only dismasted once under the British flag, and that was due to the carelessness of her mate. She was going along close-hauled in the roaring forties, when the wind shifted on to the quarter. It was night time and Captain Woodget was below. The mate, an old man, was not sufficiently on the look-out. He let her come right up, and away went the fore topmast just above the rigging and the main topmast at the cap. They happened to be pitchpine spars—Oregon spars would probably have stayed in her. Captain Woodget refused to cut anything away, but hung on to the spars and gear alongside and thus was able to refit her at sea.

Within a fortnight of her dismasting, she made a run of 313 miles under a mainsail and fore lower topsail, and a week later ran 330 miles before a moderate southerly gale.

The *Cutty Sark* has lost three rudders. The first off the Cape in her celebrated race with *Thermopylae*: the second under the Portuguese flag during a West Indian hurricane, a new one being fitted at Key West in 1909. Her third rudder she carried away on 19th June, 1915, when four days out from Lisbon for Mossamedes. She reached the Mossamedes under jury rudder, but had to wait there four months for a new rudder.

Most of the tea clippers required extra careful handling, for they usually had the sail area of ships of almost double their tonnage. Some, indeed, were so overmasted that they were dangerously crank, but the *Cutty Sark*, though she spread as much canvas in her racing days as a 1500-ton ship, was too powerful a vessel to lie down under a squall; and there was never any occasion for her crew to stand by the weather deadeye lanyards, ready to cut at the word from the "old man."

Nevertheless she was so fine that she required 400 tons of ballast to keep her upright with an empty hold. This was neglected once

c

in the London Docks, and she went over, putting her yards through the freight sheds on the wharf.

There was only one tea clipper which would stand upright with a clean swept hold, and that was the pretty little *Undine*. The others all required plenty of stiffening, and the *Cutty Sark* was no exception to the rule.

To get the best out of a tea clipper a man had to be more than a prime seaman: he had to be born with that peculiar attribute, sea sense, a quality, which one cannot properly describe in words, though it might be called an inborn, instinctive knowledge of the way of a ship in the sea—a knowledge which gives its lucky possessor the power of doing just the right thing at the right moment, of getting the last ounce of speed out of a vessel, and of being able to predict with certainty her strains and stresses, her limit of endurance in all states of wind and weather.

Most men learn to know their ships in time, but to a man who has sea sense a glance round his new vessel seems to tell him all that a less blessed sailor will take weeks to arrive at, and then, perhaps, not without one or two unpleasant experiences or risky experiments.

Thus it is that many a ship has never had justice done to her owing to the fact that she has not had officers with the true sea sense.

Such a ship often earns the reputation of being an unlucky ship, and this is specially the case with racing ships. It is exactly the same with racing yachts. No man has ever become the successful skipper of a racing yacht who has not had that elusive quality, sea sense.

One might go further and show that even machinery has not rendered this sense an unnecessary one for a seaman. Let us take tugboat men. Some of these specialists will handle big ships in the most awkward situations with an exactitude that is little short of marvellous, whilst others are just too soon or just too late in all their orders.

A curious case of this sort was once told to me by a tugboat owner. A man, whom he had promoted to a large tug from a small one, was always bungling things: when his telegraph rang, the exact and necessary moment was never hit upon. His employer was puzzled. He knew that the man had sea sense, yet his engine room telegraph seemed to paralyse it. At last he gave his bungling skipper a voice connection, and from that moment there was no more trouble—the man could use a basket of eggs as a fender and never break an egg. Apparently the tugboat man's nerves between brain and hand were too sluggish so that he was always a trifle late with the telegraph lever, but directly he was able to sing out his orders:—"A touch ahead! Stop her! Another touch ahead!" all was well.

Conrad, in that classic *The Mirror of the Seas*, makes his elderly seaman remark:—

"Ships are all right: it's the men in 'em. . . "

Cutty Sark was assuredly all right, yet the famous ship has gained rather a peculiar reputation for the way in which she got into and out of scrapes—such as small collisions, losses of anchors and rudders, narrow shaves of stranding, etc., etc.

As one writer has put it: "Deliciously blending the direst luck with the most excellent fortune."

We shall be correct in our judgment if we attribute the "direst luck" to that ever present factor in life, human error, whilst we credit the "excellent fortune" to the account of the gallant little clipper.

Yes, assuredly, Conrad's elderly seaman stated a great sea truth.

"Ships are all right; it's the men in 'em."

CHAPTER II.

THE BUILDING OF THE *CUTTY SARK*.

THERE is no form of sport which so appeals to a Britisher as a race. In truth, one cannot think of any spot on the earth, whether within the Empire or out of it, where the Britisher has not held a race of some description.

In the days of our fathers a racecourse was made of the mighty ocean itself, with the great capes of the world as rounding marks. I refer to the annual ship race from China with the first teas of the season. This was a race in which every man in any way connected with or interested in shipping was as much concerned as are the horsey fraternity in the Derby or the rowing fraternity in the Oxford and Cambridge boat race.

Huge sums were wagered on favourite ships, whose crews often risked their pay days as well as their lives; whilst the stakes received by the winning owner represented a tidy little fortune, and his proud skipper, besides pocketing a very handsome douceur knew that his reputation in his profession was made for all time. It is not surprising, therefore, that every shipowner engaged in the China trade possessed but one ambition, and that was to win the Great Ship Race, as the newspapers called it. And, just as in the Derby the prize has eluded so many, so in the Great Ship Race there were owners who, in spite of years of endeavour, had never had the luck to win what they held to be the blue ribbon of the sea.

Of these unsuccessful owners, Captain John Willis, known in the City of London as "Willis of the White Hat," was perhaps the keenest and most persevering. He had commanded his father's ships at a date when the American clippers were lords of the China seas and carried all before them. In the late fifties his *Lammermuir* had proved herself no match for Beazley's *Robin Hood* and *Friar Tuck* or Rodger's *Kate Carnie* and *Ellen Rodger*, whilst in the early sixties his *Whiteadder* was out-classed by the great trio, *Fiery Cross*, *Taeping* and *Serica*.

Nevertheless, when in the autumn of 1868 the marvellous *Thermopylae* sailed from the Thames on what was to be a record breaking maiden voyage, Jock Willis had already determined to build a clipper with the prime object of beating her. And when the account of *Thermopylae's* maiden passage to Melbourne reached home, he was no whit dismayed but full of confidence that his new ship would beat her. Willis, indeed, had good grounds for his confidence.

To begin with, he had discovered a young designer with whose talent he was greatly impressed. Secondly, he owned *The Tweed*, a vessel which he considered to be the fastest ship ever built, though she was too large for the tea trade: his idea was that the lines of *The Tweed* should be taken off and used as a guide, if they were not wholly embodied, in the design of his new ship.

The young designer upon whom old Willis pinned his hopes was Hercules Linton, who had but lately started shipbuilding at the Woodyard, Dumbarton, with a partner named Scott.

Linton, after serving his apprenticeship with Hall of Aberdeen, had risen to an important position in that firm; this position he had relinquished in order to become Lloyd's Inspector at Liverpool. Besides being a designer of great promise, Linton was well-known as a Scottish antiquarian.

It will be asked how much of the *Cutty Sark's* design came entirely from Linton's brain. His friends have claimed that the whole design was due to Linton, that he was not the man to be influenced by anyone else in such a matter. On the other hand, Willis's friends declared that the *Cutty Sark* was an absolute replica of *The Tweed* in all essentials.

But the true facts of the case are as follows:—In 1868 Captain Willis took Hercules Linton to see his favourite *The Tweed* in dry dock. Without a doubt Captain Stuart of *The Tweed* and Captain Moodie who had once been mate of *The Tweed* under Stuart and who was to command the new clipper and superintend her building, were also present.

We can well imagine the conversation that followed:— Old Jock's enthusiasm for his splendid ship, the testimony of the two captains regarding her qualities, and Linton's shrewd criticism as he took in her lines.

No fault could be found with the bow lines of *The Tweed*, in spite of the fact that she had not so much rake to her forefoot as some of the more modern tea clippers; nor was her forefoot rounded away so much as Waymouth's designs of *Thermopylae* and *Leander* or Connell's *Spindrift*.

But Linton was wholly satisfied and the *Cutty Sark* was given *The Tweed's* bow. Without a doubt the *Cutty Sark* owed most of her wonderful powers of going to windward to this bow of *The Tweed's*.

The *Thermopylae* had a great reputation for closehauled work, yet in a fair test in a dead peg to windward she could only do 85 miles to the *Cutty Sark's* 115. With her straightish stern and less rounded forefoot, the *Cutty Sark* soaked out to windward in a wonderful manner, her wake streaming away on the lee quarter.

The *Tweed's* forefoot gave the necessary grip, by means of which a vessel can eat her way out to windward, which was lost when the stem was raked aft too much and the forefoot cut away

The difference between the two types was easily noticeable for vessels like *The Tweed* and *Cutty Sark* carried their wakes to leeward when on a wind, whereas with ships which had greater rake of stem the wake was always on the weather quarter. This bow did not make *Cutty Sark* slow in stays, as one would naturally imagine, for she was well known to be one of the quickest ships coming about that ever sailed deep water.

If *The Tweed's* bow gave satisfaction to the expert, her stern did not escape criticisms. In Linton's opinion it was too barrel shaped, lacked power, and could well be improved upon. The *Cutty Sark* was therefore given a squarer stern frame and bilge with less tumble-home on top. Her stern has been criticised by some as being on the heavy side yet to the eye it fits her bow to a nicety, the proportions being admirable. And its power is very apparent especially when it is compared to the short bird-like counters of the earlier cracks in the tea trade.

The resultant qualities of this square stern were a triumph for Linton. The *Cutty Sark* proved to be much stiffer than *The Tweed*, more able to carry sail, and with a lazier, easier roll.

Most of the tea clippers were very ticklish ships to handle in a big following sea, but this was not the case with the *Cutty Sark*. Properly canvassed she would run before the heaviest of the westerlies with very small helm and without taking a drop of water over her poop, and she bore driving as no other ship that ever crossed the royal yards.

With the ends of the new clipper decided upon, the next important point was the midship section. The designers of the day were divided in opinion as to the merits of the full midship section and the cut away section with plenty of deadrise. *The Tweed* had a full midship section. *Thermopylae* was celebrated for what was called her "rocker false keel." Bernard Waymouth was probably the first designer to gain the advantage of deadrise by deepening the false keel under a moderately full body. Hall gave the new clipper *Caliph* a most unusual amount of deadwood under her bottom, Linton also gave *Cutty Sark* a good depth of false keel. But here we come to an interesting feature in *Cutty Sark's* design. Hercules Linton had a very great admiration for the Firth of Forth fishing boats, which were famed throughout the Kingdom for their speed and seaworthiness. Indeed, he was so enamoured of their qualities and shape that he used to give lectures upon their model to his fellow craftsmen.

I am pretty certain that these fine little ships influenced him in his designing of the *Cutty Sark's* bottom. Indeed he confessed as much. With this knowledge it is of interest to compare the midship sections of *Cutty Sark*, *The Tweed*, *Thermopylae*, *Sir Lancelot* and *Caliph*.

It is easy enough for a designer to recognise certain merits in other designs, but to mould them into an homogeneous whole requires not only skill and experience, but that elusive factor which is called genius. In this moulding together of the best points in *The Tweed* and the Buckhaven fishing boats, and the inspirations of his own brain, Hercules Linton was supremely successful. The result left nothing lacking. The *Cutty Sark* had good lines, her design was perfectly balanced, and if her lines gave every indication of exceptional speed, they more than hinted at her exceptional power, a quality in which she far surpassed the rest of the tea fleet.

She was "all ship" as the expression goes. Yet the *Cutty Sark* was the sharpest of all the China clippers. When the model was finished, the designers and Lloyd's surveyors, Cornish and Bernard Waymouth, probably the two foremost men in their profession, went to see it and they were both aghast at the knife-like entrance, They thought there was too much cut-away that she required more bearing forward and would therefore lack power. But they were both wrong and Linton was right. The square bilge and powerful quarters counteracted the lean bow, and the *Cutty Sark* proved herself to be a magnificent sea boat.

John Willis, who had a keen eye for a good model, approved of the specifications, and the building contract was signed at £21 per ton.

And here I come to a point which at this distance of time is very difficult to clear up. Scott & Linton were a young firm without much capital. Apparently shrewd old John Willis required a guarantee that the work on the new clipper would be properly done up to the requirements of the specification, and it is said that Mr. Peter Denny of Denny Brothers offered to become security at the price on the contract, and so the matter was settled.

In view of the life-long rivalry between *Cutty Sark* and *Thermopylae*, which have been generally admitted to be the two fastest ships that ever sailed the seas, a comparison of their measurements and specifications should be of interest.

The displacement at load draft of both clippers was given by their builders as 1970 tons.

Their registered measurements were:—

	Tons			Length	Bread'h	Depth Reg'd	Depth Moulded
	Gross	Under Deck	Net				
				Ft.	Ft.	Ft.	Ft.
Cutty Sark	963	892	921	212·5	36	21	22·5
Thermopylae	991	927	948	212	36	21	23·2

Both were built under special survey.

The scantlings I give in the Appendix. On the whole it will be noticed that *Thermopylae's* scantlings are the lighter of the two.

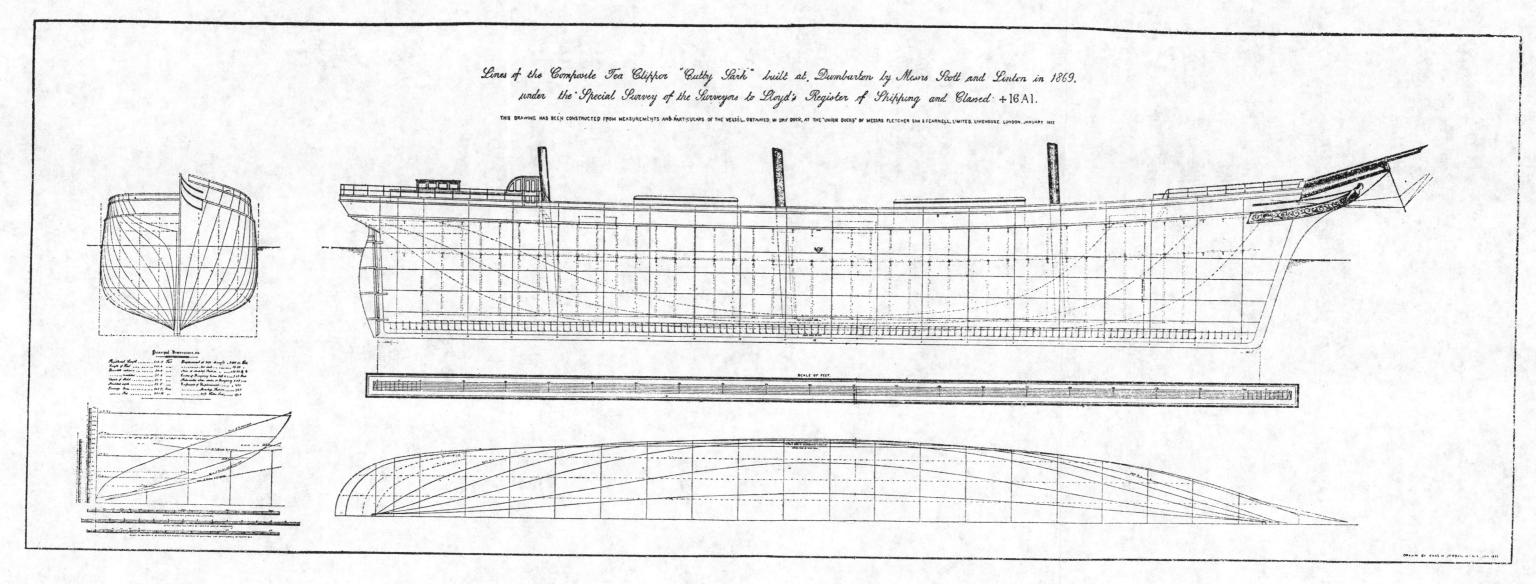

Lines of the Composite Tea Clipper "Cutty Sark" built at Dumbarton by Messrs Scott and Linton in 1869, under the Special Survey of the Surveyors to Lloyd's Register of Shipping and Classed +16 A1.

THIS DRAWING HAS BEEN CONSTRUCTED FROM MEASUREMENTS AND PARTICULARS OF THE VESSEL, OBTAINED, IN DRY DOCK, AT THE "UNION DOCKS" OF MESSRS FLETCHER SON & FEARNESS, LIMITED, LIMEHOUSE, LONDON, JANUARY 1922.

SCALE OF FEET

[See Page 24

Cutty Sark had a teak deck compared to *Thermopylae's* yellow pine, whilst *Thermopylae* had no 'tween decks laid, the *Cutty's* 'tween decks being of 3-inch yellow pine.

Knowing old White Hat's love of teak, it is not surprising to find the *Cutty Sark* with a teak deck. A teak deck only requires to be sanded down occasionally instead of the usual holystoning but it is very slippery when it is wet. Willis asked for strength and power. Waymouth evidently had the modern racing yacht designer's hatred of rigidity, for I have heard it stated that the *Thermopylae's* decks would open up when she was being heavily pressed, just like the topside planking of the Newfoundland fishing schooner, which had a habit of nipping the men as they lay in their bunks in the foc's'le. We have slowly come to recognise that the old British attribute of rigidity was not strength any more than weight necessarily means power.

Nevertheless the fact that *Cutty Sark* is still afloat with a tight bottom, whilst the *Thermopylae* lies fathoms deep off the coast of Portugal, is an eloquent testimony to the scantlings of the *Cutty Sark*.

The famous old clipper, when viewed in the same dock with the more modern sailing ships, filled the eye with her charming daintiness, yet she both looked and was a far more powerful ship than *Thermopylae*, though she could not load so large a cargo.

Finally a joiner, who worked on the *Cutty Sark* until she sailed on her maiden voyage, declares that hers were the bonniest lines he had ever seen, and not only beat *Thermopylae's* but all the famous Steele designs.

The *Cutty Sark* was far from being the only celebrated ship built in 1869. It was indeed a year in which shipbuilders were specially busy and in keen rivalry as to who should produce the finest clipper ship. Though steamers were attacking the tea trade the success of the new Suez Canal was by no means believed in by the more conservative of the sailing ship owners, with the result that no less than a dozen clippers were laid down for the object of bringing tea as speedily as possible from the ports of China.

These were *Cutty Sark. Caliph, Normancourt, Wylo, Ambassador, Eme, Duke of Abercorn, Osaka, Doune Castle, City of Hankow,*

Oberon and *Blackadder*. Ten of these ships were composite built
—one, the *City of Hankow*, had a brass bottom and iron topsides
—a transition stage between composite and entirely iron ships;
another the *Blackadder*, which was laid down in June, 1869, but
not launched until the following March, was wholly of iron; whilst
the *Oberon* was a heavily rigged 1200-ton composite ship with an
auxiliary engine. She cost Shaw & Maxton, the owners of the
celebrated clippers *Ariel* and *Titania*, a small fortune, but she was
not a success until her engine was removed.

If the steamers were already making themselves felt in the
China trade, their capture of the Colonial passenger and freight
trade was still many years distant. In 1869 men, women and children
were taking ship to the Colonies in their thousands, and the
emigration trade, which was almost entirely in the hands
of the sailing ship firms, was booming. The clippers took out
the choicest of general cargoes and brought back wool, hides,
and tallow.

It was in this year that the celebrated Loch Line started its
career by ordering the four iron clippers, *Loch Katrine*, *Loch Ness*,
Loch Tay and *Loch Earn*. The Aberdeen White Star ordered their
first iron ship, the *Patriarch* from Hood, of Aberdeen, besides the
composite clipper *Centurion*, which was expected to rival the
Thermopylae in speed. From Liverpool came the famous *Thomas
Stephens* for the passenger trade.

It is hard to say which was the finest iron sailing ship built
in 1869, but probably the most beautiful was the peerless *Golden
Fleece*, built for Carmichael by Barclay, Curle.

Of the smaller clippers, one has but to mention that wonderful
little barque of Walkers, the *Berean*; Kelso's *Deerhound*, built
by Pile under a glass roof, and the tiny *Otago*, celebrated for having
been the proud command of Joseph Conrad.

The Americans, ever conservative to their own wood, built
two ships which were sailing the seas until a recent date. These
were the well-known *Great Admiral* and Donald MacKay's last
masterpiece, the *Glory of the Seas*.

Amongst such a number of superb ships it is difficult, nay
impossible, to award the palm. Several of them were pioneers of

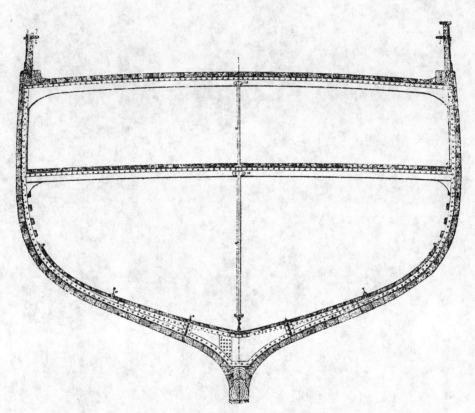

MIDSHIP SECTION OF THE "CALIPH."

[*See Page* 27

a type which became popular through their success. Others, again, such as the *Cutty Sark* herself, the *Patriarch* and the *Thomas Stephens* were never duplicated and stand out as special ships, touched with the wand of genius and therefore beyond all slavish copying.

I have given a list of these contemporaries of the *Cutty Sark* in the Appendix; most of these ships will find a future mention in this history; it is curious to see the way in which the tracks of certain ships constantly cross each other, whilst others which one would naturally expect to be in constant rivalry go their separate courses, possibly never to meet again. A ship is like a human being in this respect, or like a regiment.

In this way the names of the *Cutty Sark* and *Thermopylae* have always been linked together; yet if one had been asked in 1869 which ship would have been the *Cutty Sark's* chief rival, those in the know would undoubtedly have answered the *Caliph*.

Hercules Linton was an Aberdonian, and a large number of his men, including four of the principal foremen and two of the assistant foremen, also came from Aberdeen. One can therefore imagine the excitement in the Woodyard at Dumbarton when news came down in March, 1869, that a rival tea clipper had been laid down in Hall's yard at Aberdeen. And the interest in the rival was still further increased when it became known that she was being built for Mr. Hector, a relation of John Willis, and was to be an out and out "full blood", as the term went, with a tonnage closely approximating to that of the *Cutty Sark*.

Pride in the quickness and perfection of their work was the chief attribute of the shipwrights of those days, and the workers in the new yard at Dumbarton strained every nerve to beat the yard of world-wide reputation.

The *Caliph* was Hall's 263rd ship; with the *Cutty Sark* the young firm of Scott & Linton hoped to win their spurs. She was only their sixth ship, and their first of any size or importance. Though there was little to choose between the two ships in actual tonnage, both in design and rig they were very unlike each other.

If *Cutty Sark's* design was a great advance in one direction, *Caliph's* was equally so in another. With her midship section and ends cut away to the very limit, with more length and less depth than *Cutty Sark*, the *Caliph* was expected to be specially fast in light winds. As an aid to her sails in the calms of the China Sea, an 8 horse-power engine in her midship house was fitted with a shaft for driving two small screws, which could be lowered overboard on each side of the vessel. This, it was hoped, would prove capable of driving the ship an additional 2½ knots through the water.

In their sail and spar plans, the difference between the two vessels was specially marked. *Caliph* had a lofty narrow sail plan with three standing skysail yards, whilst *Cutty Sark* only crossed a main skysail yard and was very square, her topsails, topgallant sails and royals on fore and main being interchangeable.

The *Caliph's* sail area was 7268 yards, including jib topsail, Jamie Green, ringtail, topmast, topgallant, royal and skysail studding sails on fore and main. *Cutty Sark's* sail plan, of which I give a reproduction, works out at a good deal more.

Cutty Sark, indeed, was more heavily sparred and spread a greater sail area than any other ship in the tea trade. From the outer end of her flying jibboom to the end of her spanker boom measured 280 feet. Her mainmast from load line to truck was 151 feet in length: whilst her topmast stunsail boom was 47 feet long, 33 feet of which was outside the lower yardarm. Her stunsails indeed, were specially square, witness the following comparison with those of the *Spindrift*, nicknamed the *Giblet Pie*, owing to the length of her legs and wings.

Stunsails.			*Spindrift*	*Cutty Sark*
Fore topgallant yard	-	-	18 feet.	22 feet.
„ „ boom	-	-	28 feet.	34 „
Fore topmast yard	-	-	21 „	24 „
„ „ boom	-	-	38 „	47 „

In *Cutty Sark's* sail plan a spencer gaff will be noticed. This is a heavy weather sail, hardly ever used except when a ship is hove to in a gale of wind. The *Cutty Sark* was never hove to when racing, thus the spencer was of very little use to her. Most of the tea clippers set gaff topsails over their spankers. *Caliph* set a gaff topsail with both yard and jackyard, the topsail halliards leading

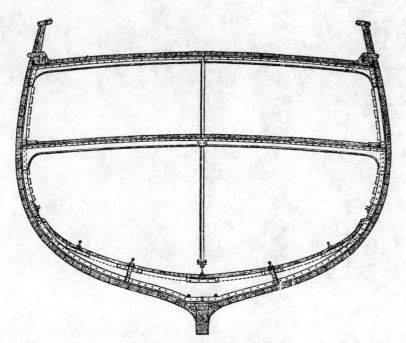

MIDSHIP SECTION OF THE "THERMOPYLAE."

[*See Page* 29

through a block at the topmost head. *Cutty Sark's* gaff topsail had even more hoist. It was jib-headed and set up to the royal masthead.

In the Appendix, I give the spar measurements of *Ariel, Titania Spindrift, Normancourt, Cutty Sark* and *Hallowe'en*. The chief points to notice are the length of *Spindrift's* mainyard, the tremendous increase in sail area given to the *Cutty Sark*, through her fore and main yards being interchangeable, and the great length of the lower masts in the three earlier clippers.

Spindrift boasted the largest mainsail in the tea trade. Its depth at the slings was 40 feet as compared to *Cutty Sark's* $35\frac{1}{4}$ and *Normancourt's* 33. *Thermopylae's* mainsail was also 40 feet in depth, though in width it could not compare with *Spindrift's Thermopylae's* mainyard being only 80 feet long against the 84 of *Spindrift*.

Unfortunately I have so far been unable to find a correct sail plan of *Thermopylae*: her sail plan has been published in an American magazine article, but it is entirely imaginary except for the measurement of the mainyard, which was probably taken from my *China Clippers*. *Thermopylae's* sail plan like *Cutty Sark's* was tremendously square, and her sail area was probably between those of *Cutty Sark* and *Spindrift*. Her main royal was 19 feet deep, as compared to 14 feet for those of *Cutty Sark* and *Spindrift*, and 15 for *Normancourt's*, but it must be remembered that *Thermopylae* never crossed a main skysail.

In devising a sail plan there is nothing more important than the proper placing and raking of masts, the table on page 30 may therefore be of interest to those who have studied the subject.

In this table the width between the masts gained by *Spindrift*, owing to her great length, is very noticeable. As regards rake, the tendency of expert opinion was to rake the masts less and less, always bearing in mind the design of the vessel. Thus *Cutty Sark's* masts had much less rake than those of *Ariel*.

Hallowe'en, which was extraordinarily fast in right winds for an iron ship, had her masts raked like those of a Chinese junk or an old East Indiaman, her foremast being raked slightly forward, her mainmast being upright and her mizen mast being raked aft.

This gave her more width between her topmasts and topgallant masts than she would otherwise have had, and this lessened the blanketing of one mast by another, which has always been a trouble in square-rigged ships.

POSITION OF MASTS.

Ship's Name	Distance from fore-end of figure-head to taffrail	Distance from fore-end of figure-head to fore-mast	Distance from after-side of fore-mast to fore-side of mainmast	Distance from after-side of mainmast to fore-side of mizen mast	Distance from after-side of mizen-mast to taffrail
	Ft.	Ft.	Ft.	Ft.	Ft.
Ariel - -	214	59	60	48	39½
Titania - -	220	60	63	50	41¼
Spindrift - -	236	62	69½	54	44
Normancourt -	212	60	58¾	47	41
Cutty Sark -	224	61¾	60½	50½	45

Another tendency in spar plans was the gradual shortening of bowsprit and jibbooms. This is well shown in the spar measurements, though *Normancourt* must be considered an exception to the rule. Nowadays we never see a bowsprit of any length, either in a square-rigged ship or a racing yacht, and many an old seaman shudders when he remembers the tremendous jibbooms of his youth, whether in ships or yachts.

Cutty Sark had iron lower masts, lower yards, and bowsprit, the rest of her spars being of Oregon pine. The *Titania* was the only tea clipper with steel lower masts; these were fitted in December, 1867, on her return from her disastrous maiden voyage.

Cutty Sark had the usual passaree swinging boom for the fore lower stunsail; her main topgallant stay was double, whilst all sails clewed up to the yardarms. All her sheaves for running gear blocks were ball bearing, then an innovation from America.

The sizes in wire and rope used may be of interest to riggers, so I give them in the Appendix. On the main, *Cutty Sark* had 5 shrouds of a side (*Ariel*, *Titania*, *Spindrift* and *Normancourt* all had 6) 1 cap backstay, 3 topmast backstays, 2 topgallant backstays, 1 royal, and 1 skysail backstay.

It is noticeable in the development of the sailing ship how the number of backstays has increased; for instance, *Ariel* and *Titania* only had one main topgallant backstay and two topmast backstays of a side.

The tea clippers were like yachts in the way in which they kept their decks and bright work; fife-rails were carved; deck houses panelled; belaying pins brass or at any rate brass-capped; rails and stanchions inlaid with brass, and ropes, where possible flemished down and pointed.

Cutty Sark's deck plan consisted of a short anchor deck forward, 22 feet long—the foc's'le for 30 men was below decks and was lighted by four ports of a side; a midship house or what was then called a Liverpool house, 27 feet 4 inches in length; a half-deck or apprentice's house just aft of the mainmast, also 27 feet 4 inches in length; a raised quarter-deck, 46 ft. 6 inches in length, with an upper poop 31 feet long on top of it, at each end of which was a companion way leading into the cabin. A donkey engine and winch occupied the forward half of the apprentice's house.

The Steele tea clippers have very low teak bulwarks, less than $3\frac{1}{2}$ feet high, but the *Cutty Sark* had bulwarks, a foot higher, of heavy iron plating, in which were six large, square swinging ports to take the water off, whilst on the teakwood pin-rail there were three handy barrel winches, two for mainsheets and tacks and one for foresheets.

The boats were carried on skids in the usual way, and were painted man-of-war fashion, black topsides and white bottoms, until a day when Captain Woodget received some new boats, which he painted all white. Old Willis, on seeing the new boats, asked Woodget why he had coated them white, when orders were that all paint was to remain the same.

The captain replied simply: "Because they look better white."

Willis said no more and white they remained.

Captain Woodget, unlike many deepwater men who hate being cramped up in a small boat, was a keen boat sailer, and kept a teak sailing boat on the skids. He also invested in steam launches. At one time he had a very smart Dartmouth-built launch; and he had another launch in Australia, which he finally sold in Brisbane.

As regards paint, the bulwarks and houses were painted white with bright panels. The lower masts and bowsprit were painted white, the upper masts and yards black, with all doublings, and mastheads, jibboom end, martingale, spanker gaff and boom, and spencer gaff white.

One of the most fascinating of dead and gone trades was that of the figure-head maker. His workshop was often dark, dingy and unpretentious, yet with its stacks of sweet-smelling timber, its carpet of chips, its rows of razor edged carving tools, and, above all, with its figure-heads in their many stages of progress, its carved head-boards and gilded gingerbread work, it was always a source of great interest to all loungers and small boys. Many a figure-head maker was an artist of great merit, though totally unknown to fame outside the shipping world.

Wood carving is far the most enthralling of all kinds of sculpture, and the figure-head maker rarely took thought of time or meals when he had an interesting job on hand. His sureness of eye and dexterity of hand were amazing. The really talented artist trusted his eye before any measuring instrument and the palm of his hand rather than a mallet, yet in the most difficult of whorls and spirals his stroke was never too strong or too weak or a hair's-breadth out of his intended course; thus a figure-head would seem to grow out of a balk of knotless timber in a way which was little short of marvellous to the ignorant spectator.

One of the prettiest examples of this highly skilled craft was adze work. Many an old time ship's carpenter could do almost anything with his adze from making a ship's topmast to shaping the most delicate of scroll designs, all flowers, leaves and elaborate spirals. But the figure-head maker rejoiced in some wonderful tools and seldom gave one an exhibition of his skill with an adze, unless he became absorbed whilst roughing out a design, then indeed the process of carving a goddess, a Turk's head or an elaborate coat-of-arms from a cube of cedarwood seemed a matter of equal ease to the wielder of that heavy weapon.

The maker of *Cutty Sark's* figure-head, F. Hellyer of Blackwall,

CAPTAIN JOHN WILLIS
"Old White Hat"

HERCULES LINTON
Designer of *Cutty Sark*

See Page 21

Photo lent by Miss Linton

"CUTTY SARK" IN DRY DOCK, 1922

[*See Page* 22

was one of the leading artists in his trade; and his conception of Nannie, the beautiful witch, her hand reached out in pursuit of Tam o' Shanter and her long black hair flying in the wind, was considered a magnificent example of his art.

Amongst the galaxy of goddesses, fairies and heroes, which graced the bows of the dainty tea clippers, Nannie held a place of honour.

Captain F. Moore, who considered himself something of an artist, tried tinting this peerless figure-head; but when old Willis saw the blush on the cheeks of Nannie, he was filled with horror at such a lapse from good taste and straightway ordered the best white enamel to be laid on top of Moore's gay colours. Coloured figure-heads in the clipper ship era were only allowable on coasters, all respectable deepwater ships abhorred the smallest deviation from the conventional white.

The *Cutty Sark's* figure-head has been photographed times without number, yet it is not her original figure-head but a vastly inferior production. The head and arm of Hellyer's Nannie were washed away many years ago, when Captain Woodget was driving the little clipper down in the roaring forties.

When the *Cutty Sark* was in port it was the custom to get a long horse's tail and put it in Nannie's hand in order to represent the old mare's tail, which the beautiful witch pulled out.

A proof of the love borne by the tea clipper owners for their ships is shown by the amount of money spent in decorating them, by the wealth of carving and gold leaf or gingerbread work, as sailors call it, which was lavished upon them.

Captain John Willis instructed Hellyer to put forward all his talent and spare no expense in portraying Burn's great poem in carved wood upon bow and stern of the *Cutty Sark*. Thus Tam o' Shanter on his grey mare "Meg" was to be seen riding along the clipper's quarter whilst the witches in very scanty attire were shown dancing in great abandon behind Nannie on the scroll work of the *Cutty's* bow.

This artistic masterpiece, however, was too much for the well-known mid-Victorian delicacy in such matters and old "White Hat" had the naked witches removed.

D

The ship's name and "Port of London" raised in letters of gold were encircled in wreaths of laurel upon her stern, whilst the punning inscription—

"Where there's a Willis away"

was blazoned upon her taffrail.

The *Cutty Sark* had two gilded rubbing strakes, the upper one being along the level of the topgallant rail and the lower along the maindeck level. Old Jock Willis was so pleased by the wonderful records set up by his ship in the wool trade that he wished to put a carved and gilded rope in teak round the famous clipper, but for some reason or other the project was never carried out.

There was one other ornament possessed by the beautiful vessel and this was the golden shirt or cutty sark which fitted over the pin at the maintruck.

Captain Willis presented this emblem to the ship after her defeat of the *Thermopylae* in the race home from Sydney in 1885. It was a challenge to the golden cock at *Thermopylae's* masthead. Captain Woodget told me that it was made out of some non-rust yellow metal. It was still aloft when the "Cutty's" mainmast went over the side off the Cape in 1917; some day perhaps it may be washed ashore on the Cape Coast, when it will certainly mystify those who find it.

Let us now try to gain some idea of the arrangements below decks. As will be seen in the plans, *Cutty Sark* had spacious 'tween decks, and she was bulkheaded off forward and aft by two stout iron collision bulkheads, which gave her two watertight compartments. So sharp was she that these bulkheads were triangle-shaped coming to a point at the keelson, on either side of which there was hardly standing room.

The *Cutty Sark* throughout her long life has always been one of the most staunch of vessels. The following are three testimonies to this fact, which I have noted.

"The *Cutty Sark* was so staunch that I think we did not use the pumps five times on the whole voyage."

"We seldom pumped her."—(1884-5.)

"Although the vessel is 25 years old, her pumps have never

been used throughout the voyage, and her cargo is coming out without a stain upon the bales."—(Hull Newspaper, 1894.)

This last refers to a wool cargo, the largest that was ever screwed into her, consisting of 5010 bales.

The only leak that she ever had, and that a very small one, was in the sternpost; probably it was due to the tearing away of her first rudder. It was discovered by the curious behaviour of the vessel herself, which showed that she was very much out of trim; and then it was found that the after compartment was full of water. This leak gave a little trouble under Bruce and the second Moore, but as soon as it could be attended to the *Cutty Sark* became as staunch as ever.

Like all the tea clippers, the *Cutty Sark* was beautifully fitted up below. Her cabins were panelled in teak and bird's-eye maple, with much fancy carving. The furniture was all of teak and the very best cabinet-maker's work. The captain rejoiced in a heavy teak four-post bed, instead of the usual bunk, and another fine piece was the saloon sideboard. Both of these bits of furniture are still in her. All the cabin doors had yellow cut-glass handles. The saloon runs athwartships, it is a neat cosy apartment with a fireplace—the mess table in the centre, over which a heavy brass lamp swings from the ridge beam of the skylight.

On top of the monkey poop, there is a large skylight for the saloon, and a smaller one aft, to light the captain's cabin. The lazarette hatch is aft on the starboard side abreast of the captain's bathroom.

The floor level of the cabins is about $2\frac{1}{2}$ feet below the raised quarter-deck.

On the small after-hatch, which is just aft of the apprentice's house, is a small booby hatch. This was a great boon to the apprentices when there was water coming aboard, as it formed a sort of breakwater for the entrance to the half-deck, the door of which faced aft.

The famous clipper, both aloft, on deck and below was fitted up like a millionaire's yacht.

The *Australian Star* reporter thus writes of her in the autumn of 1890.

"There is no apology required in introducing the *Cutty Sark*, as she lies at Circular Quay, to our readers. She is simply a picture: she is a yacht among the handsomest of merchantmen, and her appearance does not belie her."

Owners of the tea ships always made pets of their favourite clippers. Some owners, indeed, who were not regular China traders built tea clippers for the pleasure of possessing what was recognised as the thoroughbred of the seas.

Leander was always known as Somes' yacht. *Sir Lancelot* in her old age was always called the yacht of the Indian Ocean. *Normancourt* was another pet. Baring Bros. were the most liberal of owners, and never stinted the ship but gave her everything of the best without a question.

The tea ships being first class ships expected first class cargoes; but as freights fell and the competition of steamers increased, they did not always succeed in loading superfine goods.

I give a list of the *Cutty Sark's* cargoes under Willis's house-flag in the Appendix, from which it will be noticed that she not only constantly carried coal, but on one occasion case oil, on another jaggery, redwood and myrobolanes, a distinctly second class cargo, and once even scrap iron. As a rule, however, her outward cargoes were general, whilst her homeward were tea or wool.

The type of cargo makes a great difference to a vessel's speed through the water; especially is this the case with sailing ships, and therefore it must not be thought that all general cargoes were pleasant ones. Some general cargoes consisted mostly of rails and heavy machinery: these mostly were loaded in the North at Glasgow and Liverpool, but on occasions a London ship got more than she wanted of deadweight cargo.

Perhaps the most favoured of all the ships sailing from the London River were the Aberdeen White Star ships. And there was a curious reason for this. Thompson's ships, especially their early wooden ones, were constantly given Jewish names, such as:— *Maid of Judah, Jerusalem, Nineveh* and *Thyatira*. The Jewish merchants, in the City, attracted by these names, always rushed to ship their goods on the Aberdeen White Star clippers and thus Thompsons were always able to fill up with the choicest cargoes.

General cargoes to China were generally not so good as those to the Colonies. In the Colonies, with their thousands of newly landed Old Country men and women, there was always a tremendous demand for the good old British ale.

Now the easiest of all cargoes for a ship in a seaway is a liquid cargo. Old seamen used to declare that there was some affinity between the liquid inside the ship and that outside it, which helped her sailing powers in the most undeniable fashion. Thus when a captain saw numbers of cases of bottled beer, casks of brandy and barrels of rum amongst his bills of lading he was very well satisfied. I have hundreds of the *Cutty Sark's* bills of lading with their nicely engraved ships at the left hand top corner, and I think I am safe in saying that the *Cutty Sark* must have carried every product of the British Isles at one time or another from pianos to lead pipes, from coarse soda to Portland cement, from bundles of wire to cart wheels and axles, from superfine cottons and tweeds to pockets of hops and packets of matches. And in the eighties and nineties she very often took in some gunpowder at Gravesend.

I find an interesting anecdote of the *Cutty Sark* loading general cargo in Tomlinson's *London River*:—

"When my business was concerned with bills of lading and freight accounts, I was advised to ship 400 cases to Sydney, N.S.W., and one half of that consignment, my instructions ran, was to arrive a month before the other, The first lot went in the modern steel barque *Cairnbulg*. More than a fortnight later, being too young to remember that the little *Cutty Sark* had been one of the China tea clippers, I shipped the last half of the consignment in her. But she disordered all the careful plans of the consignees. She got in a fortnight ahead of the *Cairnbulg*."

The *Cutty Sark's* tea cargoes averaged about 1,325,000 lbs. The very greatest care was taken in loading a tea cargo. The lower hold and 'tween decks were thoroughly cleaned out and fumigated as soon as the previous cargo had been discharged: then they were lined with bamboo matting, ready for the chests of tea.

Perhaps the most important decision before the captain was how much stiffening he would take in in the shape of washed shingle. Most of the earlier clippers had a certain amount of fixed ballast fitting into the limber holes, but this was rarely the case in the seventies when freights were steadily dropping. Improper ballasting has cost many a fine ship her race; *Leander* once loaded down to her marks before she was half full; but as a rule the captains cut their ballasting as fine as they dared, and when as sometimes happened this was overdone, the hardly used clippers came home on their beam ends.

The Chinese stevedores with their handy mallets were wonderfully clever in stowing the chests, and at the same time wonderfully quick, for the loading of a tea cargo was always a racing matter, ship against ship, and the loss of a tide or a gap in the lighters alongside would usually turn the captain of a tea clipper into a surly bear and her mate into a roaring lion.

Cutty Sark always loaded at Shanghai or Hankow. She was usually one of the first ships on the berth and she was so favoured by the shippers that out of eight passages she was first ship away from Hankow on four occasions, first ship away from Shanghai twice and second ship from Shanghai once. In 1871 she was the first on the berth at Shanghai, but freights were only £3, and when the lighters were actually alongside, her agents, thinking that they could do better, withdrew her from the berth and sent her off to Foochow. There she found most of the tonnage already engaged and finally returned to Shanghai, by which date her agents were ready to accept the £3 freight, having lost over two months in their efforts to get more.

On her first three voyages *Cutty Sark* took general cargo to Shanghai, but on her fourth she loaded general cargo for Melbourne behind *Thermopylae*. From 1873 to 1878 she always loaded general to Sydney, from whence she took coals across to Shanghai like *Thermopylae* and most of the tea ships.

Cutty Sark usually loaded 1100 tons of coal. Regarding her wool cargoes, *Cutty Sark* first loaded wool in Newcastle, N.S.W., in December, 1883—indeed she was one of the pioneers in the Newcastle wool trade. After two trips from Newcastle, she took her first cargo of wool from Sydney, where she speedily became one of the best known of Sydney's wool clippers. Here she found herself in competition, not only with her old rivals *Thermopylae* but with much larger ships such as *The Tweed, Thomas Stephens, Samuel Plimsoll, Cimba, Patriarch, Brilliant, Trafalgar, Sir Walter Raleigh,* etc.

But not one of them could keep with her, and once again she became first favourite with the shippers. Captain Woodget was a terror to stevedores and managed to get several hundreds more bales screwed into her than Captain Moore could do in Newcastle.

Mr. W. G. Deuchar, the well-known agent, thus describes the "Cutty" loading wool:—

"*Cutty Sark* was so fine in her lines that she could not stow tallow and other cask cargo, so that she was always loaded with wool, and the largest cargo she ever carried was 4676 bales.

"In fact, Captain Woodget was so particular about the cargo carried (number of bales) that upon one occasion when I visited the ship I found him in the 'tween decks with the boss stevedore for the old firm of Talbot & Co., having a big row.

"I said, 'What is the matter, Captain Woodget?' when he turned upon me and said, 'Mr. Deuchar, they are slumming the stowage, and I have knocked the men off."

' "Why,' he said, 'we had 48 bales in this half-longer last voyage, and now they have only put in 45 bales.' The half-longer had to be pulled down and restowed; and by hard screwing the extra three bales were put in and Captain Woodget was satisfied. He always spent half the day in the ship's hold, and when not there himself he put his eldest son to watch the men.

"She usually loaded at Circular Quay, where the Japanese Mail Line now berth, and for about five years always loaded as last chance for the February wool sales.

"I remember on one occasion she had only 80 days allowed her, yet all the shippers stuck to her, and it was always a case of shut-out cargo. This trip was made in about 73 days."

Mr. Deuchar, in his mention of 4676 bales, probably refers to the cargo loaded by the *Cutty Sark* in 1891. This cargo was loaded in eight working days—a record; and it gave her a draft of 19 ft. 8 in. mean.

Two years later the stevedores determined to beat Captain Woodget and his little notebook, in which he kept the details of the stowage of all his previous cargoes. Somehow or other they managed to compress the bales until they got 5010 into her. Woodget, who knew that up till that date he had never relaxed a watchful eye on the stevedores, and firmly believed that he had always seen the utmost number crammed into her, was absolutely nonplussed and confessed himself beaten.

This cargo worked out at just over 2,000,000 lbs., and was worth about £100,000. It cost close on £800 to put on board and her freight came to about £4000. This was the voyage before old "White Hat" sold her. He complained that she was losing money; the real truth was that she, like every other sailing ship, was earning less money owing to the big drop in freights, but she was still paying a very handsome dividend per voyage in spite of the steamers cutting in and getting the cream, just as they had done in the tea trade.

The *Cutty Sark* used to take in about 200 tons of chrome ore as stiffening for a wool cargo. On one occasion as we shall see later, she had not enough stiffening and royal yards and staysails had to be sent down, yet she ran to the Lizard in 84 days.

The heaviest cargo that *Cutty Sark* has ever carried was the scrap iron, when, as Captain Woodget expressed it, she was as low in the water as a sand barge, drawing 21 feet, yet in this trim she made over 1000 miles in three days.

At New York in 1882 she loaded 26,816 cases of oil on a draft of 21 feet forward and 21 feet 2 ins. aft. And she brought home from Madras, Bimlipatam and Coconada 3310 bags of jaggery, 100 tons of redwood, 4163 horns, 115 bales of deer horns and 11,021 bags of myrobolanes on a draft of 20 ft. 4 ins. forward and 20 ft. 7 ins. aft.

Thermopylae was able to load about 100 tons more deadweight cargo than *Cutty Sark*. Thompsons, however, were very careful not to overload their ships, especially when they were racing. In 1872 *Thermopylae* only loaded 1,196,400 lbs. of tea against the *Cutty Sark's* 1,303,000 lbs. This was a special occasion and *Thermopylae* was given every chance accordingly.

Both ships, curiously enough, loaded their largest tea cargoes in the same year, 1876, when *Cutty Sark* took in 1,375,364 lbs. whilst

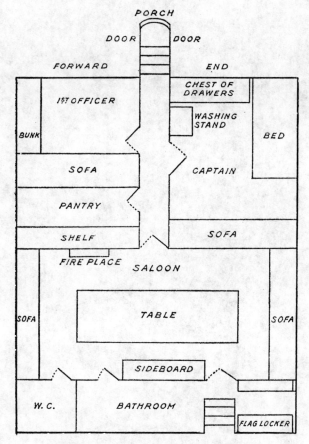

CABIN PLAN OF THE "CUTTY SARK."

[See Page 35

Thermopylae stowed 1,429,100 lbs.   *Cutty Sark's* largest coal cargo from Sydney to Shanghai was 1150 tons, *Thermopylae's* 1208 tons.

In 1885 *Cutty Sark* and *Thermopylae* loaded wool together at Sydney for the February wool sales.

Cutty Sark loaded:—

> 4465 bales of wool.
> 2342 packages of cobalt ore.
> 1345 bags of nickel ore.
> 29,772 horns.
> 122 cwt. 2 qr. 21 lbs. shank bones.
> 76 cwt. 1 qr. 20 lbs. hoofs.
> 1 cwt. of pith and 6 bales of sheepskins.

Thermopylae loaded:—

> 4638 bales of wool.
> 650 bags of chrome ore.
> 1142 bags of nickel ore.
> 19 tons 19 cwt. old iron rails.
> 15 casks of milk.
> 1 cask of sheep shears.

In the race home *Cutty Sark* beat *Thermopylae* by a clear week and made the fastest passage out of over 30 first class ships.

It is now time to say something about Captain George Moodie, who superintended the building of the *Cutty Sark* and commanded her on her first three voyages.

In choosing Moodie to command the new ship, which was being built to win the blue ribbon of the sea and lower the proud *Thermopylae's* colours, Captain John Willis picked out the most trusted of all his captains, if we except Stuart of *The Tweed*.

A native of East Wemyss, Captain Moodie was born as far back as 1829. As a boy he was always to be found amongst the hardy fishermen of the Firth, but his first genuine experience of the sea was made aboard various small vessels belonging to the Provost of Kirkcaldy. His apprenticeship papers were signed in 1847, his apprenticeship being served in the brig *Lively Maria*, belonging to the Johnstones, a well-known firm of Fife linen manufacturers, trading between West Wemyss and Riga.

In 1854 young Moodie married Janet Cassels of West Wemyss, and seven years later he gained his master's certificate.

In 1863 we find him serving as mate under Captain Stuart of *The Tweed*, on her first voyage for John Willis. It was a very successful, money-making voyage, and on her return home her mate's share in the success was rewarded—Moodie was given command of the *Laurel** in the China trade.

In 1866 Moodie took his owner out to Rangoon in the *Laurel;** here he met the *Whiteadder*, Captain F. W. Moore, who followed him in the command of the *Cutty Sark*, Captain Keay, of the *Ariel* then a new ship, loading rice for China before taking in tea for the famous 1866 race, and Captain Watt of the *Foam*, a by-gone crack—Captain Watt subsequently commanded the *Hallowe'en*.

Captain Moodie was not allowed to remain in the *Laurel** for long without promotion. Willis next gave him the *Lauderdale*† which Moodie commanded until he was needed to superintend the building of the *Cutty Sark*.

Like all sea captains, George Moodie was full of character. If he was a careful navigator, with a great deal of Scotch caution, which made him disinclined to take risks in the China seas like some of his rivals, he knew how to carry sail, and he was a magnificent seaman and a good business man, which in those days often meant the difference between a good voyage and a bad one from the owner's point of view.

Captain Moodie was very proud of his connection with the *Cutty Sark*. After his retirement from the sea, his chief interest was meteorology. He had a sharp wit, as instance this anecdote.

The Provost of Auchtermuchty met Captain Moodie in the street one day and asked him what he thought the weather was going to be.

"Wet," replied the captain shortly.

"Surely not," said the Provost, "my glass was standing at fair when I came out."

---

* *Laurel*, wood ship, 638 tons, 162 ft. long, 29·5 beam, 18·7 depth, built by Alcock of Sunderland in 1859.

† *Lauderdale*, composite ship, 851 tons, 187 ft. long, 32 ft. beam, 20 depth, built in London in 1858.

"Aye," sneered old Moodie, "and do ye think the weather cares a damn for your glass."

He could never be made to use a walking-stick as being un-seamanlike, but in his later years would totter about with his arms outstretched to steady himself.

One of the reasons that I have heard given for the failure of Scott & Linton was that Captain Moodie was so particular as to the wood and other materials used in the building of the *Cutty Sark*. Apparently his eagle eye searched every bit of wood for knots, shakes or sappy patches, and if the least defect was found it was thrown back on Scott & Linton's hands. Undoubtedly Moodie's untiring superintendence of the building is one of the reasons why the famous old ship is still afloat today and sound as a bell at that.

I have been unable to find out the exact date on which the *Cutty Sark's* keel was laid, but a joiner, who started work with Scott & Linton in January, 1869, thought she was laid down some two months prior to that date.

He also declared that in the opinion of every tradesman who worked on her, the Cutty *Sark* was a *class job.* A great deal of secrecy was used about the plans, the builders being very anxious that nothing should leak out which might be taken advantage of by the Glasgow and Greenock yards then hard at work on the *Wylo, Oberon, Normancourt, City of Hankow, Duke of Abercorn* and *Eme*, all of which were intended for the China trade.

Scott & Linton were in difficulties some three months before the launch. Every effort was made to tide over the trouble. Willis was approached, but he refused to increase his instalments. At last a day came when the weekly wage money was not forthcoming.

An old shipwright who is still living and whose claim to fame is that he built the port quarter of the *Cutty Sark,* says that one day in August Scott and Linton came into the shop and said to the men:—

"We can't pay your wages today, but it will be all right." The hands went away without a fuss and they were paid all right in ten days' time.

In the first week of September, however, the work in the Woodyard was finally suspended, the *Cutty Sark* being almost ready for launching, being planked up, caulked, and with decks laid.

On 11th September a meeting of Scott & Linton's creditors was held, in which it was decided to complete the contracts in hand, which besides the new tea clipper consisted of a three-masted schooner, which was being built alongside her. Trustees were thereupon appointed, whose first step, I expect, was to approach Denny. The course taken by the creditors in finishing the *Cutty Sark* at their own expense no doubt relieved Denny of his ignorance of this guarantee: it is probable that they were either in ignorance or else thought that they would get back part of their money by making themselves responsible for the finishing of the contract. The result was disastrous as far as they were concerned. It is rarely wise for creditors of a business in liquidation to take on its contracts.

In this case, after realising all assets, the creditors found another 4s. in the pound added to their claims. One creditor who was owed £4000 found that the finishing of the two vessels cost him another £800. Trade, however, was booming and every single creditor paid his share towards the cost of finishing the *Cutty Sark*. Denny on taking over the work replaced Scott & Linton's foremen with his own.

It has been argued that Denny's people took little interest in the work, that the *Cutty Sark* was finished in a hurry, and that some of the iron work of the riggers was defective, but I was indignantly assured not only by the workmen who are still living, but by Captain Moodie himself, that the Dennys of those days did not do scamped work and that no fault could be found with the finishing of the *Cutty Sark* by Denny Bros.

There was no doubt some delay before the yard was opened under Denny's management, as the launching of the new tea clipper did not take place until the afternoon of Monday, 23rd November.

For some days before the *Cutty Sark* was launched a dredger, belonging to the Clyde Trust, was employed in deepening the river opposite the Woodyard in order to obtain sufficient depth for a safe launch. The Dumbarton dredger happened to be absent at Girvan, which accounts for a Glasgow dredger being used.

The launch had been arranged for Saturday, but the carpenters were not ready in time. The new tea clipper was christened by Mrs. Moodie. The carpenters on the deck of the ship hoped that the bottle of wine would fail to break and thus become their perquisite, but the captain was on the lookout to prevent such an unlucky start in life for his new ship.

"Be sure an' gie a guid ca' to the bottle," he urged Mrs. Moodie. The lady followed out his instructions; the bottle was smashed to pieces on the ship's bow: the new clipper received her curious name and amidst the cheers of the spectators slipped quietly down the ways into the water. All went without a hitch. It is a superstition amongst old seamen that any hitch at a launch spells bad luck for the vessel in the future.

One of the most unlucky ships that ever sailed the seas was the *Harvey Mills*, 2186 tons, built at Thomaston, Maine, in 1876, and considered to be the finest American ship afloat. A man was killed at her launch, thus she was said to have been baptised in blood. On her maiden passage she loaded cotton at Port Royal for Liverpool. On 28th December, 1876, she lay ready for sea when she caught fire and two men were suffocated in her chain locker. The fire was got under, and giving a bond to pay the innumerable compensation claims, she sailed to New York for repairs. Two years later she ran into a hurricane and was dismasted. At the end of 1880, she ran into and sank the barque *Eta* off the coast of England. Then after paying heavy legal expenses, she once more sailed for America, was again dismasted and had to put back, finally taking twelve months to cross the Atlantic. By this time the papers were full of her. Blood-curdling yarns about the unlucky ship began to appear in print. The men she had killed haunted her, ghostly shipmates worked amongst the men both aloft and on deck, whilst in bad weather the shrieks of drowning men rang out above the roar of the storm.

At last on 12th December, 1886, she left Seattle and a few weeks later foundered off Cape Flattery taking 22 of her crew down with her, the only survivors being the mate and two seamen, who, after a terrible time clinging to floating wreckage, were picked up by the barque *Majestic*.

Though there was no hitch at the *Cutty Sark's* launch, two events occurred in the previous week which had a very considerable bearing upon her life. The first was the opening of the Suez Canal on November 16th, which in a very few years drove the sailing clippers out of the China tea trade and handed it over to the steamers The second event was the total loss of the beautiful *Spindrift*, which went ashore at Dungeness opposite the signal station the day before the *Cutty Sark* was launched. This vessel was undoubtedly one of the finest and fastest of all the tea clippers. Her untimely end not only ruined old Findlay, her owner, but broke his heart. It also deprived the *Cutty Sark* of a rival which would have taken some beating.

On the 21st December the *Cutty Sark* was towed to Greenock to be rigged out and masted. Here she was moored with her bow looking towards Cartsdyke, and right opposite the shipbuilding yard of Robert Steele.

The Steeles had just launched a new iron clipper for the East Indian trade. This was the *Ladyburn* of 1515 tons, owned by Shankland and commanded by Captain Laing, late of the *Challenge.*

Compared with *Ladyburn* the *Cutty Sark* resembled a huge yacht and was greatly admired. With the two vessels lying so close to each other the comparison must have been most interesting. The *Cutty Sark* represented the very last thing in composite building, whilst the *Ladyburn* was an early example of a type, the iron Clyde clipper type, which was shortly to cover the seas in its hundreds—nay thousands.

The black sides and gilded scroll work of the "Cutty" were a big contrast to the painted ports and pink bottom of the *Ladyburn*, and that the former looked like a yacht is easily seen when we remember that in those days no yacht was painted anything but black and gold.

The *Ladyburn* sailed for Calcutta in the second week in December; she was caught by frightful weather in the Bay of Biscay and went down with all hands.

The *Cutty Sark* did not leave Greenock until 13th January, and a fortnight later began taking in her first cargo.

There have been various assertions by writers to the papers that her iron work aloft was defective. One old hand declares that she carried some of it away on her trip round from the Clyde. This is denied by Captain Moodie. Another asserts that her mainyard came down with a run when she was using it to sling cargo aboard. A third assures me that she did not have a fair chance on her maiden voyage owing to the constant giving way of her iron work aloft. Captain Moodie himself declares that the "carries-away" were no more than usual in a new ship, but the following entries in his abstract log seem to point to a decided weakness aloft. The iron work need not have been necessarily defective, but it was very probably rather too light to stand the strain of such sail carrying as was usual in the tea trade.

March 4.—Lat. 17° 25′ N., long. 20° 10′ W. Course S. 23° W. Distance 236 miles. Fresh N.E. trades. *Fixed main topsail parrel.*

July 12.—Lat. 13° 57′ N., long 114° 31′ E. Course S. 16° W. Distance 77 miles. A fresh gale from S.W. *Found the parrel of fore topsail broken.*

Oct. 9.—Lat. 45° 28′ N., long 18° 35′. Course N. 61° E. Distance 280 miles. Wind west to N.W. strong but very unsteady in force and direction. All port stunsails set and *the broken masts and yards stand pretty stiff to it.*

Her first voyage was remarkable for light weather; on her second voyage, when a few days from Shanghai, she carried away both fore and main topsail ties and broke the cap at the fore lower masthead.

This carrying away of iron work aloft was a very common experience amongst the clippers in the early seventies, and caused many a dismasting, that of the *Blackadder* on her maiden voyage being one of the most disastrous.

Having got the *Cutty Sark* on to her loading berth for China, it is now time to begin a fresh chapter.

CHAPTER III.

IN THE CHINA TRADE

THE year 1870 opened a new era in the China Tea trade. Up till that date steamers had found it impossible to compete with the sailing ships; but with the opening of the Suez Canal and the possibliity of coaling at Singapore, Port Said, and Gibraltar, the first teas could be put on the London market by the racing steamers in less than 60 days from Shanghai, a gain of a month or more on the best times taken by the clippers in the long passage round the Cape. Nevertheless sailing ship owners were by no means discouraged and faced the future with a confidence which was rather more stout-hearted than far-sighted.

They had, however, some very good reasons for this confidence; for instance, many of the tea merchants were firmly of opinion that tea carried in iron hulls deteriorated and for this reason preferred the composite clippers, especially for their choicest brands. Besides this, the trade had grown so in volume that it was hoped there would be ample room for both sailing ships and steamers.

Thirdly, a number of shipowners in the Eastern trade were by no means sure that the Suez Canal would be a success and predicted that the steamers using the Canal would experience unexpected delays, which would add to their expenses and cut down their profits very seriously. In these days we can hardly realise the many difficulties with which those in charge of the early steamers had to contend. Undoubtedly the chief of these for ships in the Eastern trade was the task of finding stokers who could stand the ill-ventilated stokeholds in the heat of the Red Sea. At first it was thought that stoking in the Red Sea was more than any white man could endure; thus Kroomen from the West Coast of Africa were specially signed on for this object. Though probably the hardiest race in the whole Bight of Benin, these sturdy surf-boatmen collapsed in front of their furnace doors and had to be relieved at frequent intervals.

DECK OF "CUTTY SARK", 1922

(See Page 22

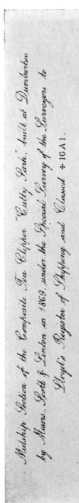

Midships Section of the Composite Tea Clipper "Cutty Sark," built at Dumbarton by Messrs. Scott & Linton in 1869, under the Special Survey of the Surveyors to Lloyd's Register of Shipping and Classed + 1GA1.

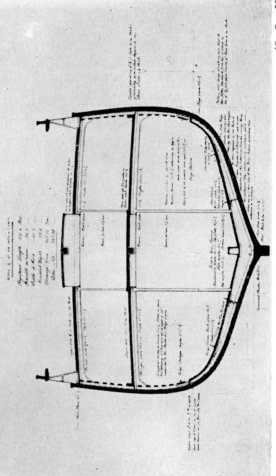

[See Page 26]

Experiments were tried with other tropical races, but with the same result. Then yellow men were tried, and finally the steam-ship owners were compelled to fall back on their own colour and make the best of it. Here we come to the triumph of the Liverpool Irishman, for it was soon realised that the Liverpool Irish stoker, the son of the Liverpool Irish Western Ocean packet-rat, was the only man who could submit to this near approach to the fires of hell and still survive. Without a doubt the Liverpool Irishman is the toughest of all the sons of man. He soon proved himself as indifferent to the stifling heat of the Red Sea as to the biting cold of the North Atlantic winter, and but for his astounding powers of endurance it is probable that the racing steamers would have had a much stiffer fight before they captured the tea trade.

In 1870 the steamers *Diomed*, *Agamemnon* and *Erl King* loaded at Hankow and the *Achilles* at Foochow. When they all reached London *via* the Suez Canal in less than 60 days, there was a rush to build steamers for the China trade. Even sailing ship owners were tempted, thus Shaw, Maxton & Co., who in 1870 had compromised with the auxiliary *Oberon*, ordered the *Lord of the Isles* and the *Galley of Lorne*, whilst Skinner began building his numerous "Castles", his short-lived *Drummond Castle* being launched in December, 1871. Skinner was a very clever and level-headed Glasgow man and had a number of irons in the fire. He also built a number of clippers on spec, most of which he sold very profitably. When he began building racing steamers, his fellow-townsmen, Allan C. Gow and McGregor, started the Glen Line in competition with his "Castles," their first steamers being the *Glengyle*, launched in 1870, and the *Glenroy*, launched in 1871.

For a few years there was a tremendous boom in these racing steamers: though at first good freights were earned, the tonnage soon threatened to overweigh the trade, then freights began to fall, profits became problematical, weak owners fell out of the struggle and gradually the trade became stabilised again, but not before the sailing ships had been driven from the China Seas.

Though the *Cutty Sark* is still afloat and still seaworthy, I do not believe that a single one of these tea steamers is in existence. Their life indeed was a very short one; they were soon shaken to

E

pieces and had to be scrapped and replaced, besides which, their losses from strandings were very heavy. In the first two or three years of the boom as many as half a dozen came to grief. The *Drummond Castle*, when barely clear of her tea port, was wrecked on the Chusan Islands; and at the subsequent enquiry at Shanghai a great deal was said about the reckless driving of racing steamers through intricate channels. The P. & O. *Sunda* was lost on a reef in the Haetan Straits, the *Gordon Castle* stranded on the Burlings, and the *Canton* on the Min Reef—to mention but a few of the casualties amongst these early steamers.*

So much for the steamers; though they were a distinct cloud on the horizon in 1870, the sailing ship owners saw no cause for despondency and hoped for many years of high freights and hard races round the Cape.

It is now time to say something about the sailing ship owners in the China trade.

When we realise that they were almost without exception retired sailing ship skippers, it is not difficult to see why they clung to their white wings with a desperate conservatism. The firm of John Willis & Son was founded by the father of the *Cutty Sark's* owner. John Willis the elder was a native of Berwick-on-Tweed. When about fourteen years of age, after a furious disagreement with his step-father, he ran away to sea and for perhaps a year served as lop-lolly boy on a coaster; such a start in sea life either broke a boy or made a man, for it was the hardest that can be imagined. After about a year, John Willis managed to escape from the North Sea and was apprenticed on a West Indian sugar drogheur. In this great trade of the eighteenth and early nineteenth centuries, he rose from boy to able seaman, from able seamen to mate, from mate to master and from master to owner. But he laid the foundations of his fortune whilst he was still a boy.

---

* Perhaps a few particulars of the first of these racing tea steamers may be found interesting:—

Erl King, 1707 tons, 250 h.p. built 1865 by Inglis for Robertson & Co.; *Lord of the Isles*, 1846 tons, 240 h,p., built in 1870 by Napier for Shaw, Maxton; *Galley of Lorne*, 1390 tons, 240 h.p. built in 1871 by Napier, for Shaw, Maxton; *Drummond Castle*, 1985 tons, 200 h.p., built in 1871 by Thomson, for Skinner; *Glengyle*, 1264 tons, 185 h.p., built by London & Glasgow Co., in 1870 for McGregor, Gow & Co.

The West India Docks were opened in 1802, when they had to be approached from the city by means of a muddy country road, thus the old hostelry of the "Blue Posts" was much frequented by shipping people, who kept the "boots" busy on their long Wellingtons. Here John Willis saw an opportunity, and whilst his ship was in the docks it was his custom to wield the blacking brush at the Blue Posts. His boot-blacking money he invested cleverly, in fiddle-strings according to one account, which he sold at a great profit to the banjo-playing darkies of the West Indies. This he always used to declare was his first trading venture. From the West Indies he brought back kegs of tamarinds and jars of ginger and sugar candy, which he sold to the well-known Wapping grocer, George Yates. And by the time John Willis obtained command he had almost saved enough money to buy a ship. Indeed the time soon came when he was able to retire from the sea and give instructions to his own captains.

The shipowners of London in the early years of the nineteenth century were divided into two classes. The first class were the magnates of the City—the great builders of East Indiamen such as Green and Wigram, who were often "India husbands" before the Company's monopoly was abolished, and when this happened ran their own passenger ships to the East, which became known as the Blackwall frigates.

The other class of London shipowner was the retired skipper, who had saved money, started in a small way with one or two ships and gradually built up a fleet.

Many of these self-made men came from North of the Tweed, and these formed a small coterie of their own, their headquarters being known as Little Scotland. The best known members of this clique of Scotsmen were John Willis, Pirrie, Brodie, James Anderson, Ross the ballastman and Maclachlan the optician.

And what characters they were! Shrewd, keen business men with a touch of Presbyterian dourness, they were yet most generous and kind-hearted where their own countrymen were concerned. Indeed one or two, notably Anderson, made it a rule never to employ any but Scotsmen.

And how they loved their ships?

John Willis the elder spent most of the day aboard his ships. Whilst his captains attended to the shore end of the business, he delighted in superintending the sailorising work aboard—directing the riggers, watching the stowage and generally poking his nose into everything—a proceeding which must have been very trying to a self-respecting mate.

When he was living at Clapton, some hour and a half's journey from the Docks, John Willis always breakfasted at seven on a bowl of porridge and a cup of "coffee royal," which was coffee laced with Jamaica rum. He was very set in his ways, and on his journey to the docks always called at the same shop for a pennorth of snuff, which was screwed up in a piece of paper—he had no affectations and the wonderful snuffboxes of those days were not in his line. Then at 8.30 to the minute he would walk aboard his ship. And nothing pleased him more than to find that his apprentices had not yet returned from their usual late breakfast ashore, of a "New Gravel Lane bullock, 50 ribs a side"—in other words a red herring, for then he was able to air his wit at their expense.

Captain John Willis the elder was a shipowner and nothing else. He hated all side lines of shipping business, which others usually combined with owning, and considered that there were only two worthy professions—"sodger or sailor". His first ships were all round-barrelled sugar-droghuers, such as the *John Willis*, *Janet Willis*, *Borderer* and *St. Abb's*. He had three sons, all of whom were brought up to the sea under the eagle eye of their father. The eldest, James, succeeded his father in the command of a West Indiaman but went missing on the passage home, after writing to his father that he had managed to get more sugar into her than ever old John had done.

The second son, after commanding his father's ships for some years, was taken into the business, and the firm became John Willis & Son. The third son, Robert, had none of the Willis character and grit; and with no incentive to make money, he soon left the sea and drifted into obscurity.

Jock Willis, known in the City as "Willis o' the White Hat" and often referred to as "Old White Hat", had a great deal of his father's character.

Decided in opinion, his speech was always straight to the point and his praise or his blame was never half-hearted, His only test of a captain was success, and bad luck he never considered an excuse for a financially unsuccessful voyage. His stock expression, for anyone in his bad books, was "scoundrel"; nevertheless he had a favourite saying:—"I would rather have a rogue than a fool as captain of my ships, because a rogue can make money for himself if he doesn't for the ship, but a fool neither makes money for himself nor the ship."

Though Jock Willis gave his captains a free hand he would never allow them any interest in their ships, neither would he allow their wives aboard though he himself was a great favourite with the ladies.

After the dismasting of the *Blackadder* on her maiden passage, and the 18 months of lawsuits with the underwriters and her builders John Willis never insured another ship.

He was very fond of teak, and made a great deal of money by buying those everlasting frigate built Indiamen, which were constructed throughout of Malabar teak. His best buy was that of the *Assaye* and *Punjaub*, the first of which he sold at a fine profit, and the second of which besides earning a fortune for herself, supplied the design for the sister ships, *Blackadder* and *Hallowe'en*, and, as we have seen, inspired the beautiful bow lines of the *Cutty Sark*.

Another fierce old sea captain turned shipowner was Killick, nicknamed the Admiral. He commanded the famous *Challenger* through the height of the American invasion of the tea trade, and made eight passages from Shanghai averaging 110 days.

Killick was a tall ramrod of a man, very blunt and plain spoken, who kept his employees very much in their place. The firm of Killick, Martin & Co. had a number of beautiful little clippers, such as the *Kaisow*, *Wylo* and *Lothair*, but they rarely entered the competition for the new teas, being content with the Japanese and New York trade.

Another of these skipper owners was Wade, of Robertson & Co., who owned the *Ada*, *Ziba* and *Eme*.

Then there was Captain Rodger, who commanded *Kate Carnie*, the first of all Steele's creations, and owned the famous *Taeping* and *Lahloo.* Rodger hailed from the Clyde, along with the MacCunn's, who owned *Sir Lancelot,* and Findlay who was broken down by the loss of the *Spindrift.* Rodger had a more philosophical nature, and, when in 1870, freights fell to £3 10s. and James MacCunn greeted him with:—"Isn't this a wretched state of things?" he replied with a quiet smile: — "Weel, James, it micht be waur."

Like many another old hand, Captain Rodger could not bear spoiling the look of a ship by giving her double topsail yards, and to the end his ships retained their single topsails.

The old friends Findlay and Rodger dropped out of the shipping business within a year or two of each other. When *Spindrift* went ashore uninsured, old Findlay, besides being nearly ruined, was so upset by the loss of the pride of his heart that his mind gradually gave way Then in 1871-2 Findlay's *Serica* was lost with all hands except the bosun, and Rodger's famous pair *Lahloo* and *Taeping* were both wrecked in the East. Rodger, thereupon, sold the *Min* and retired. But *Windhover,* the last of Findlay's fleet, with young Findlay in command—a man who was notoriously fond of the bottle—was not sold until 1880.

The voyage before she was sold, *Windhover* had a man in possession aboard whilst she lay in the S.W.I. Dock, and when she sailed no thrum mats could be found so that her hands declared that the chafing gear had been sold to pay the ship keeper—so low in the water had the firm of Findlay sunk.

There remains one other tea ship owner who requires a mention. This was the energetic Maxton, of *Falcon, Ariel* and *Titania.* Maxton had a great deal to do with the design of *Falcon,* and he considered *Ariel* and *Titania* to be the most perfect examples of the thorough-bred tea clipper. He therefore did not attempt to improve upon them but turned his attention to auxiliaries and finally to steam. He was perhaps the most brainy of all the old tea clipper captains who earned money and turned to shipowning.

In the year 1870 there were about 60 regular sailing ships in the China trade, which carried British colours; of these only about a dozen were considered thorough-bred racers or "full bloods" as they were called, namely *Taeping, Serica, Ariel, Sir Lancelot,*

Taitsing, Titania, Leander, Lahloo, Undine, Windhover, Kaisow and *Thermopylae*, every one of which was capable of 100-day passage.

In the second rank, besides several "has beens" such as *Falcon, Fiery Cross* and *Flying Spur*, there were some very fine steady-going ships, which always made good passages without ever doing anything very startling. Of these the pick were *Argonaut, Forward Ho, Belted Will, Black Prince, Maitland, Chinaman, J. R. Worcester,* and *Thyatira*.

Of the new ships *Caliph, Normancourt, Wylo, Duke of Abercorn* and *Blackadder* were out and out racers and expected to be the most dangerous rivals of the *Cutty Sark*.

The *Caliph* was undoubtedly a very fast ship indeed, but she had the misfortune to be commanded by a man of very little experience in the China trade, who failed to get a charter for the first teas and was obliged to wait until the winter for a tea cargo to New York.

On her second voyage the *Caliph* mysteriously disappeared in the China Seas, and it was believed at the time that she had been captured by pirates.

Normancourt was a beautiful little ship, designed by the celebrated Rennie, and perfectly built by Inglis. She was one of the most weatherly of all the tea clippers and with the Shewans, father and son, in command was one of the hardest sailed ships in the last days of the sailing fleet.

Blackadder was undoubtedly a very fast ship indeed, but she was thrown out of the struggle between the cracks by her various dismastings and other misfortunes.

Wylo was a lightweight flyer, much like the *Kaisow*; she specialised in the New York trade, and did not compete for the first teas of the season. She usually carried a chequer crew, half negroes, half white and was celebrated for her chantymen. Her captain, Brown, was one of the most respected master mariners in the trade. He was a bachelor, rather better educated than most shipmasters of his time, and one of the kindest and most benevolent of skippers where his crew were concerned. He was, however, a bit eccentric, and had a heart with an arrow through it tattooed on his left breast, the legend being that he had been crossed in love.

The *Duke of Abercorn* was a magnificent all round ship and her owners hoped great things of her. Though heavily rigged, she was not as sharp ended as most out and out racers, and she had the reputation of being very fast on the starboard tack, without being anything wonderful on the port, which looks as if there must have been some small fault in her building or else trim. Her passages were very consistent without being anything out of the way

She was ostensibly owned by Montgomerie, Workman, but the Smiths of the City Line were said to have had an interest in her, and also the Hamilton family probably had some shares, for her figure-head consisted of a fine portrait of the first Duke of Abercorn in his peer's robes, whilst the Hamilton arms were emblazoned on a large board amidships.

The *City of Hankow* was also built specially for the China trade by the Smiths. Though she was undoubtedly a very fast ship her passages out and home in 1870 were nothing out of the way, upon which she was relegated to the regular City round—out to Melbourne and home from Calcutta. I believe, however, that she suffered from an indifferent commander on her maiden voyage, for, on Captain Muir taking her over, she made some very fast passages both out and home, and gave both the *Cutty Sark* and *Thermopylae* good races.

The little *Ambassador*, which loaded first from Foochow in 1870, was badly overhauled and also much too small to compete against such powerful vessels as *Cutty Sark* and *Thermopylae*; whilst *Eme*, one of Connell's little beauties, never retrieved her bad first passage home, which led to so much bad language on the part of old Skipper Wade when he sacked her captain on arrival.

On the opposite page I give a table of the outward passages to China in 1869-70.

It will be noticed that the new ships *Caliph* and *Normancourt* made a very close run of it with the famous *Titania*, whilst the big *Duke of Abercorn* was badly beaten by *Sir Lancelot*.

Thermopylae, as usual, took a general cargo to Melbourne, before crossing to China. She left London on 10th November, Gravesend on the 11th and passed the Isle of Wight on 12th November. She had to beat down Channel against violent W.S.W.

gales in thick dirty weather, and did not take her departure from the Lizard until 15th November. The wind kept in her teeth down to 44° 20′ N., 15° 37′ W., when on 20th November it hauled to the N.E. She crossed the line in 28° W. on 4th December, only 19 days out from the Lizard. The meridian of the Cape was crossed in 44° 12′ S. on 23rd December, 37 days out. From this point *Thermopylae* had the wind continually from the eastward, which spoilt what otherwise might have been a record passage.

Ship	Date left	Port to	Date arrived	Days out
Undine	September 21	Shanghai	January 23	124
Caliph	October 13	,,	February 1	111
Titania	,, 14	,,	,, 1	110
Normancourt ..	,, 18	Hongkong	January 31	105
Forward Ho ..	,, 23	Shanghai	February 17	117
Lahloo	,, 28	,,	,, 3	98
Ariel	,, 29	,,	,, 14	108
Leander	November 4	,,	,, 18	106
Duke of Abercorn ..	Nov. 16 (from Liverpool	,,	March 23	127
Spindrift	November 20	Wrecked Dungeness		—
Sir Lancelot ..	,, 20	Hongkong	February 26	98
Taeping	,, 21	Shanghai	March 4	102
Belted Will ..	,, 21	Hongkong	,, 11	110
Kaisow	December 2	Shanghai	,, 11	99
Windhover ..	,, 4	,,	May 1	148
Whiteadder ..	,, 18	,,	,, 23	156
Black Prince ..	,, 18	Hongkong	April 9	112
Serica	,, 20	Shanghai	,, 10	111
Falcon	,, 23	,,	May 7	135
Flying Spur ..	January 21	,,	,, 21	120
Thyatira	February 1	,,	June 1	120
John R. Worcester ..	,, 3	,,	May 29	115
Fiery Cross ..	,, 5	Hongkong	,, 21	105
Wylo	,, 11	Foochow	,, 25	103
Cutty Sark ..	,, 16	Shanghai	,, 31	104
Blackadder ..	March 24	,,	December 11	262*

In 43° 37′ S., 77° 20′ E. she encountered a strong easterly gale, and had to be kept under reduced canvas for 10 days. Her best day's work down south was 342 knots.

* Put into Capetown dismasted

On 12th December in 29° S., 29° 46′ W., *Thermopylae* exchanged signals with *Leander*, the two ships being parted by a heavy westerly gale.

On Sunday evening, 23rd January, 1870, *Thermopylae* passed the Otway and anchored in Port Phillip on the 25th, 71 days from the Lizard.

With the exception of the ill-fated *Blackadder, Cutty Sark* was the last ship to get away, with just time to reach Shanghai before the new teas came down.

She passed through the downs about midnight on 15th February with a fresh E.N.E. wind. At 11 p.m. on the 16th Start Point bore N.N.E. 10 miles, from which she took her departure. On the 18th the fair wind shifted into S.E. and S.S.E. and it began to blow hard with a heavy head sea.

The maiden passage of a sailing ship is always an anxious one for her officers. To begin with, they have to learn her ways—to get the hang of her; and this as a rule takes time, for a ship behaves differently to every other ship, and this in every kind of wind and sea that weather can breed.

The real sailorman knows by intuition, if not by hard experience, that his trade is never completely at his finger's ends, that, though he is learning all the time, he will ever have something more to learn. And, on a maiden voyage, however great his knowledge of the way of a ship in the sea, he has ever to be on the lookout for something unexpected in the behaviour of his ship.

Then, too, the mate of a new sailing ship is sure to find that the rigger's work is far from being all that is wanted. Chafes appear where there should be none, and if these are unnoticed things soon begin to carry away. Even wire rigging has a certain amount of stretch, and as it pulls down into place requires frequent setting up. Strains on gear have to be carefully watched, especially in racing ships, and iron work, because it gives no hint of the breaking strain, is a continual cause for anxiety.

The *Cutty Sark's* crew were setting up rigging and repairing broken iron work, such as a main topsail parrel, as soon as the N.E. trade was picked up.

The gale, with the wind slowly westering, lasted until 27th February, on which day the east end of Teneriffe bore N.W. 4 miles at noon. An hour or two later the *Cutty Sark* lay becalmed.

Captain Moodie was not a lucky man with his weather, and the *Cutty Sark's* maiden voyage was specially remarkable for lack of wind. It is true that she could maintain steerage way by the flap of her sails, but she was essentially a heavy weather flyer, and the more it blew the more she liked it.

In his first hard blow, Captain Moodie had been very cautious keeping his unknown ship under small canvas, but her behaviour soon filled him with confidence and he was not long in discovering that he had something very exceptional under him from the point of view both of speed and seaworthiness.

Thus his hopes rose high, and he became confident that if only he could keep the spars in her he would not only beat the *Thermopylae* but all records in the China trade. On 1st March in the afternoon the *Cutty Sark* picked up the first of the N.E. trades, and Moodie set his skysail and royal staysails for the first time.

He seems to have made sail slowly, for he did not set his stunsails until the following day, though the trade was light, the "Cutty's" best run being on the 4th only 236 miles. On the following day with the trade still lighter, he set his royal stunsails but only made a run of 194 miles.

For the next four days the wind held at N.N.E. very light, and on the afternoon of the 9th March the doldrums set with heavy rain. This trying weather held until 17th March.

On the 13th the *Cutty Sark* lay becalmed on the line in 21° 56′ W., her week's run from the 10th to the 16th only totalling 435 miles. The S.E. trades were as light as the N.E.; they carried her to 26° S., 23° W., when she again ran into a flat calm. On the following day, 26th March, Moodie writes desperately:—

Lat. 26° 26′ S., long. 23° 47′ W.   Course S. 21° W.   Distance 15 miles.
Calm ! calm ! calm !   Sea like a mirror.

After four days of almost continual calms, the wind began to freshen from the S.E. and developed into a hard gale from right ahead with a heavy cross sea; it was not until midnight on 3rd

April that the wind at last piped up from the right quarter and gave the *Cutty Sark* her first chance to show what she could do.

On 6th April she crossed the meridian of Greenwich in 41° 40′ S., ʼ49 days out, her run for the day being 290 miles. On the 8th she made her first run of over 300 miles, her distance for the 24 hours being 304 miles. But that very afternoon the wind fell light again, and settled in the east, a dead muzzler which from a light air gradually increased to a hard gale from the S.E.

But on 12th April with the wind strong at N.N.E., the *Cutty Sark* once more got going again, and the abstract of the next week's work is worth recording:—

April 13—Lat. 44° 18′ S., long. 38° 48′ E. Course S. 83° E. Distance 298 miles. Winds N.N.E. and north, strong.

April 14—Lat. 44° 18′ S., long 47° 8′ E. Course east. Distance 360 miles. Winds north, fresh. P.M., moderate.

15—Lat. 44° 25′ S., long. 53° 22′ E. Course S. 88½° E. Distance 269 miles. Winds north to W.N.W., fresh and rainy. Distance by log 343 miles. Ship has lost these two days 76 miles by a current as both patent and common logs agree. P.M., fresh gale.

April 16—Lat. 44° 9′ S., long. 60° 22′ E. Course N. 87° E. Distance 304 miles. Winds W.N.W. and N.N.W., strong, hail showers at times. P.M., wind light.

17—Lat. 43° 23′ S., long. 66° 21′ E. Course N. 80° E. Distance 266 miles. Winds north and N.N.E. Light wind and heavy sea. Noon, strong breeze. P.M., fresh gale. Passed a ship steering east.

18—Lat. 42° 17′ S., long. 73° 51′ E. Course N. 79° E. Distance 336 miles. Winds. N.N.E. to S.E., fresh gales and dry weather. Noon, wind S.S.W., light rain. Midnight, wind S.E. strong and rain.

19—Lat. 40° 27′ S., long. 78° 14′ E. Course N. 61° E. Distance 228 miles. Winds, S.E. and south. Fresh gales and thick rainy weather. P.M., continuous rain, strong gales.

On the following day the weather still remained dirty with a sharp cross sea, the run being 228 miles, but in the afternoon it fell away to calm and left the *Cutty Sark* tumbling about in a heavy cross sea.

It remained calm with a heavy sea until the evening of the 21st when sudden squalls with heavy rain began to come up.

On the 22nd April Captain Moodie records:—

Lat. 36° 9′ S., long. 85° 37′ E. Course N. 32° E. Distance 124 miles. Winds, variable S.E. to S.S.W. with sudden squalls and heavy rain. Noon, heavy head sea, barometer falling. 4 p.m., evidently there is a hurricane ahead, shortened sail to close reefs to let it pass. 8 p.m., kept ship before the wind, being now S. by W. Midnight, barometer rising, weather getting better, but an awful sea; set foresail.

Two days later the S.E. trades were picked up, but they were very unsteady both in force and direction, the *Cutty Sark's* best day's work being 245 miles on the 27th.

On 2nd May the *Cutty Sark* passed Christmas Island and over-hauled *Wylo* and *Doune Castle*. Captain Moodie's abstract log is now of interest as showing the *Cutty Sark's* performances in very light airs against other well-known ships.

May 3—At 6 a.m., Java Head bearing N.N.W. Noon, Java Head bore north 12 miles. Wind, east and variable. P.M., faint airs and calms. Ships *Wylo* and *Doune Castle* in company. (The *Cutty Sark's* passage to Java Head was 76 days, a very fine performance considering the unfavourable weather. The *Wylo* had taken 81 days and the *Doune Castle* 98 days.)

May 4—At 1 p.m. hove to off Anjer. Light variable airs and calms. 8 p.m., passed North Watcher.

5—Faint variable airs and calms, with thunder squalls. Ships *Wylo* and *Thyatira* in company. (The *Cutty Sark* has thus caught *Thyatira*, which sailed a fortnight ahead of her.) 10 p.m., passed Shoal Water Island.

6—Noon, West Hook bore east 2 miles. Winds, variable, faint airs and squalls. At daylight found ship inside of Six Islands. Must have been strong easterly current. Numerous coral shoals. *Wylo* and *Thyatira* in same position.

7—Lat. 1° 39′ S., long. 107° 18′ E. Winds, variable, faint airs and hot sultry weather. Nine vessels in company. Signalled barque *Crested Wave*, Cardiff to Shanghai, 108 days.

8—Lat. 0° 2′ N., long. 106° 58′ E. Course N. 8° W. Distance 104 miles. Winds, variable and south, faint airs, calms and hot sultry weather. Signalled ship *Fiery Cross*, London to Hongkong. (*Cutty Sark* had made 10 days on the *Fiery Cross*.) Noon, St. Barbe Island E. by N. $\frac{3}{4}$° N., 16 miles.

9—Lat. 2° N., long. 107° E. Course N. 1° E. Distance 118 miles. Current 21 miles E.N.E. Wind, south, light breezes and hot sultry weather. Ship *Wylo* still in sight astern.

10—Lat. 4° 34' N., long 107° 12' E. Course N. 5° E. Distance 155 miles.
Current 10 miles N.E. Wind, variable, light breezes and cloudy.
5 a.m., sharp squall from westward. Noon, light breeze from S.W.
Ship *Wylo* out of sight.

Light airs and calms continued until 23rd May, when
with Samisana Island in sight, the wind came strong from
N.E. and for two days the *Cutty Sark* had to battle with a
fresh head gale. On the 24th the wind died away again,
and the *Cutty Sark* took another week drifting slowly towards
her port.

On 25th May when the *Cutty Sark* was off the north end of
Formosa, about opposite Foochowfoo, the *Wylo* made her port,
having come up inside the Island whilst *Cutty Sark* was outside.
As the latter approached the Saddle Islands, the sea gradually
assumed the tint of peasoup, the colour being due to the yellow
mud from the Yangtze River, which caused geographers to name
this bit of the China Seas the Yellow Sea.

With a light southerly air, the *Cutty Sark* rounded the Saddles
at 1 a.m. on 31st May, 104 days out. At 5 a.m. a pilot was picked
up, and as the ship headed for the light vessel, she began to overhaul numbers of junks, the largest of which boasted as many as
seven masts. These Chinese coasters must have opened their eyes
at the way in which this "three piecey bamboo" slipped ahead
in the light wind. They had the advantage of the clipper in being
able to cut across the flats with their shallow draft and leeboards.
Shanghai pilots charged 3 taels a foot of draft, a matter of close
on £20 for the "Cutty."

With the aid of a tug the new clipper successfully negotiated
the celebrated Woosung bar, a frequent cause of delay for vessels
bound in or out of Shanghai.

When the British were threatening Shanghai in 1842, the Chinese
sank a number of junks in this place in order to block the river.
This barrage of junks, though it did not save the city, soon silted
up into a mud bar, which afterwards proved a great inconvenience
to navigation, both *Cutty Sark* and *Thermopylae* stuck on it more
than once, and in 1873 *Duke of Abercorn* had all her false keel ripped
off by it.

Shanghai means "out of the sea". The city lies 12 miles up the river from Woosung. As the *Cutty Sark* began to breast the "chow-chow" water, crowds of sampans gathered on her quarters and endeavoured to hook on; and no sooner was her anchor down than swarms of Chinks, the touts of every imaginable trade that could interest the sailor, came bundling aboard.

Those who have only seen the Shanghai River under present day conditions can have no idea of its picturesqueness in 1870, with its thousands of junks and dozens of tall ships.

The anchorage for foreign shipping lay opposite the Bund with its stone jetties, its palatial hongs and busy godowns. Where in 1843 a few piratical-looking opium schooners lay opposite to a muddy shore with their hammock nettings triced up and the tompions out of their pop-guns, in 1870 the stately men-of-war sparkled in the sunshine as they lay peacefully moored with awnings spread and boat booms out, whilst on either side of them floated the famous tea clippers, their masts raking the skies, their jibbooms casting shadows on the water some 60 to 70 feet beyond their figure-heads, and their yards squared by lift and brace to a mathematical exactness.

Sampans waddled to and fro like water beetles, whilst smart gigs, their yoke lines held by the sunburnt fists of burly, hard-faced skippers in shore-going rig of tall chimney-pot hat and black cloth coat, dashed between the shipping and the landing places.

Snatches of chanties rang across the water from the merchantmen.

> Hi ! Hi ! Hi ! Ching ! Ching ! Ching !
> Chinaman son of a gun,
> Me no likee him

roared the "Cutty's" apprentices, quick to adapt their songs to the pidgin lingo of the Flowery Land.

The almond-eyed coolies, with their own working songs, were quick to retaliate in like badinage. But aboard the stately British man-of-war ahead nought was heard but the shrill pipe of the bosun's whistle and the quick double patter of bare feet on the white decks, a contrast to the picturesque if violent language of the irritable bucko mate on the tall Yankee Cape Horner, which lay astern.

The spotless cleanliness of these windjammers, their sparkling brass-work, their yacht-like decks, and their varnished carved teak rails and stanchions would have dazzled the modern eye used, as it is, to the smoke and grime, the oily waterways and smutty paint of even the smartest of steam-driven vessels.

In the days of sail, seamen, from captain to cabin-boy, took a special pride in the appearance of their ships, and in harbour a good officer considered himself disgraced if so much as a ropeyarn was out of place.

An Irish pennant aloft or a spot on the deck brought forth a grunt of horror from the "old man", a sulphurous outburst from the mate, a whirlwind of blows from the bosun and a stream of outraged abuse and contemptuous sarcasm from the foc'sle, all of which combined to give the offender many days of mental and bodily pain.

Not only had one to satisfy one's own pride, but one had to contend in a never ending rivalry with one's neighbours, and if one of these happened to fly the Stars and Stripes, only slave driving with endless sand and canvas and holystones could hope to approach his standard of ship-keeping.

Yet not even the most fastidious Yank could find many faults with the way in which a British tea clipper was kept up.

· · · · · · · ·

The *Cutty Sark*, having discharged her outward cargo and taken in her shingle ballast, was put on the berth for the new teas. From the start she had captured the hearts of the shippers, and she was the first sailing ship to load at Shanghai, a great honour for a new, untried ship.

Owing to the opening of the Suez Canal and the number of steamers loading new teas, freights for sailing ships, after opening at £3 10s. per 50 cubic feet, soon dropped to £3 and even £2 10s.

The *Cutty Sark* and *Serica* both managed to fill their holds at £3 10s., but none of the other ships succeeded in getting more than £3. Captain Dalrymple of the *Duke of Abercorn* was evidently

"SPINDRIFT" SAIL PLAN

Lent by W. McAlpine, Esq.

[See Page 46

CAPTAIN MOODIE

[*See Page* 53

full of confidence that his ship could beat any other ship in Shanghai on the race home, and he proceeded to challenge every clipper which was going to load new teas. This sporting spirit led to a great deal of betting amongst the shipping fraternity, and finally the crews of the *Cutty Sark*, *Duke of Abercorn*, *Serica*, *Forward Ho*, *Argonaut*, *Ethiopian* and *John R. Worcester* wagered a month's pay, to go to the ship which made the quickest passage from Shanghai to the Channel.

This wager was easily won by the *Cutty Sark*, in spite of a passage, which, owing to poor winds, by no means contented Captain Moodie. The *Cutty Sark* had no opportunity of trying her paces with the *Thermopylae*, as that ship went to Foochow for a cargo and did not sail until more than a month after the *Cutty Sark*.

The tea was very slow in coming down from the interior in 1870, especially at Foochow, thus there was very great rivalry amongst the first class ships as to which should have her hold full first. Besides *Thermopylae*, *Sir Lancelot* and *Windhover* of the old cracks, the new untried clippers *Ambassador*, *Wylo*, *Norman-court*, the *Caliph* and *Eme* were all competitors for new teas at Foochow.

Captain Kemball, of the *Thermopylae*, had his wife on board —a rare occurrence in a tea ship. Mrs. Kemball like many a sea captain's wife took a great interest in her husband's business and what is more knew a great deal about it, but she could not help boasting about the famous clipper, and this rather got on the nerves of the other skippers, who were frequently entertained in the cabin of the *Thermopylae*. At last, when she celebrated the filling of the *Thermopylae's* lower hold by a party, some coarsish wit broke from one or two of the rougher spirits amongst the tea commanders which effectually silenced her inclination to boast.

I believe it was about this time that the *Thermopylae* had her gear stolen. Finding that the night watchman was asleep, river thieves crept aboard the clipper and cast off all the braces and other running gear belayed on the topgallants rail, then dropped the ends quietly overboard; these at once trailed away on the tide and the thieves promptly cut them off as close to the ship as they dared, and got successfully away with their booty. Next morning

F

at daybreak, when it was discovered that the yards were loose and pointing in every direction as if the ship were in mourning, there was a nice hullaballoo.

Thermopylae seemed unfortunate in the choice of night watchmen, for she lost her golden clock on her maiden voyage in the same way, stolen, it was said, by an enterprising seaman from the *Taeping*.

It will be noticed from the table of tea passages on page 85 that the little *Ambassador* succeeded in being first ship away from Foochow, beating *Thermopylae* by five days, in spite of Mrs. Kemball's efforts.

But we must return to the Shanghai River and the *Cutty Sark*. Early on the morning of 25th June, the inhabitants of Shanghai were startled by the firing of guns. A moment's thought, however, told the experienced what this portended.

As it had not the regular sound of men-of-war saluting, it must be the departure of a tea ship, a ceremony which was never allowed to go by without a general cannonade.

Those who could afford the time rushed out on to the Bund and beheld the *Cutty Sark*, first tea ship of the year, towing away to sea with flags flying and her signal guns spouting white smoke.

This ceremony of departure was not considered an unmixed blessing by the local inhabitants.

In 1868 a wad from one of the *Argonaut's* guns blew a hole through a passing junk's mainsail, large enough to drive a coach through, and, landing on the quarter of a neighbouring ship, knocked away some of her ginger-bread work. Whilst in 1873 a correspondent to the *Shanghai Evening Courier* complained that the noise of the *Thermopylae's* guns, being fired off right abreast of the English settlement, so startled his pony that it nearly put him into the river.

Nevertheless it was an occasion greatly beloved and most strictly observed by the old-time seaman. It was a ceremony of friendliness in which every ship took part and akin to the cheering between racing yachts at the end of a race. The homeward-bounder towed proudly away to cheer and to be cheered by each ship, as she passed, whilst the anchorage reverberated with the roar of the saluting guns.

TEA PASSAGES 1870.

Ship	Freight	Cargo lbs.	Port from	Date left	Passed Anjer	Channel	Date	Docked	Days
Taeping	£3 10s.	1,215,190	Whampoa	June 9	July 7	Scilly	Oct. 5	Sept. 29	112
Titania	£5 10s.	1,305,812	Hankow	Woosung June 18		Beachy	Oct. 12	Oct. 8	112
Cutty Sark	£3 10s.	929,110	Shanghai	June 25	August 2	Deal	Oct. 22	Oct. 13	110
Serica	£3 10s.	1,325,984	,,	,, 28				Oct. 24	118
Forward Ho	£3	1,060,838	,,	,, 28				Oct. 25	119
Ethiopian	£3	1,102,691	,,	July 1		Scilly	Nov. 8	Nov. 12	134
J. R. Worcester	£3		,,	,, 5		Deal	Nov. 7	Nov. 8	125
Argonaut	£3		,,	,, 8				Nov. 15	130
Eliza Shaw	£3		,,	,, 13				Nov. 16	126
Belted Will	£3	1,535,378	Whampoa	,, 16	August 13			Oct. 25	101
Duke of Abercorn	£3		Shanghai	,, 18	Pitts Passage August 24	Scilly	Nov. 9	Nov. 14	119
Doune Castle		892,229	,,	,, 23	Manipa St. August 26	Deal	Nov. 23	Nov. 24	124
Ambassador		1,406,425	Foochow	,, 25	Pitts passage August 24	Deal	Nov. 15	Nov. 17	115
Thermopylae			Shanghai	,, 30	August 28			Nov. 12	105
Undine			Foochow	,, 30		Cape Clear	Nov. 5	Nov. 14	105
Sir Lancelot		1,002,648	,,	August 2	September 8		Nov. 12	Nov. 14	104
Normancourt		1,326,833	,,	,, 3	,, 8	Start	Nov. 12	Nov. 16	105
Eme		1,182,251	Shanghai	,, 3		Plymouth	Dec. 1	Dec. 13	133
Thyatira		934,192	,,	,, 12	September 27			Dec. 8	118
Wylo		1,064,645	Foochow	,, 18	25			Dec. 12	112
Chinaman		1,259,896	,,	,, 27	26			Jan. 13	108
Windhover		1,050,142	Shanghai	,, 31	October 9			Dec. 8	99
Wild Deer		360,851	Foochow	,, 31		Deal	Dec. 7	Jan. 3	125
Falcon		995,495	Shanghai	September 2				Dec. 19	108
Huntly Castle		1,626,567	Foochow	,, 2				Jan. 3	123
Maitland		822,359	Shanghai	,, 10	October 6			Dec. 30	111
City of Hankow		911,600	Macao	,, 14	October 17			Jan. 12	122
Fiery Cross		1,137,000	Foochow	,, 16				Jan. 10	117
Flying Spur		1,081,200	Shanghai	,, 22	October 21			Jan. 20	120
Leander		1,085,500	Foochow	October 12		Deal	Jan. 17	Jan. 18	98
Lahloo			,,	,, 12				Jan. 18	98
Kaisow			,,	,, 26				Feb. 2	99
Taitsing			,,	November 3				March 4	121
Whiteadder			,,	,, 9				Feb. 20	103

Though the *Cutty Sark* was the first ship away from Shanghai, there was one ship beating down the China Sea ahead of her. This was the beautiful *Titania*, which had loaded at Hankow, and passed Woosung exactly a week before the *Cutty Sark*. The latter crossed the bar at 10 a.m. on the 25th and anchored for the night 3 miles S. by W. ½ W. of the Amherst Rocks.

On the following morning at 4 a.m. Captain Moodie weighed anchor and made sail with a light southerly wind blowing right in his teeth. By noon the southerly wind had increased to a strong breeze and the Barren Islands bore W.S.W. 14 miles. Captain Moodie soon found that he had to keep his yards jammed on the backstays with never a hint of a slant, and with a strong N.E. current against him.

Though the *Cutty Sark* did well under the conditions, for she was a marvellous ship on a wind, it was slow, nerve-trying work. For the first week the wind kept from moderate to fresh, but nailed firm in the S.S.W., whilst Moodie beat doggedly south, tack and tack. Then it fell away in force, and squalls and calms were mixed indiscriminately, but always with the wind coming out of the south.

On 1st July *Cutty Sark* was tacked off Tamsui Harbour, Formosa; at 10 a.m. on the 2nd Turnabout Island bore N. by W. 8 miles: two days later the westernmost of the Pescadores bore E. by S. 12 miles.

And here I think Captain Moodie made a serious mistake, for instead of hugging the China Coast, so as to work to westward of the Paracels and be in a position to use the land and sea breezes off the Cochin China coast, he kept to the eastward of the Formosa Bank and the Pratas, and worked due south against light head winds and the strength of the foul current.

On the 8th July the *Cutty Sark* lay becalmed for 18 hours about 25 to 30 miles due north of the Scarborough Shoal. When the wind came again, it came in squalls from the S.W. to S.E., some of which were very violent. Captain Moodie now steered almost due west, apparently heading at last for the Cochin China coast and aiming to pass south of the Macclesfield Bank. His abstract log reads as follows:—

July 9—Lat. 15° 22′ N., long. 117° 35′ E. Course S. 42° W. Distance 58 miles. Wind, faint airs and calms. 6 a.m., light breeze from west. 2 p.m., sharp squall from southward.

10—Lat. 15° 29′ N., long. 115° 50′ E. Course N. 86° W. Distance 102 miles. Wind S.W. very unsettled. 4 a.m., a violent squall struck us from S.W. and veered round to S.E. Fore topsail and fore top-gallant sail were both split. Noon, dry but squally looking. Wind fresh from S.W. P.M., baffling winds and calms.

11—Lat. 15° 11′ N., long. 114° 53′ E. Course S. 71° W. Distance 56 miles. Baffling winds and calms with heavy showers of rain. Wind flying about right round the compass, light airs. P.M., violent squalls from S.E. and N.W. catching the ship aback very suddenly before the yards could be hauled round. Midnight, more settled.

12—Lat. 13° 57′ N., long. 114° 31, E. Course S. 16° W. Distance 77 miles. A fresh gale but less squally from S.W. Found the parrel of fore topsail broken. Noon, fresh gale and dry. 3 p.m., a ship in sight about 10 miles S.W. of us, supposed one of the tea clippers. (It could only have been the *Titania*. It will be noticed that Captain Moodie has once more put his ship on the starboard tack.)

13—Lat. 12° 56′ N., long. 113° 42′ E. Course S. 38° W. Distance 78 miles. A fresh gale and dry but cloudy, wind S.W. and S.S.W. A very sharp sea running, P.M., strong gales with an overwhelming sea, ship plunging heavily.

14—Lat. 13° 9′ N., long. 111° 48′ E. Course N. 83° W. Distance 112 miles. Current N. 9° E., 27 miles. Wind, S.W., begins strong gale and very heavy sea. At daylight more moderate. P.M., wind very unsettled sometimes blowing a gale.

Captain Moodie had once more tacked to the westward and with the strong current on his beam could make no better than N. 83° W. On the following day with the wind moderate to fresh but still squally and uncertain, he again went about and headed south. This time he kept his luff through a week of calms and light airs until he made the Natunas.

On the 19th he writes:—"From noon to midnight, nearly calm; at least the ship had not steerage way most of that time." And on the following day he bursts out with:—"In all my sailing about the China Sea, I have never experienced such weather: the principal complaint all the way down has been want of wind with three days' exception."

On the 23rd July the *Cutty Sark* was tacked at 8 a.m. about 10 miles off the south-east end of Great Natuna. Captain Moodie shaped a course between the Natunas and made no attempt to work the land and sea breezes on the Borneo coast. On the 24th the *Cutty Sark* had to be twice shortened down to lower topsails and foresail for violent squalls, which blew with the strength of a hard gale for some two or three hours.

On the following day Direction Island was passed and at 9.30 p.m. the *Cutty Sark* overhauled a steamer, which was heading for the Karamata Passage and left her astern. Three days later, when the ship was conveniently placed for a beat through Gaspar Straits, Captain Moodie headed off east with the wind light to calm from the S.W. In thus rounding Billiton instead of making a dash for the straits, Captain Moodie sacrificed three days, on one of which it was so calm that the *Cutty Sark* only covered 13 miles in the 24 hours.

On 2nd August at 9 a.m. the *Cutty Sark* was hove to off Anjer, whilst letters were sent ashore to be posted. Captain Moodie had taken 37 days to Anjer, having had to beat the whole distance against 728 miles of N.E. current. Considering that he kept in the strength of the foul current, made no attempt to work the back eddy and land and sea breezes of the Cochin China and Borneo coasts and then wasted four days in the Karamata Strait in preference to beating through Gaspar Straits, it is surprising that the *Cutty Sark* did so well. If Captain Moodie had steered the course which was generally favoured by racing captains, he would probably have reached Anjer in less than 30 days.

Cutty Sark did not pick up the S.E. trades until 6th August in 12° 26' S., 97° 57' E., her captain writing with disgust:—"This ship is apparently doomed to light winds, for the legitimate winds seem to flag at our appearance. Here we are in the middle of calms, where it ought to be blowing a steady, strong S.E. trade."

However on the 6th the wind at last came out of the S.E. and straightway the *Cutty Sark* began to step out, the captain's log recording:—

Aug. 7—lat. 14° 2' S., long. 93° 5' E. Course S. 71½° W. Distance 303 miles.
  Wind, S.E. and S.S.E., a strong breeze and overcast. 5 a.m., broke

fore topmast studding sail boom. At daylight sent aloft another.
At 10 a.m. broke this other boom, and as I had very few spars left me
had to go without studding sails. The wind hangs far to the southward.

8—Lat. 10° 10′ S., long. 87° 45′ E. Course S. 89° W. Distance 311 miles.
Winds, S.E. and S.S.E., a strong breeze and dull drizzly weather.
There must be some peculiarity about this ship as the patent log
has been put over frequently and has always shown from 14 to 15½
knots and we find by observation that she has made about 13 on
an average. Our luck won't go past us.

9—Lat. 15° 12′ S., long. 82° 21′ E. Course S. 79° W. Distance 320 miles.
Current N.E. 35 miles, winds, S.S.E. and south, very unsettled with
unsteady winds—the strangest trade winds I have seen for some
time. I was trying to set the lower studding sail, just before the
sail was properly set the boom broke. This day it is very plain that
a current has been setting to the N.E. 35 miles in the 24 hours. Dull
weather, drizzling rain at times.

10—Lat. 16° 36′ S., long. 77° 5′ E. Course S. 74° W. Distance 314 miles.
Current N.N.E. 35 miles. Wind, S.S.E. strong breeze, more settled
and steady, P.M., moderate breeze and clear. Set all studding sails
fore and aft.

The very next day the wind petered out, and Captain Moodie
writes:—"The old music again, sails clashing against the masts for
want of wind." With light winds, the *Cutty Sark* had no further
opportunity of making big runs this side of the Cape, and Captain
Moodie's remarks clearly show the state of affairs.

Aug. 12—Sails clashing against the masts. Very pleasant to people not in a hurry.

13—Wind baffling at times. This is the first time the ship has made the course
she has been steered. She has always been to north and east of her
position, but today she is S.E. of where she should be.

14—Light winds appear to be the legitimate heritage of this ship.

15—(Passing Mauritius).—Light winds with a confused cross sea. Noon, sails
clashing about.

16—Nearly calm.

17—Nearly calm.

18—About as much wind as will blow the smoke of a cigar away.

19—A black squall from southward, but the wind did not come in a sudden
burst but very gently.

20—Nearly calm at times.

21—Sails clashing against the masts. If they do not get worn one way they
will another. During the voyage for one day that they have been full, they have
been two clashing about.

22—Light baffling airs.

And so it continues. Nevertheless the *Cutty Sark* managed to round the Cape on 28th August, 26 days from Anjer, which was a very good performance, considering that *Ariel's* best run from Anjer to the Cape was 25 in 1866, *Thermopylae's* 23 in 1869, and *Sir Lancelot's* 25 in 1869. For three days the *Cutty Sark* was held up to the southard of the Cape by a strong gale from N.N.W. right ahead. The rest of the passage was without incident, though Captain Moodie still growled in his log about the continual lightness of the wind and the "*Cutty Sark* music," as he called the noise of the sails clashing against the masts. The S.E. trades were light, and the *Cutty Sark* crossed the N.E. trades in four days. Her times were as follows.—

Sept. 8—Midnight, passed St. Helena, about 4 miles off shore—11 days from the Cape.
  12—10 p.m., passed Ascension about 4 miles off shore.
  16—Crossed the equator in 20° 25′ W.—8 days from St. Helena.
  25—Passed Cape Verde Islands—9 days from the equator.

Oct. 6—At midnight, Flores (Azores) bearing N.N.E.
  12—9.30 p.m., Beachy Head bearing N.N.E. 10 miles—6 days from Western Isles.

The *Cutty Sark* came racing up Channel before a strong S.W. gale with the usual thick rainy weather, and Captain Moodie's landfall was the Beachy Head light. At 1 a.m. on the 13th the Ness was rounded, when Captain Moodie had to heave his ship to and wait until daylight for a pilot. It was still blowing a hard gale with severe squalls. A pilot managed to get aboard at 6.30, and an hour later the *Cutty Sark* was forced to anchor in the Downs as it was blowing too hard to be able to tow. However Captain Moodie managed to get into the Thames during the day. From the Shanghai pilot, the passage was 109 days, which, considering the extremely unfavourable weather, was recognised as a very fine performance.

It was the best passage made that year in the height of the S.W. monsoon, and none of the ships which had wagered a month's pay came anywhere near it, their times being—*Serica* 118 days, *Ethiopian* 134 days, *John R. Worcester* 125 days, *Forward Ho* 119 days, *Argonaut* 130 days, *Duke of Abercorn* 114 days.

Though both Captain Moodie and John Willis were disappointed with the actual time, they were satisfied that they had a vessel which, given the opportunity, could beat the *Thermopylae* or any other ship in the China trade.

The *Cutty Sark* came into port with fishes on masts and yards; on 9th October Captain Moodie wrote in the log:—"Wind west to N.W., mostly strong, ship is sometimes going over 14 knots. All port studding sails set and the broken masts and yards pretty stiff to it." No doubt the old man could carry sail, but at the same time it was evident that the ship required strengthening aloft for she had proved herself able to bear being driven almost without limit.

Of the other ships only *Normancourt* had definitely won her spurs. Racing against the *Thermopylae* and *Sir Lancelot*, she should have made the best passage of the three; she was off the Start 101 days out, but then unfortunately she had a dead muzzler to port, which *Thermopylae* and *Sir Lancelot* just escaped.

Ambassador, *Duke of Abercorn*, *Eme* and *Doune Castle* all took the long eastern port route *via* Pitts Passage and *Wylo*, leaving Foochow on 18th August, took 40 days to Anjer, but made the good run home from thence of 76 days.

It is difficult to compare the passages of the ships which sailed in the strength of the S.W. monsoons with those which sailed later in the favourable N.E. monsoon, and the passages of *Windhover*, *Leander*, *Lahloo* and *Kaisow* were probably less meritorious than those of *Titania* and *Cutty Sark*.

Windhover actually made the fastest passage of the year; she took her departure from the White Dogs at 4 p.m. on 1st September, passed Anjer on 26th September, 25 days out, arrived in the Downs early on 7th December and docked at 1 p.m. on the 8th, 97 days 20 hours from her Foochow pilot.

Ariel had an unlucky voyage. When bound from Yokohama to load tea, she went over on her beam ends in a severe gale on 26th April. Captain Courtenay was compelled to cut away his topmasts to save his ship. He then put back to Yokohama, where it took a long time to refit. Finally, having missed her chance to load new teas, the *Ariel* took a cargo from Yokohama for New York, where she arrived on 26th January, 1871.

The *Caliph* did not get away from Foochow until all the other tea ships had gone. She also was glad to get a New York cargo, and arrived there on 3rd March, 1871.

Ariel left New York on 7th February, 1871, and arrived in the Thames on 7th March, 28 days out; whilst *Caliph* left New York on 1st April, and arrived London 22nd April, 21 days out.

I have treated *Cutty Sark's* maiden voyage at some length, but space will not permit of this in the future and I shall have to confine myself to describing the most interesting features of future voyages.

But in 1871 both *Cutty Sark* and *Thermopylae* made such fine outward passages that I have been induced to give the abstracts of them in the Appendix.

The evenness of their times to the Cape meridian are worth noting, *Cutty Sark* crossed the line 19 days from the Downs; *Thermopylae* being 20 days; both ships crossed the Greenwich meridian in 38 days and the Cape meridian in 41 days from the Downs.

Cutty Sark took the long eastern route to China *via* the Manipa Strait. Off the Ombay Passage she overhauled *Taeping* and *Titania* having gained 24 days on *Taeping* and a fortnight on *Titania*. Captain Moodie was again unlucky in the China Sea or he should have done the passage in about 90 days. At any rate it was considered an extremely fine performance.

1871 was the only year in which *Cutty Sark* had time to make any coastal intermediate passages; leaving Shanghai on 28th February, she anchored in Hongkong Harbour at 4 p.m. on the 3rd March, 68 hours from the Saddle Islands. At Hongkong she received orders to go to Bangkok for rice. On 4th March she took her departure from the Gap Rock and at 11 a.m. on 13th March she anchored 3 miles outside the bar of the Bangkok River; 8 days 14½ hours from Hongkong.

The town of Bangkok lies some 40 miles up the river. It is one of the hottest, most mosquito-ridden places in the world and is celebrated for its swarms of fireflies, which feed on the foliage of a certain local tree, and on moonless nights transforms the pestilential place into a perfect fairyland of tiny lights. In 1871 the port was somewhat notorious for its German grog shops, and possessed few others attractions for sailors.

Here *Cutty Sark* found a very interesting vessel, a smart little brig, which was hove down ashore for repairs. This was the *Leonora*, owned and commanded by Bully Hayes, the South Sea pirate. The *Leonora* had originally been the *Waterlily* of Aberdeen, an opium clipper. In 1868 she put into Manila, damaged by weather. She was then condemned and sold. She was next heard of as arriving in Shanghai on 8th March, 1869, from Ascension, with her new owner, C. A. Williams, on board. Her master at this date was the notorious American blackbirder, Captain Ben Pease, known as the first man to recruit black labour for the Fijis. He was one of the many semi-piratical adventurers who thronged the China Seas and the South Sea Islands before the days of the cable.

A book, more thrilling than any fiction, could be written about these wild, lawless characters, who supplied the gossip for all the ports from Shanghai to Sydney. These mid-Victorian gentlemen of fortune stopped at nothing from robbing copra stations to women stealing, from plundering junks to schooner wrecking. They invariably paid their bills with the topsail sheet and sold their cargoes for their own benefit in ports, which were far away from their consignees.

Of these modern pirates, Ben Pease was one of the leading lights, a very shifty, close-eyed customer indeed. He was not an engaging ruffian like Bully Hayes, neither had he the romantic touch of a certain Captain Proctor, who retained some traces of gentle birth.

Proctor to pick out one of his aliases, was very well known in the treaty ports during the seventies. He commanded the usual rakish looking craft, whose business was more or less of a mystery and like most of his kind he was usually very short of ready cash.

It was his habit to lounge about Shanghai with a pair of great Danes at his heels, and no doubt he reckoned on these animals making his arrest a difficult one, should one of his little speculations come to light unexpectedly. He had, however, plenty of nerve, and was a constant visitor of the midshipman's mess whenever he was in port with a man-of-war. On these occasions he spun the most lurid yarns and swallowed an incredible number of drinks, to the fascination of the youngsters, but, at parting, he was not above cadging provisions from their meagre store, and it was even whispered that he could tempt rope and paint from the bosun's locker.

This man was an Englishman. His record was tame and mild compared to that of a certain Down Easter who had held command in the Yankee Cape Horn fleet.

Roughly the last buccaneer's record was as follows:— Retired from the sea at the age of 35 and started farming in California; a year later killed a man who had been too polite to his wife; fled to sea; turned up in the China Sea in command of a piratical schooner and started sinking junks and plundering coast towns; he once held a whole village in check single-handed whilst his crew carried off a boat-load of young women. His cruelty was phenomenal, his favourite amusement being the tieing of two Chinks together by their pig-tails, slinging them across a spring-stay, and making them fight for their lives with knives, the victor being given his freedom. He had a crew of white men, riff-raff from the Pacific ports, and a few Cantonese servants to do the dirty work. He was careful not to touch a white trader, but he waged such war on the inoffensive trading junk that even the comic opera Chinese frigates were compelled to up anchor and go in search of him.

At last he was caught in the act of scuttling a captured junk by a British man-of-war. He was unwise enough to return her fire and promptly had his schooner sunk under him. With four of his men he clung to the wreck for two days and then was picked up by a Spanish brig. He at once captured the unsuspecting Spaniard and resumed his war on junks. For nearly another year he managed to elude capture by shifting from ship to ship as he captured them. It was believed that he replenished his stores and ammunition from his secret cache, which was said to be a coral reef some three days' sail from Hongkong. In the end he was captured by an inquisitive British gunboat, and executed with his crew at Hongkong. His nerve broke at last and he died a whimpering coward.

These later day pirates of the Pacific were more crafty than daring as a rule. They generally combined the suave methods of the swell mobsman with the low cunning of a sneak thief, and they never hesitated to hide their tracks, when necessary, by killing a man or scuttling a ship.

Their history has never been written, neither probably could the material be got together, but they were worthy successors of Avery and Bartholomew Roberts, of Captain Kidd and that scarlet ruffian, Teach, known as Blackbeard.

To return to the history of the *Cutty Sark's* neighbour in Bangkok —the *Waterlily* was sold in Shanghai to Glover, Dow & Co., who retained Pease in command, whilst they renamed the brig the *Pioneer*. A year later, in March, 1870, the *Pioneer* turned up at Apia, Samoa. Meanwhile, probably because Ben Pease saw to it that all profits went into his own pocket, Glover, Dow & Co., became insolvent. And here for the first time Bully Hayes comes on the scene. He apparently bought the brig at Apia from the firm's assignees for a small sum in cash and the cancellation of a claim for wages. On 1st April the *Pioneer* left Apia with both Pease and Hayes on board. It was not likely that two such consummate ruffians would agree for long, and a few months later Pease had disappeared and the *Pioneer*, under the new name of *Leonora*, was left in the hands of Bully Hayes, a past-master at obtaining a ship for nothing. March 1871, found the *Leonora* bound to Hongkong with rice from Saigon, but Hayes got ashore on Cape St. James, and on refloating his vessel altered his course for Bangkok, where he knew no questions would be asked and that he would find it easier to repay for repairs with his cargo than at Hongkong.

The *Leonora* arrived at Bangkok on 29th March, and after being repaired, caulked and coppered, left on 27th April with a clean swept hold, having cleared for Saigon.

Bully Hayes was not heard of again until he turned up at Apia in February, 1872, in spite of the fact that every man-of-war in the Pacific had instructions concerning him. The rest of his adventures and the wreck of the *Leonora* are related in Rolf Boldrewood's *Modern Buccaneer* and Louis Becke's *South Sea Reminiscences*.

But the following description of the *Leonora* may be of interest

The *Leonora* measured 218 tons, and had been built in Aberdeen for the opium trade. Her sail plan was a large one with single topsails fitted with Cunningham's patent reefing gear.

She originally carried eight guns, and during her opium running days had more than once beaten off Chinese pirates. Bully Hayes reduced this battery to one gun, on finding how much his cannons were appreciated by his friends amongst the South Sea Islands chiefs.

She had a large foc's'le, for she carried between 25 and 30 men before the mast, consisting of Kanakas, half-castes and Malays, with only one European, a Scotchman named John McDonald.

The bulkhead of the foc's'le was loopholed for rifles and thus commanded the fore 'tween decks, which were often crowded with wild Islanders, recruited often by force for Bully Hayes' own plantations.

On the main deck there was a large house, divided up into cook's galley, boats crews' quarters, and cabins for the mates, of whom the first was a Dane and the second a Fiji half caste named Billy Hicks. On top of this house was a whale-boat in chocks, alongside of which stood two sentries, a most necessary precaution for a man in Bully Hayes' trade. The *Leonora* had the reputation of being one of the fastest ships in the Islands, but she would have had no chance against the *Cutty Sark*, even in the light winds of the China Sea.

It is curious to think of the respectable tea clipper lying at anchor close to the piratical brig.

Did Captain Moodie swap yarns with the notorious Bully Hayes in the local ship chandler's? It is more than likely: and no doubt the bluff simple-minded captain of the tea clipper was as completely hoodwinked by the suave talk and easy bonhomie of the famous South Sea pirate as everyone else, for Bully Hayes was that type of plausible ruffian, the classic example of whom is Long John Silver in Stevenson's *Treasure Island*.

The *Cutty Sark* left Bangkok with a rice cargo—possibly some of it from the hold of the *Leonora*—on 3rd April, and after the usual light weather passage anchored in Hongkong harbour on the 21st, 18 days from the Gulf of Siam. Her passages up and down the coast in 1871 proved that she was as fast as, if not faster, than the most celebrated of the light weather flyers. Of these, *Taeping* with her single topsails was considered to be about the best.

In 1871 *Taeping* left Shanghai on 25th February and arrived Bangkok on 11th March. The *Cutty Sark*, leaving Shanghai on 28th February, in spite of a 24 hours stay at Hongkong, arrived at Bangkok only two days behind her.

The following times for the passage from Hongkong to Bangkok at the same time of year are interesting as a comparison:—

1869 *Sir Lancelot* left Hongkong January 27 arrived Bangkok February 5 9 days
1870 *Caliph*   „   „   March 7 „   „   March 19 12 „
 „ *Sir Lancelot*   „   „   „   13 „   „   „   24 11 „
 „ *Leander*   „   „   „   10 „   „   „   19 9 „
 „ *Lahloo*   „   „   „   30 „   „   April 13 14 „
1871 *Cutty Sark* left Hongkong March 4 8.30 p.m. arrived Bangkok March 13 11 a.m., 8 days. 14 hrs. 30 min.

On the return journey to Hongkong, *Cutty Sark* and *Taeping* left the river on the same date, 3rd April, and the hard weather flyer *Cutty Sark* beat the light weather flyer *Taeping* in a fair and square drifting match of light easterly winds, by three days, the *Taeping* arriving Hongkong on 24th March, 21 days out. The *Sir Lancelot* also took 21 days on this passage in 1869.

The *Taeping* and *Cutty Sark* were the only front rank ships which went to Bangkok in 1871.

The *Titania* did two trips between Hongkong and Saigon before going to her tea port. She left Shanghai 20th February, Hongkong 28th February and arrived Saigon 6th March—six days from Hongkong. Left Saigon 15th March and arrived Hongkong 30th March—15 days out. Her second trip was of about the same duration.

The *Cutty Sark*, after spending a month in Hongkong harbour, left in ballast on 23rd May and anchored in the Shanghai River on 2nd June, 10 days from Hongkong. She was immediately laid on the berth to load new teas alongside of *Thermopylae, Forward Ho* and *Undine*.

It was a very bad year for tea freights on account of the competition of many new steamers, the best rate being only £3 per 50 cubic feet. This did not satisfy Jardine, Matheson & Co., the *Cutty Sark's* agents, and when the tea lighters were actually alongside they withdrew her from the berth and sent her down to Foochow to see what could be done there.

Leaving Shanghai on 7th July *Cutty Sark* dropped her pilot off the lightship at 7 p.m. and on the 10th at 7 p.m. anchored under Matson's Island, a sailing time of three days. At Foochow Captain Moodie found the *Duke of Abercorn* loading for London. This vessel had also given up Shanghai in disgust. She left Shanghai on 24th June and arrived Foochow on 3rd July, nine days out; another coastal victory for the *Cutty Sark*.

Captain Moodie found freights as bad and charters as difficult in Foochow as they were at Shanghai.

The *Sir Lancelot*, which by the way was in mourning for her owner and had her figure-head, gilt streak and gingerbread work painted over a dull kind of blue, had arrived at Foochow the day before the "Cutty," whilst *Lahloo* arrived the day after. Four ships, *Titania*, *Ziba*, *Harlaw* and *Maitland* had already sailed, the steamers had taken a much greater quantity of tea than ever before, and there was not much more expected.

Lahloo had her charter already fixed, and things looked hopeless for *Cutty Sark* and *Sir Lancelot*. The latter did not waste any time and left at once for Shanghai, but Moodie, having just come from Shanghai, felt compelled to wait a bit. He waited three weeks, and then up-anchored on 30th July, and was back in Shanghai on 4th August.

It was now getting late in the season, *Sir Lancelot* had sailed with a cargo for New York, and the only "full blood" still on the berth was the beautiful *Ariel*.

Cutty Sark, after wasting two months in an effort to get more was at last compelled to accept the despised £3, and started loading lighter for lighter with the *Ariel*.

This was the only year in which *Cutty Sark* was not one of the first ships away from China. It was a great pity that her agents did not allow her to load in June with the *Thermopylae*, for the whole shipping world were looking forward to a fair race between these two, and many knowing judges considered that the *Cutty Sark* could lower the *Thermopylae's* colours, a proceeding which no other ship in the world at that date was pronounced capable of doing.

As it happened, the *Cutty Sark* found herself pitted against the *Ariel*, a worthy antagonist enough, if Captain Keay had been

"TAEPING," PAGODA ANCHORAGE, FOOCHOW

[See Page 54

"CUTTY SARK" OFF HONGKONG, 1871

Painting by a Chinaman

See Page 74

at the helm; but this year *Ariel* had a new skipper, Captain Talbot, and was therefore an unknown quantity, the unfortunate Courtenay being displaced after his disastrous voyage in 1870.

Both ships got under weigh, on 2nd September, but the *Cutty Sark* broke her windlass. This was not repaired until 3.30 p.m., so that she missed the tide over the bar, and was compelled to wait at Halfway Point until the following day.

At 3 p.m. on the 3rd the *Cutty Sark* passed Woosung, and at 7 p.m. anchored off the Beacon.

At 3 a.m. on the 4th she weighed and proceeded in tow of the *Rocket*, and at 8 a.m. when off the Tongsha lightship she cast off the tug and made all plain sail. Two hours later the wind dropped and with the tide against her she was compelled to anchor. At 3 p.m. she again weighed and made sail, Mr. Wilson, the pilot leaving the ship at 5 p.m. For the first five days she had the benefit of the N.E. monsoon, and on the 8th caught and passed the *Caller Ou*, which had left Shanghai on 31st August.

On the 10th the monsoon petered out, and the *Cutty Sark* ran into a fresh southerly gale with a high sea into which she pitched violently, and split her fore topsail, main topgallant sail, inner jib, and flying jib. This lulled away on the 12th September into the usual S.W. monsoon weather.

Captain Moodie pursued the same tactics down the China Sea as in 1870, keeping in mid stream on the strength of the northerly current and going round Billiton instead of through Gaspar Straits, so that the *Cutty Sark* took over 30 days to Anjer.

The passage, except for very bad weather off the Cape, was without incident.

Oct.   6—Abreast of Anjer, 32 days out.
      12—Best run in the S.E. trades, 322 miles.
      19—Passed Mauritius, 13 days from Anjer.
      20—P.M., wind came from the westward.

Captain Moodie writes:—"First time I have met with westerly winds so far north in this part of the ocean in all my 15 years coming these voyages." From this date until she rounded the Cape, the *Cutty Sark* had a very heavy head sea to contend against.

G

Oct. 28—Lat. 30° 2' S., long. 37° 16' E. Course S. 58° W. Distance, 202. 6 a.m., a hard gale from S.W. with very confused sea. Ship taking large quantities of water aboard taking it in at both bow and stern at the same time P.M., bent best foresail, the other being split.

30—6 a.m., wind increased to a strong gale from N.E. with a tremendous heavy cross sea. Ship half burying herself, leeside of deck completely full of water.

The wind lulled right away to a calm on the 31st and the *Cutty Sark* threatened to thrash her sails to pieces as she pitched and rolled in a gigantic sea. On the 2nd in 35° 16' S., 24° 9' E., the wind again came out of the westward, a strong gale, and the *Cutty Sark* had to be snugged down to three lower topsails. "It is more like the month of November in the North Atlantic than summer in the Southern Ocean," wrote Captain Moodie.

On the 3rd it was still blowing a hard gale from the west with a very heavy sea, and the clipper dished one up over her poop, which filled the cabin through the skylight.

On the 4th November she only made 22 miles, and Captain Moodie remarks:—"Squalls from all points lasting a few minutes then calm—then all aback again, about every quarter of an hour: the ship is most of the time going astern with the sea flying in pyramids: sails thrashing themselves to pieces." At 4 p.m. on the 5th, Cape Agulhas bore N. by E., 18 miles, and the Cape of Good Hope light showed N.E. by E. at midnight, the *Cutty Sark* being 30 days from Anjer.

Nov. 9—Passed the *Woodlark*, which had left Shanghai on 25th July.

15—Passed the *Everest*, which had left Shanghai on 16th August.

16—7 p.m., passed west of St. Helena, 11 days from the Cape.

20—Passed Ascension.

24—Crossed the line, 19 days from the Cape.

30—Passed Cape Verde, 6 days from the equator.

Dec. 12—Passed the Western Isles, 18 days from the equator.

16—Sent all stunsail booms and skysail yard down.

18—Lat. 48° 5' N., long. 9° 33' W. Course W. 65½° E. Distance 323 miles. Wind S.W. strong.

19—6 p.m., Start Point bearing N.E., 7 days from Azores, 44 days from the Cape.

20—4 a.m., St. Catherine's N.N.E. Noon, Beachy Head abeam. 1.30 p.m., passed Dungeness, blowing a hard gale. 2.15 p.m., got a pilot in East Bay. 4 p.m., passed through the Downs. 6 p.m., compelled to anchor off North Foreland 90 fathoms of chain out. 10 p.m., gale began to abate. In getting underweigh again the chain parted about 10 to 12 fathoms from the anchor.

During the whole passage of 107 days nothing was seen of the *Ariel*, which did not arrive for another week.

Underneath I give a table for the 1871 tea passages. *Titania* was the heroine of the year. *Sir Lancelot, Wylo, Eme, Taitsing, Yangtze, Fiery Cross* and *Flying Spur* all left China or Japan for New York. The *Yangtze* was wrecked on the Paracels, Captain Smith and six of her men being drowned.

TEA PASSAGES 1871.

Ship	Freig't	Cargo lbs.	Port from	Date left	Passed Anjer	Arrived Channel	Docked	Days out
Thermopylae	£3	1,361,300	Shanghai	June 22	July 22		Oct. 9	106
Forward Ho	£3	1,301,100	,,	,, 22	,,	Oct. 19	,, 20	118
Undine	£3	1,010,600	,,	,, 27			,, 16	111
Titania	£3	1,250,000	Foochow	July 1	July 26		,, 2	93
Ziba	£3	731,800	,,	,, 4			Nov. 6	125
Harlaw	£3	1,141,800	,,	,, 7	Aug. 5		,, 8	124
Maitland	£3	1,090,100	,,	,, 8		Nov. 8	,, 9	124
Whinfell		1,113,100	Shanghai	,, 8			,, 25	139
Fire Queen		993,500	Foochow	,, 10			,, 24	137
Normancourt ..			Macao	,, 15	Aug. 8		Nov. 3	111
Argonaut		1,531,000	Shanghai	,, 16	,, 21		,, 8	115
Duke of Abercorn ..		1,500,500	Foochow	,, 24		Prawle Pt. Nov. 9	,, 11	110
Lahloo		1,120,000	,,	,, 27	Sept. 2		Nov. 17	116
Ambassador		971,900	Whampoa	Aug. 30	Oct. 6		Jan. 1	125
Cutty Sark	£3	1,315,100	Shanghai	Sept. 4	,, 5	N. Foreland Dec. 20.	Dec. 21	108
Ariel	£3	1,221,500	,,	,, 4			,, 27	114
Thyatira			Foochow	,, 30	Oct. 26		Jan. 16	108

Kaisow loaded at Batavia for the Texel, *Belted Will* at Manila and the *Blackadder* at Penang. The dates of this unlucky vessel's maiden voyage are worth recording:—

BLACKADDER'S MAIDEN VOYAGE.

1870.   March 24—Left the Downs.
      April   3—Passed Madeira, 10 days out.
              11—Sighted St. Antonia, 18 days out.
              19—Crossed the equator, 26 days out.
              27—Passed Trinidad, 34 days out.

May   10—Dismasted.
      14—Sighted Tristan d'Acunha, 51 days out.
      20—Crossed Greenwich meridian, 57 days out.
      25—Sighted Table Mountain.
      26—Anchored Simon's Bay, 63 days out. Refitted.
Sept.   10—Passed Anjer.
Dec.   7—Collided with French mail steamer, *Volga*; both ships staggered
          into port with their fore compartments full of water.
      11—Arrived Shanghai.
1871. July   23—Left Penang—had been in collision there and lost her jib-boom.
      Nov.   17—Arrived London, 117 days out.

The *Cutty Sark* left London for Shanghai in the spring of 1872 with the redoubtable *Sir Lancelot* close on her heels. *Cutty Sark* passed through the Downs on 8th February, casting off her tug at 7 p.m., and at 4 p.m. the next day she sent her pilot ashore in a fishing smack when off Start Point.

The *Sir Lancelot* left Gravesend on 10th February. On the 19th February *Cutty Sark* had Madeira in sight, and after experiencing a very light N.E. trade crossed the line on 4th March in 23° W. *Sir Lancelot* did not cross the line until the 14th. The *Cutty Sark* was in company with the smart little *City of Delhi* for three days in the doldrums, but on picking up the S.E. trades in 4° 20′ S. on 7th March ran the *City* under the horizon astern in a few hours.

On 22nd March *Cutty Sark* sighted Tristan d'Acunha, and crossed the Greenwich meridian on the 25th, 44 days out. She then had five days of calm weather and thick fog and did not cross the Cape meridian until 1st April.

Her best work on the passage was made from 42° 9′ S., 49° 46′ E. to 41° 37′ S., 70° 9′ E. on 10th, 11th, and 12th April, before a strong N.W. to west gale, her runs by dead reckoning being 320, 363, and 306, but sights gave 76 miles of current against her.

On the 23rd April, when a day from Christmas Island, she made a run of 307 miles in the S.E. trades. At noon on the 26th she passed Anjer, 76 days out, but at 6.30 p.m. was obliged to anchor 2 miles east of the Button owing to calm and a strong current from the N.E. She passed through Gaspar Straits on 29th April, had light winds and calms to 18° 30′ N. and then the N.E. monsoon strong. On 23rd May, at 8 a.m. she was off Amoy. On 28th

May with a moderate easterly breeze and thick rain she made Senhouse Island, sailed through the Pass at noon, picked up her pilot at 2.30 p.m., passed the light-vessel an hour later and at 5.30 anchored 6 miles below the Beacon, 108 days out. *Sir Lancelot* did not arrive until 4th June.

Of the other outward passages there is not much to remark. *Thermopylae* again made a very fine run out to Melbourne. Leaving London on 14th November, 1871, she passed the Lizards on the 17th, then had light winds right down to the equator which was crossed on 10th December, in 28° W., 23 days from the Lizards.

The S.E. trades were light and were followed by a long spell of doldrums, but *Thermopylae* managed to cross the meridian of the Cape on 30th December, 43 days out. Running the easting down, her two best days totalled 336 and 334 knots. On the meridian of the Leeuwin, the wind blew very hard from the west for 12 hours, during which time *Thermopylae* had to be kept under two close-reefed topsails and foresail. She passed the Otway on the night of 22nd January, 1872, and anchored in Hobson's Bay on the afternoon of the 23rd, 67 days out.

Blackadder, after her disastrous maiden voyage, distinguished herself by making the best passage of the season to Shanghai. Her first captain, Robinson, had been told to pack up and clear out in very forcible language by old Jock Willis, and he was replaced by the reliable Captain Moore, who was really Willis's ship's-husband or, as they now call it, superintendent. Moore left Seal at 2 p.m. on 3rd January, 1872, was off Dartmouth on 5th January, passed Anjer 23rd March, 77 days out and arrived Shanghai 7th April.

The other passages to Shanghai were:—

Titania	arrived	February	9—108 days out.	
Undine	„	March	14—117	„
Argonaut	„	March	18—109	„
Normancourt	„	April	9—118	„
(Going by the long route round Australia.)				
Lahloo	arrived	April	23—128 days out.	
Duke of Abercorn	arrived	May	15—126 days out.	

The beautiful *Ariel* went missing this year. She left London on 31st January with a new man in command, Captain Cachenaille, and was never heard of again It was suggested that she either crashed into an iceberg or else was pooped and foundered whilst running her easting down.

The last of the tea clippers, the little *Lothair*, came to sad grief this year. It was her second voyage, she went out to Yokohama, left Kobe on 10th June for Hongkong and Foochow, left Foochow in ballast for Kobe again on 22nd July, and put into Yokohama on 20th August, under jury rig, having lost her main and mizen masts and her fore topmast.

It is probable that like the *Ambassador*, which was also built by Walker, she was over-hatted, for on her maiden passage out to Japan she limped into Yokohama on 27th January, 1871, having lost her topgallant masts and yards off the Cape on 14th September, 1870.

For her first two voyages *Lothair* was commanded by a Captain Peacock, but after her second dismasting he was replaced by Captain Orchard.

This year the *Cutty Sark* and *Thermopylae* met for the first time. The two ships loaded together at Shanghai and sailed from Woosung on the same day. Both captains were confident of victory, but nevertheless prepared their ships carefully for the race.

Captain Kemball, whose average cargo of tea was 1,390,000 lbs., only loaded 1,196,400; whilst Moodie, though he did not cut it down quite as much, took 20,000 lbs. less than usual.

As a test of their cargo capacity, in deadweight, it is noticeable that *Thermopylae* usually loaded 1200 tons of coal against the *Cutty Sark's* 1100 tons. It is therefore very easy to see that Kemball was giving his vessel every advantage, and that when she left Shanghai she must have been "flying light."

There was tremendous competition as to which would be ready for sea first, and this was won by the *Cutty Sark*, literally by a tide; but as it happened a thick fog held up both vessels for three days.

Cutty Sark's last chest of tea was stowed on the afternoon of the 17th June; at 7 p.m. she weighed her anchor and dropped down to Halfway Point, where she was obliged to anchor for the night. On the morning of the 18th *Cutty Sark* crossed Woosung bar with *Thermopylae* close behind her. *Sir Lancelot* was also in company, on her way to Foochow. The wind was strong from the S.E. with rain and a thick fog, and all three vessels were compelled to anchor close to the lightship for the night.

On the 19th it was blowing a full gale from the S.E., with heavy rain and fog. At noon it was cleared a little whereupon *Cutty Sark's* pilot weighed anchor and dropped down 6 or 7 miles with the ebb. But at 3 p.m. the fog closed down again and she had to be brought to an anchor.

The same thing happened on the 20th. It cleared a bit at anchor again at 5.30 p.m. On the 21st at daybreak it was at last noon, the *Cutty Sark* weighed and made sail, but was obliged to clear to the horizon with a moderate east to E.N.E. wind. At 7 a.m. the pilot left the ship and at 10.30 a.m. sail was made with Amherst Rocks bearing E.N.E. By noon the fog was thick again, but at 2 p.m. it cleared sufficiently to show the North Saddle Island, and at 2.30 p.m. the *Cutty Sark* was kept away for the Senhouse Pass. At 5 p.m. Bitt Rock was passed and at 8.45 p.m. departure was taken from the Leaconna Hummocks, bearing N.E. by E. $\frac{1}{2}$ E., 2 miles.

A light E.N.E. breeze was carried through the night, but at 8 a.m. on the 22nd when the *Cutty Sark* had gained an offing of close on 50 miles, a calm set in with fog and rain. With an horizon of a few ships' lengths, nothing was, of course, seen of the *Thermopylae*.

The calm and fog held until 2 a.m. on the 23rd June, when a light wind from the west sprang up, which soon began to increase rapidly and haul to the N.W. Soon after 6 a.m. the *Cutty Sark's* fore top-gallant sail went to rags, and by noon it was blowing a hard gale from the north, before which the clipper made good progress.

At midnight Tungying Island was in sight bearing W.N.W.; at 2 a.m. on the 24th Alligator Rock bore N.W. by W. At noon Ocksen Rock bore N.W. by W. 5 miles, and at 8 p.m. the Chapel Island light off Amoy was in sight. The northerly breeze held until 8 a.m. on the 25th, when the wind became baffling, torrents of rain began to fall, and it looked very black and threatening in the south-west. At midnight the wind came out of the S.E. in light airs, and the weather remained very unsettled and threatening with the wind gradually veering to S.W. and W.S.W., through the whole of the 26th.

At 1 p.m. when the *Cutty Sark* was abreast of Hongkong, the *Thermopylae* was sighted to the N.W. on the former's port quarter. Both ships hoisted their ensigns to show that they recognised each other, and great was the excitement of their crews. Throughout the afternoon the wind was very light from the S.W., and the *Thermopylae*, apparently holding a better wind, steadily gained on the *Cutty Sark*, until at sunset she was hull down on the latter's port bow.

For the next three days the wind kept in the S.W. quarter, very light as a rule, but with constant squalls and heavy rain, whilst immense masses of cloud hung above the racing ships.

At daybreak on the 27th the *Thermopylae* was still in sight, but the *Cutty Sark* had done well in the night for she was now hull down again on the latter's port quarter. But again the green clipper gained on her rival during the day and in the afternoon was 6 miles to the S.S.W. of *Cutty Sark*, both vessels heading about S. by E. on a wind and experiencing frequent heavy squalls with torrents of rain.

On the morning of the 29th both vessels passed to leeward of the Egeria Bank (Macclesfield Bank), and in the afternoon, with the wind falling very light, the *Cutty Sark* tacked to the westward.

On the 30th, after a calm night, the wind came away again strong and squally from the S.S.W., and at noon the *Thermopylae* bore north from the *Cutty Sark*.

On 1st July Captain Moodie got an observation of the sun— the second only since leaving—and this showed him to be 74 miles N.E. of his dead reckoning, which was due to the usual northerly current during the S.W. monsoon.

The two ships had now parted company, but the *Cutty Sark's* crew were comforted by the fact that when last seen the *Thermopylae* was astern.

At 1 p.m. on the 1st a strong gale came on very rapidly, and again the *Cutty Sark's* fore topgallant sail was split to pieces. This

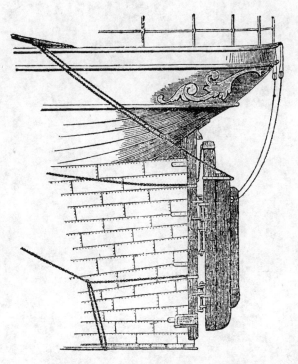

"CUTTY SARK'S" JURY RUDDER.

[*See Page* 96

gale, however, soon blew itself out and for the next week Willis's clipper beat slowly south against light airs from S.S.E. to S.S.W.

Captain Moodie would have done better if he had steered in under the lee of the Cochin China coast, where he could have worked the land and sea breezes and been out of the current.

As it was he kept too far off, and from the 2nd July, when he was in 14° 17′ N., 111° 17′ E., to the 7th, when he was abreast of Cape Padaran, he had 20 miles a day of northerly current.

On 8th July, he stood away for the Borneo coast, passing to the east of the Minerva Bank. A strong W.S.W. breeze, at times blowing a fresh gale with very heavy squalls, carried the *Cutty Sark* across the China Sea to Cape Sirik on the Borneo coast in three days at the expense of a fore topsail and two topgallant sails, which were split in the squalls.

From Cape Sirik, which was about 50 miles due south on the 10th, Captain Moodie tacked to the westward instead of steering for the Api Passage along the Borneo coast, which would have been the course adopted by Captain Keay and other crack clipper ship masters. Moodie, however, making no better than a due west course, passed close to the southward of the Great Natuna and did not tack to the southward again until he was in 20 27′ N., 107° E.

On 15th July, when abreast of Direction Island, the *Cutty Sark* again sighted the *Thermopylae*, about 8 miles to the N.N.W., the wind being very faint from the east. All that afternoon the *Thermopylae* gradually dropped astern, but on the following morning she was still in sight from the topsail yard. On the 16th however, she picked up a good deal, though she was still some way astern when the two ships entered Stolzes Channel, Gaspar Straits, on the morning of the 17th. All that day the *Cutty Sark* and *Thermopylae* were beating through the Straits with a very light south-easterly wind in their teeth. At 11 p.m. *Cutty Sark*, the leader, passed Shoalwater Island, with the wind freshening from the E.S.E.

On the 18th the wind began to be baffling with ugly squalls, and *Cutty Sark* had rather an alarming experience with several waterspouts, which so interfered with her that she had to take in sail and bear away off her course. This contretemps set her to leeward and let the *Thermopylae* by so that at noon on the 19th *Thermopylae* was about 3 miles ahead; and she passed Anjer 1½ miles ahead of the *Cutty Sark*. Captain Kemball did not stop, but Moodie hove to at 6 p.m. for a couple of hours and went ashore for letters.

The two ships were 28 days from the Shanghai pilot to Anjer, and Captain Moodie was well satisfied with his performance, for Kemball was well known for his clever navigation and splendid times down the China Sea.

From Anjer light N.E. airs with spells of calm held up both clippers until 25th July. At 2 p.m. on that date, with Keeling Island in sight to the north from the topsail yard, the *Cutty Sark* at last picked up the trade blowing fresh from E.S.E. *Thermopylae*, when last seen, was 3 miles W. by S. of *Cutty Sark*, but with strong winds the latter's power at once began to tell and she went romping ahead with three consecutive runs of 340, 327 and 320, and the two racers did not meet again.

From Keeling Island to 28° 49′ S., 39° 54′ E. (noon sights on 7th August) the *Cutty Sark* made the fine average of 260 miles a day, and had run close on 400 miles ahead of the *Thermopylae*. But at 1 p.m. on the 7th the wind took off, as if cut by a knife, as Moodie expressed it, and for the next 30 hours *Cutty Sark* slatted her sails in baffling airs and calms. Then, on the 9th, the wind began to breeze up, with all the signs of a sudden shift to the west with a very heavy westerly swell.

On the 10th Moodie snugged his ships down, and after another 24 hours of unsettled squally weather with the usual black sky and much lightning flying about, the wind rushed furiously out of the western quarter at midnight on the 11th, a hard gale with very heavy seas. During the next three days both wind and sea increased, the wind hauling from west to N.E. and back again to west, where it settled down on the 13th in real earnest. During that afternoon the *Cutty Sark's* fore and main lower topsails both went to pieces. The 14th was a repetition of the 13th, the battered clipper head-reaching in a tremendous sea, the wind west, a hard gale with howling squalls.

On the following day at 6.30 a.m. a heavy sea broke under the stern of the ship and tore the rudder from its eye-bolts. As luck would have it, this was the last effort of the gale, for by noon the wind had begun to moderate and Captain Moodie was able to try a spar over the stern but soon found that it would not steer the ship. By midnight the weather had cleared up with the wind dropping light and almost south.

The question was what to do next?

The owner's brother, Robert Willis, was on board, going the voyage for his health, and he immediately besought Captain Moodie to put into the nearest South African port. But Moodie was made of sterner stuff and declared for a jury rudder.

The argument between the two almost came to blows, but the captain had his way and told his owner's brother he could go to the devil.

A spare spar, which would either have made a jibboom or a main topgallant yard, was picked out and cut into three pieces, the longer piece to make a jury rudder-post with the shorter pieces to make the blade of the rudder.*

---

* Captain Moodie's description of his jury rudder.—"The making of the rudder was, however, the only simple part of it, the connecting it to the post and securing it to the ship so that it would work and be of sufficient strength for use when placed was the most difficult part of the job. The connection was made by putting eye-bolts in both rudderposts and rudder, and placing them so that the one would just clear the other; a large bolt (an awning stanchion) was then passed through them and clenched on both ends; in this way we had five eye-bolts in each, locked with two strong bolts which would bear considerable weight. The securing of the whole to the ship was of the next importance, and it was soon apparent that this could not be done in the way usually recommended, viz., by placing chains along the ship's bottom and leading into the hawse pipes; in the first place, the *Cutty Sark* is too sharp for chain to lie along the keel, and in the next place the length of the ship is too great, it would be difficult to bind the post tightly to the vessel owing to the great length of chain. I therefore concluded to take both the guys into the after mooring pipe, fitting the lower one with a bridle under the keel, 16 feet from the heel of the ship, so that from the post to the bridle there was a little down-pull which prevented post and rudder from rising.

"The next thing to be done was to get the steering gear secure to the rudder, for the trunk was too small to admit anything but the false sternpost, which came about 2½ feet above the deck, and being wedged round formed a good support. The steering gear had therefore to be secured to the back of the rudder and led to a spar placed across the ship, about 15 feet before the taffrail, which led the steering chains clear of the counter, and then inboard to the wheel. Of course all the gear was attached to both rudder and post before they were put over the stern. Having a small model of the ship I took all the measurements for the chains by that, which enabled me to place them pretty near the truth "

Perhaps I should give here the captain's abstract log to show the weather in which the jury rudder was made and shipped.

Aug. 15—Lat. 34° 26' S., long. 28° 1' E. At 6.30 a.m. a heavy sea struck the rudder and carried it away from the trunk downwards. Noon, wind more moderate, tried a spar over the stern but would not steer the ship. Thereupon began construction of a jury rudder with a spare spar 70 feet long.

16—Lat. 34° 13' S., long. 28° 24' E. Light winds from south. P.M., strong breeze from E.N.E. Constructing jury rudder and sternpost as fast as possible.

17—Lat. 34° 43' S., long. 28° 25' E. Strong winds from east to E.S.E. constructing jury rudder and sternpost.

18—Lat. 34° 58' S., long. 28° 11' E. Strong winds from E.N.E. Constructing jury rudder and sternpost.

19—Lat. 34° 51' S., long. 27° 58' E. Strong winds from N.E. Constructing jury rudder and sternpost.

20—Lat. 34° 38' S., long. 27° 36' E. Light wind from westward. Noon, strong westerly breeze and clear. About 2 p.m. shipped jury rudder and sternpost, a difficult job as there was a good deal of sea on.

It will be noticed that whilst the rudder was being constructed with the *Cutty Sark* hove to and making no way, strong fair winds prevailed which carried the *Thermopylae* round the Cape; but immediately the rudder was shipped the wind came out of the west again in gale strength. During the whole time there was a heavy sea running, which added greatly to the difficulties of the work.

As luck would have it, there were two stowaways on board, one happened to be an English carpenter, the other a Scotch black-smith. Whilst the English carpenter helped with the shaping of the spars, the Scotch blacksmith forged the bolts and bars from the ship's awning stanchions, whilst Moodie's son, Alexander Moodie, an apprentice, kept the bellows going.

The *Cutty Sark* was rolling heavily in the trough of the sea all the time, and as there was more water coming aboard on the lee roll than on the weather one, the forge was set up on the weather side of the deck, but, even so, it was constantly being upset and washed away.

On one occasion the whole fire upset into the shirt of young Moodie, and he carried the scars for the rest of his life. At the same time the water took the feet from under the blacksmith, who was hanging on to a red hot bar. As the sea washed him away, the unfortunate man went sailing past the end of the house, still grimly clutching the bar, but holding it as far from his own nose as possible. Its hissing end just missed the sailmaker's face as he sat on his door-sill.

But such difficulties were treated in regular sailor fashion. The sailmaker remarked grimly that at any rate the blacksmith had a good match to light his pipe. The blacksmith swore at young Moodie for not saving the fire; and the apprentice retorted that he was in just as much a hurry to get the red hot cinders off his chest as the blacksmith was to keep the red hot bar off his nose.

And so the work went on.

In order to get the jury rudder in place, Captain Moodie used a kedge anchor, weighing 5½ cwts., as a sinker. This was hung to the heel of the rudder-post by a slip rope and a block, with a rove line hooked to the anchor, so that it might be hauled on board after being detached.

Owing to the sea running this anchor caused a lot of trouble, as it was difficult to keep it clear of the guys: then, before the rudder was in place, the slip rope chafed through, and as, by some means or other, the hauling line for getting the anchor aboard had not been made fast, away went the anchor to the bottom of the Southern Ocean. At this juncture, we may well conclude that the skipper's language kept all hands from catching cold. The difficulty now was to get the rudder in place, for the broken ropes kept washing about as the ship rolled and fouling the chains.

Nevertheless at last the rudder was fixed to the old man's satisfaction. It was, however, impossible to make sail at once, for it was breezing up harder from the westward every minute, and by noon on the 21st it was blowing a hard gale. However, that afternoon it cleared up and sail was made before a light easterly air, and to every one's delight the ship was found to steer very well.

But Moodie's bad luck still held and the poor little *Cutty Sark* was not yet clear of hard gales and Cape seas. On the 23rd August she rounded Agulhas before a stiff breeze from the southward.

That very afternoon, however, the wind began to haul to the westward and the glass to fall. By the afternoon of the 24th it was
blowing a strong gale from N.W., in which the ship had to be hove
to in order to preserve the jury rudder. This gale, which gradually
hauled to the north, lasted on and off until the 31st August, on
which date the *Cutty Sark* was in lat. 32° 33' S., long. 14° 19' E.,
having only covered 465 miles in the eight days since passing
Agulhas.

After running into that disastrous head gale on the 11th August
Cutty Sark had only totalled 1027 miles, her runs being 77, 83, 0,
0, 0, 0, 19, 14, 23, 36, 116, 194, 149, 51, 17, 11, 19, 77, 57, 84. Without any favour from the winds, she had covered the distance between
these two positions on her two previous homeward passages in a
week, we may therefore reckon that already the loss of her rudder
had cost her an extra 13 days on the passage.

Let us now try to see how the *Thermopylae* was getting along.
It is a little difficult to trace her passage because Captain Kemball
kept his latitude and longitude a dead secret from every man on
board, and, as we shall see later, even refused to produce his log
book, after his arrival home, in order that it might be compared
with that of the *Cutty Sark*. However we are not quite check-mated.
The *Thermopylae* was spoken on 22nd August in 32° S., 13° E.,
by the *Paula*, which arrived at St. Helena on 5th September; and
on the following day in 31° 43' S., 13° E., by another ship. We
thus see that on the day the *Cutty Sark* rounded Agulhas the
Thermopylae was roughly 500 miles ahead, a couple of days' work in
the S.E. trades, but to give an ample margin, say, three days ahead.
And if we note that the *Cutty Sark* lost a whole week covering
50 miles, after she lost her rudder, we may safely conclude that
she was from three to four days ahead when the rudder went.
Thermopylae probably rounded Agulhas on 20th or 21st August,
and passed St. Helena on 4th September.

It is worth while noting that from 32° S., 13° E., to Gravesend,
the *Thermopylae* took 50 days, whilst from 32-33° S., 14° 19' E.
to Gravesend the *Cutty Sark*, in spite of having to keep her speed
down to about 8 or 9 knots, only took 48 days.

There was another ship which made very good running with

the *Thermopylae* this year, and that was the *Duke of Abercorn*, which left Foochow on 18th June, the day *Cutty Sark* and *Thermopylae* left Shanghai. *Duke of Abercorn* was spoken by the *India* in 34° S., 15° E., on 23rd August, the day on which *Thermopylae* was in 21° 43′ S., 13° E., and she beat her home by a day, arriving Gravesend at 9.15 p.m. on 10th October.

The long spell of bad weather off the Cape played havoc with Moodie's jury rudder, but in spite of the fact that several eye-bolts holding the rudder to the post carried away as well as the stanchions which connected the steering chains to the back of the rudder, the steering was successfully accomplished by using two emergency wire pennants, which were shackled on to an eye-bolt at the back of the rudder.

The ship steered well enough as long as the wind was aft, but with beam winds it was often necessary to reduce sail and keep the speed down to about 8 knots as at anything over that the *Cutty Sark* threatened to run away with her crew.

On 1st September the normal weather for running down to St. Helena set in. The Island was passed at 9 a.m. on 9th September, from which date with fine fresh trades the *Cutty Sark* put in some very good work for a lame duck. She passed Ascension on the 12th and crossed the line on the 15th September in 18° 52′ W., an average speed of $8\frac{1}{2}$ knots from St. Helena. On the 17th the trades gave out and the usual doldrum weather was encountered.

On 20th the last of the eye-bolts on the rudder gave way and the whole contrivance had to be got aboard for repairs. Moodie was now getting very short of material and was compelled to use flat pieces of iron to replace the eye-bolts, between which the stanchions rods were fitted. The chain guys, which had rusted away owing to the action of the copper on the ship's bottom, were replaced by heavy wire pennants parcelled over with canvas. The steering chains, also, were rove through spare topsail sheet blocks. This made the steering heavier work but it was easier on the gear.

The band for the slings of the topgallant yard was taken off and riveted on to the jury rudder, so as to bind it all together.

All hands worked with a will and the rudder was ready for lowering into position on the 21st. A light easterly breeze was blowing, and by clever manoeuvring of his ship Captain Moodie managed to get the rudder into place without any of the previous contretemps.

As soon as the rudder was dropped over the stern the sails were filled, and as the ship gathered headway the whole contrivance streamed away astern. The sails were then laid aback and the rudder hauled close up to the trunk, the weight of the chains and wires sinking it sufficiently. As soon as the *Cutty Sark* began to gather sternway, the slack of the guys was got in, the heel of the rudder sinking in the process, so that the head was easily hauled up through the trunk.

It was a delicate operation, but owing to the handiness of the *Cutty Sark*, the fine seamanship of Captain Moodie and the smartness of his crew, everything went without a hitch.

The N.E. trades were picked up on the 25th September and on the following day the *Cutty Sark* was becalmed for a few hours, whilst she passed to leeward of the Cape Verde. The trades proved of fine strength, but as the ship steered wildly on a wind when going over 8 knots the royals had to be taken in and speed kept down to under 200 miles a day.

On 6th October Fayal bore S. by E. ½ E. 35 miles, the *Cutty Sark* being 21 days from the line and 10 days from Cape Verde.

The weather from the Azores to the Channel was very unfavourable for a lame duck, but the *Cutty Sark* forced her way against strong gales from north to N.E. without mishap.

On 16th October Portland bore north at noon, the wind blowing from the N.N.W., a strong gale with hard squalls, the *Cutty Sark* being 10 days from the Western Isles, and having had her yards on the backstays all the way from 42° N., 21° W. Dungeness was passed on the 17th and Gravesend reached at 9 p.m. on the 18th; the *Cutty Sark* being 119 days from her pilot and 122 days from Shanghai.

Her performance in making the Channel from the Cape under jury rudder in 54 days was looked upon as a great piece of work, and congratulations were showered upon Captain Moodie.

Though *Thermopylae* had arrived first, the shipping world gave all the credit of the race to *Cutty Sark*. Captain Moodie was almost

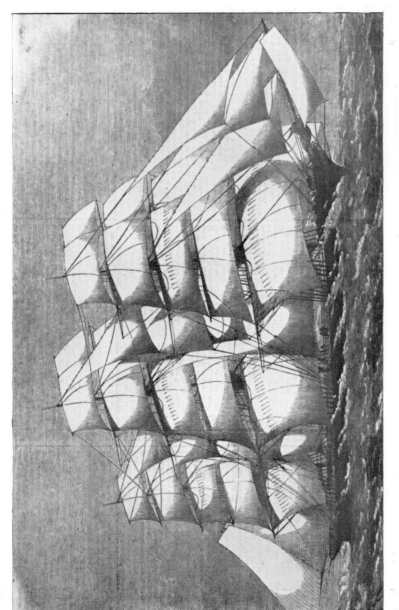

" ARIEL "

[See Page 81

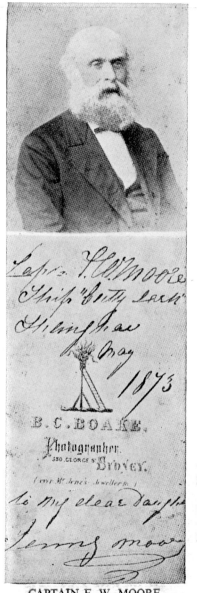

CAPTAIN F. W. MOORE

[See Page 103

worn out when he arrived but Captain Kemball's officers declared that the latter's anxiety was so great that life was hardly worth living aboard the *Thermopylae*, especially after leaving the Cape.

Kemball at first tried to insist that the *Thermopylae* was leading when *Cutty Sark* lost her rudder, but when Willis, Moodie and Linton went to the White Star office with the *Cutty Sark's* log book and challenged Kemball to produce the *Thermopylae's* he refused to do so, and it had to be admitted that the *Thermopylae* was badly beaten. Even her officers agreed that their ship was no match for the *Cutty Sark* in fresh winds, and Kemball had to put up with a lot of chaff, and, what was harder to bear, commiseration in the captains' room at Lloyd's.

Meanwhile Captain Moodie resigned the command of the *Cutty Sark* to the consternation of old White Hat. On being asked his reason, he explained the cause of his row with Robert Willis. At which old Jock waxed mightily indignant and declared that as long as he lived his brother should never have another voyage on any of his ships.

And he tried his best to get Moodie to alter his decision, even offering to build him the finest iron ship which could be produced. But Moodie was firm, and left the sea for steam, taking a command in the State Line of Glasgow, which finished by swallowing up a good part of his savings.

The tea passages of this year are given on the following page. *Normancourt*, after weathering out a severe typhoon which cost her a whole suit of sails, made the best passage of the season.

Several famous ships came to grief. The *Lahloo*, which left Shanghai on 30th June, was wrecked on Sandalwood Island on 31st July, through the fault of the second mate, who was in charge of the deck.

Serica left Hongkong on 2nd November and was wrecked on the Paracels, her whole ship's company except the bosun perishing. Captain Innes and eight men died from privation and exposure on a raft, which they had constructed, whilst the remainder, numbering 19, were drowned on the Triton Rocks, where their raft went to pieces.

H

Taeping, when bound from Amoy to New York, was lost on Ladds Reef, her mate's boat and six men being the only ones that were picked up.

TEA PASSAGES 1872.

Ship	Freig't	Cargo lbs.	Port from	Date left	Passed Anjer	Arrived Channel	Docked	Days out
Titania			Macao	May 25			Sept. 19	116
Duke of Abercorn ..		1,585,200	Foochow	June 18			Oct. 10	114
Cutty Sark	£3 10	1,303,000	Shanghai	„ 18	July 19	Portland Oct. 16	Oct. 18	122
Thermopylae	£3 10	1,196,400	„	„ 18	„ 19		„ 11	115
Undine	£3 10	1,128,600	„	„ 24		Prawle Pt. Oct. 15	„ 17	115
Blackadder		1,394,300	Foochow	„ 28		Deal Oct. 26	„ 28	122
Argonaut	£3 10	1,544,100	Shanghai	July 2			„ 27	117
Sir Lancelot		1,218,200	Foochow	„ 7			Nov. 6	122
Maitland		1,110,300	„	„ 19			„ 6	111
Ambassador		880,800	„	„ 23		Deal Nov. 7	„ 8	108
Falcon		909,800	Macao	Aug. 4	Sept. 6		„ 21	109
Doune Castle		1,282,000	Shanghai	„ 1			Dec. 1	122
Harlaw			Foochow	„ 1	Sept. 8		Nov. 21	112
Taitsung		1,084,300	Shanghai	., 8			„ 30	114
Thyatira..			„	Sept. 5			Jan. 6	123
Normancourt			Macao	„ 14	Oct. 5	Lizard Dec. 17	Dec. 19	96
Ziba			Foochow	Oct. 4			Jan. 16	107
Eme			„	„ 1	Oct. 26		„ 14	102

CHAPTER IV.

IN THE CHINA TRADE.

Continued

IN the year 1873 the fact that the steamers had come to stay in the China trade was forced without further doubt, upon the minds of the sailing ship owners, and they recognised that not only were the "steam kettles" going to take all the first teas, but a great deal of the export trade to China as well.

Thus in the autumn of 1872 we notice other tea ships besides the Aberdeen White Star clippers loading general cargoes for Australia.

The run out to Australia, with its long spell of easting in the roaring forties, was far from being a suitable one for the smaller tea ships: indeed the only China clippers which were really fitted for it were the *Cutty Sark, Thermopylae, Duke of Abercorn, Forward Ho,* and the two sister ships, *Blackadder* and *Hallowe'en.*

The beautiful Steele clippers were often really dangerous when heavily pressed in a big sea such as one finds in the Southern Ocean, and had a way of squatting down by the stern until the quarter-deck was under water, then if not quickly relieved of their after canvas they would sweep their decks clean. The cause was clear enough: they were too fine and had not enough bearing aft.

Let me try to illustrate this trying quality by a few anecdotes from Captain Keay's reminiscences of the time when he was in command of the *Ariel.*

He became aware of *Ariel's* propensity for throwing water over aft before he was a day out on his maiden passage.

I will use his own words, from a lecture which he gave some years ago to the boys of the training ship *Conway.*

"After casting off the tug near the Tuskar, we made sail and stood to the S.S.W., then tacked to W.N.W.: the wind hauled to south so that she came up to W.S.W., heading into the old S.W. short sea, wind moderate and topgallant sails set: presently she dipped her tail when seas took her forward and threw a cascade completely over the taffrail and wheel and helmsman in a most surprising way, as if for a bit of fun. I said nothing, and fortunately the man at the wheel was a cool fellow and took it calmly after the first douche we both got. I took in her topgallant sails and ended her capers that time.

"Again running east, about 42° S. latitude, carrying main topgallant sail, gale and sea quarterly with a turbulent confused swell she began to sit down aft and the sea, curling over both quarters filled the decks to the rails. I quickly took in main topgallant and all sail off the mizen, and she rose kindly to her work like one relieved of a load.

"Another time homeward bound off the Cape, the wind had been N.W., a strong gale with the ship under low canvas. It lulled off to near calm, then hauled to W. and S.W., moderate but looking ugly.

"I waited an hour or so for expected renewal of the gale, then, being eager to get along, set more sail.

"Before reefed under topsails and reefed foresail could be set properly, the gale burst on us from south. I called all hands and we struggled for fully two hours to furl all except lower fore and mizen topsails, but had to let the foresail hang in the gear and spilling lines and call the men down from aloft.

"To see—as well as the dismal darkness and blinding seas and spray would allow us—how she went into and over the mountainous nor-west seas as we steered about N.N.W. was a caution.

"The log was hove after the men came down from aloft, and she was going 10 knots, with only lower topsails at fore and main, into a howling gale from south against that fearful sea.

"I was secured near the helmsman, and he had a rope round him with scope enough for his arms.

"The binnacle light was washed out several times, but the splendid man at the wheel kept her going all right. He steered by the feel of the wind on his back and neck and a little help now and then till we could see the compass again.

"When the first green seas came along the deck, the hen coops, which, under the monkey poop close aft, were snug enough in most weathers, were in an instant all swept overboard; and the piteous, loud scream of the fowls was like a human cry in agony, though hushed in a moment.

"T'was very eerie, I assure you, and never to be forgotten.

"Next day there was a hard gale from about south, and we gave her more canvas. In the afternoon she had too much and began that sitting down trick, the starboard quarter going clean under water.

"I sang out:—'Let go the topsail halliards.' But no one could get near the mizen topsail halliards, and it took me up to the neck letting them go.

"She presently rose and went dancing along gaily towards St. Helena and home. 'The girls have got hold of the tow rope,' we used to say in those days, and Jack fancied he saw them skipping merrily ahead, looking slyly over their shoulders."

The above is a vivid enough picture of a typical tea clipper in bad weather; but, as we shall see later, *Cutty Sark* was a very different vessel, whilst *Thermopylae* had already proved herself to be the best passage maker in the Melbourne trade.

Hallowe'en, also, had won her spurs in the roaring forties on her maiden passage in 1872, when she went out to Sydney in 72 days and took a wool cargo home instead of crossing to China, being too late for a tea cargo.

In 1873 there were several desperate races out to the Colonies. The first two ships of the tea fleet to load for Melbourne were *Titania* and *Thermopylae*. The owners of *Titania*, with their knowledge of a tea clipper's habits when running heavy, had wisely cut down her big sail plan before she sailed, her lower yards being reduced as much as 10 feet and the rest in proportion.

Notwithstanding this, her captain was very chary of carrying sail in the roaring forties, with the result that *Thermopylae* overhauled her hand over fist.

Captain Dowdy left *Titania* on the completion of her 1872 voyage in order to take command of Maxton's tea steamer *Lord of the Isles*. He was succeeded in *Titania* by a man named Hunt, who apparently was not a success, for he only had her one voyage and made the worst homeward passage of her existence.

In comparing the passages of ships on the Australia run I shall resort to a system of tables, which show at a glance the positions of the ships with regard to each other, and will commence with a table, comparing the passages of *Titania* and *Thermopylae*.

Details of Passages 1892-3.	*Titania*	*Thermopylae*
Left London	October 25	November 16
Off the Start	November 2	—
Off the Lizard	—	November 17
Off Cape Finisterre ..	November 14	—
Off Madeira	—	Dec. 2 (to Leeward.)
N.E. trades	Very poor	Good. Lost in 6° N.
Crossed equator	Dec. 8 in 26° W.	Dec. 12 in 27° W.
S.E. trades	Favourable, lost off Trinidad	Moderate, lost in 20° S.
Crossed Cape meridian ..	December 23	Dec. 31 in 44° S.
Ran down easting in ..	42° to 45° S.	46° S.
Passed Cape Leeuwin meridian	—	January 19
Passed Cape Otway ..	1 a.m. Jan. 24	8 a.m. Jan. 25
Anchored Hobson's Bay	January 24	Forenoon Jan. 26
Days out from departure	83	70

The winter of 1872-3 was not as favourable a season as usual for vessels bound south, and none of the ships made specially good runs.

It is but fair to say also that cargoes to the Colonies this year were very heavy, and many of the ships were overloaded. *Thermopylae* took out 1600 tons of general cargo and was much deeper in the water than usual. This was also the case with *Cutty Sark*, which the Australian shipping reporters considered to be quite "out of flying trim" on her arrival.

In this way, the passenger carrying ships had a great advantage over the tea clippers, who filled their 'tween decks with freight.

The passages of *Titania* and *Thermopylae* were more of a chase than a race, but *Cutty Sark* on her first trip to the Colonies had a very interesting race, not only with two of her tea rivals, *Blackadder* and *Duke of Abercorn*, but with the celebrated *Thomas Stephens* which was considered to be one of the very fastest passenger ships to the Colonies.

Before giving a table of this contest, I must give *Cutty Sark's* new captain a short notice.

Old Willis was very nonplussed at Moodie's "pigheadedness", as he called it, in giving up the command, for there were few men to whom he was willing to trust his beloved *Cutty Sark*, and at last he was compelled to fall back on trusty Captain W. F. Moore, his superintendent, who had just brought home the *Blackadder* and shown that that unlucky vessel could be coaxed into a good humour.

Captain Jock gave the command of his "hoodoo" ship to Sam Bissett, who had been mate of her on her maiden voyage. Sam Bissett was a rare good man, as good a seaman as could be found in the Port of London, and he had another first rate man, Henderson as his mate, yet, as Captain Moodie would have expressed it, the *Blackadder's* luck would not go past her.

Captain F. W. Moore, who now took command of the *Cutty Sark*, had had a very long experience of the China trade. As far back as 1853 he was bosun of the *Merse* under Captain Shewan; in 1856 he was second mate of *Lammermuir*, and from 1857 to 1860 mate of the *Lammermuir*.

His last command was the *Whiteadder* from 1865 to 1869, he then came ashore to act as ships'-husband to Willis's fleet. But in 1872 "old White Hat" had to ask him to go to sea again in the *Blackadder*, as that vessel evidently required a very experienced man in charge; then, as a favour Moore took the *Cutty Sark* for a voyage.

Captain Moore was more celebrated for the way in which he kept his ships than for carrying on—indeed, he had few equals at making a ship look her best, and he kept the *Cutty Sark* like a yacht, so that she was noticed for her smart appearance amongst a fleet of perfectly kept ships. But Moore was an old man and he had outgrown the thrill of driving a vessel, and did not fancy hanging on to his topgallant sails when other ships were reefing topsails, which was what the *Cutty Sark* rejoiced in.

Nor did he care about taking risks or cutting corners in the China Sea. He was as safe a navigator as he was a seaman; and with his position assured, he was content to let the *Cutty Sark* go her natural speed without making any attempt to spur her.

Yet if there was ever a vessel that liked the spur it was the *Cutty Sark*, and there is no doubt that with a little more help from her captain the clipper would have saved a good many days on each of her 1873 passages.

Duke of Abercorn should have been far ahead of the *Blackadder*, *Cutty Sark*, and *Thomas Stephens* with her long start in the run to Australia, but from 21st November until 2nd December, when Scilly bore N.N.E. 80 miles, she was hove to in a terrific S.W. gale, during which the barometer went down to 28.60. *Cutty Sark* and *Blackadder* also experienced this gale in the Channel, but *Thomas Stephens* came away with a fair wind.

The *Cutty Sark*, though very deeply laden, made several consecutive runs of over 310 miles a day. It was Captain Moore's first visit to Melbourne for over 20 years. *Blackadder* was evidently

Details of Passages 1872-3	*Duke of Abercorn*	*Blackadder*	*Cutty Sark*	*Thomas Stephens*
Left London ..	November 15	November 21	November 26	December 2
Off the Start ..	—	December 3	December 4	—
Off the Lizard ..	—	—	—	December 4
Scillies N.N.E. 80 miles	December 2	—	—	—
Off Madeira ..	—	December 11	—	—
N.E. trades ..	Moderate	Strong, best run 306	Strong, lost in 4° 30′ N.	—
Crossed the line	Dec. 22 in 30° W.	December 24	Dec 23 in 28° 30′ W.	Dec. 25 in 27° W.
S.E. trades ..	Fair, lost in 21° S.	Light, lost in 22° S.	Very scant, S.S.E. for 8 days	Very indifferent
Passed Trinidad	—	January 1	—	—
Tristan d'Acunha	January 13	—	—	—
Crossed Meridian Greenwich ..	—	—	Jan. 18 in 47° S.	Jan. 17 in 43° S.
Greenwich Cape	Jan. 20 in 45° S.	Jan 20 in 40° S.	—	—
Ran down easting in	45° S.	46° and 47° S.	46° and 47° S.	47° S.
Best run.. ..	—	320	320	—
On meridian Cape Leeuwin ..	—	February 5	—	—
Off the Otway ..	—	—	February 10	February 10
Off S.W. Cape, Tasmania ..	February 17	February 10	—	—
Anchored Port .. Phillip ..	—	—	Feb. 11, p.m. at Queenscliff	Feb. 11, noon
Anchored Sydney	Feb. 23, p.m.	Feb. 23, p.m.	—	—
Days out ..	83	83	69	69

driven hard by Sam Bissett, for besides a run of 320, she made one of 316 and three of 300, and she covered 7255 miles in 30 days, an average of 242 miles a day or 10 miles an hour from 20° W. to Tasmania, but then had light winds and calms to port.

Thomas Stephens distinguished herself by bringing papers, two days later in date than those of the last mail. She also landed a Shorthorn bull in very good condition.

Cutty Sark and *Thomas Stephens* both had no difficulty in keeping ahead of the crack Loch liner, *Loch Tay*, which left Greenock on 2nd December, and reached Port Phillip 19th February. *Forward Ho* arrived at Melbourne on 7th March, 75 days out from New York, having made two consecutive runs of 332 and 312.

The best passage to China this year was made by the *Wylo*, which arrived Hongkong on 27th June, 99 days from the river Elbe. The other ships sailing to China direct were *Sir Lancelot, Undine, Maitland, Windhover, Normancourt, Kaisow* and *Lothair. Lothair* had a new master, Captain Orchard, who drove her out to Hongkong in 101 days, arriving 26th October. She lost a man overboard running her easting down, but was not as unfortunate as *Leander*, which had two men washed overboard and her helmsman's thigh broken and wheel smashed up.

This year *Leander* found herself pitted against *Hallowe'en*, which loaded wool home in 1872, and thus had not yet had any testing against the China cracks.

It will be noticed from the following table that, though *Leander* had all the best of it as long as the wind was light to moderate, *Hallowe'en* raced ahead in the roaring forties. Both vessels had trouble. On 26th April, in 17° S., 30° 24'. W. *Hallowe'en* was struck by a violent S.E. squall, which carried away her bowsprit, fore topmast and main topgallant mast. The fitting of new spars was a work of some difficulty, nevertheless by 1st May she was all ship-shape again.

Leander ran into a heavy Sly. gale in 45° E. on 21st May. On the 23rd with the barometer down to 28.3, the wind suddenly fell light. The ship's head was kept to the N.E., whilst a terrific sea rolled aboard fore and aft. By noon it was blowing a fierce W.S.W. gale, the ship scudding before it under reefed main topsail, lower fore topsail, foresail and fore topmast staysail. The squalls were furious, with short lulls in between. During one of the lulls a heavy sea came up astern, and breaking over the taffrail smashed the wheel in halves and fractured the thigh of one of the helmsmen.

Shortly after this, a huge dollop struck the port quarter, heeling the *Leander* over until her starboard upper dead-eyes were under water, and in the return roll two men were swept overboard and drowned.

Details of passages 1873	*Hallowe'en*	*Leander*
Off Dungeness	March 23	
Off the Start	March 24	March 22
Crossed the equator	April 18 in 22° 28′ W.	April 12 in 26° W.
Crossed meridian of Greenwich	May 14	May 7
Crossed meridian of Cape ..	May 17	May 11
Ran down easting in	44	40 to 44
Off the Otway	June 10	June 13
Off Gabo Island	June 13	June 18
Arrived Sydney	June 15	June 22
Days out	84	92

With the growing demand in China for coal, all the tea ships loaded coal either at Newcastle or Sydney for Chinese ports, the rate being round about 44s.

CROSS PASSAGES 1873.

Ship	Cargo coal in tons.	Port from	Date left	Port to	Date arrived	Days out
Titania	1190	Newcastle	Mar. 21	Shanghai	May 3	43
Thermopylae ..	1200	Sydney	,, 21	,,	,, 3	43
Blackadder ..	1230	,,	,, 26	,,	,, 25	60
Cutty Sark ..	1200	,,	April 1	,,	,, 12	41
Duke of Abercorn	1600	,,	,, 10	,,	,, 29	49
Argonaut	1485	Newcastle	,, 16	,,	June 4	49
Forward Ho ..	1300	,,	,, 20	,,	,, 9	50
Ambassador ..	1038	,,	May 31	,,	July 18	48
Harlaw	1136	Sydney	June 6	,,	,, 17	41
Doune Castle ..	1274	,,	,, 19	,,	July 23	35
Thyatira	—	Newcastle	June 10	,,	Aug. 25	45
Leander	1000	Sydney	July 30	,,	Sept. 13	45
Hallowe'en ..	1300	,,	Aug. 9	,,	,, 13	35

The passage up the Pacific is a light weather one with delightful summer sailing until the China Sea is reached, when the dreaded typhoon may bring what has been a pleasant trip to a disastrous end.

It is curious the way in which the ships kept in pairs in 1873. *Titania* and *Thermopylae*, leaving Australia on the same day, arrived Woosung together without ever sighting each other during the passage; indeed the former never saw a single vessel all the way to the Saddle Islands.

Titania was able to get up to Shanghai without delay, but *Thermopylae* stuck fast on the bar. Twenty-one feet of water had been signalled as the soundings on the bar and as *Thermopylae* was only drawing 3 inches more, Captain Kemball thought that he could easily drag his keel through that amount of mud, but he was mistaken, and before *Thermopylae* would come off cargo boats had to be sent down to lighten her.

Cutty Sark and *Blackadder*, the next pair to cross the Pacific, encountered a severe typhoon off the Ladrones; *Cutty Sark* came through safely but *Blackadder* came badly to grief.

May 2nd found the barometer steadily falling aboard the *Blackadder*, with a fresh S.E. gale, dull cloudy weather and a big S.E. sea making. By 2 a.m. on the 3rd the weather was looking very wild and threatening with both wind and sea rapidly increasing. The barometer was down to 29.50, having dropped steadily from 29.80 in the 24 hours. Calling all hands, Captain Bissett shortened sail to three close-reefed topsails and foresail. By 3 a.m. the sea had grown very heavy and confused and thick rain was falling. At 5 a.m. the barometer registered 28.90, the wind was still at S.E., and with the weather growing worse every minute, the *Blackadder* was put under a lower main topsail and hove to on the starboard tack. At 6 a.m. the barometer was 28.60 and still falling. The main trysail was now set as the ship showed an inclination to fall off. At 9 a.m., with the barometer at 28.50, the S.E. wind suddenly increased to hurricane force with a hideous sea. With a difficulty which may be imagined, all hands managed to furl the main lower topsail. At 10 a.m. with the ship more under water than above it, a successful effort was made to lash a tarpaulin in the mizen rigging. The position by account at noon was 21° 30′ N., 140° 20′ E., with the barometer down to 28.40. At 2.30 p.m. in a terrific squall of wind and rain, the ship was hove down on her beam ends, with the water over the lee sheer poles and half covering the hatches.

The decks were swept clean, the skylight torn off the poop, and all the iron parts to leeward washed away.

Instead of freeing herself and bringing her spars to windward, the *Blackadder* showed signs of settling whereupon Captain Bissett gave the order to cut away the topgallant masts. As this had no effect, the topmasts were next sent over the side. And still the *Blackadder* lay on her beam ends, whilst it was quite impossible to clear away the wreck owing to the force of the wind and the terrific sea. It was impossible to stand up even by holding on to rail or rope, and the spray and rain drove over the ship in such clouds that the fore end of the vessel could not be seen from the poop. In this desperate situation, the mainyard broke adrift, and a cry for axes to the main lanyards was passed from mouth to mouth. As soon as the lanyards were cut, the mast broke 3 feet below the deck beams, tore a great hole in the deck, and stove two boats in its fall. A third boat was picked out of her skids by a sea and smashed to splinters on the deck.

The loss of the mast relieved the ship and she became a little easier, though the sea began to pour through the hole in the deck. The two mates and the carpenter, together with an apprentice to pass the nails, were now lashed to stanchions and ring-bolts, whilst they endeavoured to nail a tarpaulin over the gap. This job took over two hours, during which the struggling men spent half their time under water as sea after sea swept over them.

On one occasion, when the water had run off, the apprentice was found clinging to the mate's leg, with Henderson's great bulk on top of him (he weighed 18 stone) whilst the nails had mostly found their way inside the carpenter's shirt. The air was blue with what each one thought of the situation, and when Chips hit the second mate's fingers instead of the nail heads, his hammer strokes made uncertain by the violent movement of the ship, the language became more and more lurid. And when the third mate came to help and was promptly set down on the mate's head by an invading sea, the top limit of exasperation was reached. After going through the Chinese alphabet about 50 times, the mate sat up with a freely bleeding nose, whereupon he proceeded to express his opinion in the Japanese alphabet also, and one could almost smell the brimstone.

Meanwhile almost as desperate a struggle was going on down in the hold, where the men were trying to trim the coal over to windward; whilst, lashed to the binnacle, Captain Bissett strained his eyes in a vain effort to pierce the smothering rain and spray and detect the first sign of any change. This did not come until midnight, when the wind began to veer to the southward and slowly moderate as the barometer slowly rose.

At 4 a.m. on the 4th May it was still blowing a strong gale from the south with a very maelstrom of a sea, in which the *Blackadder* tumbled and tossed and strained like a buck jumper. Captain Bissett kept her on the starboard tack, whilst the wind hauled to N.W., round by S.W., and gradually eased. No spars were standing except the fore lower mast, mizen lower mast, bowsprit and crossjack yard, and all hands were soon busy setting up a jury mainmast and sending yards aloft on fore and mizen.

The *Blackadder* had 1400 miles to cover under jury rig and it took her 21 days. On arrival at Shanghai Captain Bissett was anxious to get his ship into dry dock, for he feared the hull might have been damaged by the masts and spars washing about alongside during the typhoon; but he found that the *Duke of Abercorn* had first call on the Tunkadoo Dry Dock.

Like the *Thermopylae*, the "Duke" had grounded in trying to cross Woosung bar, and it was found that nearly all her false keel had been knocked away and some of her metal torn off. The *Blackadder*, therefore, after discharging her coal, was removed to the "lower limits" to await her turn at the dock.

Meanwhile a fine number of first class ships began to collect at Shanghai; and there was great rivalry amongst them when the 4th July came round and the usual ship dressing and other celebrations to honour the day of America's independence took place.

In the ship decorations Captain Moore and the crew of the *Cutty Sark* specially distinguished themselves, the *Hongkong Times* remarking—"The decorations of the ships of all nations in the honour of the Anniversary of America's independence has been unusually brilliant this year, conspicuous amongst them being the British ship *Cutty Sark*, whose crew must have been at work all night to produce her display of this morning."

The first ships on the berth to load tea at Shanghai this year were the *Sir Lancelot, Cutty Sark, Thermopylae* and *Titania*, the very pick of the fleet, and China newspaper correspondents wrote that "this clipper ocean race would be watched with an interest like to that awakened of yore by *Taeping* and *Ariel, Serica, Lahloo, Spindrift* and *Fiery Cross*."

Unfortunately 1873 was a year of continual bad weather in the China Sea, with a regular succession of typhoons, and the shipping reports were full of wrecks, founderings and dismastings.

Of the four cracks, *Sir Lancelot* was the first to hoist the Blue Peter, and *Cutty Sark* came next, beating the *Thermopylae* in a loading race of two days.

When *Cutty Sark* left Shanghai the weather was very bad, with a falling barometer, and she was hardly to sea before lame ducks began to come into Woosung, reporting terrific weather outside.

The American barque *Conquest*, from Manila to 'Frisco, was passed under jury rig, on her way into Shanghai for repairs, having been dismasted off the Saddles. A dismasted junk lay off the Beacon in charge of the pilot boat *Ruby*.

A raft with 15 men on board was sighted from Gutzlaff Island, drifting about 6 miles off the land, and H.M.S. *Mosquito* was sent out from Shanghai, but failed to find it.

Harlaw, which was bound from Shanghai to 'Frisco, put back owing to stress of weather, whilst the *Northampton* arrived at Woosung from Sydney, having carried away her topgallant masts on the 9th.

The weather was no better when *Thermopylae* left Shanghai at noon on the 11th. Two tugboats were requisitioned to tow her down against the strong flood tide, but they could not hold her, and as soon as her anchor was off the ground she took a sheer in towards the Poontug shore and stuck in the mud by her forefoot for an hour and a half. *Thermopylae* was hardly clear of the river before a rumour began to circulate through Shanghai that *Cutty Sark* had been wrecked about the Chusan Group.

The weather and the amount of distressed shipping no doubt helped to spread the report, which luckily was not verified.

Captain Moore, however, was having a hard time beating south against a southerly gale, which culminated in a typhoon off Formosa on the 20th, which devastated Amoy.

The log of *Undine*, which was on the other side of this typhoon, is worth quoting, as I have not *Cutty Sark's*.

Sunday, July 20. Clipper Ship *Undine*. Captain Vowell.

4 a.m.—Slight swell making from S.E. Wind N.N.E. Force 6.

8 a.m.—Scud passing very rapidly from N.E., north and N.E. by N. Force 5. Strong sea making from S.E. Typhoon appearance.

Noon.—Lat. 22° 9′ N., long. 118° 57′ E. Wind N.E. by N. Force 5.

2.30 p.m.—Kept away S. by W. to get to the southward of the centre. Wind N. by E. Force 6-10.

4 p.m.—Squalls getting very heavy. Wind N. by N. 6.10.

5.15 p.m.—Barometer 29.30; 6.45 p.m., bar. 29.40; 7.15 p.m., 29.33; 9 p.m., 29.45.

6 p.m.—Scudding under lower fore topsail—11 knots.

8 p.m.—Squalls terrific, like thunder, could hear nothing for the howli of the wind. The wind westering as the ship scuds southward. Wind N. by W. Force 10-11.

10 p.m.—Squalls moderating, wind getting well to the westward. Bar. 29.54.

Midnight.—Ship leaving the centre fast. Wind N.N.W. to W.S.W. Force 11-9.

Monday, July 21.

2 a.m.—Gradually moderating with continuous rain, barometer rising steadily.

4 a.m.—Wind west. Force 9-8.

8 a.m.—Wind S.W. Force 7.

Noon.—Lat. account 20° 39′ N., long. account 119° 26′ E. Wind S.S.W. Force 7. Continuous rain. Barometer stationary.

4 p.m.—Wind S. by W. Force 7.

8 p.m.—Wind south to S.E. variable. Force 7-3.

10 p.m.—Continuous rain. Weather looking bad but barometer steadily rising.

Midnight.—Wind S. by W. Force 5.

Cutty Sark, having weathered this typhoon successfully, had a very unfavourable run to Anjer, which she did not pass until 12 days after *Thermopylae*.

Captain Kemball had probably as good a record in the China

Seas as any racing skipper, and he never made a bad run to **Anjer** in the *Thermopylae*, as is shown by the following times:—

1869	Left	Foochow	July	3	passed	Anjer	July 28—25 days.
1870	„	„	„	29	„	„	Aug. 23—25 „
1871	„	Shanghai	June	22	„	„	July 22—30 „
1872	„	„	„	18	„	„	July 19—31 „
1873	„	„	„	11	„	„	Aug. 8—28 „
1874	„	„	„	17	„	„	Aug. 14—28 „

Cutty Sark, on the other hand, was never given a good start by her skippers and never made anything better than an average run to Anjer.

In 1873 she was spoken by the barque *Hopewell* on 20th August at the North end of the Sunda Straits, and reported that she had struck an uncharted reef that morning in the Java Sea.

Moore's tea passage was a disappointing one; Kemball, indeed, was the only one of the early starters who made a good passage, the worst of all being made by *Titania*, whose captain was replaced at the end of the voyage.

I have related how *Cutty Sark* was sighted by the mail steamer *Garonne* off the Cape Verdes in my first chapter.

The *Garonne* spoke her on 16th October in 14° N., 25° W., the *Cutty Sark* running home from Cape Verde latitude to Deal in 17 days, a very good performance.

Before turning to *Cutty Sark's* fifth voyage, it behoves me to relate what happened to the stricken *Blackadder* and other ships in this year of disasters.

The *Blackadder*, after refitting and remasting in the Tunkadoo Dock, found that no shipper would trust her with a tea cargo, and she was at last compelled to go to Iloilo, where she loaded sugar for Boston. She left Iloilo on 22nd October, and at 4 p.m. on 3rd November got hard and fast on an uncharted reef near the Island of Banquey. The wind was coming in squalls from the S.W. and she soon began to pound heavily. After failing to move her by jettisoning some of his cargo, Captain Bissett at length abandoned ship, and transferred his crew to the *Albyn's Isle*, which was in company. But no sooner were her crew aboard the other ship before a squall took the *Blackadder* aback and forced her off the

"BLACKADDER," DISMASTED IN TYPHOON, 1873

From drawings in colour by one of her crew

[*See Page* 108

"HALLOWE'EN"

"BLACKADDER"

See Page 122

reef stern first; then away she went as if the spirit of mischief were steering her and it took the *Albyn's Isle* all of four hours to catch her.

After this effort on the part of the *Blackadder's* demon, she had light winds and calms, and her natural speed was slowed down very much because her iron bottom had now become very foul. It was not long before provisions began to run short and for the last two months and eleven days of the passage the crew had nothing to live upon but the sugar cargo; thus when the *Blackadder* at last arrived at Boston after a very long passage, 28 of her ship's company were suffering from blind scurvy.

The American doctor ordered vegetables but no meat; as may well be imagined this was far from popular with starving men, and, as one of them put it, "we started to moo and moo to such an extent both day and night that at last Captain Bissett sent beef and mutton aboard, with the horns on top to show that it was genuine." These horns, after being boiled clean, were nailed at the mastheads, and it was decorated in this guise that the *Blackadder* eventually arrived in the London River.

The one ship to distinguish herself in 1873 was the *Hallowe'en*. She made a very good run up the Pacific from Sydney, during which she caught her old antagonist *Leander*, and ran neck and neck with her to port. *Leander* reported sighting the *Doune Castle* under jury masts when 30 miles east of Leaconna. *Doune Castle* had left Shanghai in ballast on 3rd September for Hongkong, having been chartered to load tea at Whampoa for New York.

About 9 a.m. on the 3rd when she was about 80 miles south of Barren Rocks and running south before an N.N.E. gale under close-reefed topsails and foresail, *Doune Castle* was struck by a terrific squall, which threw her on her beam ends; then, as she struggled to bring her spars to windward, a second squall came down on her, and all her ballast fell over to starboard. The ship lay down until she was submerged up to the main hatch and her crew had to clamber out on to her side.

Captain McDiarmid managed to cut away his masts, and this saved the ship. He next let go his port anchor, and paying out 105 fathoms of chain brought her head to wind. It was possible then for all hands to get below to trim the ballast over. On the following day it was blowing a terrific gale with an appalling sea; the cable broke at the hawse pipe, and until a sea anchor could be rigged the ship drifted at the mercy of wind and wave. The weather improved on the 6th and for the next few days all hands were busy rigging jury masts, but on the 12th, with Leaconna in sight, another typhoon burst upon the ship, and at 1 p.m. Captain McDiarmid was compelled to bear up and run dead before it in order to keep his jury masts on end.

All that night the *Doune Castle* was run to the southward, with the barometer down to 28.70; but at 8 a.m. on the 13th, when 60 miles to the east of the north end of Formosa, the wind shifted suddenly into the S.W., blew harder than ever, and the ship had to be run to the north again. The typhoon took off about 10 p.m. on the 14th, and with light winds and calms the battered *Doune Castle* did not make Woosung until the 20th.

Another ship, which had a narrow escape this year, was the *Argonaut.* She stranded on the Pescadores and was compelled to jettison 3000 cases of tea before she got off.

Even *Kaisow* was not safe from a mishap, though at anchor at Shanghai, for on the night of 15th July, during a strong southerly gale, she was fouled by an American gunboat and had her jibboom taken out of her.

On *Cutty Sark's* arrival home in 1873, Captain Moore once more retired from the sea and resumed his duties as Willis's superintendent. He was succeeded by Captain W. E. Tiptaft.

Tiptaft was a native of Coldstream, and had served practically all his sea time in Willis's ships. In 1865 he was an A.B. on the *Whiteadder*, two years later we find him second mate of the same ship and in 1870 he succeeded Captain Moore in the command of her. In 1873 he had the *Merse*, and left this slow old Sunderland-built ship to take over the flyer of the fleet.

Tiptaft was a quiet, modest man, without any of the qualities of a ship driver, so that the whole time she was under him the *Cutty Sark* never had a chance of showing her best foot. Though it is true that he never made a bad passage, we may be certain that if Woodget had had her instead of Tiptaft every passage would have been from 10 to 20 days better.

Below I give particulars of the 1873 tea passages:

Ship	Freig't	Cargo lbs.	Port from	Date left	Passed Anjer	Arrived Channel	Docked	Days out
Sir Lancelot	£4	1,228,548	Shanghai	June 28			Nov. 1	127
Maitland	£4	1,145,153	Foochow	July 6			,, 3	120
Cutty Sark	£4	1,353,072	Shanghai	,, 9	Aug. 20	Deal Nov. 2	,, 3	117
Thermopylae	£4	1,417,117	,,	,, 11	,, 8	Gravesend Oct. 19	Oct. 20	101
Undine	£4	1,156,600	Foochow	,, 16			Nov. 26	133
Forward Ho	£4	1,388,700	,,	,, 23			Dec. 1	131
Titania	£3 10	1,391,492	Shanghai	Aug. 2	Sept. 17		,, 18	138
Normancourt	£4	1,147,700	Foochow	,, 4	,, 5		Nov. 28	116
Argonaut	£4	1,465,000	,,	,, 9	,, 14		,, 18	111
Kaisow	£3 10	1,098,900	Shanghai	,, 9			Dec. 2	115
Duke of Abercorn ..	£4	1,565,900	Foochow	,, 25	Sept. 29		,, 17	114
Ambassador		842,900	,,	Sept. 23	Oct. 24		Jan 15	114
*Hallowe'en**	£2 10		Shanghai	Nov. 19	Dec. 6	Deal Feb. 16	Feb. 17	90
Thyatira			Foochow	,, 2			Feb. 16	106
Lothair			Whampoa	Dec. 11			Mar. 19	98

* *Hallowe'en's* cargo consisted of—5508 chests tea, 11075 half chests tea, 2917 boxes tea, 955 boxes of wax, 62 packages of hats.

In December, 1873, *Cutty Sark* loaded her first cargo for Sydney. Winds in the South Atlantic and Southern Ocean were very unfavourable and light in the winter of 1873-4 and no outstanding passage were made by ships sailing for the Colonies in the Autumn of 1873.

Details of Passages 1873-4	*City of Hankow* Capt. Muir	*Thermopylae* Capt. Kemball	*Cutty Sark* Capt. Tiptaft
Left Docks		December 1	—
Left Downs	November 29	December 2	December 13
Off Portland	December 3	—	—
Off the Start	—	December 6	December 15
N.E. trades	Light, only lasted 4 days	Very light	Light to moderate
Crossed equator ..	Jan. 1 (in 30 30 W.	December 30	Jan. 4 (in 33° W.)
S.E. trades	Good	Moderate	Very poor
Crossed Cape meridian	Jan. 21 (in 42 S.)	Jan. 20 (in 44 S.)	January 30
Easting in	45-47°	45°-47°	40°
Off Otway	—	Feb. 15, 8 p.m.	—
Off S.W. Cape Tasmania	—	—	February 25
Anchored Hobson's Bay	Feb. 19, p.m.	Feb. 16, 10 a.m.	—
Anchored Sydney ..	—	—	March 4
Days out	78	72	79

There were, however, one or two interesting races. *City of Hankow* distinguished herself by running a close race with *Thermopylae*. It was the longest passage which Thompson's champion had yet made to Melbourne. During the whole trip her royals were only furled once, and that but for a few hours. *Cutty Sark* was close on the heels of these two ships, but could not catch them. Captain Tiptaft sailed a bad track running down his easting; he did not go further than 40° S., and was badly held up by calms and light baffling winds, nevertheless the *Cutty Sark* took the same number of days to the S.W. Cape Tasmania as *Thermopylae* to Hobson's Bay.

Of the other tea clippers, which made outward passages to the Colonies the following were the times:—

Sir Lancelot left the Start January 1 arrived Sydney March 26—84 days out.

Forward Ho left Plymouth January 18 arrived Sydney April 9—81 days out.

Normancourt left Lizard January 9 arrived Sydney April 8—89 days out.

Kaisow left Lizard January 10 arrived Melbourne April 6—86 days out.

Titania left St. Alban's Head January 21 arrived Adelaide April 17—86 days out.

Argonaut left Lizard February 6 arrived Melbourne April 24—77 days out.

Duke of Abercorn left Deal January 28 arrived Sydney April 27—89 days out.

Hallowe'en left Start April 9 arrived Sydney June 22—74 days out.

Leander left Isle of Wight April 27 arrived Sydney July 10—74 days out.

The most exciting race was between *Normancourt* and *Kaisow*, which proved to be very equally matched, being in company on and off from Beachy Head to the Greenwich meridian.

The *Hallowe'en* in her passage to Sydney made some of the biggest runs of her life. She was chartered by Messrs. Potter & Co. for £2400 and loaded a general cargo consisting of deadweight 412 tons, merchandise 1240 tons, liquids 54 tons, and bottled beer 50 tons on a draught in dock of 18 ft. forward, 18 ft. 10 ins. aft. Her abstract reads as follows:—

April 6—6 a.m., left the Downs.

 9—Put Mr. Stuart, Channel pilot, on board a trawler off the Start.

 11—4 a.m., took departure from the Lizard.

 30—Crossed the equator in 24° W.

May 19—Crossed Greenwich meridian in 40° 30′ S.

 20—Lat. 39° 54′ S., long. 6° 29′ E. Course N. 83° E. Distance 338 miles. Strong W.N.W. gale, severe squalls.

May 28—Lat. 42° 50' S., long 44° 34' E. Course S. 81° E. Distance 300 miles.
Fresh and gusty N.N.W. to W.S.W. All sail set.

30—Lat. 43° 26' S., long. 57° 41' E. Course S. 88° E. Distance 341 miles.
Strong breezes. N.N.W. to N.W. by W.

June 3—Lat. 43° 23' S., long. 78° 21' E. Course N. 85° E. Distance 328 miles.
Blowing strong and gusty from N. by E. to N.N.W.

4—Lat. 43° 12' S., long. 85° 21' E. Course N. 88° E. Distance 312 miles.
Strong steady Nly. breeze. All sail set.

5—Lat. 42° 59' S., long. 93° 33' E. Course N. 88° E. Distance 360 miles.
Strong N.N.W. breeze. Water smooth. Carry topgallant sails.

6—Lat. 42° 41' S., long. 99° 55' E. Course N. 86° E. Distance 280 miles.
Fresh steady N.N.W. breeze. All plain sail.

7—Lat. 42° 31' S., long. 106° 58' E. Course N. 88° E. Distance 314 miles.
Strong N.N.W. breeze under topgallant sails and main royal.

8—Lat. 42° 2' S., long. 113° 55' E. Course N. 86° E. Distance 310 miles.
Blowing strong north to N.N.E. Heavy gusts at times.

9—Lat. 41° 43' S., long. 119° 40' E. Course N. 86° E. Distance 257 miles.
Fresh N.N.E. gale. First reef in topsails.

17—5 p.m., on meridian of S.W. Cape, Tasmania.

22—11 p.m., anchored Port Jackson. (Lizard to Sydney 14,349 miles in 72 days.

Cutty Sark was the first of the tea ships to arrive in Shanghai in 1874, but Tiptaft on his first trip up the Pacific made a sad mess of it and did not give the ship a chance. Leaving Sydney on 26th March with 1100 tons of coal, she did not reach Shanghai until 19th May, being very nearly caught by the *Thermopylae* which left Sydney with 1200 tons of coal on 11th April and arrived Woosung, 41 days out, only three days behind the *Cutty Sark.*

The unlucky ship this year was the *Titania*, which also had a new commander, Captain England. *Titania* left Sydney for Hongkong on 2nd July. On 3rd August the barometer began to fall rapidly whilst sea and wind were making from S.W. On the 4th the weather steadily grew worse, and by the 5th all preparations were made for a typhoon. At noon the vessel was in 17° N., 133° E. By 8 p.m. the storm was at its worst with all the usual terrors, and at 10.30 p.m. it became necessary to cut away the masts in order to save the ship.

Titania arrived Hongkong on 27th August under jury masts; the hull was not damaged but the only spar which was intact was the bowsprit and the cost of repairs was estimated at $23,000. This misfortune threw *Titania* out of the contest for the first teas and she never loaded another cargo in the S.W. monsoons.

It is sad to notice how one by one the "full bloods" drop out, until at last practically only *Cutty Sark* and *Thermopylae* continued to load regularly in June or July.

This year, Jardine, Matheson, *Cutty Sark's* agents, made a new departure and sent the clipper up to Hankow to load amongst the tea steamers, which now numbered something like a dozen. It was still strongly felt that a few cargoes of new teas sent by way of the Cape in sailing ships would fetch good prices in the London market, and as Hankow was becoming the earliest and most favoured tea port, Jardine, Matheson picked out their best ship and sent her up the river, the *Cutty Sark* leaving Shanghai in tow on 27th May.

Hankow is upwards of 600 miles from the sea, and the trip up and down the Yangtze was often a dangerous one owing to the strength of the freshets and the big rise and fall of the tide. The anchorage at Hankow was also often very uncomfortable. The best berths lay just below the settlement about 1½ cables from the bank in from 7 to 10 fathoms. In the high-level season these were very bad indeed, and at all times it was necessary to sight anchors constantly or they became so embedded in the soft mud that they could not be weighed.

There is not much to say about the tea passages this year. Captain Tiptaft, with no need to hurry, took things easy and went by the long eastern route through Pitt's Passage. *Cutty Sark* was spoken on 12th September, in 20° S., 1° E., 80 days out from her Woosung pilot, and as she was the first ship to arrive in the Thames by way of the Cape there was a very good demand for her teas.

Thermopylae, with the ever hustling Kemball, made the best passage in the S.W. monsoon, whilst *Hallowe'en* repeated her fine running in the N.E. monsoon.

It was Kemball's last voyage in the *Thermopylae*. He left her to superintend the building and take command of the *Aristides*, the flagship of the Aberdeen White Star fleet for many years. He was succeeded in *Thermopylae* by Charlie Matheson, his first officer.

Hallowe'en repeated the splendid time of her previous year, and showed that it was no fluke.

I have the details of her cargo, which may be of interest. On a draught of water of 17 ft. 2 ins. forward, and 17 ft. 11 ins. aft, she loaded:—

3649 chests of tea
4941 half chests   } = 720 tons at £3 freight = £2160.
  200 boxes.

1010 chests of tea
6182 half chests
  203 boxes   } = 658 tons at £3 10s. freight=£2303.
  401 bales of strawbraid
    9 packages of effects
  577 bales of silk   = 82 tons at £4 freight = £328.

    Total 17,172 packages   = 1460 tons = £4791.
      of 50 cubic ft.

On arrival in London she turned out 1532 tons of cargo. Her abstract reads as follows:—

Oct. 21—6 a.m., weighed; 10 a.m., tug left; 3 p.m. pilot left; 10 p.m., off North Saddle.

Nov. 2—Off Tambelan Island at noon. 6 p.m., Direction Island S.E. 30 miles.
6—6.30 p.m., anchored Gaspar Island N. by E. Current S.S.E. 1½ knots.
7—6 a.m., weighed; 9.30, off Leat Lighthouse; noon, Entrance Pt. N.N.W. Wind moderate west to W.S.W. Tacking occasionally.
9—9 p.m., anchored. North Island S. by W. 5 miles.
10—6 a.m., weighed. At noon, tacked off Anjer.

Dec. 8—5 p.m., passed Cape of Good Hope, 4 miles off.
19—7 a.m., signalled St. Helena.
27—Crossed equator in 20° W.

Jan 4—'75. Passed Cape Verde.
13—Terceira bearing North.
18—11.40 p.m., passed the Start. Distance from Shanghai Lightship. 14,738 miles, 89 days out.
19—Strong Wly. gale. 4 p.m. hove-to off Dungeness. 9.30 p.m., anchored Margate Roads.
20—7.30 a.m., engaged tug *Fergus McKever* for £50.
—11.30 p.m., arrived at East India Dock.

PASSAGES 1874.

Ship	Freight	Cargo lbs.	Port from	Date left	Anjer	Arrived Deal	Days out
Cutty Sark ..	£5-£4	1,270,651	Hankow	Woosung Pilot June 24		Oct. 20	118
Thermopylae ..	£3 10-£3	1,315,825	Shanghai	July 15	Aug. 14	,, 27	104
Sir Lancelot ..	£3 10-£3	1,149,957	,,	,, 31		Nov. 19	124
Ascalon	£3 10-£3	1,000,000	Foochow	,, 24		,, 25	124
Normancourt ..	£3 10-£3	1,184,625	,,	,, 27	Aug. 30	,, 17	113
Forward Ho ..	£3 10-£3	1,373,907	,,	Aug. 4		Dec. 13	131
Kaisow	£3	1,100,000	Shanghai	,, 18	Sept. 30	,, 27	131
Lothair	£3	1,300,000	,,	,, 22	Oct. 4	,, 28	128
Wylo	£3	1,300,000	,,	,, 31	,, 12	Jan. 5	127
Undine		1,108,416	Foochow	Sept. 12		,, 3	113
Duke of Abercorn	£3	1,543,395	Shanghai	,, 17	Oct. 25	,, 6	111
Hallowe'en ..	£3 10-£3	1,091,708	,,	Oct. 21	Nov. 10	,, 20	91
Titania			Hongkong	Jan. 31'75		May 11	100

Both *Cutty Sark* and *Thermopylae* made splendid passages to Australia in the winter of 1874-5. *Cutty Sark* passed Tasmania 66 days out, and if she had only been favoured by the wind in her run north would probably have broken—at any rate equalled —the record to Sydney; whilst *Thermopylae*, leaving the Lizard 10 days later was only 64 days to Melbourne.

Cutty Sark had a very interesting race with the *City of Hankow* and *Thomas Stephens*; the three vessels keeping very close together down to the roaring forties, when *Cutty Sark* raced ahead, taking only 25 days from the Cape Meridian to the South-West Cape, Tasmania.

Three times during the passage she was in company with *City of Hankow*, the last being on 1st December in 44° S., 3° 10' E. *City of Hankow* was also in company with *Thomas Stephens* on several occasions between the Lizard and the line. Below I give the abstracts of the four passages.

City of Hankow had rather an advantage over *Cutty Sark* and *Thomas Stephens*, for she was in beautiful trim with a light general cargo of liquids, etc. The *Thomas Stephens* was loaded very deep this year, and drew 11 inches more than on her previous outward passage. Her appearance was much admired by seafaring men, as she sailed into port on the afternoon of 31st January, a black ship with painted ports; for up to this date she had always been painted an ugly drab colour.

Thermopylae had the satisfaction of beating the November mail. She averaged 262 knots from 13th January to port. In 35° E., during a hard S.W. gale, she carried away her main topsail yard and had her port quarter life-boat washed away.

Cutty Sark's was the best passage of the year to Sydney, and in a favourable season a comparison with those of other tea clippers clearly shows her greater power. *Normancourt* arrived Port Jackson on 11th March, 82 days out: *Lothair* on 28th April, 91 days out; and *Hallowe'en* on 12th May, 82 days out.

Details of Passages. 1874-5	*Cutty Sark* Capt. Tiptaft	*City of Hankow* Capt. Muir	*Thomas Stephens* Capt. Bloomfield	*Thermopylae* Capt. Matheson
Gravesend	November 14	November 17	November 18	November 29
Downs	November 14	—	—	December 1
St. Catherine's ..	November 16	—	—	—
Down Channel ..	Had to beat	down Channel against S.W. gales		Fair wind
Down Channel ..	*Cutty Sark* lost	a man overboard	off St. Catherine's	—
Start	November 21	—	—	—
Lizard	—	November 21	November 22	December 2
Madeira	—	November 29	November 29	
N.E. trades	Very baffling	Only lasted 2 d'ys	Very light	Fair
7° 51' N., 26° 40' W.	—	December 7	December 7	—
Equator	Dec. 11 (in 26 W.)	Dec. 11 (in 29° W.)	Dec. 11 (in 29° W.)	December 25
S.E. trades	3° S. to 24° S. Good	Strong, lost off Trinidad	Fair, lost off Trinidad	Good
44° S., 3° 10' E. ..	December 31	December 31	—	—
Cape Meridian ..	Jan. 1 (43° 30' S.)	Jan. 3 (44° 27' S.)	Jan. 5 (41° 15' S.)	January 14
Easting in	45° 30'	44°-46°	44°-46°	45°
Best run	—	—	—	348
Leeuwin	—	Jan. 20 (44° 30' S.)	Jan. 23 (45° 51' S.)	—
S.W. Cape Tasmania	Jan 26 (66 d'ys)	—	—	—
Otway	—	—	Jan. 31 a.m.	—
Anchored Melbourne	—	Jan. 30 (3 p.m.)	Jan. 31 (p.m.)	February 4
Anchored Sydney ..	February 2	—	—	—
Days out	73	70	70	64

There were, however, two very good passages out to China. *Sir Lancelot*, after having had her spars cut down, 8 feet being taken off the mainmast, left the Channel 28th December, 1874, and arrived Shanghai 7th April, 100 days out. This was beaten by *Kaisow*, which left Deal 5th March, Lizard 10th March, Equator 29th March, meridian of the Cape 23rd April, Anjer 23rd May and anchored Hongkong on 10th June, only 92 days from the Lizard. She had a light weather passage except for the last two days, but *Kaisow* was a flyer in light winds and it just suited her.

There is not much of interest in the coal passages from Sydney this year. Tiptaft made an average passage. Leaving Sydney with 1100 tons of coal, he reached Shanghai on 14th April, 48 days out.

Matheson left Sydney on 26th March with 1100 tons of coal and made the run to Nagasaki in 42 days. From Nagasaki he ran down to Foochow for a tea charter, arriving in the Min River on 4th June, 8 days out. *Wylo* arrived Shanghai 25th July 40 days out from Sydney, and *Normancourt* on 26th May, 43 days out from Sydney.

Blackadder was now commanded by Gentleman White. She arrived very early on the China Coast and made a couple of quick coal trips between Shanghai and Nagasaki, averaging 4 days each passage. The first round trip, including 10 days in Nagasaki, occupied 17 days, and she beat this on the second by 2 days.

The tea passages this year present little of interest. The fleet was gradually growing smaller and there was no racing.

Sir Lancelot left Shanghai on 5th May for New York, and made the run in under 100 days, her whole voyage only totalling 9 months 2 days.

Kaisow loaded at Bangkok, whilst *Duke of Abercorn*, going straight to Yokohama from London joined the Japan ships. *City of Hankow* crossed to 'Frisco from Sydney. *Titania* and *Windhover* both missed the season, as they did not leave London for Shanghai until August.

It is worth noting that only *Cutty Sark* and *Thermopylae* were able to keep to time, and make the round voyage in under 12 months with unfailing regularity. Every other ship was thrown out through delay from one cause or another.

Shanghai was steadily losing its position as a great tea port all through the seventies. It is also of interest to compare the shipping in Shanghai at the commencement of the tea season. Let us take an average year in the early sixties and compare it with an average year in the early seventies.

On 20th May, 1862, there were 85 merchantmen and 21 men-of-war in port—the merchantmen consisting of 27 steamers, 18 ships, 21 barques, 8 schooners and 3 luggers.

On 20th May, 1874, there were only 22 steamers, 8 sailing ships and 8 men-of-war.

Ten years later and there was not a British sailing ship in port *Cutty Sark* again loaded at Hankow, following 14 tea-lader steamers down the Yangtze, and she was again the first sailing ship to land new teas in London. Her voyage was without incident, Tiptaft again went the long eastern route. She was spoken on 28th August in 34° 40' S., 24° 12' E. and docked on 22nd October. The two sister ships, *Blackadder* and *Hallowe'en*, were the only other clippers to load at Hankow. In the table of tea passages I give the times from Woosung not from Hankow, as the passage down the Yangtze often took a week.

TEA PASSAGES 1875.

Ship		Fr'ght	Cargo lbs.	Port from	Date left	Anjer	Arrived		Days Out
Cutty Sark	..	£4	1,347,699	Woosung	June 21	—	Deal Oct.	21	121
Thermopylae	..		1,413,000	Foochow	July 8		Deal Oct.	31	115
Blackadder	..	£4	1,200,300	Woosung	July 19		Deal Nov.	22	126
Black Prince	..		1,041,420	Foochow	July 20		Falmouth Dec.	6	139
Forward Ho	..		1,383,104	Foochow	July 29		Docked Nov.	16	110
Undine ..	..	£3 10	1,300,000	Shanhgai	Aug. 23		Docked Dec.	17	116
Normancourt	..	£3 10		Shanghai	Sept. 2	Oct. 10	Downs Dec.	31	120
Jerusalem	..			Foochow	Nov. 9		Docked Feb.	18	101
Hallowe'en	..			Woosung	Nov. 23		Docked Feb.	24	92

On the outward run to Australia in 1875-6, *Cutty Sark* had a very interesting race with *Thermopylae,* the abstract details are given on page 124.

On her seventh voyage *Cutty Sark* had a hard driving second mate named Webster, who had been master in the Aberdeen White Star Line. He gave it to her whenever he got the chance, but even so her crew considered that she would have saved several days on her outward passages if only Captain Tiptaft had held on to his canvas.

The start was unfortunate. At Gravesend *Cutty Sark* came into collision with the *Somersetshire*, whereby she lost an anchor, 15 fathoms of chain and her main topgallant mast. This accident necessitated a return to dock for repairs. These were quickly effected but the new main topgallant mast was a short one and no skysail yard could be crossed, so that the *Cutty Sark* was compelled to go the voyage without her skysail,

On the second start light winds were experienced down Channel, the herald of a spell of easterly weather. From being light at east, the wind regularly backed to N.E. and the *Thermopylae* came romping down Channel behind the *Cutty Sark* in the midst of tearing snow squalls.

In the Bay of Biscay, the wind came W.N.W. and carried both vessels quickly south as far as 19° N., 20° W. Whilst crossing

Details Outward Passages 1875-6	*Cutty Sark*	*Thermopylae*
Left London	November 21	November 30
Put back for repairs after collision	November 22	—
Left London again	November 25	—
Landed Pilot off Portland ..	November 27	—
Off the Lizard	November 29	December 3
N.E. trades	Good	Good from 16° to 6° N.
Spoke and passed *Honoruri* ..	—	—
London to New Zealand in 20° 50′ N., 19° 54′ W.	December 10	—
Spoke and passed *Cleveland* ..	—	—
London to Melbourne, in 6° 59′ N. 22° 11′ W.	December 17	—
Picked up S.E. trades	4° 50′ N. 22° 43′ W.	2° N.
Crossed equator	December 21	Dec. 24 in 29° W.
Lost S.E. trades	22° 50′ S., 31° 46′ W.	23° S.
Spoken in 25° 23′ S., 31° 50′ W.	December 30	—
Spoken in 31° S., 31° 50′ W. ..	January 1	—
Crossed Cape Meridian	January 13	Jan. 14 in 45° S.
Ran down easting in	45° S.	45° S.
Best Work	2163 miles in 6 days	270 miles a day from from 22° W. to 100 E.
Crossed 113° E.	—	January 29
Passed Cape Otway	February 1	Feb. 7, 5 p.m.
Passed S.W. Cape, Tasmania ..	February 4	—
Arrived Melbourne	—	Feb. 9, 9 a.m.
Arrived Sydney	February 12	—
Days out	75	68

the Bay *Cutty Sark* fell in with a Belfast ship, in ballast with a heavy list, evidently abandoned. The clipper hove to for a few hours close to the derelict, but no sign of life could be seen so the *Cutty Sark* at length filled away on her course without boarding her.

Between Madeira and Teneriffe the *Cutty Sark* overhauled and passed a south-bound Castle Line steamer. The clipper was doing 14 to 15 knots under main royal with fresh trades, she rose the steamer in the morning and left her hull down before dark.

In running their easting down both *Cutty Sark* and *Thermopylae* had strong northerly winds. In covering 2163 miles in six days, the *Cutty Sark* accomplished a record. On several of these days the log recorded 370 miles. The log line was marked to 15½ knots and the *Cutty Sark* took it all out easily. It came to be quite a common saying aboard—"15½ knots and two apprentices," as it took two stalwart apprentices to hold the reel.

If only *Cutty Sark* had carried the wind through Bass Straits she would have broken the record to Sydney, but when she was about 50 miles south of Melbourne it came on to blow hard from the eastward, whereupon Tiptaft put his helm up and ran south, preferring to round Tasmania rather than wait for a slant or an ease up in a gale. As it happened this manoeuvre spoilt his passage. for on the other side of Tasmania he found light northerly airs, and it took the *Cutty Sark* eight days to beat from the South West Cape to Sydney Heads.

Thermopylae, which was in excellent trim with her Plimsoll load-line showing well above the water, also made excellent running in the roaring forties and crossed the meridian of the Leeuwin a day ahead of her record passage, but on 7th February she was becalmed all night off the Otway and did not make Port Phillip Heads until 5 p.m. on 8th February, but could not enter until the following morning owing to the thick, foggy weather.

In the run from Sydney to China *Cutty Sark* had very light winds whilst *Thermopylae* had more wind than was pleasant. Leaving Sydney with 992 tons of coal on 5th March, *Cutty Sark* did not reach Shanghai until 23rd April, 49 days out. *Thermopylae* left Sydney on 28th March with 1200 tons of coal for Petropalovski but was obliged to put into Hongkong on 13th May, after a severe battering in which she had lost most of her sails.

Of the other outward passages the next best to Sydney was made by *Blackadder*, her sister ship *Hallowe'en* making the best passage to China.

Blackadder left Deal, 27th December, passed the Lizard 1st January, equator 20th January, meridian of the Cape 1st February, and S.W. Cape, Tasmania, on 5th March a fine run of 63 days from the Lizard, but from Tasmania she had even worse treatment than *Cutty Sark* and did not reach Sydney until 6.30 p.m. on 20th March. She took out two thoroughbred horses for Messrs. Gangar, which came through the voyage in first rate condition.

Hallowe'en, sailing direct to Shanghai, made the splendid passage of 96 days from the Lizard; her abstract records:—

Passed the Lizards ..	..	..	..	March 20
Passed Madeira	..	..	..	March 26
Crossed equator	..	..	..	April 9
Crossed meridian of Greenwich	..	..	April 29
Best run 306 miles	..	..	..	May 13
Abreast of Anjer	..	..	..	June 1
Shanghai pilot 6 a.m.	..	..	..	June 23
Anchored Shanghai ..	..	..	..	June 24

Hallowe'en was a very fast vessel in all winds, but she was also a very lucky vessel, for Captain Fowler, was not a driver like Captain Watt, and under him she rarely made any very big runs, though her passages were nearly always excellent.

In noting the tea passages in 1876, one might almost call it:— "*Cutty Sark* first, the rest nowhere."

Cutty Sark left Shanghai on 14th May for Hankow, where she was actually favoured by the shippers before half the tea steamers, 12 loading behind her. The only other sailing ships to load at Hankow this year were the usual pair *Hallowe'en* (for London) and her chum ship *Leander* (for New York). They always loaded silk as well as tea and leaving in the N.E. monsoon received the benefit of the reduced insurance rates.

This year the *Cutty Sark* on leaving Hankow was obliged to abandon her anchors in the Yangtze mud. *Hallowe'en* had still a worse experience when she was ready to sail, for, in swinging to the ebb tide, she grounded athwart the river and in this helpless predicament had to take the whole strength of the ebb and current upon her broadside, whilst *Leander*, moored just below her, was kept sheering about in every direction by the force of the eddies caused by the *Hallowe'en's* opposition to the stream. However, *Hallowe'en* with her extra thick plating came to no harm and floated all right when the flood made in the afternoon.

In the list of tea passages this year, I have included the names of the steamers to show the proud position of the *Cutty Sark*.

TEA PASSAGES 1876.

Ship	Cargo	Freight	Departure from	Date left	Anjer or Singap'e	Arrived	D'ys out
S.S. *Glenartney* ..	about 2,000,000	£3 15-£3	10 Woosung	May 19	May 27	London July 1	42
S.S. *Hankow* ..	,,	,,	,,	,, 20	,, 29		
S.S. *Glenearn* ..	,,	,,	,,	,, 23	,, 23		
S.S. *Fleurs Castle*	,,	,,	,,	,, 25	June 6		
S.S. *Cawdor Castle*	,,	,,	,,	June 3	,, 12		
S.S. *Galley of Lorne*	,,	,,	,,	,, 8	,, 18		
Cutty Sark ..	1,375,364	£4 5	,,	,, 9	July 15	Start Sept. 25	108
S.S. *Glenfinlas* ..	about 2,000,000	£3 15-£3	10 Foochow	,, 9	June 17		
S.S. *Glenlyon* ..	,,	,,	Woosung	,, 10	,, 20		
S.S. *Viking* ..	,,	,,	Foochow	,, 18			
S.S. *Braemar Castle* followed by S.S. *Teheran, Flintshire, Glavens, Thibet, Anchises, Glenfalloch*, etc.							
Windhover ..	1,202,200	£3	Shanghai	July 20	—	London Nov.25	128
Thermopylae ..	1,429,100	£3	Foochow	,, 28	Sept. 4	Scilly Nov. 21	115
Blackadder ..	1,109,500	£3	Shanghai	Aug. 5	—	Dec. 8	125
Undine ..	1,102,060	£3	,,	Sept. 7	—	Dec. 27	111
Hallowe'en ..			Woosung	Nov. 13	—	Feb. 23	102
Black Prince ..			Shanghai	,, 28	—	Mar. 14	106
Normancourt ..			,,	Jan 30	—	Start May 17	107

Of the ships not mentioned in this list, *Titania* left Shanghai on 27th March for New York. *Sir Lancelot,* which made a bad profitless voyage, went out to Otago from London, arrived Shanghai from Dunedin on 24th June, and finally loaded at Yokohama for St. Nazaire. She left Japan on 23rd August and passed Plymouth 28th December, 127 days out.

The abstract of *Cutty Sark's* passage gives:—

Left Hankow..	..	..	June 4
Left Woosung	..	..	June 9
Passed Anjer	..	..	July 15—36 days out.
Passed the Cape	..	..	Aug. 11—27 days from Anjer.
Passed St. Helena ..	..	..	Aug. 19—8 days from Cape.
Passed Ascension	..	..	Aug. 23
Passed equator	..	..	Aug. 27—8 days from St. Helena.
Passed Start ..	..	..	Sept. 25—108 days out.
Docked	..	..	Sept. 26—109 days out.

Having left her anchors in the Hankow mud, *Cutty Sark* was obliged to hang on to her tug at Woosung until others could be procured at Shanghai. At last two were obtained, of which one was large enough for a ship of 3000 tons whilst the other was not much bigger than a small kedge.

The *Cutty Sark* made a magnificient run up Channel, taking only 24 hours from Start Point to the anchorage off Southend Pier.

Of the New York ships, *Leander* made the best run, leaving Woosung on 11th January, 1877, she arrived New York on 20th April, 99 days out.

There was no interesting race to Australia for the *Cutty Sark* in 1876-7, and both she and *Thermopylae* were not favoured by the wind, either north of the line or south. Though their passages were separated by a couple of months, I have put them together in the following table, as any comparison between the great rivals is always of interest.

Cutty Sark	Date	*Thermopylae*	Date
Left London	Oct. 21	Left London	Dec. 16
Passed Lizard	Oct. 22	Ushant bore South	Dec. 22
Light N. and N.E. winds to Madeira		N.W. breeze to Finisterre.. ..	
No. N.E. trades, light, variable ..		S.W. gales to Canaries, passed ..	Jan. 8
Airs and calms from Madeira ..		N.E. trades from 28° N. to 8° N.	
Crossed equator in 27° W.	Nov. 19	Crossed equator in 22° W. ..	Jan. 24
(Up to equator had not made a run of		Very light S.E. trades from line ..	
200 miles)		to 23° S.	
S.E. trades from 4° N.; favourable ..		From 235 to Cape N.W. winds and	
Sighted Martin Vaz	Nov. 26	thick weather	
Sighted Tristan d'Acunha	Dec. 4	Crossed Cape meridian in 43° S.	Feb. 12
Crossed Greenwich meridian, 41° S. ..	Dec. 7		
Ran down easting in 45° to 47° S. ..		Ran down easting in 45° S. ..	
Moderate N.W. winds and fine ..		Light westerly winds and fine ..	
Rounded S.W. Cape Tasmania ..	Jan. 3	Passed meridian Leeuwin ..	Mar. 4
Head winds to Sydney		Off Otway	Mar. 11
Arrived Sydney	Jan. 10	Arrived Melbourne	Mar. 12
(10 months 5 days from date of leaving			
Sydney 1876)			
Days out	80	Days out	80

Cutty Sark took the China mail across to Shanghai this year, leaving Sydney on 30th January with 1025 tons of coal, she arrived Shanghai 18th March, 47 days out.

Thermopylae, with more favourable winds, left Sydney with 1208 tons of coal on 23rd April and arrived Shanghai on 14th June, 42 days out.

J. S. WALLACE, "CUTTY SARK" 1880

[*See Page* 137

"DUKE OF ABERCORN"

"SALAMIS"

[See Page 138

1877 we may consider as the last year in which sailing ships paid a dividend on a tea cargo. As usual *Cutty Sark* was the favoured vessel, and loaded at Hankow amongst the steamers, but Tiptaft was far from hurrying himself, and took the long eastern route instead of going for Sunda Straits and giving his ship a chance across the strength of the S.E. trades. However, he made a good average run up the Atlantic, being 34 days from Ascension to Scilly.

Sir Lancelot made the best run of the New York ships arriving New York on 2nd April, 95 days from Shanghai, *Thermopylae* and *Forward Ho,* with good luck in the China Seas, made quick passages; *Hallowe'en,* as usual, kept up her average in the N.E. monsoon. It was, however, a depressing year, in which sailing ships were forced to see that their days in the tea trade were numbered.

TEA PASSAGES 1877.

Ship		Freight	Cargo	Left	Date left	Anjer			Arrived in dock	Days out
Cutty Sark	..	£4 5	1,334,000	Woosung	June 6	Scilly Oct. 6			Oct. 11	127
Windhover	..	£4	1,115,000	,,	,, 20				,, 23	125
Thermopylae	..	£3		Shanghai	July 10	Lizard Oct. 18			,, 20	102
Forward Ho	..	£2 15	1,227,223	,,	,, 30	Anjer Aug. 29			Nov. 16	109
Woolahra ..	..	£2		,,	Oct. 23	,, Nov. 23			Feb. 20	120
Blackadder	..	£2		,,	,, 26	,, ,, 17			,, 16	114
Wylo ..	..			Foochow	,, 30	,, ,, 20			,, 18	111
Jerusalem	..			,,	Nov. 6				,, 20	106
Centurion ..	..			Shanghai	,, 20	Anjer Dec. 15			Mar. 27	129
Hallowe'en	..			Woosung	Jan. 7				April 16	97

Titania again missed the season; arriving Shanghai on 19th December from London, she failed to get a charter until the following year's tea came down. Whilst *Normancourt,* after spending six months on the coast, had the indignity of being cut down to a barque and also had to wait for the 1878 season.

In a long life ships can no more expect to escape trouble than a human being, but the *Cutty Sark* was always celebrated for the way in which fortune favoured her when it seemed as if the worst must happen.

Her escape from disaster in the great winter gale of November, 1877, is a very good illustration of her luck. She cleared from London for Sydney with a crew of 28 hands on 3rd November, and left Gravesend on the 4th. In the Channel she found a strong S.W.

K

wind with thick rain and a falling glass. With the weather showing every sign of an approaching depression from the Atlantic, Captain Tiptaft and his pilot decided that it would be wiser to put back until the S.W. gale had blown itself out; and so, in company with a large fleet, which included several steamers and the fine ships *Star of Albion* and *Blair Athole*, the *Cutty Sark* ran back to the Downs, where she anchored on 8th November.

During the 9th and 10th she lay quietly to a single anchor with the promised storm still brewing. By Sunday, the 11th, it was blowing a hard, vicious S.W. gale, and there were no less than 60 ships besides several large steamers taking shelter in the Downs. Captain Tiptaft now moored his vessel with 105 fathoms on his starboard anchor and 60 fathoms on his port, whilst another 100 fathoms of cable for each anchor were got up and ranged on deck in case of emergency.

By sunset on Saturday the Channel ports from Margate to the Lizard were reporting wind of hurricane strength, whilst the life-boat crews were being called out along the whole length of the coast.

Amongst the crowded shipping in the Downs pandemonium reigned. Blue lights, flares and rockets began to show in every direction, as cables parted and ships began to go adrift; and whilst they were hustling to man the life-boats ashore, out of the blackness to sea there came at regular intervals the dull boom of gunfire, which, penetrating through the scream and howl of the raging gale, told of a ship in dire distress—a large steamer was on the Shingles, firing guns and burning flares.

In the pitchy darkness with the hurricane at its height, those ashore could only wait and pray, dodge flying chimney pots and falling trees, but when day broke the tragedy of the night at sea became revealed. There were no less than five ships ashore in Pegwell Bay; Margate was full of dismasted coasters; a large barque had sunk off Broadstairs and only her topgallant masts showed; another barque was on the Goodwins, whilst the steamer stranded near the Tongue Light still signalled for assistance.

As the wind took off, the Deal boatmen with spare anchors and chains launched their galleys off Deal beach through the boiling surf in their well-known fashion, and braving the heavy sea which rolled through the Downs saved many a ship. All through the night collisions in the crowded roads had been a recurring nightmare; drifting ships had crashed into those which still had hold of the ground, and carried them away in their turn; ships ground together, till their spars came down upon their crews; men leaped from ship to ship in their panic, and several of those vessels which had come ashore, contained strangers, often of foreign nationalities, who had sprung aboard them in the darkness and the terror.

Besides the brave galley punts, all the life-boats were out, whilst Coastguards and longshoremen were busy in every direction hauling men through the surf from stranded vessels.

Then as the tide made, small knots of men and weeping women showed where the breakers had rolled up the bodies of seamen and tossed them in the yellow froth on the edge of the screaming shingle. Noon came, and with it the Calais boat, battened down and with half-a-dozen men at her helm. As huge seas were sweeping over the Admiralty pier she made for the harbour and berthed amidst the cheers of a huge crowd, which had been anxiously awaiting her appearance.

Meanwhile what of the *Cutty Sark*? At 11.30 a.m. on Monday a special telegram was sent from Deal announcing that she was no longer in the Downs. In truth only one vessel had ridden out the gale; of all the shipping that had been riding in the Downs on Sunday, only the *Star of Albion* could be seen still at anchor on her old bearing on Monday morning.

Let us now see what happened to the *Cutty Sark*. At 10.35 p.m. when the hurricane was at its height, both cables parted. Then before the *Cutty Sark* could be got under control she ran foul of a brig on her port bow. There was a crash, the ships ground together for a moment, and then drifted apart in the darkness. A minute later and there was another crash: this time it was a vessel to starboard.

We can scarcely imagine a more trying situation. The pitch blackness, the roaring wind and blinding rain, the flying sprays, and in the midst of it the *Cutty Sark* drifting helpless and crashing into unseen neighbours.

Captain Tiptaft's first order was to run up the fore topmast staysail, his idea being to get her off the wind. "Sheet home the fore and main lower topsails," was the next command, but then it was discovered that the port bulwarks were stove, rail and head boards gone, and the port fore braces all adrift, with the yards swinging madly at every roll.

The main lower topsail, however, was sheeted home, and a course set to carry her through the Gull Stream, then as soon as she was to the northward of the Goodwin Sands, the *Cutty Sark* was hove to on the starboard tack with her head to the southward.

Not knowing what further damage might have been done in the two collisions, Captain Tiptaft now began to fire rockets and burn blue lights for assistance.

These were seen at 4.30 a.m. by the tugboat *Macgregor* which was some distance to the S.W. of the Kentish Knock. It took the *Macgregor* an hour's steaming at full speed to get up to the *Cutty Sark*, which by this time had drifted dangerously close to the sands, being just off the South Kentish Knock buoy. In fact the *Macgregor* only just got hold of her in time. Between midnight and 5 a.m. the storm had been at its worst. The main lower topsail had soon blown to rags, the upper topsail had then been set, but by the time the tug appeared this also had split and threatened to blow away at any moment. It requires a sailor of the sail to thoroughly realise all the strain and stress of that awful night. Luckily at 5 am. the wind began to take off, though it continued to blow very hard from the W.S.W. with a very nasty sea. However, after about half-an-hour's strenuous work with some fine seamanship on the part of the tug men, the *Macgregor's* rope was got aboard the *Cutty Sark*, and the steamer began to tow. It was soon found that in spite of a tremendous head of steam, noted as 27 lbs., the *Macgregor* could only move the *Cutty Sark* about one knot through the water, whereupon Tiptaft began signalling for another tug. It was not until 10 a.m. on Monday morning that another tugboat was obtained and during the intervening five hours the *Macgregor* had only made 6 miles over the ground. The second tug was the *Benachie*; and between them they were able to get the *Cutty Sark* through the Princes Channel to an anchorage off Greenhithe by 7 p.m. Here she was moored for the night and on the following morning was towed up to London and placed in safety at the East India Dock entrance.

In the usual litigation which followed the salving of the *Cutty Sark*, the value of the ship with her cargo and freight was agreed at £85,000. The case was tried before Sir R. J. Phillimore and Captain Were and Bayly on 28th November; the tugs claimed £8000 and were awarded £3000.

Many other lawsuits resulted from this famous gale, fought between the owners of ships which had been in the numerous collisions. Luckily for old White Hat, though one damaged ship did sue the *Cutty Sark*, there was not enough evidence to identify her. I may add that the trusty carpenter of Willis's famous clipper, a man who had helped to build her and had been in her since her launch, did find a piece of the name-board of a vessel lying on the *Cutty Sark's* deck close to where her bulwarks were stove, but, with an eye to his owner's advantage, he thoughtfully slid this piece of evidence overboard without saying a word about it at the time.

This action probably saved old Jock some hundreds of pounds, for the vessel to which it referred had been dismasted and badly damaged through a collision during the hurricane.

Some of the *Cutty Sark's* cargo was broken out in order to see what damage had been done, but she was found to be quite unhurt beyond her bulwarks, head boards and a stove plank or two; and by the end of the month she was once more ready for sea.

The delay gave the *Cutty Sark* the chance of a race with her rival *Thermopylae*, which left London on 28th November, put back to the Downs on 29th November owing to bad weather in the Channel, and finally left Deal on 2nd December, the day on which *Cutty Sark* left the Docks, thus the *Cutty Sark* started her passage close on the heels of the *Thermopylae*.

Thermopylae, with her usual luck, carried a strong N.E. wind right away from Deal to the Bay of Biscay, and passed the Lizard only 24 hours from the Downs, having outdistanced a huge fleet of wind-bound ships which were racing down Channel. *Cutty Sark* just missed this favourable slant, and in the run to the line lost eight days on *Thermopylae*, which crossed the equator only 17 days out from the Lizard.

In the table giving the abstracts of the two passages I have included that of the *Baron Aberdare*, for the sake of comparison with a large first-class, iron passenger ship, built for speed and with that advantage in trim over the tea clippers which is given by passenger accommodation.

Baron Aberdare was one of James MacCunn's three "Barons," known as the Baronial Line. She was built in 1874 and measured 1630 tons, being commanded by Captain Bloomfield who had made his reputation in the *Thomas Stephens*.

Though noted for her speed *Baron Aberdare* was still more noted for her evil luck. Wm. Watson of Sunderland, her builder, went bankrupt over her, and before she sailed on her maiden voyage she capsized in the Victoria Dock; the historic lawsuit, MacCunn *v.* the London Dock Co., which followed, resulting in the latter being compelled to pay the whole claim and very heavy costs.

It will be noticed that *Cutty Sark* and *Baron Aberdare* left the Docks together, passed the Lizard on the same day and crossed the line on the same day, but as soon as they were south of the equator *Cutty Sark* began to go ahead, and soon outdistanced what should have been the more powerful ship of the two in strong winds.

The *Cutty Sark*, after an average passage down the Atlantic, again showed her marvellous powers in the roaring forties, and after giving *Thermopylae* eight days' start from the equator not only overhauled her, but rounded the South Cape, Tasmania, more than 24 hours before the *Thermopylae* passed the Otway, which was a most decisive victory for Willis's clipper. After making the best passage of the year to Sydney, *Cutty Sark* proceeded to make the best passage up the Pacific.

It will be noticed that *Salamis*, which was supposed to be *Thermopylae's* iron double, also adventured across to Shanghai in the hopes of a tea cargo. It was her second attempt to gain a place amongst the tea ships. She had tried in 1876, but had been compelled to content herself with a Hongkong cargo, making the run home from Hongkong in the N.E. monsoon in 110 days. The year

1878 happened to be one of general depression and gloom in commercial circles, and *Salamis* found things in Shanghai to be if anything worse than in Sydney.

Date	Thermopylae	Cutty Sark	Baron Aberdare
Nov. 28	Passed Deal		
,, 29	Put back to the Downs ..		
Dec. 9	Left the Downs	Left Dock	Left Dock
,, 3	Passed the Lizard.. ..		Sigd. St. Catherine's
,, 4		Off Torbay	
,, 5		Landed pilot off Dartmouth	
,, 6		Passed the Lizard	Passed the Lizard
	Variable winds to Finisterre then N.W.	Variable winds, N. to S.S.E. to 37° N.	
	Strong N.E. trades, lost 6° N.	Favourable N.E. trades	Strong N.E. trades 29° N. to 4° N.
,, 19		Sighted Bonavista (Cape Verde)	
,, 20	Crossed equator in 27° N.		
,, 28		Crossed equator in 26° W.	Crossed equator in 31° 44' W.
	S.E. trade light, lost in 17° S.	S.E. trade light but favourable	S.E. trade light.
Jan. 6		Sighted Trinidad Island	
,, 15		Crossed Greenwich Meridian in 41° S.	
,, 17	Crs'd Cape meridian in 41° S.		
,, 19			Crs'd Cape meridian in 42° 34' S.
	Ran easting down in 44½° S	Ran easting down in 46° S.	Ran easting down in 45° 46' S.
	Moderate Westerly winds.	Moderate N. to N.W. winds, heavy rain.	Moderate Westerly winds to 103° E.
Jan. 21		Spoken in 44° 20' S. 26° 33' E.	
Feb. 2	Crossed Meridian 120° E. thence Easterly winds	Easterly winds from 103° E.	Easterly winds from 103° E.
,, 13		Rounded S. Cape Tasmania	
,, 14	Passed Otway 11 p.m. ..		
,, 15	Entered Port Phillip 8 a.m.		Off Cape Northumberland
,, 16		Anchored Neutral Bay	
,, 19			Anchored Melbourne

	Lizard to Line	Line to Cape	Cape to Otway or S. Cape, Tasmania	Lizard to Port
Thermopylae ..	17	28	28	74 (Melbourne)
Cutty Sark ..	22	21	26	72 (Sydney)
Baron Aberdare ..	22	22	31	75 (Melbourne)

The smart little *Harlaw* after running out to Sydney from the Lizard in 78 days, on her passage to Shanghai ran on the Tungshaw Bank, and was abandoned on her beam ends in 4 fathoms of water.

A sign of the badness of the year was shown by *The Tweed* actually loading coals instead of wool or jute

Cutty Sark found *Titania* and the iron clipper *Serapis* on the loading berth at Shanghai, with freights no better than 30s. per 50 cubic feet.

As usual *Cutty Sark* was sent up to Hankow as soon as she had got rid of her coal. Here she found that she had been forestalled in her favoured position by the little *Ambassador* and *Windhover*, which were filling up very slowly at 50s.

PACIFIC PASSAGES 1878.

Ship	Cargo Tons of Coal	Left Sydney	Destination	Date arrived	Days out
Cutty Sark	1019	Mar. 13	Shanghai	April 22	40
Thermopylae	1194	April 5	Shanghai	May 23	48
The Tweed	2050	May 16	Hongkong	July 15	60
Harlaw	1169	June 22	Wrecked	July 31	—
Salamis	1200	July 22	Shanghai	Sept. 12	52
Blackadder	1060	July 30	Shanghai	Sept. 24	56
Hallowe'en	1140	Oct. 4	Shanghai	Nov. 18	45

Ambassador, with her small capacity, did manage to fill her hold, but neither *Windhover* nor *Cutty Sark* succeeded in completing their cargo at Hankow and were finally compelled to leave for Shanghai in the hopes of picking up the remainder.

Windhover only wanted a few hundreds and these she managed to get in Shanghai at the miserable rate of 25s.; *Cutty Sark* was not so fortunate as she was obliged to leave Hankow with only 625,000 lbs. in her hold.

For the second time she had to abandon her anchors to the Yangtze mud, and broke her port hawse pipe in a desperate effort to weigh them.

On arriving at Shanghai on 27th August, she found *Titania*, *Serapis*, *Taitsing* and *Thermopylae* taking all the tea available at 35s. per cubic feet.

Salamis had also been put on the loading berth as soon as she arrived, but both she and the *Cutty Sark* were soon withdrawn, and whilst *Salamis* tried for a general cargo at 30s., Tiptaft decided to make a coal trip across to Japan. The only life in the Eastern trade this year was that of coals between Nagasaki and Shanghai.

Cutty Sark left Shanghai 19th September and arrived Nagasaki 26th September, seven days out; left Nagasaki 9th October, and arrived back at Woosung 12th October, three days out. The round trip was a tempestuous one, with more than one typhoon causing destruction to shipping on the Japan coast, but *Cutty Sark* came through unscathed, although she left Shanghai on the tail of one typhoon and raced back in front of another.

After being delayed some days by lack of water on the bar, she arrived at Shanghai to find no better prospect of completing her tea cargo. It was at this important juncture in her fortunes that Tiptaft fell ill and died. His fellow shipmates declared that the worry of this bad season killed him, and that it was heart disease aggravated by worry that was probably the correct diagnosis.

Tiptaft was succeeded by his chief mate, Wallace, a very different character to his late commander. Wallace besides being a grand seaman was as hard a carrier of sail as Tiptaft was the reverse. He was one of those jovial souls, full of jokes and high spirits; a trifle easy-going as far as discipline went and therefore very popular with his crew. He always had a pleasant word for everybody: his apprentices adored him for his friendliness and for the trouble he took to teach them their profession, a very unusual quality in a skipper of that date.

Wallace took over the command of the *Cutty Sark* with the determination to give her a real chance to break a record, for he knew that he had the fastest ship that was sailing the seas.

However, he found it quite impossible to get a tea cargo in Shanghai. The crop was a very small one, having failed in many districts, and practically all of it had been already taken.

The few tea passages in 1878 were as follows:—

Ship	Freight	Port from	Date left	Reported	on		Arrived		Days out
Ambassador	50/-	Woosung	Aug. 18	Anjer	Oct. 10	London	Dec. 31		135
Windhover ..	50/- 25/-	,,	Sept. 1	,,	Oct. 7	,,	Dec. 31		121
Titania	30/-	Shanghai	,, 22	,,	Oct. 25	,,	Dec. 31		100
Serapis ..	30/-	,,	,, 22	,,	Nov. 7	,,	Feb. 8		140
Wylo ..		Foochow	,, 22	,,	Oct. 22	,,	Jan. 15		115
Taitsing ..	35/-	Shanghai	Oct. 3	,,	Nov. 6	Portland	Jan. 28		117
Thermopylae	35/-	,,	Nov. 27	,,	Dec. 19	London	Mar. 17		110

For the first time *Cutty Sark* and *Hallowe'en*, the favourite ships in the trade with the exception of *Thermopylae*, were left in the cold. The unlucky *Salamis* failed even to get a general cargo at 30s. and finally sailed in ballast for Australia, a-seeking. She was followed in turn by *Hallowe'en* and *Cutty Sark*. *Blackadder* managed to get a charter from Singapore home, whilst *Sir Lancelot* and *Undine* stuck to the Japan trade.

PASSAGES TO AUSTRALIA FROM SHANGHAI.

Salamis	*Hallowe'en*	*Cutty Sark*
Left Shanghai Nov. 26 N.E. monsoon to Pulo Sapute, then light variable winds to Sunda Anchored off Sumatra Dec. 15	Left Shanghai Dec. 19 Passed Saddles Dec. 23 Passed Sunda Strait on Jan. 9, 21 days out Passed the Otway Feb. 13	Left Shanghai, Dec. 31 Light N.E. monsoon to Jan. 12 Passed through Gaspar Straits, Jan. 13 Reported Anjer Jan. 16, 16 days out.
Passed Anjer Dec. 27 Cleared Java Hd. Dec. 29 Carried S.E. trades from 14° S. to 32° S. Best run 336 miles Anchored Queenscliff Jan. 26, 1879, for orders Left Queenscliff Feb. 17 arrived Sydney Feb. 22	Had violent E.S.E. gale on Feb. 15 off Horn.	Mod. S.E. trade from 15 to 31 S. Ran easting down in 44° S., light variable winds between N.W. and S.W. Rounded South Cape Tas. Feb. 11. Light winds and fine weather to Feb. 15. 40 miles S.E. of Sydney Feb. 15 Heavy gale began Feb. 15. backing from E.S.E. to S.W. blowing hurricane force for 56 hours, then light airs and calms to port.
Passage to Queenscliff 61 days.	Arrived Sydney Feb. 18 58 days out.	Arrived Sydney Feb. 20 51 days out.

Salamis left Shanghai with *Thermopylae*, and the two ships had a level race down the China Sea; but on arriving off the north end of the Straits of Sunda on 15th December, only 19 days out, the two green clippers found a fleet of 37 sail vainly trying to get to the S.W. of Thwarttheway Island in the face of a very strong N.E. current.

Several attempts were made, but again and again both ships had to give it up and run back to an anchorage off Sumatra. At last *Thermopylae* succeeded, and reported off Anjer on 19th December. *Salamis* was held up some days longer, and did not clear Java Head until 29th December, but she left the rest of the fleet still struggling to leeward of Thwarttheway.

Wallace's first passage was a magnificent one; the *Cutty Sark's* being only 16 days to Anjer, 42 to the South Cape, Tasmania, and 46 to 40 miles S.E. of Sydney.

But for the southerly buster off Sydney, she would have caught and possibly beaten *Hallowe'en* into port. The three seekers all loaded coal at Sydney for Shanghai and this time *Salamis* gave the tea ships an example of what she could do, whilst *Cutty Sark* again showed up *Hallowe'en*.

Ship				Tons of Coal	Left	Arrived	Days
Hallowe'en	..	..	..	1100	Sydney March 11	Shanghai May 2	52
Cutty Sark	..	..	..	1150	Sydney March 18	Shanghai May 2	45
Salamis	..	..	..	1200	Sydney March 20	Shanghai April 28	39

Cutty Sark grounded in crossing the bar, and hung there for a tide, suing 7 feet, but came off with the aid of three tugs without having to discharge any cargo. She was barely safely to an anchor at Shanghai before a small iron barque, the *Queen of the West*, came bumping into her after crushing the boats of the U.S. gunboat *Palos* and taking the foremast out of a junk. *Cutty Sark* was only slightly damaged, but the *Queen of the West* came out of the melee with several of her plates cracked and her main rail torn away

The three ships from Sydney soon discovered that the tea trade was likely to be no better than in 1878, for when the market opened not a single sailing ship was engaged either in Shanghai or Hankow.

Fowler resigned himself to his fate and put the *Hallowe'en* on the berth for general cargo at 35s. per 50 cubic feet, but Wallace would have none of it, and left on 12th June in ballast for Manila, whilst Captain Phillip took *Salamis* off to Foochow. He did not find things any better at Foochow and was finally compelled to return to Australia in hopes of a wool cargo; leaving Foochow on 6th July, he had a very light weather passage and was 64 days getting to Melbourne, where he managed to get a wool charter.

Thermopylae wisely did not cross from Sydney in 1879 but loaded wool home; and it so happened that she was able to race her iron sister, and beat her, though it is probable that *Salamis* was handicapped by a foul bottom.

The freight rates from Shanghai and Foochow for tea were only 30s., and *Hallowe'en* actually loaded a general cargo at 5s. better.

Thermopylae ..	Left Sydney	Nov. 18	Arrived London	Feb. 7	81 days
Salamis	Left Melbourne	Nov. 19	Passed Prawle Pt.	Mar. 5	106 days

It was not a favourable season as regards wind, and several ships made the longest passages of their careers. It must, however, be noted that some of the captains took things very easy, for instance *Leander* stayed two and *Hallowe'en* three days at St. Helena.

Below I give my last table of homeward passages from the China Seas: I have included the Philippine ships. It will be noticed how the clippers were driven out of the tea trade into the jute and sugar trade of Philippines. *Cutty Sark*, indeed, had made her last tea passages. *Thermopylae* only made one more—in 1881-2 from Foochow. Of the rest *Hallowe'en* and *Leander*, a pair which kept together in an extraordinary way, alone persevered into the eighties but they always loaded as much silk and other Chinese exports as tea.

Ship	Port from	Date left	Anjer	Cape	St. Helena	Port to	Date arrived	Days out
Doune Castle ..	Manila	July 17	Aug. 16			Liverpool	Nov. 13	119
Undine ..	Foochow	Aug. 12	Sept. 30		Nov. 20	London	Jan. 4	145
Lothair ..	Cebu	Aug. 21				New York	Dec. 1	102
Windhover ..	Shanghai	Sept. 3		Nov. 25	Dec. 6	London	Jan. 26	145
Cutty Sark ..	Manila	,, 23		Nov. 25		New York	Jan. 12	111
Hallowe'en ..	Shanghai	,, 24		Dec. 19	Dec. 27	London	Feb. 6	135
Leander ..	Shanghai	,, 29	Nov. 2		Dec. 27	London	Feb. 6	128
Taitsing ..	Shanghai	Oct. 3				Portland	Jan. 25	117
Normancourt	Foochow	,, 8	Nov. 2			London	Feb. 4	117
Sir Lancelot ..	Foochow	,, 22				London	,, 27	128
Ambassador ..	Manila	,, 23				London	,, 29	129
Titania ..	Manila	,, 25				New York	,, 14	112
Wylo	Yokohama	,, 25	Nov. 20			New York	,, 14	112

Cutty Sark overtook and signalled *Windhover* off the Cape, but did not stop at St. Helena. In his book *The Clipper Ship 'Sheila,'* the late Captain Angel has recorded a race between the *Sheila* and the *Cutty Sark* in the Indian Ocean. This race is purely imaginary. *Sheila* did indeed meet the *Cutty Sark*, though not in the Indian Ocean but in New York, where Captain Angel and Captain Wallace became great friends.

Sheila left Calcutta for Trinidad on 30th July, 1879, stopped at St. Helena which she left on 7th October, and arrived New York from Trinidad on 29th December, so that it was impossible that the two vessels could have met as Captain Angel describes.

Nor did the episode refer to any other passage of the *Cutty Sark's.* There are several other races with famous ships recorded in *The Clipper Ship 'Sheila,'* but they also are entirely imaginary.

Cutty Sark left New York for London on 14th February, 1880, Captain Wallace being determined to break the record of the Atlantic if he were given the chance. He left Sandy Hook in a cyclone, which speedily stripped the *Cutty Sark* of her foresail, two lower topsails and an upper topsail. At the height of the storm the ship was hove to for 18 hours, during which time new sails were bent with incredible difficulty.

On 24th February in 45° N., 36° W., when the weather had begun to moderate with the wind at south, the *Cutty Sark* fell in with a derelict, which proved to be the *Ulster* of St. John's, N.B., a blue-nose timber ship, abandoned, all boats gone, decks level with the water and swept clean. Captain Wallace ran close under her stern, but seeing no signs of life proceeded.

Soon after passing the derelict, a thick sou-wester was picked up, which carried the *Cutty Sark* to the Wight.

It was an anxious passage for Captain Wallace; he had a sight about the longitude of the Western Isles, but never got another and had to trust to his dead reckoning, seeing nothing until he made St. Catherine's.

Deal was passed on 5th March, and the *Cutty Sark* got into the river the same day, 19 days out from New York. Her crew declared that her actual running time was 10 days from Sandy Hook to the Wight, which they claimed as a record, but I hardly think this can be allowed.

However, she beat all her rivals in the run across the Atlantic, the next best being *Titania*, which, leaving New York on 9th March, was off St. Catherine's on 1st April, 22 days out.

CHAPTER V.

A HELL-SHIP VOYAGE.

WE now come to the second period in the life of the *Cutty Sark*.

Her failure to get a tea cargo for London in either 1878 or 1879 had convinced John Willis that the tea trade was finally shut to the clippers and that henceforth his famous ship must go a-seeking and be content with less lucrative freights.

He came to the reluctant conclusion that her racing days were over, little suspecting that she would find all the racing he could wish for in the wool trade, and was destined to make an even greater name for herself in the roaring forties than she had done in the China Seas.

Old Jock was deceived by the opinion, freely expressed in shipping circles, that the graceful, yacht-like tea clippers were not powerful enough and a trifle too small for the big seas and westerly gales of the Southern Ocean.

Most of the tea clipper owners still looked to the Eastern trade as their only chance of paying their way. Already the clippers were beginning to jostle with the leisurely "Country" traders on the Coromandel coast, in the Gulf of Martaban, and in the Java Sea.

Many a famous ship was contented with sugar droghuing. *Sir Lancelot* and *Leander* fell entirely to the Indian coasting trade. *Titania*, on the other hand, after one or two voyages with Manila jute and the palm tree sugar of the Coromandel coast, was rescued by the Hudson Bay Company and put into their Vancouver trade, where for voyage after voyage she braved the greybeards of the Horn. *Lothair*, after years in the Japan trade, went to the West Coast of South America, whilst *Windhover*, after falling into the hands of the brokers, made her name in the cross Pacific trade between 'Frisco and the Australias. *Hallowe'en* alone hung on to the China trade to the end.

142

Of all the tea ships only three were to become regular wool clippers, the two great rivals *Cutty Sark* and *Thermopylae*, and the unlucky *Blackadder* which specialised in the Brisbane trade.

But before the little *Cutty Sark* was allowed to settle down as a crack wool clipper she had to undergo an experience which no sea novelist would have dared to put on paper for fear of being accused of melodramatic tendencies.

On his arrival in New York, Captain Wallace, to his infinite disgust, received a letter from Jock Willis, announcing that the *Cutty Sark* was to be cut down on her arrival home.

Thus it came about that in March, 1880, 9 feet 6 ins. were cut off her lower masts, 7 feet off her lower yards and her upper masts and yards were shortened in proportion, whilst her skysail yard disappeared altogether.

It will no doubt be asked what effect this reduction in sail area had upon the "Cutty's" speed.

In strong winds it had no effect at all, for under such conditions she could henceforth carry her royals when they would have been fast under her original plan; but the reduction took at least a knot off her speed in light winds and she lost those ghosting powers, which were such a well-known hall-mark of the China clipper.

In future we shall occasionally find ships able to keep company with her in light winds, though they would begin to drop astern fast enough directly the breeze freshened.

It was in the roaring forties, running her easting down, that she actually benefited by the reduced sail plan. With the big following seas which come chasing up from astern in those latitudes, the lower sails drop into the mast becalmed, as the vessel dives into the hollow, and it is therefore of the greatest importance for a ship to be able to hang on to her topgallant sails until the very last moment.

With her big sail plan the *Cutty Sark* could not carry her topgallant sails when it was blowing hard and even had to reef her topsails, but with her reduced sail plan she was able to carry topgallant sails running before a fresh gale.

Indeed, Captain Woodget made a practice of driving her under a main royal when other ships were snugged down to lower topsails;

and more than once ships lying hove to under a goose-winged main topsail had the mortification of seeing this little clipper of perhaps their tonnage foam by at the rate of 16 or 17 knots.

The cutting down of her spars was thus not such a great handicap as it would appear to be as far as the wool trade was concerned; but on her first two voyages after being cut down it was a handicap, for they took her to the catspaws and calms of the Java Sea and Bay of Bengal.

Yet, on her first passage after being cut down, under the hard-driving Captain Wallace, *Cutty Sark* went out to Anjer in 69 days from Lundy Island, arriving some days before any orders came out from her owner, who was far from expecting such a wonderful run from his clipper racer.

In the spring of 1880 orders for the best Welsh steam coal to supply their fleet in Japanese waters were sent over to England by the American Navy Department.

The coal was wanted as soon as possible and big freights were offered in order to attract clipper ships, which would race out with it to Japan.

Uncertain as to what he would do with his cut down tea clipper, John Willis jumped gladly at the American offer, and thus we find the *Cutty Sark* leaving London in ballast on 6th May, 1880, bound to Wales in order to load steam coal for the American fleet in the Pacific.

Besides a new outfit of sails, spars and rigging, the *Cutty Sark* left London with a new set of apprentices, hastily collected from Willis's other ships, which happened to be at home.

Of these apprentices McCausland joined from the *Zenobia*, Sankey and Bill Barton from the *Fantasie*—better known as the old Steele-built clipper *Eliza Shaw*—Fullerton from the *Whiteadder*, and Stanton from Green's *Carlisle Castle*, whilst Parton and Kirby were first voyagers. With regard to the rest of the ship's company, jovial Captain Wallace remained in command.

The mate, though a Scotsman, was a regular bucko of "Down East" style—one of those hard-fibred, despotic characters which were more common in the virile days of sail than in these luxurious days of steam.

"CUTTY SARK"

See Page 157

Photo by Captain Woodget

"CUTTY SARK," DRYING SAILS, SYDNEY HARBOUR

[See Page 172

The second mate was a rather colourless young Englishman, who was so short-sighted that Captain Wallace nearly always stood his watch with him. The third mate was an apprentice out of his time, who had failed to pass as second mate and had signed on as O.S. He lived in the half-deck.

The carpenter was one of those seamen, who, having fallen in love with a ship, look upon her in the light of a sweetheart and sign in her regularly voyage after voyage.

Chips had been in the *Cutty Sark* since her launch, He knew every timber and bolt and was a very privileged person, a favourite of "Old White Hat," a trusted adviser of Captain Wallace, and an oracle in the "Cutty's" half-deck.

The sailmaker was a big German, of that well-known type called "squareheads," who one and all answer to the name of "Dutchy."

Of the crew with which she left London we need say little. The short experience of Mr. Bucko Smith in the trip round to Wales was sufficient to send them and their bags flying over the rail directly the *Cutty Sark* reached the coal port of Penarth, where she arrived on 22nd May.

Captain Wallace found the usual difficulty in picking a crew at a Welsh coal port, his task being not rendered any easier by the sinister reputation of his mate. Finally he had to content himself with a very scratch lot of nationalities, consisting of 5 Englishmen, 3 Danes, 3 niggers (two of them steam-boat men) 2 Greeks and an Italian.

With cook and steward the *Cutty Sark* thus had her complement of 28 souls, one of the Englishmen serving as bosun.

Wallace sailed from Penarth on 4th June—a Friday, and at once a member of the crew began to prophesy the well-known consequences. This man was something of a character, a veritable sea croaker, a cross-grained, sour-tempered seamen of a type which used to flourish in sailing ship foc's'les. His conversation ran entirely in the minor key; he was a pessimist of pessimists: his yarns were all concerned with mutiny and murder, with shipwrecks and disaster, with foul weather and fearful diseases, whilst he was superstitious to the last degree.

L

The man seemed to nurse a thousand wrongs within his hairy breast, to see death and destruction ever within an arm's length and to expect nothing else than hell and damnation for everyone within his ken. He was one of those hard-bitten sailors who required next to no sleep, and during the night watches below he would pace the deck muttering to himself for hour after hour. Naturally enough he was a prime seaman; there was no fear in his composition; he had brooded so upon horrors that nothing could daunt him, and no Liverpool packet-rat was ever tougher or more enduring.

The apprentices of the *Cutty Sark* were not long in finding a suitable nickname for this queer old man of the sea, whose prophecies of evil were soon to be so amply fulfilled. There was something so uncanny about him that the boys likened him to the Flying Dutchman, and he was soon known on board as Vanderdecken.

The first of his prophecies was almost instantly confirmed. The *Cutty Sark* was barely to sea on that fatal Friday before she was compelled to anchor in the Severn, whilst a wild sou-west gale shrieked up the Bristol Channel for three days of flying scud, raging seas and howling winds, which tested her ground tackle to the utmost.

The gale over, the pilot was dropped and departure taken from Lundy Island on 7th June. To the secret disgust of Vanderdecken, the *Cutty Sark* carried a strong fair wind to Cape Finisterre, then good N.E. trades gave her the course to the line. In the strength of the trades *Cutty Sark* fell in with *Titania*, which had left London on 3rd June.

Both ships were bound to Anjer for orders. For the next four days, the two famous tea clippers with every rag set raced side by side. It was *Titania's* best point of sailing and the two ships proved to be so evenly matched that there was little to choose between them. *Titania* had been stripped of her racing sails and spars as far back as 1872, as much as 10 feet being cut off her lower masts, yet this did not affect her speed in strong winds any more than it did that of the *Cutty Sark*.

It would have been hard to find two more perfect ships of their size and type, and we may well imagine the wonderful picture they must have made as they raced south, neck and neck, in that lovely trade weather. A morning came, however, when their courses differed and they gradually parted company, with the understanding that it was to be a race to Anjer.

Soon after this the *Cutty Sark* raised the Peak of Teneriffe, standing up like a black cone upon the horizon. This was the well-known mirage, for the Peak was over 150 miles away, and as the sun rose higher in the heavens the cone gradually disappeared.

The *Cutty Sark* made a splendid run to the line, but the usual work of shifting sail, as soon as the doldrums were reached, gave her bucko mate a splendid chance of working up his watch in proper "hellion" fashion.

His spite was chiefly vented upon the three darkies, especially one of them named John Francis, who was particularly incapable and clumsy. In shifting the mainsail this man managed to get his hand badly crushed in a buntline block. The pain roused his temper and he began to talk back at the mate, who was swearing at him from the deck with all the sting and concentrated venom in his composition.

Then the mate's watch began to show their sympathy for the nigger and very shortly the whole ship was in an uproar. By the time that the hands came down from bending the mainsail, matters had grown to such a pitch that Captain Wallace called his officers and apprentices aft and gave them arms. He then turned to the angry foremast crowd and boldly declaring that he meant to put a stop to the trouble once and for all, ordered Francis to apologise to the mate or else take a hiding from him.

The nigger, who saw red where the mate was concerned, flung off his coat in defiance. A ring was at once formed just forward of the poop. The nigger and the mate flung themselves upon each other with all the fury and lack of rules usual in sea fights, whilst the captain flourished his revolver and threatened to shoot the first man who attempted to interfere.

The two belligerents pounded away at each other for about a quarter of an hour without much result; then Captain Wallace stopped the fight and sent the hands forward with the caution that he would put the next man in irons whom he caught abusing his officers.

This method of preserving discipline at least cleared the air; Captain Wallace had acted with decision, moreover, he was very popular with all hands: and henceforth, though the bucko mate was far from mending his ways and still vented his spite on the niggers, both watches worked keenly to make a record trip.

This fight on the *Cutty Sark* reminds me of the famous battle between Captain Tom Bowling of the *Invercargill* and Brighton Bill. I give the story as it was given to me by one of the onlookers.

"Captain Bowling was a man of prodigious strength, and I have seen him take hold of a small anvil by the point and with a stiff arm raise it straight above his head. On one occasion, whilst I was with him, he had some trouble with a big A.B., known as 'Brighton Bill' after his home town.

"Bowling said something pretty sharp, and Bill retorted, 'It is only your coat that protects you.' At which Bowling said sharply: —'Come on to the quarter-deck at 4 bells (6 o'clock) and I will take my coat off.

"We were in the south-east trades and the weather was fine, so at 4 bells all hands came aft to watch the fight. Both men stripped to the waist and they fought for two hours, but Bowling was just a bit better than the other man, so he was considered to have won. It was a Homeric combat such as is given few men the chance to witness, for both men were as hard as nails (though Bowling was a man well over 50 at the time) and both knew something about handling themselves.

"But ever after that no man dared say a word against Tom Bowling whilst Brighton Bill was about. I believe he afterwards sailed with Bowling as bosun."

It may be of interest to add that Captain Bowling was an old China clipper man; and when he retired from the sea had been 30 years in command of sailing ships out of 50 years afloat.

With the "old man" driving the ship and his bucko mate driving her crew, the *Cutty Sark* made a splendid run to the Cape meridian.

The first of really heavy easting weather occurred in 42° 30′ S., 23° 00′ E. when the wind began to come out of the sou'-west in heavier and heavier squalls: then it gradually settled down to a blow of hurricane force, straight from the west. This was just the weather to bring out the daring and resourcefulness of Captain Wallace and show the *Cutty Sark* at her best.

The "old man" hung grimly on to his canvas until a particularly vicious squall tore his brand new fore and main topgallant sails from the boltrope; at the same moment the lower fore topsail sheet carried away and that sail went to tatters.

By this time a tremendous sea was running whose long hill-like ridges rolled up astern until it seemed that the "Cutty" must be pooped and swept out of existence. But in such a case the *Cutty Sark* was always game and running beautifully, lifting clear of each sea with a buoyancy which roused the enthusiasm of her crew.

Whilst she was in the trough her topsails fell into the mast, absolutely becalmed by the hissing crests of the great combers; then as she rose, the sails filled with a clap of thunder which shook the ship from stern to stem and threatened to tear the masts out of her.

The gale was about at its worst, when the men were sent aloft to bend a new lower fore topsail, which was swayed aloft to the tune of "Blow! Boys! Blow!"

> Oh, blow, my boys, I long to hear you
> > Blow, boys, blow!
> Oh, sing, my boys, 'twill always cheer you,
> > Blow, my bully boys, blow!
> With a gallant ship and a bully crew:
> > Blow, boys, blow!
> We're just the boys to pull her through;
> > Blow, my bully boys, blow!
> Oh, blow, my boys, no cause for growling:
> > Blow, boys, blow!
> Though up aloft the wind is howling;
> > Blow, my bully boys, blow!
> Oh, blow my boys, no finer weather;
> > Blow, boys, blow!
> A long strong pull, and all together;
> > Blow, my bully boys, blow'

Then blow today, and all tomorrow;
        Blow, boys, blow!
With cheery hearts, no thought of sorrow;
        Blow, my bully boys, blow!
For up aloft this sail must go;
        Blow, boys, blow!
What if the wind blow high or low;
        Blow, my bully boys, blow!

There is nothing like a chanty to put heart into men in bad weather, and up went the topsail in its stops, all ready for bending—but it was another matter to bend it.

For two hours the hands aloft fought to bend that sail, between gasps for breath, which was torn from their lungs by the storm fiend, they swore at the wind, they swore at each other in that mental irritation which is common at such moments.

Finger nails were torn in their effort to hold on to the bagging canvas. The sweat ran off their cheeks into the necks of their oil-skins. The footrope swung and dipped as they braced themselves against the tilting yard, and strove to pass the rovings under the jackstay. The task seemed an impossibility, but that topsail had to be set in order to keep the *Cutty Sark* ahead of those monstrous chasing seas, and set it eventually was.

Whilst the battle raged aloft, one green sea did succeed in coming in over the stern and swept the length of the deck so that to the men on the yard there was nought to be seen but three masts sticking out of a maelstrom of boiling foam. Then, with deck ports clanging, the gallant little ship cleared herself and rushed headlong into the yawning hollow. Hardly was the topsail sheeted home before the gale settled down into a steady blow.

On the morning of the second day three test heaves of the log were taken, when the *Cutty Sark* seemed to be doing her best, and $17\frac{1}{2}$, 17 and $17\frac{1}{2}$ knots were recorded, whilst 16 knots were constantly on the log slate.

As usual the little clipper steered beautifully. Under foresail and fore lower topsail, the two main topsails and sometimes a main topgallant sail, the mizen lower topsail and two headsails (for safety in case of a broach-to), she almost steered herself, yet it looked alarming enough to the man going aft to relieve the wheel. But in spite of the overtaking seas bumping under her stern as she rose on top of them, the *Cutty Sark* neither kicked nor yawned but piked along dead before it.

And during the whole of this strenuous time her mixed crew played up most gallantly, their only wish being to give the ship her chance and break the record.

At the first sign of a lull there came a call to stick out all three topgallant sails and out tumbled the watch below, gallantly indifferent to risk of life and limb or to the loss of their hard earned sleep.

Wallace, the sail carrier, had hung on to his topgallant sails to the last moment and he set them again at the very first opportunity: indeed no sooner had the storm spent its intensity than he sheeted home his royals.

The strongest part of the blow lasted for three days, and in those short days of easting the *Cutty Sark* ran 1050 miles—an average of 350 miles a day or $14\frac{1}{2}$ knots for 72 hours.

．　　．　　．　　．　　．　　．　　．

Captain Wallace was one of those skippers who took an interest in their apprentices. On Sundays it was his custom to ask a couple of them to dinner, and we may guess how the boys appreciated the treat.

Most captains believed in the hardening process, which they themselves had to undergo in their youth.

An apprentice in the *Lothair* under the stern Captain Orchard recounts that the only time his captain spoke to him during the whole voyage was to rebuke him for dropping ropeyarns on the sacred poop when he was serving the eyes of the ratlines in the mizen rigging.

Unfortunately for the boy, the captain had hardly finished speaking when down came another ropeyarn, which landed at the autocrat's feet, whereupon Orchard burst out with:—"Damn you, if you drop another ropeyarn on the poop I'll send you out of this altogether." After this threat we may be certain that the apprentice made sure of his ends going over the rail and not inboard.

Two of Wallace's apprentices used to take sights regularly, and the captain was at pains to help them with their navigation.

The subject of navigation, indeed, suddenly assumed unusual importance, for, as the *Cutty Sark* neared the longitude of St. Paul's Island the chronometers began to differ by five minutes in their rate, and Captain Wallace had no means of knowing which of the two was right. No ship was sighted: Tristan d'Acunha had been kept below the horizon and St. Paul's Island was given a wide berth.

The *Cutty Sark* continued to make good time, and it was soon necessary to haul up for Sunda Straits. The shift of helm caused the chief tragedy of this tragic voyage. It was the middle watch. The *Cutty Sark* was on the starboard tack, with a nice wholesail breeze from the south-east. The mate's watch was on deck, the troublesome nigger, John Francis, being on the look-out. At 3 a.m. Captain Wallace gave the orders to alter course from east to N.N.E. This meant squaring her in. Whilst the watch manned the fore-sheet, the mate sang out to the nigger on the foc's'le-head to let go the tack. But the order was not obeyed. Again the mate sang out. And again the look-out took not the least notice. This was more than the bucko could stand, and he went forward "on the jump," his mouth full of strong language and his heart full of rage.

Apparently the darkey met him with not only an insolent tongue but a raised capstan bar. There was a short sharp struggle, whilst the mate gained possession of the bar. Then it was the irate officer's turn, and without a moment's hesitation he brought it down on the man's head with such force that John Francis dropped senseless to the deck. It must have been a shrewd blow, for a black man's skull is notoriously hard, yet Francis never regained consciousness and died on the third day after the blow had been struck.

He was buried at sea, the captain reading the service. Though the nigger was far from being popular amongst his shipmates, the mate was still less popular. The ship suddenly became very silent. With gloomy faces and angry, bitter hearts the foremast crowd went about their work, in sullen silence; whilst the afterguard, sensing the atmosphere forward, were uneasy and full of foreboding.

The mate retired to his cabin and was not seen again on deck for the rest of the passage, Captain Wallace taking his watch

The *Cutty Sark* was now barely a week from Anjer, but, owing to the error in his chronometers, Captain Wallace dared not lay a direct course for Java Head, but, allowing a margin of about 80 miles, did not haul in for the land until he was in the latitude of the Straits.

A nice fresh sea breeze took the *Cutty Sark* in under the shadow of Krakatoa and then died away. And whilst she lay becalmed to leeward, her crew had the mortification of seeing their rival, the *Titania*, glide up the Straits before a nice little air of wind. Thus, through the error in her chronometers, the *Cutty Sark* went about a hundred miles out of her way and lost the race with *Titania* by 12 hours, both ships anchoring off Anjer on the same day.

The *Cutty Sark* had made a very good run out, being only 72 days from Penarth to Anjer, and 69 days from her departure from Lundy Island.

Whilst *Titania* continued her passage to Hongkong, where she arrived on 16th September, *Cutty Sark* had to wait for orders for old Willis had not expected a run of this speed from his cut-down clipper, and Captain Wallace, though he thought that his destination would be Yokohama, found that there was no telegram awaiting him at Anjer confirming this.

This telegram did not arrive until 29th August

Whilst the *Cutty Sark* lay off Anjer awaiting her belated orders, the mate took the opportunity of persuading his kind-hearted captain to help him to escape.

An American ship, the *Colorada,* had just arrived from Hamburg and lay at anchor ahead of the *Cutty Sark*. Captain Wallace found that the "old man" of the *Colorada* was quite ready to take the "Cutty's" bucko mate aboard, being only too glad to get hold of a man-handler of such reputation.

The next question was how to smuggle the mate aboard the *Colorada* without the knowledge of the "Cutty's" crowd; for it was known aft that the friends of the murdered nigger, headed by old Vanderdecken, had sworn that they would see the mate brought to book.

They were hoodwinked in this fashion. Early one morning some native bumboats came alongside to starboard, whereupon the "old man" supplied the hands with some money, and both watches were soon busy bargaining over the side for packets of jaggery and bunches of small onions, for bananas and pineapples, for Java sparrows and screaming parrakeets.

Whilst this hullaballoo was going on, the mate, unnoticed by the excited men waging their brisk bargains with the gesticulating and screeching Malays, sneaked up on deck and quietly dropped into a sampan, or it may have been the *Colorada's* boat, which had cautiously dropped under the "Cutty's" port quarter. This escape of the *Cutty Sark's* mate has been a well-known yarn in ships' foc's'les for many years. Gradually it has been embroidered and enlarged upon until at last the celebrated Joseph Conrad was tempted to put it into one of his books.

But the version which stated that the mate swam off to the *Colorada* was an absurd one, for the Straits are infested with sharks and he would have had to swim against wind and current. The mate made the trip to the Down Easter in a boat. But he had hardly got safely away from the *Cutty Sark* and hidden aboard the *Colorada* before his escape was discovered.

It turned out that one of the men had noticed him with a bundle in his hand, skulking about behind the deckhouse at 7.30 a.m., just after the bumboats had come alongside, and the foc's'le was not long in putting two and two together. Led by old Vanderdecken, they at once refused work, declaring that they would not turn to until the mate was found. In spite of his popularity, Captain Wallace was unable to pacify them, and he at last agreed to take some of the men ashore to see the authorities.

Men before the mast had small chance of getting fair play ashore in those days. The native police were certainly ordered to search all the ships lying off Anjer for the missing mate, but the crew of the *Cutty Sark* were not allowed to join in the search. There was a good deal of fuss, with, of course, no result.

The crew of the now notorious clipper were by no means satisfied with the steps taken by the authorities ashore—they knew they had been hoodwinked and so they still refused to turn to.

The *Cutty Sark* had now been at Anjer a week, and at the psychological moment the belated orders arrived—she was to proceed to Yokohama.

It was now time to get underweigh, but not a member of the foc's'le would touch a capstan bar. Whereupon Wallace determined to up anchor and set sail as best he could with the aid of his devoted apprentices and petty officers; so the capstan was manned by the half-deck, carpenter, cook, steward and sailmaker.

The more determined of the crew immediately tried to interfere, but again Wallace acted with decision—the afterguard were given arms and the ringleaders of the crew, four in all, were captured and clapped in irons. At which the remainder of the crew retired sulkily to the foc's'le whilst six boys and four men set to work on the long weary job of weighing the anchor in that steamy, enervating heat.

The anchor was barely off the ground before a light draught of air gave the "Cutty" steerage way and carried her out of Anjer Roads into the Java Sea. It was the 5th September. Scarcely, however, was the *Cutty Sark* clear of the land before she ran into a clock calm which lasted on and off for three days. The ship now rang with old Vanderdecken's prophecies of disaster. He described the evils which would happen to the poor little *Cutty Sark* and all on board with such a wealth of detailed horror that some of the hands became really frightened. The whole ship's company felt tragedy in the air and it was not long in coming.

Captain Wallace had no sooner helped his mate to escape than he realised in what a predicament he had placed himself. He saw an official investigation looming ahead at Yokohama, in which there was little doubt but that he would be held responsible for the mate's escape, and the very best that he could expect was the suspension of his certificate. He had an old mother and a young wife dependent upon him, and the future for them as well as for himself looked black indeed.

The worry of it all so preyed upon the once jovial skipper that all hands began to pity his care-worn face. Ever since the escape of the mate he had been unable to sleep. Night and day he stood gazing out to sea or walked with bowed head up and down the poop in a misery which was plain to see.

His friends in the half-deck watched him furtively with anxious eyes. There was no more singing in the dog watches—only the ceaseless drone of that croaker, Vanderdecken, mingled with the lazy flapping of the listless, calm-ridden sails. The ship had lost all life. The calm aggravated the tension aboard. The sullen crew, still athirst for vengeance upon the missing mate, kept forward and allowed the half-deck to do what work was necessary. Discipline had grown lax under the influence of the captain's indifference to all around him, the steamy heat and the stagnant calm.

It was not a situation that could possibly last; something had to happen soon. One or two of the wisest recognised that the captain's mind and body could not stand the strain much longer. The reliable "Chips" stood watch with his skipper, ready to stand by his beloved ship and her unfortunate captain, but uncertain how to act in order to relieve the strain.

The scene was laid and the climax was at hand.

On the fourth day after leaving Anjer, the watch had just been called at 4 a.m., when the captain, who was standing at the break of the poop with the carpenter, turned to his faithful petty officer and asked if the second mate was on deck.

"Chips" replied that he was just coming up. Whereupon Captain Wallace left the carpenter and walked aft: called the helmsman's attention to the course; then deliberately stepped on to the taffrail and jumped overboard.

At the moment the *Cutty Sark* was sneaking along at about two knots before a faint draught of air. The man at the wheel quickly threw over two life-buoys and put the helm down. The crew, who had for so long refused work, flung themselves upon a boat, which had been used at Anjer and was still in the davits, and had it in the water in record time.

The sea was as calm as a mill-pond. The life-buoys were picked up, but no trace of the captain was ever found, though a number of sharks swimming furiously about gave only too clear an indication of his fate.

Thus passed a splendid seaman, a kind and capable shipmaster, and a man whose death was regretted by everyone aboard. The crew took the death of their captain greatly to heart and blamed themselves bitterly for refusing duty. The half-deck lamented the loss of a true friend, whilst the *Cutty Sark* had been deprived of a skipper who understood her every mood and had proved that he knew how to get every ounce of speed out of her. Tragedies and misfortunes have a way of piling up. The *Cutty Sark* had sailed on a Friday, and old Vanderdecken's evil prophecies were fast beginning to mature; her run of bad luck had now fairly started, from henceforth there was to be no let up until the voyage was ended.

As soon as the boat was hoisted up and all hope of saving the captain abandoned, a consultation of all hands was held. The crew wanted the second mate to take the ship on to Yokohama, but that young man was quite unfit for such a responsibility; his navigation was very shaky, and his eyesight was so bad that he was compelled to ask Sankey, the star navigator amongst the apprentices to help him in taking sights. There was evidently nothing for it but to head back for Anjer, and in that calm weather it took the *Cutty Sark* four days to regain the anchorage.

Nor were these four days without accident. When close to the Cap and Button Rocks and without a breath of wind, the *Cutty Sark* was caught in a strong tide-race, which swept her stern first round the north-west side of Thwarttheway Island.

The steep rocky sides of that well-known island rose sheer up from a great depth, and so close to the shore was the *Cutty Sark* taken by the current that her yards had to be braced up to avoid striking the towering cliffs. Luckily there were no out-lying reefs and the deep sea lead gave no bottom; but it was sufficiently alarming to make old Vanderdecken declare that the ship was bewitched. However, the island, so well named Thwarttheway, was cleared without mishap. A light breeze then sprang up and allowed the *Cutty Sark* to head in for the anchorage.

The inexperienced second mate next proceeded to anchor too far out and dropped his hook upon a shelving rock which terminated abruptly in deep water. The next day he was compelled to move the ship on to better holding ground nearer the land.

The *Cutty Sark* now had another week of idleness whilst cables passed to and fro between the incapable second mate and the mystified John Willis, who had, of course, heard nothing of the killing of the nigger and the escape of the mate.

Whilst the second mate spent his days between the ship and the telegraph station, little work beyond wetting down the decks was done on board; but the lucky apprentices who manned the boat enjoyed many a stroll through the small native town and Dutch colony, which was so shortly afterwards to be wiped out by the appalling eruption of the extinct volcano of Krakatao. At first Willis, who was loath to forfeit such a good charter, wanted the second mate to proceed to Yokohama, but the man, if without grit, knew his own limitations and refused to undertake the responsibility. At last orders came out for the *Cutty Sark* to proceed to Singapore in charge of a Dutch pilot.

The next excitement was the working of the *Cutty Sark* through the narrow Banka Strait. The ship was put under "Calashee" watch, which meant that all hands stood by ready for a call to work ship, but no other work was done. The straits are narrow, not much wider than a large river in places; and what with tides and currents, rocks and shoals, calms and squalls and sudden shifts of wind, the ship had to be handled smartly. Nor did the bewitched clipper get through without one close call. With no wind and helpless in the grip of a strong current, the *Cutty Sark* drifted by some sunken rocks on which the surf was boiling.

For a few moments the hearts of all on board stood still, then, with her usual luck in extricating herself from almost certain disaster, the "Cutty" slid by the reef just clear of the broken water but so close to the jagged fangs which showed above the surf that the meanest thrower aboard could have tossed a biscuit on to them.

But for this scare the passage was a most enjoyable one. For the most part a gentle fair wind prevailed, which made it ideal sailing. Nor was the weather too warm, and amply clad in broad brimmed hats, rolled up dungaree pants and open throated shirts, the ship's company lounged about the decks as if on a yachting cruise. With the double tragedy but just beneath the horizon, the crew nevertheless were able to enjoy the trip with the usual sailor's shortness of memory for the unpleasant. A week of this idyllic sailing brought the *Cutty Sark* into Singapore harbour, and on 18th September she once more dropped her anchor.

Singapore, already all agog with the *Jeddah* disaster and the dismasting of the *Bates Family*, received a still greater thrill when the cause of the famous *Cutty Sark's* first visit to the port began to get abroad. The story of the *Jeddah* has been immortalised in Joseph Conrad's great classic *Lord Jim*—it was a most disgraceful one, the captain and officers abandoning the ship in a panic and leaving over a thousand souls, native crew and pilgrims aboard a sinking ship, as they thought, to perish. The chief officer of the *Jeddah** arrived at Singapore on 15th September, and he plays the part of "Lord Jim" in Conrad's story.

The *Bates Family* disaster was more curious than disgraceful. She was a well-known Liverpool ship, notorious for her straight steamer stem, upon which the whole family of Bates was carved, forming a gigantic figure-head, which drew attention to her wherever she went. Being bound from Newport to Calcutta with coal, she was dismasted on 6th September in a very odd way. The iron jackstay on her foreyard chafed through the forestay, which suddenly carried away. At which the foremast fell back on the mainmast, the mainmast on the mizen, and the mizen in its turn upon the wheel, so that all three masts lay fore and aft along the deck like masts of a bottle ship before it is put into the bottle. On the deck everything was smashed up by the fall of the masts—boats, deck-houses, skylights, wheel and even rudder, whilst the bowsprit broke short off as well.

It is difficult to imagine a more complete smash up. On the following day the *British India* came along whereupon the captain of the *Bates Family* determined to abandon his ship, and taking the circumstances into consideration the Court acquitted him of all blame. The *British India* transferred the crew of the *Bates Family* to the *Copenhagen* on the 10th, which duly landed them at Algoa Bay, whilst the *British India* brought the news to Singapore.*

---

* *Jeddah* iron screw brig 993 tons net register, 1541 tons gross register, built by Denny of Dumbarton in 1872, owned by the Singapore Steamship Co.

Bates Family, iron ship (converted steamer) 2154 tons, built in Hull, 1859; owners E. Bates & Sons, Liverpool.

The *Cutty Sark* was tied up to the Tanga Paka wharf, where a gang of Chinese coolies proceeded to unload the coals, which they shovelled into baskets and ran ashore, slung on bamboo poles.

An enquiry into the tragedy was now held, which resulted in the crew being given the option of their discharge. Only a few availed themselves of this concession, but chief amongst them was old Vanderdecken, who openly declared that henceforth his object in life would be to run down the mate and bring him to justice, for he was certain that the *Cutty Sark* would have no luck until the nigger killer was under lock and key.

Those remaining on board were far from sorry when they saw old Vanderdecken bundle over the rail, for they had begun to think that there was something uncanny about the queer old man and his prophecies, which had come true in such a tragic manner—in fact, many considered that he was the Jonah at the root of all the trouble.

Whether old Vanderdecken ran the mate to ground at San Franscisco or in a London pub does not very much matter, but the mate at any rate owed his arrest to being recognised by one of the crew, and was tried in London some two years later and sentenced to seven years imprisonment for manslaughter.

I give the account of the trial in the Appendix.

At Singapore the poor-spirited second mate was promoted chief, and a new second mate and hands signed on, to replace those who had taken their discharge. Finally a new captain arrived on the scene. Curiously enough his name was Bruce. It was surely a coincidence that he should follow Wallace.

When the news came over the wires that his famous clipper was held up at Anjer for want of a captain, Jock Willis was puzzled how to find a suitable man within reach of Java Straits.

The *Hallowe'en* happened to be at Hongkong, so old White Hat cabled to Captain Fowler and asked if he considered his chief officer, Bruce, capable of taking command of the *Cutty Sark*.

Fowler hated his chief officer like poison and was only too delighted to get rid of him, so he immediately wired back a laconic "Yes."

And thus it came about that one day, whilst the *Cutty Sark* was still discharging her coal, her crew were surprised to see a fat

"CUTTY SARK" RUNNING DOWN TO ST. HELENA

From a painting by J. Everett in possession of the Author

[*See Page* 182

"CUTTY SARK" IN MID-OCEAN

[See Page 221

little man with an uneasy look coming up the companion ladder, who announced himself to the newly promoted mate as the ship's new commander. There could hardly have been found a greater contrast to Captain Wallace than Captain Bruce.

Bruce was no carrier of sail, no hero at sea. Boastful ashore, he was timid to a degree on the water, and was that great rarity amongst sailormen, a real downright physical coward.

As long as there was a fair wind and it was not too strong, he would strut about the deck and talk big about carrying sail: but when it came on to blow, or the glass fell, or he was nearing land, his nerve went entirely—the fat little man collapsed like a pricked balloon and with pale face and shaking hands would retire below and leave his chief officer in charge. Like most cowards he was not only a bully but a hypocrite. He affected to be deeply religious and even went to the extent of holding daily prayer meetings aboard; these however, were interrupted by long spells which were far from the least hint of piety, when the bottle was his only love and the most horrible blasphemy his chief form of conversation.

He was one of those peculiar followers of the sea, who keep a shore face and a sea face. On shore he aped the sanctimonious type of black-gloved, smug-faced evangelist, but he could never keep this role up for long at sea where his bullying nature and a craving for strong drink soon obtained the upper hand.

Indeed he was a kind of nautical Jekyll and Hyde. Bruce had, however, one good quality or rather we should call it, qualification. He was particularly skilled at navigation, which made his peculiar dread of a landfall the more difficult to understand. Whilst he was in charge of the *Cutty Sark*, he made a complete set of chronometer records from a series of lunar observations: he corrected the deviation charts and also the displacement tables to check the loading of ballast: and when he was in an amiable frame of mind, which was not very often, he gave the navigators amongst the apprentices some valuable lessons in the higher realms of navigation.

The cargo of the *Cutty Sark* was but half out when the ss. *Glencoe* came alongside to take the remainder. This ship was one of the steam supplanters of the tea clippers, and with a cargo of

M

tea on board was actually racing home against another steamer called the *Sultan of India*. One may imagine the disgust of the *Cutty Sark's* crew when they found that they had to provide the means of propulsion for one of those contemptible steam kettles which had driven the beautiful clippers out of the China tea trade. The half-deck, with all the devotion of youth for their ship, were specially indignant.

"The miserable thieves," groaned the senior apprentice, "that tea belongs to us and the *Titania* and the *Thermopylae*."

"Shade of Tam o' Shanter!" burst forth another, voicing a common exclamation aboard the *Cutty Sark*, "to think that that dirty ditch at Suez should be the means of turning the 'Cutty' into a collier for those fair weather sailors!"

The *Glencoe*, however, soon showed that she was racing in her own mechanical fashion. Double gangs of coolies were put on and her steam hoists were brought into use. Indeed so quickly was the coal removed from the *Cutty Sark's* hold to the steamer's bunkers that stiffening ballast had to be rushed into the clipper to preserve her stability.

The hold of the *Cutty Sark* was barely empty before orders came out for her to proceed in ballast to Calcutta, whereupon more stiffening was taken in and the royal yards sent down on deck.

On 1st October the clipper once more stood out to sea and headed up the Malacca Straits under a native pilot. It was a case of working land and sea breezes in narrow shoal waters. Calms succeeded squalls with dreary monotony whilst numerous water-spouts, running before the wind, infringed all rules of the road and frequently compelled the *Cutty Sark* to luff or bear up out of her course and give them right of way.

The tides, too, had to be taken into consideration. The ship was usually headed inshore towards sunset, so as to be able to anchor at nightfall. The anchor was given just enough chain to keep the vessel from drifting, the sails were roughly furled and an anchor watch set, the rest of the ship's company going below to snatch what sleep they could before the call of "Up anchor!" which usually came about 1 a.m.

This "circus," as the apprentices called it, continued for a fortnight, during which time there was only one mishap, which was due to the leadsman calling 7 fathoms for 17. The order was given to let go and away went the chain over windlass and through hawse-pipe until the sparks were flying: and we may guess the weary time they had heaving up again.

The chief amusement on board was catching boobies, which in their well-known foolish way would settle on the yards and allow one to catch them at will. When the pilot left, on the *Cutty Sark* gaining the open sea, he took a number of these birds as provender for his journey back to Singapore.

"Calashee" watch is all very well as a novelty, but all hands were glad enough to get back to sea watch when the *Cutty Sark* left these narrow waters for the Bay of Bengal.

As soon as the ship had cleared the Andaman Islands, the new captain began to come out of his shell and show one side of his double nature—the religious side.

Prayer meetings became the order of the day, at which the sanctimonious little hypocrite preached unctuously against intemperance and all the other various temptations which beset the sailor.

However, as the *Cutty Sark* approached the Sandheads the old man's interest in the morals of his crew rapidly faded before his peculiar dread of a landfall. For some days before sighting the pilot brig, the miserable little coward was a prey to his imagination. He was torn between the fear of a stranding and the dread of a cyclone. He watched the barometer with bulging eyes and quivering lips, though the weather had every appearance of being set fair.

Day after day he sent his amazed crew aloft to shorten sail for no apparent reason: night after night he laid the vessel to. He seemed to be in the grip of a nerve-destroying panic, and all hands watched his weakness with a growing contempt.

At last the pilot brig was sighted, and straightway that despicable old man regained his self-esteem and once more strutted the deck like a turkey-cock. Presently a powerful Hooghly tug took hold and away went the *Cutty Sark* up the celebrated river.

Making port is one of the most enjoyable and interesting of all the sensations, which this world has provided for man. Whether it be the familiar white cliffs of old England, the towering heads of Sydney, the lovely bays of 'Frisco, Auckland or Rio, or the wide entrance of one of the world's greatest rivers, one's interest is always intense. But for sudden change from the open sea there is nothing that can compare with the first night's anchorage in the Hooghly.

Surrounded by miles upon miles of unseen jungle, the senses of hearing and smell alone give one the first never to be forgotten impression of a strange and wonderful land. For the night is laden with the heavy scent of the tropics, and the still night air vibrates with the noise of wild beasts—the deep roar of the wandering tiger, the whining cry of the jackal, the short distinctive note of the lone hyena or the sudden grunt of an angry boar, roused from his bed by a pack of hunting dogs in full cry upon the line of a terrified sambhur.

And all the while the turbid waters of the great river rush gurgling and chattering by, their lapping occasionally overnoised by the sudden splash of a river porpoise or flapping turtle or perhaps the swish of a great mugger of the Sunderbunds, as, with a whisk of his tail, he slips off a neighbouring sandbank.

Nor is sleep easy for another reason; the ship indeed, resounds to the hum of a myriad of mosquitoes and the slap and damn of the fresh-faced English boys.

The lordly Hooghly pilot and his attendant leadsman, the passage of the dreaded James and Mary Shoal, the shifting sands and zigzag turns, the native craft and busy life of the Calcutta River have all been described at length by every sailor scribe who has ever traded there—suffice to say that the *Cutty Sark* arrived without further incident at the Garden Reach anchorage on 11th November, 1880, and the following day took her place in the mooring tiers of Princeps Ghat, those well-known Esplanade moorings, which at that date were crowded with magnificent sailing ships.

The *Cutty Sark* lay on these moorings for no less than four idle months, for the famous little clipper was out of her beat and found a great difficulty in getting a cargo.

The crew were paid off. Both mates took their departure, and only the apprentices and the faithful carpenter remained out of the ship's company which had left England. Luckily it was the best time of year, and for those who remained on board passed happily enough. Cleaning ship, painting, caulking, paying and scraping deck seams and sundry carpenter's repairing jobs formed the usual day's work. Fortunately for the half-deck there was no mate to hustle them and Captain Bruce was too busy ashore working up a reputation for godliness to trouble much about what work was being done aboard.

Thus the "Cutty's" apprentices had a very different experience to those of *The Tweed*, which just about two years later lay just above the Pepper Box at the Esplanade moorings for almost as long a time as the *Cutty Sark* in 1880.

Old man White of *The Tweed* kept his boys at work from 6 a.m. to 6 p.m. in the heat of the sun. *The Tweed* had come round from Manila in ballast and had not only worked through the Malacca Straits by means of slow, laborious kedging, but had sailed up the Hooghly instead of being towed.

Whilst she lay at Manila, old White ordered her topsides to be scraped and planed. The work was started at Manila but it had to be finished in Calcutta, and so the boys spent their days in the blazing sun on stages over the side. This treatment so roused the ire of the more humane skippers that they even remonstrated with White.

On one occasion the apprentices were at work on the stern. The big stern windows were open and Captain White was inside. The captain of another ship who was passing in his boat sang out, "Hello, boys, hard at it again?"

"Yes, sir," replied the perspiring apprentices meekly. Whereupon he yelled out in a voice which Captain White must have heard with ease.

"It's an infernal d—d shame the way in which you boys are being worked."

The Tweed's boys with their skipper within dared make no reply, nor did the speech have any effect on Captain White's stony heart. As soon as *The Tweed's* topsides were finished, her apprentices were sent aloft to black-varnish the yards. No brushes were served out, so they had to use swabs. The black varnish in that heat burnt wherever it touched the skin; and as the boys slapped at their faces with their varnish covered hands in a vain attempt to keep the mosquitoes at bay, the sun burnt the skin off both hands and faces. Then the backstays, which were new, owing to her dismasting on the passage out to Sydney, had to be served over; and every week the teak decks were holystoned and all paint work scrubbed with sand and canvas.

To return to the *Cutty Sark* in the year 1880; ships came and went, and still she remained without a cargo, with her harbour dues steadily mounting up. Yet her apprentices did not repine. They made many new friends and met many old shipmates, for one or two of them were *Conway* boys and Calcutta was a favourite port for Liverpool ships, which generally had *Conway* boys in their half-decks.

The residents of Calcutta, at that date, took a personal interest in the hundreds of apprentices who manned the magnificent sailing ships in the river. Not only did they help the Seamen's Mission, but they did their best to entertain the boys and keep them out of mischief. The people of Calcutta had not yet had time to forget how in the Mutiny they had been saved by the officers and crews of the sailing ships in the Hooghly. Yes, the apprentices undoubtedly enjoyed themselves. One of their never-failing amusements was to toss into the air two pieces of meat attached together by a piece of string and watch the tug of war between two Bromley kites, when the birds caught the meat in the air. The pigeons of the Fort, also, flocked round the *Cutty Sark*, but they were not so easily beguiled as the kites. The apprentices had two thorns in their flesh. In spite of smudges of smoke, of evil-smelling face greases and many other devices, the mosquitoes continued to feed handsomely; whilst the boatmen at the pier end spent their nights in Koran chanting—that monotonous droning sing-song, which one cannot help listening to however sleepy one may be.

On Christmas day all the ships were dressed in flags, bunches of evergreen at their mastheads and yardarms, whilst their half-decks were feasted right royally at the Seamen's Home. Then came the New Year, when most of the officers and apprentices attended the midnight church service ashore. At midnight a gun was fired from the fort, and immediately hundreds of ships along the waterfront began ringing their bells like a vast fog-bound fleet. This, with the peeling of the church bells and the firing of rockets, lasted for half-an-hour then a sudden silence reigned—the good ship "New Year" had reached Calcutta in her voyage round the world in chase of that once famous clipper, the "Old Year."

A few weeks later there was a total eclipse of the moon, which roused terror in the minds of the natives. They believed that an evil spirit was trying to get possession of that luminary, and they immediately began to do all in their power to stop it. From all over the city and the surrounding countryside there came a dismal moaning, like that of so many lost souls. Thousands of voices began to chant suitable passages from the Koran. Amongst the mooring tiers, the country ships vied with each other as to which crew could make the most din; whilst on the river bank solitary natives would suddenly spring to their feet, fire off ancient guns at the disappearing moon, and then squat down again to reload.

As the shadows steadily crept over the moon the panic grew; thousands gave way to despair, and the noise began to resemble the wailing of a lost world. By midnight the moon was completely obscured, and the moaning came in waves upon waves of misery, rising and falling like the breathing of the Universe itself.

Then, as the shadows thinned and the first clear beam of light broke out, the whole native population plucked up hope again and concentrated their efforts on a grand attack, in which guns were fired as fast as they could be loaded, tom-toms were beaten in a frenzy, and screams and uncouth battle cries rent the air. And as soon as this attack was seen to be taking effect, joyous shouts burst forth from thousands of parched throats.

The battle was not over until 4 a.m. There was little chance of sleep in the "Cutty's" half-deck that night, especially as she had a country ship alongside of her; and the night-watchman was the only one aboard who really appreciated the battle and the resulting victory. It was shortly after the eclipse that news arrived that the *Cutty Sark* had at last procured a cargo; and soon a gang of cargo wallahs could be seen stowing jute, castor-oil and tea, or smoking their hookahs and hubble-bubbles about the decks.

The tea turned out to be the first tea ever shipped from India to Australia. It consisted of the choicest Indian brands and the greatest care was taken over its stowage. Owing to her well-known reputation for speed, the *Cutty Sark* was also entrusted with the Australian mail, though if the postal authorities had known of Bruce's lack of nerve they would undoubtedly have preferred a slower vessel with a captain whose reputation for passage making had been proved.

With the arrival of the cargo the new mates made their appearance. For the remainder of this tragic voyage, the new first mate, as we shall see, played second villain to his captain, but the second mate was one of those quiet level-headed men who possess that hidden strength of character only shown when the urgency of the occasion demands it—he, indeed, beginning with a minor, colourless part, ended up as hero of the piece.

The rest of the new actors in the next act of the *Cutty Sark* drama were mostly shilling a month men, who had shipped for the run to Australia.

The chief villain, that double-faced Captain Bruce, had been very busy playing the part of Jekyll during the "Cutty's" long stay in Calcutta, and so successfully had he managed to deceive the good people of that famous city by his shipboard church services, his pious demeanour, and his voluble panegyrics on temperance and chastity that they presented him with a gold watch as a testimony of their esteem.

Cutty Sark's new mate was a rank atheist, who believed that there was no good in anything, yet, strange to say, we find him from the first the boon companion of his captain, whom he rivalled in every kind of villainy and debauchery, from robbing the ship to robbing her crew, from cruel hazing to attempted murder, and from steady soaking to delirium tremens.

On 5th March, 1881, the *Cutty Sark* cleared for Melbourne. She first of all dropped down to moorings at Garden Reach, where the tail end of a very severe but short-lived cyclone gave her cables a testing which would have amply satisfied Lloyd's. Departure was taken from the Sandheads on 9th March. The wind held S.S.W. moderate until 1° 34′ N., 90° 25′ E. The equator was crossed the following day with the wind coming in fierce squalls from the east. The passage as far as the roaring forties passed without incident, but as soon as the *Cutty Sark* began to reel off the knots under the influence of the brave westerlies, her captain's nerve gave out and he fell down with a bad attack of the funks. Twice he humiliated the gallant ship, in weather that she loved, by heaving her to under a goose-winged main topsail. The first time was on 6th May in 110° E. and the second time on 8th May. It is true that on the second occasion the glass fell very low and remained so for a day, yet there was no indication of bad weather from either sea or sky. It just happened that she had run into a large area of low atmosphere, which gradually readjusted itself without disturbance.

However, although a nice little fair wind was blowing, the nerve-racking Bruce kept the *Cutty Sark* hove to with a sail in the mizen rigging as long as the barometer remained low.

Shortly after this, the *Cutty Sark* showed herself very difficult to handle—she refused to lay to the wind just as if she had made up her mind that she had had enough of being hove to whilst favouring winds were blowing and meant to put a stop to such unusual bridling of her eagerness to throw the miles behind her.

The old man was now in a great fright. It was, however, very noticeable to a seaman that the vessel was very much down by the stern and investigation into the cause of this soon led to the discovery that the after watertight compartment was full of water.

What had happened was this:—There was a slight leak near the sternpost, so a hole had been bored in the watertight bulkhead to allow the water to get through to the well, where the main pumps could deal with it. This hole had somehow got plugged up, thus the water could not escape and the compartment gradually filled. As soon as this was remedied, the clipper lost her obstinate fit and her captain's cheeks regained their colour.

Directly the *Cutty Sark* arrived within a hundred miles of Cape Otway, fear of the land began to overwhelm Captain Bruce, just as it had done when the vessel was nearing the Sandheads.

The man was really to be pitied, he could not sleep. He was apparently afraid to trust his officers and he dared not leave the deck. For day after day and night after night he kept the unfortunate ship standing off and on; finally when a fair, strong west wind began to blow straight for Melbourne, the poor little ship was kept head-reaching under a lower main topsail between Cape Otway and the Tasmanian coast, whilst her old man tottered about the poop almost crazy with sheer funk.

During the time that the *Cutty Sark* was drifting in this sorry fashion, the *Cingalese*, a ship which had left Calcutta a week behind her, and which the *Cutty Sark* could have sailed rings round, came foaming by under reefed upper topsails; and we may imagine the humiliation aboard Willis's crack clipper when a cheer of derision reached her from the passing ship.

The *Cutty Sark* at last made enough leeway to take her within sight of the land, and a Melbourne pilot was picked up. No sooner was the responsibility off the captain's shoulders than everything was cracked on her, and the "Cutty" made such a grand showing of her powers as she sailed up the coast to Port Phillip Heads that the pilot showered compliments into the gratified ears of the undeserving Bruce. The anchor had no sooner been dropped at Queenscliff than a real gale came up and raised a nasty choppy sea, which at times threatened to put the *Cutty Sark* on the shore. However she rode it out safely, and as soon as it had moderated sailed up to Williamstown and anchored off the pier on 14th May.

We now come to an incident which shows up the mate's character. Knowing that most of the hands had shipped for the run, he determined to "work their old irons" for the last time; so, on the day that the *Cutty Sark* arrived off Williamstown, he gave out that the rigging was to be tarred down on the morrow. The men, however, considered that they had fulfilled their agreement with the letting go of the anchor, and took the mate's order as an imposition and a final attempt at hazing.

That night, after a lot of talk, the boldest of them broke into the paint locker and dumped the tar barrel overboard. But the mate was not going to be beaten: he managed, by boiling up the remnants from tarpots with salt water, to make about a couple of gallons of a dirty, muddy substitute, and with this in their pots he hustled the men aloft. This was far from being a wise proceeding. It was a clincher to their many grievances against the mate, and the men went up the ratlines in a very ugly mood. Presently, down came a pot from aloft, scattering the mate's filthy compound in its passage over the white lower masts and landing with a final splutter of its contents over the deck and bright work.

This was followed by another, and then another: others of the men aloft took their revenge by smearing the tar over every-thing and making an awful mess of the rigging. The wretched apprentices had a rare time of it later on scraping the stains off masts, decks and bright work, but the ship could not be cleaned up in time; on the following day the ill-used *Cutty Sark* was hauled along-side Sandridge Railway Pier in this dishevelled condition instead of her usual yacht-like trim.

On the first night alongside the wharf the third tragic death of the voyage occurred. In spite of the "sheoak net" under the gangway, a foremast hand managed to get into the water and was drowned. It was believed that he had staggered off the pier end after an over-indulgence in bad whisky. The body was washed ashore a week later: no friend or relative could be found, so the man's clothes and effects were sold in the usual way aboard the ship.

The *Cutty Sark* only remained long enough at Port Phillip to discharge her Melbourne cargo; but there was time enough for the apprentices to join in the usual skirmish between the sailors in port and the larrikins; and it was found that a stone tied up in a handkerchief was a handy weapon to put in one's pocket before going up town at night.

Melbourne was still full of excitement over the recent capture of the Kelly gang and the exposure of the *Star of India* swindle. With reference to the latter, one of the "Cutty's" apprentices gained distinction because he had seen the *Star of India* in Mauritius two years before. During the last year or so the whole world had been on the look-out for the stolen ship and her capture had been due to the wit of a Melbourne detective who, on boarding a strange steamer of about her known tonnage, noticed that the number on the main hatch had been tampered with. The police, at his summons, only just got on board in time, for the steamer was found to have steam up, ready to clear out at a moment's notice, and would have done so but for the fact that her captain, the chief conspirator, happened to be ashore.

The *Cutty Sark* lost an apprentice at Melbourne, for Staunton decided to leave the sea after his experience of two bucko mates and took a steamer passage home.

Sail was made from Port Phillip on 5th June, and with a nice fair wind splendid time was made to the Heads and out through the "Rip," but the *Cutty Sark* had hardly made her number off Judgment Rock before the wind headed her, and in tack and tack up the coast under such a skipper as Bruce it is not surprising that she took a week to Sydney Heads.

In Sydney the *Cutty Sark* found the flagship of her line, *The Tweed*, which under Gentleman White had made a 90-day run from the start and was loading for Hongkong.

A few days later *Thermopylae* arrived at Port Jackson, 86 days out from the Channel, and she was followed by the sister ships *Blackadder* and *Hallowe'en*.

These two had raced home from Foochow in 1880, their times being:—

Blackadder left Foochow 26th September arriving London 3rd February—130 days.

Hallowe'en left Foochow 1st October arrived London 4th February—126 days.

The three famous clippers all loaded coal for Shanghai with the prospect of a fine race up the Pacific, but with their knowledge of Captain Bruce and his lack of nerve, the *Cutty Sark's* crew had little spirit for it with but faint hopes of beating their rivals on this fine weather passage.

The bunks in the half-deck were once more filled up, one vacant bunk being taken by a young Sydney-sider, whose joy at going his first trip to sea in such a famous ship was soon to be effectually quenched; the other bunk was filled by a stranded apprentice, out of his time, who signed on as O.S.

Captain Bruce was also obliged to ship a number of hands in Sydney to fill up his complement and supply the places of the shilling a month men. This was a costly job, for A.B.'s wages out of Sydney were equal to those received by the second mate of the *Cutty Sark*. These expensive hands, indeed, were the cause of much of the trouble which was to fall upon the poor little ship.

Of the four clippers, *Cutty Sark* was the first away on 2nd July. She was hardly at sea before it was noticed that the old man and the mate, who had so far been at everlasting loggerheads, had made a truce and were giving vent to a peculiar and most suspicious chumminess. This alliance between such a pair of devils was at once recognised as ominous of coming trouble, and the old hands in the half-deck prepared to stand from under. The first result of this sinister entente was a drinking bout—both captain and mate being plainly drunk for all hands to see before the ship had gained an offing. The ranting hypocrisy had dropped from Bruce like a cast-off cloak, and he showed himself in the unmistakable colours of Hyde; it only needed this encouragement from the "old man" to set that limb of Satan, the mate, going to the utmost extremes, and the poor little *Cutty Sark* became a real Hell afloat.

Every method of working up the crew was resorted to by the conspirators. The afternoon watch below became a thing of the past. All hands spent the afternoon at sand and canvasing the wood work, cleaning off varnish by the most dreary, back-breaking, God-for-saken method, that was ever devised by man. The mate, also, soon showed himself a past master at finding unnecessary night work.

One wretched apprentice who fell into his bad books was kept aloft at every possible opportunity, doing up gaskets, overhauling buntlines, etc.; and the boy would no sooner reach the deck than he would be pounced upon by the mate and sent aloft again.

It is hard to beat a half-deck of sailing ship apprentices; and, determined to outwit the mate and save themselves from these worked up jobs, the apprentices held a council of war, where it was decided that whenever any of them were sent aloft, they would not come down until they had rectified anything that needed attention. Thus it came about that when the mate looked aloft in search of work in the night watches, he found a growing difficulty in discovering any—gaskets were always made up, buntlines and leach-lines were always well overhauled, Irish pennants were nowhere in sight, no stops were broken, no clinches adrift, all was as it should be—and it made him tired.

Whereupon he put a stop to shaking down on deck at night, and to catch an apprentice having a quiet doss in the shadow of the rail gave him a pleasure which soon palled, when he discovered that the young rascals were only pretending on purpose to fool him.

This hazing of the half-deck was of course only sheer spite and devilment; his hazing of the men forward had a deeper purpose —the ship had to be made so disagreeable for those expensive Sydney hands that even in such a bad place for stranded sailormen as Shanghai they would be ready to run as soon as the anchor was down. But the men knew well enough the reason for this shining up of old irons, and though they growled and small shindies were of constant occurrence, they stuck it out in a way which roused the mate to still further efforts.

It was a light weather passage as far as the Loochoo Islands, where a high cross sea was encountered—the aftermath of a typhoon whose wake the clipper crossed. As the *Cutty Sark* approached the Saddles, the "old man" was struck down by his customary "land fever", but after the usual delay a pilot was picked up and the *Cutty Sark* was brought to an anchor below Shanghai on 17th August.

The passages of the four ships were as follows:—

Ship	Cargo Tons of Coal	From	Date Left	To	Date arrived	Days out
Cutty Sark	1100	Sydney	July 2	Shanghai	Aug. 17	46
Thermopylae ..	1200	,,	,, 7	,,	,, 25	49
Hallowe'en	1100	,,	,, 27	,,	Sept. 9	44
Blackadder	1130	,,	,, 28	,,	,, 15	49

Cutty Sark negotiated Woosung bar successfully, but both *Thermopylae* and *Hallowe'en* stuck fast, and *Thermopylae* had to discharge 150 tons of coal before she could be got off.

The *Titania* was very nearly lost at Manila two days after the *Cutty Sark* had reached Shanghai. She arrived at Manila on

18th August from the Channel. On the following day a severe typhoon passed over Manila, doing immense damage to the shipping. *Titania* went ashore near the Maleron, where she luckily stranded on sand, and so she was able to be refloated again. Another typhoon blew over Shanghai on 27th August, and a great number of cargo boats were lost. A typhoon in Shanghai was fortunately a rarity, but it always meant great destruction and loss of life, along the river; as the flood tide overflowed its banks, houses and sampans were overwhelmed, and when the tide turned the wreckage drifted out to sea with numbers of helpless wretches clinging to it with no chance of rescue; and the ghoul-like river thieves made the tragedy still more horrible. During one typhoon, which passed over Shanghai the calm centre was crowded by myriads of birds, and a ship which passed through it reported that their terrified screaming was enough to unnerve the strongest.

This rare experience I also find recorded in the log of the East Indiaman *Buckinghamshire*, caught in a cyclone in 10° N., 75′ E. on 19th April, 1847. The entry in her log book is so interesting that I am tempted to transcribe it:—

Monday, 19th April, 1847. Ship *Buckinghamshire*. London to Bombay
April 19.—2 a.m. Course N.N.W. $\frac{1}{2}$ W. Wind S. by W. Strong gale, squally and lightning.

3 a.m. Wind south. Barometer 29.50. At daylight passed a vessel with loss of topmasts and mizenmast, showing a British Ensign inverted. She proved afterwards to be the *Mermaid*, Rogers, from Bombay. She ran on shore the next day 5 miles below Vingorla.

At 8 a.m. passed an Arab ship with loss of jibboom and foretop-gallant mast, on starboard tack.

10 a.m. Threatening weather and the barometer falling rapidly. Furled mizen topsail, main topsail blew away. At noon gale having augmented to an extraordinary degree, kept the ship before it. Barometer 28.35. The gale blowing furiously and veering to the eastward; cut the foresail from the yard and hauled it on deck: the foretopsail blew entirely away.

At 0.30 p.m. the ship was inclined to broach to, cut away the mizenmast and kept her before the wind: blowing a hurricane; the main topmast blew away; the hurricane increasing and the foremast bending to its force. About 1 p.m. the foremast fell over to starboard; a most furious gust blew away the mainmast near the deck; the quarterboats blew away, the starboard or large cutter flying across the poop; the poop ports having been blown in, the violence of the wind blew down the bulkheads, destroying everything in the cabin. The ship covered with spray and labouring excessively in a tremendous sea, the rapidity of her motion tearing everything on the different decks and in the hold adrift. Men unable to stand on their legs or hear one another shout.

2 p.m. The wind, which had been for the last half hour indescribably furious, suddenly ceased entirely. The barometer in the calm continued to stand at 28.08. The fore and mainmast, which had got under the bottom were now cut adrift.

The ship covered with aquatic birds, thousands of them dying on the deck.

About 4 p.m. the wind, which had ceased at E.S.E. or east, began to blow with equal fury from W.N.W. The ship was again enveloped with the sea and labouring with a violence nothing could resist; 3½ feet of water in the hold. 9 p.m. Wind abating and barometer rising to 28.96. Midnight, moderate wind at west. Barometer 29.1.

Daylight. Squally at west. Commenced rigging a jury foremast. Crew at the pumps.

9 a.m. Saw Vingorla Rocks bearing N.E. ½ E.

To return to Shanghai and the *Cutty Sark*: The cargo was discharged at American Town, and the necessary ballast having been taken in, the ship dropped down to her anchorage again. Yet there had been few desertions and it was now necessary for the mate to make a final effort to get rid of his expensive crew. What with the coal dust on top of oil, the hold was in a pretty state, and here was the mate's opportunity. All hands, from dawn to dusk, were kept at sand and canvasing the hold, whilst the mate washed the sand off with quantities of hose water: and after knock-off time, it was a case of pump ship for two to three hours every night in order to get all this water and slush out of her.

This routine had the effect of driving a few more men out of the ship, but the mate's chance was a short-lived one, for the work was most effectually put a stop to by that dreadful scourge Asiatic cholera.

The ship's last day alongside the wharf had been liberty day, and the infection had been picked up in some of the low dives ashore; thus the ship had not been many days at her anchorage

CAPTAIN E. MOORE

[See Page 194

CAPTAIN WOODGET

[See Page 211

CAPTAIN WOODGET'S COLLIES ON THE POOP OF THE "CUTTY SARK"

BREAK OF THE POOP, "CUTTY SARK"

[*See Page* 214

before man after man fell down with this terrible illness. The "old man" was comfortably housed ashore, and the senior apprentice was sent off, post haste, in a sampan to notify him and bring along a doctor. By the time he got back it was found that out of the whole ship's company only the two mates, the petty officers and two of the apprentices were free from infection, whilst two of the men were in a dying condition and succumbed shortly after reaching hospital.

Whilst all those affected were hurried off to the isolation hospital the yellow flag was run up to the foremast head and the *Cutty Sark* put in quarantine. The ship had at once to be fumigated. Sulphur was burnt in the hold, and all clothing and bedding had to be hung up in the smoke for two days. All communications with the shore was, of course, cut off, provisions being slung aboard from a sampan, which kept as far away from the ship as it could.

Three weeks later the *Cutty Sark* was allowed out of quarantine, and the sick men, with the exception of one apprentice, who was so ill that he had to be invalided home, came aboard looking more like skeletons than seamen.

Finally Captain Bruce, who had been playing the role of the respectable Dr. Jekyll ashore, came aboard with a clean bill of health and straightaway assumed his more natural character of Hyde. The men, who could scarcely crawl around the decks, were at once ordered to turn to cleaning up the hold with sand and canvas. They promptly refused to work.

The *Cutty Sark* was now lying below Woosung, all ready to go to sea.

The two schemers now congratulated themselves, for they considered that at last they had accomplished their object in getting rid of the expensive Sydney seamen, in that they could jail them for mutiny. Captain Bruce hurried back to Shanghai in a sampan, and in his best Jekyll manner put his case before the judge; but he soon found that he had gone too far and could not fool the Court. The judge held an investigation, took the evidence of the hospital doctor, and, after censuring the captain severely, ordered that no more than the necessary work was to be done for a fortnight and that special provisions were to be served out to the convalescents.

N

But a little more—the testimony of the men themselves—and Bruce would have been relieved of his command. He came back to his ship like a whipped cur. Before he left three of the men had been put in irons—to these he came begging and whining for mercy, wailing over his dependent family, blaming the mate, and promising all sorts of redress.

The sailor has ever been the most forgiving soul alive, and so the matter was dropped and taken no further. Before the outbreak of cholera, the *Cutty Sark* had received orders to cross the Pacific and load grain at Portland, Oregon—a new departure for a crack tea clipper, but one which was taken that year by the *Sir Lancelot* which went across to Portland, O., from Honolulu. But owing to the delay caused by the cholera, *Cutty Sark's* orders were cancelled and she was told to proceed to Zebu for a jute cargo.

Before we take leave of Shanghai, it might be of interest to note a few of the expenses incurred by a ship in those days.

EXPENSES OF A TEA CLIPPER IN SHANGHAI 1881.

Tonnage dues ½ a tael per ton.
Pilotage—5 tales per foot of draft.
Towage inwards—210 taels.
Water—50 cents per 100 gallons.
Discharging coal cargo—5 cents a ton.
Attendant Sampan—50 cents a day.
Loading a tea cargo—1 tael per 10 tons.

Fowls—2 dollars a dozen.
Ship's washing—3 dollars.
Consul's fees—$2.50.
Commission—1 per cent.
Brokerage—1 per cent.
Exchange—5/1⅛ per tael.

3 taels per 100 packages of tea.

The *Cutty Sark* was barely to sea before Sankey, her senior apprentice, went down with cholera; luckily the attack was a mild one, but the ship was off the Island of Luzon before he was able to crawl around again.

Bruce, with his usual lack of judgment, started to work south through the narrow waters, which lie between Luzon and Mindanao. The deep rock-bound straits with their strong currents and numerous reefs were swept by a southerly breeze, so that the *Cutty Sark* had a foul wind to contend against, and the narrowness of the channel necessitated tacking ship several times a watch.

Such ticklish work was too much for the weak nerves of Captain Bruce, and he grew so sick with fright that the mate, a villain, who at any rate did not lack courage, was obliged to take charge. But it was no use, the attempts to cut through had to be abandoned and a course was shaped round the southern end of Mindanao, which at least gave more sea room.

In coasting round Mindanao, the ship's company were treated to one of the finest sights in the world, a volcano in full eruption.

It was towards the end of October that the *Cutty Sark* at last dropped her anchor in Zebu roadstead, where she found four ships, including MacCunn's *Guinevere*, waiting to load. This meant that her turn would not come for close on six weeks.

The anchorage off Zebu is poor holding ground in a shallow bay, which is but slightly protected by an island lying offshore and is wide open to the south and east. A variable current sets in through the channel, which, however carefully a vessel is cast or tended, makes a foul hawse a certainty before long, and it was found that every few days the anchors had drawn together and had to be hove up and laid out again.

Beyond this trouble, the time passed pleasantly at Zebu. Captain Bruce had not recovered from his fright in Shanghai and was playing the part of Dr. Jekyll to the best of his ability: he allowed the men two hours off work at noon, and even attempted to start his religious services again. But here he was unsuccessful; neither the apprentices nor foremast hands, who by this time well knew his Hyde-like nature, would have anything to do with this hypocrisy. The trail of the shark had been too clear, albeit for the moment his fin was out of sight. No one was deceived though all were glad of the welcome respite, but it was recognised that the transforming mixture, whether it was gin, whisky or the local fire-water, was too handy to his elbow for Dr. Jekyll to last long.

Presently the cargo began to come alongside—a nice clean lot of baled jute. The native stevedores were a decent crew of men, intelligent, rather good looking with regular features and straight black hair—a good-tempered, hard-working crowd if properly handled. And they were properly handled, for the second mate was put in charge of the loading with the senior apprentice overlooking the gang in the hold and another apprentice tallying.

The second mate, indeed, handled the stowing gang with tact and kindness instead of the usual blasphemous hazing and brutality. An easy was allowed occasionally, whilst a plug of tobacco, cut up in small pieces and distributed amongst the Manila men, set them singing cheerily at their work. The result was a well-stowed cargo with very little space lost.

The apprentices who manned the captain's boat did not find much of interest ashore. Zebu is celebrated for two reasons—the great navigator, Magellan, met his death on the island of Matkan across the Strait, and a monument to his memory, erected by Queen Isabella II., was to be seen at Zebu. Secondly, the beautiful sponge, called "Venus' Flower Basket", and by the Spaniards "Regaderas," is only to be found in one spot in the whole world and that is off the island of Matkan.

The town of Zebu in 1881 was a straggling mass of tumble-down shanties and bamboo huts, with but few fine buildings. It was ruled with a rod of iron by the Spanish priests, whose orders were enforced by Spanish soldiery. Both priests and soldiers might well have been contemporaries of Pizarro. Religion consisted in magnificent processions and the scattering of dispensation papers, which were eagerly scrambled for by the superstitious natives.

The business of the place was, of course, in the hands of the hard-headed Scot, the shrewd Yankee, the smooth-faced German and the wily Chink. The exports were jute, hemp, sugar, coffee and tobacco. These were cultivated with some difficulty, owing to the scarcity of labour, as the natives were not enamoured of field work.

With few attractions ashore, the *Cutty Sark's* apprentices took to ship visiting by the simple method of swimming. This was not difficult as the ships were all anchored within a few cables' lengths of each other.

One Sunday two of the boys went over the side in order to swim to a ship 200 yards away, but the tide was making against them and they had the hardest swim of their lives. Finding that they could make no headway, they were compelled to turn inshore and work up inside the strength of the current, thus it took them $2\frac{1}{2}$ hours to reach their goal. But they were rewarded for their long swim by being asked to dinner by the friendly captain of the ship. The return journey was a very different matter. The boys dived off the stern of the ship they were visiting, and came up under the "Cutty's" bows.

The *Cutty Sark* was not to leave Zebu without an adventure of some sort; and presently it came along in the shape of the tail-end of a typhoon. All hands were called out one night by the watch-man to find a tremendous wind blowing and the ship snubbing her nose into a nasty choppy sea. The weather grew rapidly worse. The choppiness was succeeded by heavy rollers, which came hurtling in through the Straits in long foam-capped ridges, and fell upon the beach with a deafening roar. Then a Nova Scotia-man to windward began to drag, and dropped down upon the vessel which lay ahead of the "Cutty." This vessel slacked out her chain to get clear of the Bluenose and in a moment was down alongside the *Cutty Sark*.

It was now the latter's turn to veer away on her cables. Unfortunately, the day before, the compressors had been painted and screwed down on the cable with the result that as soon as the chain was slacked on the windlass there was a bad jam.

Here was a nice kettle of fish. The other ship was jumping about alongside, and that cable had to be cleared. Who would go in under the foc's'le-head and clear the chain? The crowd forward would have none of it and retreated aft. The bosun, also, hastily removed himself from the neighbourhood of the windlass: and it remained for the second mate and the two senior apprentices to take hold of the job. So in they went under the "Cutty's" anchor deck, armed with crowbars and a lantern. A little careful prising did the trick. Away went the cable, flying round the windlass like a fiery serpent with sparks shooting in every direction, whilst the second mate and apprentices flattened themselves against the ship's side and wished for day.

A stopper had been put on the cable, 60 fathoms from the windlass, and when this had run out the ship was brought up with a jerk, which must have torn the windlass from its bed if the two anchors had not dragged until they were in line.

The next morning the harbour was a sight. A huge surf was

breaking on the beach, in which all the native craft, which had dragged ashore in the night, were being pounded to pieces. The Nova Scotia-man had managed to bring up just outside a line of breakers, which were bursting on a coral reef—here he hung, literally within the jaws of death, at the end of 120 fathoms of chain. The other shipping, being more protected from the sea which swept in from the open, had come to no harm. There would have been no hope for any ship in that gigantic surf, and the *Cutty Sark* and her companions had every cause to be thankful for a narrow escape from destruction.

No sooner was the *Cutty Sark* loaded and ready for sea than orders arrived for her to go to New York instead of London. Whether this disappointment was the cause or not, at any rate the spirit of evil once more broke out aboard.

The mate and bosun, with the connivance of the "old man," brought a supply of native spirits on board and in less than no time had all hands forward fighting drunk. The plot was soon apparent. A quarrel was picked with one of the two remaining Sydney hands which soon led to blows and a lot of wild talk. Whereupon the captain ran up the signal for the police-boat, and after being well pounded by the butts of the policemen's rifles the unfortunate Australian was taken ashore and locked up.

The next day he was brought before the British vice-Consul, who, as is the way with our Consular service, was anything but a Britisher. The mate and the bosun appeared against the seaman, and stated that the man was a dangerous character who had already incited the men to mutiny in Shanghai, and that it would not be safe for the ship if he was allowed to resume his duty on board. No one else was allowed ashore to give evidence on behalf of the wretched man.

The Consul was either completely deceived by the glibness of the mate or else was a party to the miscarriage of justice, for the unfortunate man was sentenced to two month's imprisonment. A native was shipped in his place at the cheap rate of £1 a month, and the conspirators came on board chuckling over the success of their vile plot. But the crew were far from being deceived and the *Cutty Sark* went to sea with her crowd in a very sullen humour.

The ship had to make sail from her anchorage. The heaving up of two anchors and a big scope of chain was a long weary job. It was a case where a good chanty would have helped the labour and halved the time; yet not the slighest sound came from the *Cutty Sark's* crew. There is no greater sign of discontent and of trouble brewing than that of a deep water crew working in silence.

The "old man" naturally wanted the canvas on her quickly, but there was no hurrying the men—they took their time, and the apprentice who had been sent to the wheel had been over four hours at the helm before the last sail was set and he was relieved.

But a fair wind and pleasant sailing in summer seas very soon blunted the memory of past injustice and lulled all hands into a more contented frame of mind. It was the best time of year— December—the *Cutty Sark* having got her clearance papers on 6th December. The course was set past Bohol and the Sulu Islands for Gaspar Straits.

With a steady favourable wind, the *Cutty Sark* made a quick run to Anjer. Careful navigation was needed and a good look-out was a necessity, for the course lay through a sea of volcanic rocks and coral reefs, where the charts were unreliable, for the bottom owing to the numerous submarine earthquakes was always shifting. Indications of constant volcanic upheaval were given by the numerous patches of pumice stone, which were met with floating on the water. At other times colonies of large grey water snakes wriggled about all round the ship. Very often the bottom of clear white coral was plainly visible, and the sea changed in colour from the deepest blue to a chalky emerald green, as the soundings varied from those of the Sulu Deep to those of reefs, which at low water showed their foam-ringed heads above the surface.

The Gaspar Straits were threaded, and once more the *Cutty Sark* found herself in the Java Sea with all its fateful associations. the Cap and Button Rocks were passed, old Thwarttheway was left behind, and then—just when all hands were expecting the *Cutty Sark* to carry the fair wind until she struck the S.E. trades, the course was altered and on 3rd January the hook was dropped in Anjer Roads. As there was no need to call for orders, this halt in the Straits of tragic memory cast a spell of uneasiness over the vessel and the old hands could not but feel that the evil spirit which had been following "nine fathom deep," had come to the surface again.   Nor were their fears wide of the mark.   Dr. Jekyll went ashore, but the sinister Hyde returned aboard with a boat-load of "sham-shaw," the local tangle-foot.   Once more the devil stalked the decks of the unfortunate *Cutty Sark*.

The "old man," mate and steward were speedily drunk.   It was now late in the day; wind and tide had turned to the eastward, nevertheless the befuddled captain ordered the ship to be got under-weigh.   The anchor was hove up and the sails set, then with her yards on the backstays the *Cutty Sark* was headed out of the anchorage.   The wind was light and failing, and on the very first board the current set her so much to leeward that it was easy to see that there was no hope of making any progress till the tide turned.   Nevertheless she was put about every hour until dark, whilst the current steadily drifted her back into the waters which she had lately come through, and every tack in the failing wind and strong tide stood her into greater danger.

The mate, who, although drunk, was sufficiently clearheaded to see the senseless folly of his superior, after a furious row retired to his cabin to sulk and finish his share of the sham-shaw.   But the besotted Bruce strutted the deck with all the confidence and pigheadedness of a drunkard.

At last, when it was almost dark, the *Cutty Sark*, through her captain's faulty handling, missed stays and the next moment was rushed stern first past the Cap Rock in the grip of the current.

This narrow escape of a smash up brought matters to a head, The crew went to the second mate and demanded that he should take charge.   After a hurried consultation with the two senior apprentices, it was decided to resort to craft, for to take forcible charge of a vessel from her captain needs to be justified before the authorities, or it is nothing less than mutiny.   They decided that the only way to save the ship was to render the captain so incapable that he would not know what was going on.

Thereupon the second mate got hold of a bottle of the fatal grog and plied his fuddled captain with it until he was senseless.

We can imagine the scene. The *Cutty Sark* stealing along like the witch that she was into the darkness, which was full of hidden dangers of reef and rock. The false carousal on the poop, where the second mate, with a strained smile which was meant to be a convivial grin, kept replenishing the trembling tumbler of his sodden captain, whose meaningless babble grew less and less as his senses left him.

The third mate, at the break of the poop, straining his eyes into the short tropic twilight, watching out for the ship, but with his ears intent on what was going on behind him. The anxious faces of the crew, as they watched the effect of the stratagem from the main deck and muttered their comments in low tones. The white face of the helmsman as he peered round the corner of the monkey poop in order to get a view of the drugging, then the sudden creak of the rudder chains as he spun the wheel to keep the "Cutty" out of the wind. And there were other sounds, significant of the crisis—the stertorous snores of the mate, sleeping the sleep of drunkenness in his cabin at the fore-end of the poop—the hullaballoo of the crazy steward as he ran amuck amongst his cups and saucers —then a sudden slating aloft as the fitful breeze dropped and as quickly came again.

The drama was played successfully to a finish: and as soon as the second mate had worked his will upon his incapable commander, a rush was made for the chart. An anchorage, some 20 miles back opposite Cape St. Nicholas, was speedily found, the yards swung, and the *Cutty Sark* headed for it. Next the cabin was ransacked for grog, and every bottle found was hurled overboard by the second and third mates, in their determination to save the ship from another catastrophe.

Then the crazy steward had to be dealt with. He was bundled into his room and the key turned upon him. Finally, with a sigh of relief from all hands, the anchor was dropped, the sails furled and an anchor watch set, whilst everyone else turned in.

For two days the *Cutty Sark* lay at anchor opposite Cape St. Nicholas, and during all that time not a hand's turn was done on board.

On the second day the captain wandered up on deck and gaped to find the *Cutty Sark* lying quietly at anchor off the Sumatra Coast, but he dared ask no questions. The mate, who still had some of the fatal fire water stowed away in his berth, refused to leave his cabin, pretending that he kept to it on account of his row with his partner in villainy.

The date was 5th January. A nice fair wind was blowing, at sight of which Bruce plucked up courage and ordered the ship to be got underweigh.

The anchor was hardly off the ground and the *Cutty Sark* beginning to move through the water with about half her sails set, when the *Blackadder* came flying past under a cloud of canvas bound for New York with Shanghai tea.

The *Blackadder* had managed to load a cargo at 45s. She had left Shanghai on 18th December, and was about the last of that season's ships.*

The *Blackadder* must have wondered what on earth the crack ship of her line was doing under short canvas when a nice leading breeze was blowing through the Straits.

Bruce followed Captain Moore, keeping in the wake of the *Blackadder* until Java Head was astern, when the two ships parted company.

The *Cutty Sark* was hardly clear of the land before a new grievance set the whole ship's company in the dumps—the supply of sugar gave out.

It was no use growling, because there was no more sugar on board: but to be out of sugar when less than a month out from a sugar port prepared the crew for more trouble. It was now the half-decks' turn to run foul of the "old man." When the *Cutty*

---

* Of the others, *Thermopylae* left Foochow on 30th October, was off Cape Recife on 21st December and reached London on 15th February—107 days out. She had the honour of beating *The Tweed*, which, leaving Hongkong on 29th October, did not arrive in the Thames until 2nd March, 124 days out. *Leander* also loaded at Foochow. She had been nearly lost on 16th November 1880. She ran ashore near Port Phillip Heads and scraped off 15 feet of her false keel and several sheets of copper before she was refloated. She left Foochow on 5th November, 1881, and reached London on 17th February—104 days out.

Hallowe'en left Shanghai on 27th November, passed Anjer on 18th December, and anchored at Gravesend on 11th March, 103 days out, whilst *Titania*, after her stranding in the typhoon, was repaired and loaded at Manila, which she left on 19th November, arriving at Gravesend on, 5th March, 106 days out. The rest of the clippers were widely scattered. *Taitsing* followed *Sir Lancelot* to Portland, Oregon; *Whiteadder* came home from Calcutta; *Kaisow* loaded at Iloilo whilst *Lothair* made her usual run from Japan to New York.

Sark had anchored off Anjer, the apprentices had driven the usual trade with the bumboats alongside and by parting with various items of clothing had managed to lay in a large stock of bananas. The boys, from sheer kindness of heart, had made a practice of shoving a few bananas through the mate's port-hole, as they passed on their way to the wheel. These the mate, who still sulked in his cabin, was only too glad to eat, but the vicious little rat of a steward, who like all sailing-ship stewards was always at war with the half-deck, was only too glad to report the presence of banana skins in the mate's cabin and explain to the captain how they got there.

The latter at once assumed his most pompous manner and gave the apprentices a severe rating for the heinous crime of aiding and abetting the mate in his insubordination.

The half-deck with the diplomacy earned by hard experience took their rating meekly but with the usual tongue in the cheek. Though to all appearances the most penitent sinners in the captain's presence, they laughingly mimicked his effort at righteous indignation as soon as they reached their own quarters. Their only regret came when the bananas were finished.

The *Cutty Sark* had barely taken the S.E. trades before another cut was made in the rations—all hands being put on half allowance of lime juice; and a rumour crept round the ship that provisions were short all round, though the steward, who knew that such was the case, did his best to deny it, under orders from the "old man."

In the fine weather of the S.E. trades, and with all the transforming mixture over the side, it was the turn for Dr. Jekyll to appear upon the scene again. The captain and mate patched up their row, and with a sudden change of front showed themselves very friendly with the two senior apprentices. Bruce, whose one accomplishment was navigation, set to work to instruct the boys in the higher paths of that science. Lunars became the rage; stars were taken every night; and the talk swung from double altitudes to lines of bearing.

There was, of course, a reason for all this "sucking up," as the boys called it. Both Bruce and his mate were anxious to find out what had really happened in Sunda Straits.

But the two lads, being thoroughly skilled in sea diplomacy, were not to be drawn and they kept their lips tight shut. It was in vain that hints were dropped. Neither the captain nor the mate succeeded in finding out how the *Cutty Sark* came to be anchored opposite Cape St. Nicholas when she should have been to the westward of Krakatoa.

The two culprits were doubtless very uneasy. They knew that they had hopelessly overstepped the mark again, and that, if the facts came out, their reign on the *Cutty Sark* would be over for good and all. Whether they were rendered desperate and the tragedy which was next to happen on the *Cutty Sark* was intentional or accidental can never be known.

At 7.30 a.m. one morning the *Cutty Sark* was bowling along with a 12-knot breeze on the quarter. The weather clew of the mainsail was hauled up in order to allow the foresail to draw better and steady the steering, and the third mate and one of the hands were at work in the main rigging. Suddenly without any warning the heavy clew spectacle with its tack and sheet blocks came down with a run and fell full upon the two at work in the rigging—the mate had let go the clew-garnet! The third mate, who had his arm round one of the shrouds, managed to hang on, but the seaman was knocked backwards and overboard.

In a moment the cry of "man overboard!" rang through the ship, and the watch below, who were at breakfast, came tumbling out on deck. The helmsman, without orders, put the helm down and threw the life-buoys over the stern.

Luckily for the ship, the third mate kept his presence of mind, and jumping out of the rigging let go the weather forebraces. As it was, when the sails came aback on the main, the main topgallant stay went and the main topgallant mast was badly sprung.

It was a ticklish business lowering a boat and getting it safely away from the ship's side. However, the boat went clear, and pulled about for an hour or so in charge of the bosun without seeing a sign of the man or even the two lifebuoys.

This seaman was the last of the expensive Sydney hands!!

The mate did his best to explain the accident, but he could not escape condemnation, and foul play was the verdict of both foc's'le and half-deck; whilst Sankey, who had so nearly been the second victim of the mate's so-called carelessness, never trusted his superior officer again and kept a sharp eye open for the next accident. He argued that he knew too much and that it would be a great relief to the two rascals if by some means or other he could also be sent " on the line" cruise.

The *Cutty Sark* was favoured by the weather, and if Bruce had dared to let the gallant vessel have her head she would have made a fine run to New York from Anjer, but even in the steady trades he would not give her a chance. The coast of Africa was made about East London and the land kept close aboard until Table Mountain was on the quarter, then the yards were squared and stunsail booms rigged out for the run down to St. Helena.

With the voyage nearing its end, the policy of conciliation was again promoted aft and all past troubles smoothed over as much as possible. But this did not last for long, owing to the captain's false economy which prevented him from the necessary reprovisioning at Zebu and kept him from buying fresh provisions at Anjer or Capetown; indeed, though he knew how low the stock was, he made no attempt to call in at St. Helena, which was sighted and passed on 27th February. On the very next day all hands were put on half allowance. Once more Bruce had been guilty of a big blunder in tactics. He had badly overrated the docility and long-suffering of his crew. It was now time to clean and paint the ship for port, but the crew at once refused to do a hand's turn more than was absolutely necessary in managing the ship.

At this the evil spirit came aboard again. The mate started working up jobs and tried to keep his watch for ever on the run, whilst the captain began to interfere with the second mate and abuse him before the men. Though Bruce had failed to get the apprentices to talk he had managed to gain some idea of what had happened in Sunda Straits by incessant questioning of the man at the wheel. He saw clearly that the second mate had him in his power and clumsily took the very course to bring things to a head.

For some time the second mate said nothing and bore his captain's interference and continual slanging with stoical indifference, then, one day, he suddenly rounded on him and said quietly but decidedly that if Captain Bruce was not satisfied he could take over the watch.

The fat little hypocrite blustered and swore, but the second mate was unmoved—either he was going to run his watch or the captain could and he would retire to his cabin. This called the "old man's" hand, as usual his nerve failed him at the crisis, and henceforth he left the second mate alone and made no further attempt at interference in the ship's work.

As the *Cutty Sark* approached the equator, the shortage of provisions grew more and more serious, until at last there was nothing left but some weevily bread and some tainted pork. The beef was all gone, the groceries were down to vanishing point and there was very little lime-juice. Luckily for the half-starved crew, the *Cutty Sark* was in a part of the ocean where ships are usually numerous. The first ship was encountered on the line in 20° W. She was a German, and some very fat smoked pork was obtained from her. What her crew could have thought, as the clipper filled her mainsail and went streaking away from her, history does not relate, neither what tale was told by Captain Bruce to account for his being out of provisions when bound north, only a week's sail from St. Helena and but three days from Ascension with its turtles. A few days later some cornmeal biscuits were cadged from a Frenchman. These were as hard as stone and when soaked in water became something like glue, but so fine drawn had the "Cutty's" crew become that any kind of food was acceptable.

Whilst the ship was in the doldrums, Bruce ordered the full allowance to be served out again in the hopes that the men would get on with the work of painting the ship for port. But it was no use. In vain the mate kept both watches on deck in the afternoon, the men had made up their minds to do as little as possible and they simply laughed at any attempt at playing the bucko, whilst the lack of food had so taken the life out of the half-deck and the boys were so down in the blues that they did not care what happened.

It soon became necessary to reduce the rations again, and in the N.E. trades they were cut down first to half allowance and then to a quarter of the full allowance. The men were now rendered desperate for want of food. They even came to the second mate and tried to persuade him to take charge again and put into the

Bermudas, but he put them off as best he could. Nevertheless the "old man" got wind of this attempt, and pretending that the second mate was trying to start a mutiny, he called the third mate and apprentices into the cabin one by one and ordered them to reveal all they knew under pain of being put in irons. But they, one and all, refused to say a word and dared him to put them in irons. His bluff had failed and he knew it. The man was now half crazy as he saw his day of reckoning approaching. How much longer the men would have kept quiet if H.M.S. *Thalia* had not hove in sight it is hard to say. The man-of-war was sighted running before the wind under a press of sail, being bound for the West Indies, and she was almost abeam before she distinguished the urgent signal:—"Short of provisions," flying from the "Cutty's" peak.

Then, indeed, she acted as if she was racing against time in a sail evolution. Rounding to close under the *Cutty Sark's* lee, she clewed up, hauled down and furled as she put her helm down, the calls of the bosun's pipes being plainly audible on the clipper as she lay bobbing to the seas with her mainyard aback.

Captain Bruce went himself in the boat in order to explain the situation to the Captain of the *Thalia*, but what excuses he could find for being out of provisions in a clipper ship of *Cutty Sark's* notoriety it is hard to imagine. Yet he was so anxious that only his version of the cause should be heard on board the man-of-war that he took the unusual step for a shipmaster of leaving his vessel in mid-ocean.

Whilst Bruce was aboard the *Thalia*, an animated flag talk was carried on between the two ships, and the "Cutty's" apprentices were very proud when they found they could keep pace with the trained signallers of the warship. They even obtained a dropped flag rate for their chronometers.

Presently a boat came alongside from the *Thalia*, which proved to be piled up with provisions, which had been specially cooked. These gave a pretty clear indication of the pitiful tale which Captain Bruce must have spread aboard the man-of-war. There was also a fine present of tobacco in the boat.

Then the two ships swung their mainyards and filled away on their respective courses, the *Cutty Sark's* cheer of gratitude to the open-handed man-of-war receiving three ringing British cheers in reply.   And now with their port close aboard and their hunger allayed, the crew of the *Cutty Sark* regained their good temper and once more peace reigned aboard.   For the first time for many weeks songs were heard in the second dog watch, whilst the captain and mate, both on their best behaviour, yarned good humouredly with the second and third mates, whom but a short while before they would have been glad to have seen over the side.

With the American coast close over the bow, Bruce had a final attack of land fever and kept the *Cutty Sark* hanging about offshore for a couple of days in cold foggy weather.

This raw Western Ocean climate chilled the ship's company to the bone after their long spell of the tropics.   The Manila man, especially shrivelled up in his light clothing.   This man had turned out a capable seaman and a first rate worker and was popular with all hands so that he did not have to go cold for long, for with the usual generosity of sailors, clothes were thrown at him and he was soon able to wrap himself up like a mummy, the half-deck even presenting him with a complete suit of cricketing flannels.

In due course a pilot was picked up and a tugboat engaged. The *Cutty Sark* was barely inside the Narrows before a howling snow squall came down upon her, and for two days she lay at anchor in a gale which coated her rigging with ice; finally she was berthed almost under the span of the Brooklyn Bridge on 10th April, 125 days from Zebu, and this Hell-ship voyage was over.

Its numerous tragic events would probably never have come to light if Captain Bruce, with his usual bad judgment, had not been foolish enough to refuse the second mate his discharge.   Whereupon that long suffering second officer at once laid a complaint before the Consul and demanded an investigation, which ended in the captain and mate having their certificates suspended whilst the second mate and crew were discharged, the apprentices sent home, and an allowance of money, reckoned at one-fourth of a day's food allowance from the date the *Cutty Sark* had left Anjer, was paid to all hands.

Such was the ending of what was undoubtedly the most disastrous and adventurous voyage of the *Cutty Sark's* career.

J. SELBY, MATE OF THE "CUTTY SARK"

[*See Page* 234

SMITH, A.B. AT THE WHEEL OF THE "CUTTY SARK"

THE WHEEL OF THE "CUTTY SARK," 1922

CHAPTER VI.

UNDER CAPTAIN MOORE.

OLD Jock Willis must have used some very strong language, when for the second time in one voyage he received a cable stating that the *Cutty Sark* was without either master or chief officer. The urgency of the case was increased by the fact that the clipper was already taking in a cargo of case oil for the East and would be ready to sail in a very short time. John Willis solved his difficulty by transferring the *Blackadder's* complement bodily across to the *Cutty Sark*. This consisted of Captain F. Moore, his chief officer, six apprentices, cook, steward and an A.B. named Drew. Captain Moore had made the run from Shanghai *via* Amoy to New York in 105 days, arriving on 2nd April, thus beating Bruce from the Straits of Sunda by eight days. In this turn over the *Blackadder* was sacrificed to the *Cutty Sark*, and she did not get away from New York until 16th May having loaded for Sydney.

Captain F. Moore was no relation of Willis's superintendent, and had not been very long in Willis's employ; in fact, beyond taking the *Coldstream* from Newport round to London the *Blackadder* was his first command in Willis's fleet. But his record with this ill-starred vessel in the round voyage, London, Melbourne, Sydney. Shanghai and Amoy to New York, had been so free from unwelcome incidents that he had quite gained the confidence of old Jock. His previous record, also, proved his worth and capacity.

After serving his time (five years) in the Tyne coal trade with London and the Baltic, he had worked up from mate to master in colliers sailing to the Mediterranean from South Shields, then after a few years as a chief officer in steam he left the steamer *Leda* in 1873 to take command of the little 433-ton barque, *Teviot*, in the Mauritius and Eastern trade. His next command was Lidgett's *Dilharee*, a composite ship of 1293 tons, which eventually came to grief in the Columbia River. And it was from the *Dilharee* that he went to the *Blackadder* in the spring of 1881.

Captain Moore was the very opposite of Captain Bruce, both in character and appearance. Tall, bearded and dignified, with a quiet reserved manner and a very deep bass voice, Moore was not only a fine looking man but a fine seaman, a capable shipmaster and a clever navigator.

It has been contended that he was not a driver such as the *Cutty Sark* required; but this is not altogether fair to Moore, for when he took over the ill-used clipper he found her quite denuded of bosun's stores, whilst her rigging and gear were in a very bad and neglected state, which Willis, smarting under the loss incurred by Bruce's mismanagement, refused to put right, so that practically for the whole time that Moore had the "Cutty" he dared not carry sail owing to the rotten gear. Nevertheless his two voyages to Newcastle were exceedingly good; and if his first voyage in the *Cutty Sark* showed nothing in the way of fast passages, we must remember that besides having a very heavy outward cargo Moore had no need to hurry, and was also compelled to rest content with the clipper's natural speed, whilst he took every opportunity to put things right after the neglect of Bruce and his evil satellite.

I have the official log of the *Cutty Sark's* 1882-3 voyage, and it is as free from incident as her previous voyage was full of incident. The clipper loaded 26,816 cases of oil on a draft of 21 feet. On 1st May at 4 p.m. the *Blackadder* contingent, headed by Mr. Sybret, the mate, came aboard. It may be of interest to say a few words about some of her apprentices, for ever since she had been cut down and her complement reduced from over 30 to 23 all told, her apprentices formed the backbone of her crew. The *Cutty Sark* was a very easy working ship, yet if it had not been for her regular half dozen or more of sturdy boys she would never have been able to make those records, which gave her fame in the wool trade.

The apprentices transferred from the *Blackadder* were Fred Royatt, Gordon, Paramor, Jacques, Jackson and Sykes. Of these Jacques, who afterwards became third and then second mate, was probably the leading spirit. He not only knew his work but always jumped to the fore in times of emergency, being a natural commander of men. He joined the Eastern Telegraph Company from the *Cutty Sark*, and died on the West Coast of Africa when chief of the *John Pender*.

Jackson was a son of the well-known manager of the London and Shanghai Bank. He was noted for his curly hair and the great care he took of his appearance, being the most immaculate of brass-bounders whenever he went ashore. Like Jacques, he was a fine seaman. He joined the P. & O. afterwards, and was chief officer of the *Nubia* in 1903, but died shortly after in Australia. Sykes was the son of a clergyman, a most lovable boy, always bright and willing, and a great favourite with all hands. He also joined the P. &. O. from the "Cutty," but died in Bombay of enteric about 1891.

The other three are so far as I know still alive and flourishing.

The crew, making 9 A.B.'s with Drew, came aboard at 5 p.m. on 2nd May, and the *Cutty Sark* was unmoored and towed to an anchorage off the Battery.

On 3rd May the carpenter joined and the hatches were battened down. Captain Moore and the pilot came aboard at 4 p.m. on 4th May, and the ship was at once towed away to sea by the *F. W. Kendy*.

At 8 p.m. the tug was cast off and sail made to a nice S.W. breeze. At 10 p.m. Sandy Hook Lightship bore N. by W. $\frac{1}{2}$ W. and the sea watch was set. Twenty-four hours later found the *Cutty Sark* filling her decks in a fresh S.W. gale, and by noon on the 6th she had run 641 miles from her departure. The sea had, however, taken toll of her decks in the stormy weather. Two panels of the starboard topgallant rail had been burst in, the starboard boat was stove and the bow of the gig smashed, the harness cask was washed out of its lashings and overboard, and finally the mainmast coat burst, a quantity of water getting below by this means. The breeze worked round to the N.E. and continued strong until the 10th, when the *Cutty Sark* was in 29° 42' N., 47° 39' W. From this date pleasant trade weather was encountered until the 24th, when she ran into the doldrums in 6° N. Instead of keeping on the port tack for Cape San Roque, in accordance with Maury's advice, Moore wasted some time in trying to get to the eastward, and the *Cutty Sark* did not cross the equator until the 1st June.

With the most weatherly ship ever launched, Moore had nothing to fear from being back-strapped under Cape San Roque, though from 2° 25′ N. to 12° S. he had about 100 miles of westerly current.

As a contrast to his passage, in 1853 at the same time of the year the lucky *Flying Cloud* had fresh squally easterly winds from 20° N. to the line, which distance was covered in five days. Knowing he had a fast weatherly ship, Captain Creary boldly kept on the port tack all the way and his boldness paid.

As an example of a slow passage at this time of year, the *Francis F. Jenness* in 1852 took 70 days to the equator from Philadelphia, being no less than 33 days between 10° N. and the line.

Whilst the *Cutty Sark* is crossing the S.E. trades, which were picked up on 2nd June, let us see what her rivals were doing.

Thermopylae, under Henderson, left the Lizards on 21st March. crossed the line on 7th April, 16½ days out, and arrived in Port Jackson on 2nd June, 73 days out.

Titania passed Dover on 2nd May, and arrived Brisbane on 30th July, 89 days out.

Leander left London on 18th April, passed Anjer 12th July and arrived Shanghai 15th August, 119 days out.

Hallowe'en passed Prawle Point on 30th May, and arrived Sydney, 31st August, 93 days out.

Lothair made the fine passage of 95 days from the Downs to Hongkong under Tom Boulton, arriving Hongkong on 15th September.

Sir Lancelot under Shortland left Astoria on 3rd April, arrived in the Downs on 21st August for Hull; left Shields on 4th October, Beachy Head 6th October, and arrived Anjer on 27th December. From there she went to Calcutta, and leaving the Hooghly on 20th April, 1883, under a new captain, McDonald, arrived at Rouen on 2nd September, 1883. From Rouen she went to the Clyde and loaded for Mauritius; she left the Clyde on 23rd December, and was not seen again in an English port having become a country trader between Calcutta, Bombay and Mauritius.

The *Cutty Sark* crossed the meridian of Greenwich on 28th June, and was not very far away from *The Tweed* when Willis's flagship was dismasted.

The Tweed had left the Channel on 26th April, under Gentleman White, so named because he never appeared on deck except in a reefer suit with stiff white shirt and collar, and never went ashore without his tall hat.

Her chief officer was a man named Norrie, a splendid seaman who rather aped the bucko. Her second mate was a better musician than a sailor, but otherwise she had a splendid crew including 11 apprentices, some of whom were afterwards on the *Cutty Sark*, and 40 men before the mast, 20 of whom were working their way out to Australia at 1s. per month. Her leading seaman was Tony Robson that wonderful Chinese sailorman, who was afterwards cook in the *Cutty Sark* for many years. Her petty officers were experts, such as could not be found in these days.

The Tweed was on the meridian of the Cape, bowling along on the port tack under every stitch she could carry, when between 10 and 11, it being the second mate's watch, the wind shifted in a squall and caught the officer of the watch napping.

"All aback forward!" yelled the look-out, then immediately after—"Foremast gone by the board." *The Tweed* went over on her starboard beam ends, and in the blackness of the night the noise of the spars breaking, the sails flogging and the wind shrieking raised a pandemonium which sent all hands rushing on deck. The fore topmast carried away just above the cap of the lower mast, and took with it the foreyard, jibboom, main topgallant mast and upper and lower main topsail yards but left the mizen undamaged.

An attempt was at first made to save the spars, and the cat-fall rigged to the foremast head for that purpose, but in the end everything had to be cut away to avoid the ship being damaged by the spars bumping about alongside.

As soon as it was daylight, the ship was got before the wind, and under her mainsail alone she made the phenomenal run of 240 miles to noon the next day, whilst her crew were busy jury-rigging her.

A spare fore topmast was soon aloft, and spare spars were swayed up for a foreyard and topsail yards, whilst the main topsail yards were fished. Under this jury rig the gallant old ship covered 2000 miles in a week, and reached Sydney on 28th July, only 93 days out.

Here the wrathful White sacked his second mate; but that incompetent sailor, who could play almost any musical instrument, became the leader of the best orchestra in Sydney within a week, with probably three or four times the pay he had been receiving as second mate of *The Tweed.*

The Tweed was very nearly dismasted again on her passage home from Calcutta this voyage. Off the Western Islands she was running before a hard westerly blow of almost hurricane force, doing 16 knots by the patent log under a goose-winged lower main topsail, when she took a sea over the port quarter, which smashed the quarter boat on the skids, and gutted all the cabins on that side of the poop, taking their whole contents overboard with the exception of the mate's monkey, which clung like grim death to a stanchion.

This scared old White, and he resolved to heave to. As he watched for a smooth before putting the helm down, the rare order was heard "Stand by for your lives!" The ship was brought to the wind successfully; but she was no sooner hove to than it was discovered that the rigging had stretched very badly, and the back-stays had to be frapped together as quickly as possible in order to save the masts, as the slack of the lanyards could not be taken up until the weather moderated.

The very same thing happened to the *Cutty Sark* during her passage to Anjer, her rigging also got slack during a blow and had to be frapped across. Though Moore snugged her down directly she was doing 12 knots, if not before, her log is full of split sails and other casualties aloft. Her lanyards were found to be in a very bad state and all had to be renewed; as to the condition of her sails the following extracts tell the tale:—

May 20—Starboard side of main topgallant sail ripped up for several cloths.

     25—Clewed up lower mizen topsail to repair the leeches.

     27—Shifted mizen royal for repairs.

     31—Shifted fore topgallant sail for repairs.

      6—Port head earing of mainsail carried away.

June 4—Split fore royal.

     11—Parrel of main topgallant sail carried away.

     18—Lower topsails, fore and mizen upper topsails, and main topmast staysail blown to pieces, main topgallant sail split, crossjack all to pieces, starboard side of both fore sail and mainsail all split, inner and flying jibs ripped up the leech.

19—Split mizen staysail, bent on main topmast stay to keep the ship steady.

23—Hauled the mainsail up to reef, during which time it split from head to foot. Starboard fore topsail sheet carried away and topsail split from head to foot.

By this time half the watch were kept hard at it repairing sails; whilst for a week the *Cutty Sark* had to be content with a lower fore topsail bent on the mainyard in lieu of a mainsail.

Whilst the *Cutty Sark* was in the roaring forties, the toll of sails continued; on 9th July during an N.E. gale the lower fore topsail burst its bolt rope and the portside went to pieces, whilst the fore topmast staysail was blown clean out of the hanks. A few days later the foresail ripped up the middle, and so the ripping of her worn-out canvas continued.

It is therefore not surprising to find that she had a longish run to Anjer, and made no day's work of 300 miles.

The anchor was dropped off Anjer on 2nd August. At 5 p.m. on the 3rd orders came off for the ship to proceed to Samarang. She was immediately got underweigh, and after a weary beat to windward in light airs against a strong current along the north coast of Java, arrived off Samarang on 20th August.

Here the cargo was unloaded by coolies, whilst those of the crew, who were not laid up by fever, spent the time in cleaning and painting ship.

At last on 5th October with 295 tons of stiffening on board, the *Cutty Sark* set sail in ballast for Madras. By this time half her crew were down with fever and they did not recover until the ship was well out into the Indian Ocean.

Anjer was passed on 13th October, and as the "Cutty" slipped past Krakatoa Island that afternoon, her crew little thought that within less than a year it was to be torn asunder by the famous eruption of its volcano, which had been so long asleep.

The British ship *Charles Bal* was actually within sight of Krakatoa when the explosion split the island in twain.

Captain Watson's description of his experience is worth recording. At 7 p.m. on 22nd August in 15° 30′ S., 10° 5′ E., the *Charles*

Bal suddenly ran into a milk-white sea, which coming from ahead gradually extended until it touched the horizon all round. The sky, also, gave forth a silvery glare, somewhat like an Aurora display, the cumulus clouds, which showed here and there, being edged with a pinky light.

These phenomena continued to recur until the 25th when the *Charles Bal* made Java Head; the land was seen to be covered with thick dark clouds, pierced continually and in every direction by forked lightning.

Princes Island was passed at 9 a.m. on the 26th, and by noon a small portion, along the water's edge, of the N.E. corner of Krakatoa could be made out, the rest of the island being covered by a dense, black cloud.

The wind was S.W. with fine weather. By 2.30 the eruption was noticed to be growing steadily in violence; masses of black cloud being whirled to the N.E. at amazing speed, whilst the noise resembled heavy artillery fire at a second's interval one moment and the next a crackling and hissing as if of a mighty and furious fire.

At 4.15 p.m. the *Charles Bal* was only 10 miles south of the volcano, which was belching out what looked like blinding rain in a tornada-like squall of wind, and the glare was like that from countless millions of red hot ashes. The wind was moderate at W.S.W., and Captain Watson now shortened sail to lower topsail and fore sail, being more than troubled for his ship's safety, as the roaring noise increased and every feature of the eruption grew more terrifying.

By 5 o'clock the sky had been completely covered in by a pall of black smoke, which shrouded the ship in a smothering darkness. A hail of pumice stone now began to fall—it was quite hot to the touch and many of the pieces were so large that the skylights had to be covered, whilst the crew of the *Charles Bal* had hurriedly to don boots and sou-westers to protect their feet and their heads.

For an hour these brickbats fell without ceasing; they were then followed by smaller stones and ashes and dust, which last blinded the eyes and speedily covered the decks to a depth of 3 or 4 inches, and all the time an intense blackness covered the sky, sea and land.

Captain Watson now hove his ship to, not daring to hold his course in face of the stupendous cataclysm ahead. The *Charles Bal* was abreast of the Fourth Point—at least it was believed that the light had been caught sight of for a moment.

At this point Captain Watson described his situation as a truly fearful one. Sand and stones still fell without ceasing. The blackness over the doomed island was continually broken by sudden bursts of light as the volcano roared in explosion after explosion, whilst all around the ship every kind of lightning zigzagged, flared and dazzled.

With the wind now blowing strongly from the S.W., the *Charles Bal* was put on the port tack, and gradually head-reached away from the Java Shore until at 11 p.m. Krakatoa bore W.N.W. 11 miles off, and the eruption was in plain observation of her crew.

Chains of fire were noticed ascending and descending between the island and the black pall above it, at the same time balls of white fire rolled away from the S.W. end in a continuous stream. The wind blew strong, hot, choking and sulphurous, with the suffocating smell of burning cinders. Some of the lumps which were bombarding the ship seemed to be made of red hot iron. Captain Watson kept a man in the chains with a leadline, and the lead came up quite warm from a bottom of 30 fathoms.

From midnight to 4 a.m. the *Charles Bal* might well have been off the Mouth of Hell itself. The choking winds held strong but unsteady between S.S.W. and W.S.W. The pitch blackness on every side was pierced every other second by a blaze of fire as Krakatoa burst forth with a roaring and a thundering, which clattered, banged and rumbled as if the whole earth were being shattered to pieces.

Electricity ran everywhere. The mastheads and yardarms of the *Charles Bal* were studded with corposants, whilst a peculiar lurid pink flame seemed to come down out of the clouds until it appeared to be resting on the trucks of the masts.

At 6 a.m. the eruption grew somewhat less violent and it became light enough to make out the Java shore. The Fourth Point lighthouse was passed at 8 a.m. The *Charles Bal* hoisted her number but got no answer. At 8.30 she passed close enough to Anjer to make out the houses, but no movement of any kind could be detected ashore.

At 10.15 a.m. the ship passed within half a mile of the Button Island. The weather for the moment was finer, no ashes or cinders were falling, the sea showed like glass under the lee of the island and the wind was south-east, light. An hour later a fearful explosion came from Krakatoa, now over 30 miles distant; and for the first time the crew of the *Charles Bal* took notice of an earthquake wave. Four times this wall of water rolled up, sweeping right over the southern end of the Button, and rising half way up its north and east sides, whilst it could be seen running high over the Java shore. With this wave the wind came strong out of the S.W. by S., whilst the sky was rapidly covered in by dense clouds of smoke, and by 11.30 a.m. the darkness had become so thick that it could be felt.

The ship was running N.E. by N. 7 knots under three lower topsails. Two ships had been sighted to the north and N.W. just before the sky closed in—they were the barques *Norham Castle* and *Sir Robert Sale*—so Captain Watson put out his sidelights, placed two men on the look-out forward and gave his two mates instructions to watch on either quarter.

Once more the heavens began to rain stones and sand, and, in addition, mud, which was so thick and sticky that a man had to be specially employed washing it off the binnacle glass. At noon the atmosphere was so dense and impenetrable that men standing together could not see each other, and the crew had to grope their way about the decks as if in the thickest, blackest fog.

This terrifying state of things continued until 2 p.m., when the fall of mud ceased, though there was no diminution in the thunderings of the volcano, in the wild play of the lightning or in the brilliant glare of the flaming sky above Krakatoa.

Soon after 2 p.m. the lower yards were distinguished, and by 5 West Island and the horizon ahead were visible. But the sky remained dark and heavy, sand fell at times, and the roaring of the volcano continued very distinct, though by this time the *Charles Bal* was fully 65 to 70 miles away, with the North Watcher in sight over the bow.

The ship came out of the ordeal without any serious damage,

but she looked as if she had been covered with cement from truck to waterline, her spars, sails, blocks and ropes being all coated with a mixture of mud and sand, which stuck like so much melted glue.

The last ship to take orders from Anjer was Carmichael's *Medea*. She had to plough her way through a sea of pumice stone in order to reach Batavia. Here she was anchored in pitch blackness whilst Captain Thomson landed in the Dutch Custom-house officer's boat. On the way to the shore, the final outburst, the one which probably split the island, occurred, and a glare went up into the sky which was so bright that human eyes could not bear it, then came the thunderous report in roll on roll of ear-shattering sound, such as has been reckoned to be the greatest ever heard upon this earth.

This was followed by the tidal waves, which caught the *Charles Bal* off the Button. The first wave picked up the boat and, without breaking, deposited it on top of a goods shed where its terrified occupants lay prone until the water had subsided.

The *Jason*, of the same line, was one of the first ships to arrive off Anjer after the eruption. She found the Straits completely changed, there were islands where there should have been none, and some familiar landmarks had disappeared altogether, whilst the ramshackle town of Anjer was absolutely wiped out.

Captain Richardson landed. At first he could find no sign of life whatever, but at last a half-demented native was encountered.

To the captain's stupified enquiry:—"Where is Anjer?" the native replied in tones of terror:—"Anjer gone; wave come; all gone, all gone!" and straightway fled in a panic, as if he feared a second convulsion of Nature.

Captain Richardson estimated that the wave must have been 60 feet in height from the evidence of wreckage on the top of a solitary palm tree, which stood some distance from the beach.

It is a fascinating subject, this eruption of Krakatoa, but it behoves me to get back to the *Cutty Sark*.

She made the anchorage off Madras at 10 a.m. on 7th November after an uneventful passage.

Here the *Cutty Sark* lay until 28th December, when she sailed for Bimlipatam with 3310 bags of jaggery or palm sugar, stuff which is like black mud and not much nicer to handle, and 100 tons of redwood in her hold.

A few items in her expenses at Madras may be of interest:—

Port dues were 2½ annas a ton and light dues 1 anna a ton. Deputy Collector's Customs for shipping cargo came to 9 rupees 7 annas 7 pie. Boat hire cost 2 rupees a day. The dubash's account was 30 rupees; for clearing the ship 5 rupees went to the Deputy Collector of Customs and another 7½ to the Deputy Master Attendant's Department. Dunnage mats, of which Captain Moore bought 1000, cost 9 rupees a hundred; the crew's tailor came to 290 rupees; the captain's hotel expenses were 20 rupees, whilst in the items bought under sea stock I notice 34 loaves of bread at 1½ annas a loaf and a number of chickens at 8 annas a fowl.

The *Cutty Sark* arrived in Bimlipatam Roads on 8th January, 1883. Here she took in 6240 bags of myrobolanes—a kind of dye nut—and 4163 buffalo horns.

At midnight on 21st January she proceeded for Coconada, and after a pleasant sail in light airs arrived in the road and brought up in 7 fathoms with the lighthouse bearing N.W. by W. distant about 4 miles. The *Cutty Sark* was kept close inshore all the way, but the big Liverpool ship *Andromeda* once took 28 days to make the distance between Bimlipatam and Coconada, having stood off-shore and got into bad weather.

The homeward cargo was now completed with 4781 bags of myrobolanes or myrabolums and 115 bales of deer horns, her draft when ready for sea being 20 ft. 4 ins. forward and 20 ft. 7 ins. aft.

The *Cutty Sark* set sail out of Coconada Bay on 31st January, 1883. She was no sooner to sea than it became necessary to pump the ship to get rid of the drainage from the cargo, which ran into the hold from the palm sugar in the shape of molasses. This is one of the drawbacks to a load of jaggery, which never stops draining a thick treacly fluid into the bilges; thus the pumps had to be manned pretty nearly every day during the first half of the passage, a most unusual proceeding on the staunch little *Cutty Sark*.

With a very foul bottom after her long sojourn in the calm waters of the Java Sea and Bay of Bengal, the *Cutty Sark* had no chance of making a quick run home.

The days passed monotonously as she wandered slowly South. On 6th March in 26° 43' S., 53° 34' E. she fell in with *Taitsing*, 42 days out from the Philippines and bound for Liverpool. The wind was light and variable with a heavy S.W. swell, and the two Willis ships kept close to each other for four days.

The *Cutty Sark* was off Agulhas on 19th March, where Captain Moore was compelled to heave to in a strong W.N.W. gale with heavy sea, which lasted for 36 hours, during most of which the clipper was kept head reaching under lower topsails and staysails. One very heavy sea was shipped on the 20th which split the bulwarks forward and the teak rail at the break of the topgallant fo'c'sle.

By noon on the 22nd the weather had moderated and with the wind swinging into the S.E., sail was piled on her for the run to St. Helena, where the *Cutty Sark* was brought to an anchor on 5th April, whilst Captain Moore hurried ashore for some necessary stores. After a halt of six hours the clipper resumed her passage and at 4 p.m. on the 6th once more fell in with the *Taitsing*. With the wind very light from the south east, the *Taitsing* again managed to hold on to the *Cutty Sark* for three days.

Ascension was passed at 6 p.m. on 10th April; the equator crossed on the 13th, and after a long spell of catspaws and calms the N.E. trades were picked up on the 25th April in 4° 18' N. After a moderate run across the trades, very light winds were carried to 40° N., 29° W. (18th May) where strong head winds (N.E. to E.N.E.) increasing at times to gale strength, held up the *Cutty Sark* till 26th May, in 45° N., 23° W., whence she had light airs and calms to port.

The Lizard was sighted on 31st May, the tug *Challenge* took hold on 1st June off St. Catherine's, and the *Cutty Sark* was made fast in the London Dock on 2nd June, after a light weather and somewhat weary passage of 122 days.

The *Taitsing*, which had left Zebu on 23rd January, arrived Liverpool on 1st June, thus showing very level running with the *Cutty Sark*. This beautiful little ship, one of the celebrated five in the 1886 race, was wrecked on her next voyage. She left Swansea with coals for Zanzibar and was totally lost on Querimba Island in September, 1883, her crew being rescued by H.M.S. *Ranger* and landed at Zanzibar.

We now come to *Cutty Sark's* first wool voyage. From this date she once more became a racing ship in rivalry not only with her old antagonist *Thermopylae,* but with the crack wool clippers, especially those in the Sydney trade such as *Patriarch, Brilliant, Cimba, Samuel Plimsoll, Woollahra, Sir Walter Raleigh* and *Rodney,* and as we shall see, they, one and all, had to admit defeat.

In July, 1883, she loaded general cargo for Newcastle, N.S.W. On 15th July *Cutty Sark* left Gravesend; she passed Deal on the 16th and after being detained in the Channel by light head winds and fog, she took her departure from the Lizard on 23rd July. The voyage was devoid of incident, Newcastle being reached on 10th October, 79 days out from the Lizard.

Cutty Sark was one of the first ships to load wool at Newcastle, which she left on 28th December with 4289 bales of wool and 12 casks of tallow.

This was the clipper's first wool cargo, and her smallest with one exception. I have no details of her homeward run, though I think the following encounter ocurred this voyage; I have taken it from the P.S.N.C. Magazine. A retired sea-captain writes:—

"I was coming up by the Azores on the *E. S. Hocken,* 275 tons register, barquentine rigged, brand new. Weather fine and clear, beam wind fresh, all sails drawing. Fell in with her ladyship 'Short Chemise,' otherwise *Cutty Sark.* We were close to from 7 a.m. till 4 p.m., and could talk without flags. At 4 p.m. wind drew more aft and increased to moderate gale with moderate sea. Our log said 12½.

"At 6.10 p.m. the *Cutty Sark* was hull down and still carried royals, whilst the *E. S. Hocken* was still doing 12½ under topgallant sails. We were in Fowey in 8½ days, but the 'Cutty' was berthed in London in four, total distance being about 1400 miles."

The *Cutty Sark* anchored off Deal on 20th March, 82 days out from Newcastle. Not only was it the best wool passage of the year, but she beat all the ships sailing about the same time by from 25 days to over a month, as witness the table on page 207.

The *Cutty Sark* again loaded for Newcastle in 1884, taking

in 1285 tons of general cargo and 90 tons of gunpowder, which, as usual, was shipped at Gravesend.

A word or two about her personnel. Dimint was chief officer and Egan second, both these men had risen from the foc's'le, they were good seamen, though not very strong on discipline.

Ship	Left		Arrived		Days
Orontes	Sydney,	Dec. 22	Deal	April 26	125
La Hogue	—	,, 26	,,	April 12	107
Cutty Sark	Newcastle,	,, 28	,,	Mar. 20	82
Dharwar	Sydney	,, 29	,,	April 21	113
Cimba	Sydney	,, 29	,,	April 15	107
Christiana Thompson	Sydney	,, 29	,,	April 21	113

The *Cutty Sark* had a specially hefty lot of apprentices this voyage; Jacques was now senior apprentice and third mate, whilst Jackson and Sykes were also third year boys. Millett and Farnham came from *The Tweed*, and were second year boys. Then there was Chittenden, who achieved fame in the war by sinking a submarine, by which he gained a D.S.O.; Vaughan, a red headed youth, and a first voyager, who came from the Channel Islands.

With 8 strong boys, the A.B.'s were cut down to 8, thus keeping the complement at 23 all told.

Before the voyage was over the 8 apprentices gained the upper hand over the 8 A.B.'s. The hands at first thought they could boss the apprentices, but the latter possessed a pair of boxing gloves, which were brought out in the tropics. After giving the men a good chance of seeing how they handled themselves, the boys went forward and challenged the whole foc's'le, but there were no takers and ever after this the boys saw to it that the men had all the dirty jobs.

John Willis rather prided himself in his boys and he invariably came down to see his ships off, when it became the custom for the apprentices to line the rail, as the ship began to move behind the tug, and with raised hats gave their employer a "Good-bye, sir." To which Old Jock always raised his white hat in response, with a cheery "Good-bye, my lads."

The *Cutty Sark* left the East India Dock on 15th June, 1884, took in her gunpowder at Gravesend and passed Deal the same day. Mrs. Moore went as far as Dover with her husband, and I believe this was the only occasion on which the *Cutty Sark* had a lady on board at sea.

Off Dover the mainyard was backed whilst Mrs. Moore and the pilot went over the side. And they were scarcely in the boat before the captain sang out "square the mainyard," and the *Cutty Sark* was off down Channel with a moderate breeze.

Several noted ships had sailed from the Thames ahead of the "Cutty." The new crew of the latter, like all old sailors, swore by their last ships, and though they had, of course, heard of the *Cutty Sark's* performances, they were not willing to admit she could sail until they noticed ship after ship being overhauled and left behind.

Beachy Head was passed early on 16th June, and the Lizards on the 18th, the wind falling light. Indeed it was a light weather passage all the way down to the Cape, the line was crossed about 25 days out, and the "Cutty" was spoken in 9° S., 33° W. on 21st July. The mate took the opportunity of the fine weather to chip and scrape the cable on deck and to tar down fore and aft. During the unpleasant job of tarring down young Chittenden was nearly the means of a tar pot falling on his skipper. The boy had made his tar pot fast to the fore royal halliards and had come down on deck for something: before he returned to his job, the mate lowered the royal yard down; the lanyard of the pot carried away and down it came smothering the sails in its passage and only just missing Captain Moore, who happened to be forward, smoking a cigar.

The *Cutty Sark's* gear was in worse shape than ever this voyage, and whenever the "old man" attempted to hurry her something invariably carried away.

The main topgallant chain sheets carried away three times in one watch: they had been tinkered up so often that they were practically composed of repair links. Nevertheless some good runs were made under reefed topsails in the roaring forties, though the *Cutty Sark* did not come through unscathed, as I have a Newcastle bill for repairs to bulwarks, for straightening stanchions and providing new ones, and also for repairing the poop rails. This damage was caused by a big sea which flooded the poop and jammed the

"THOMAS STEPHENS"

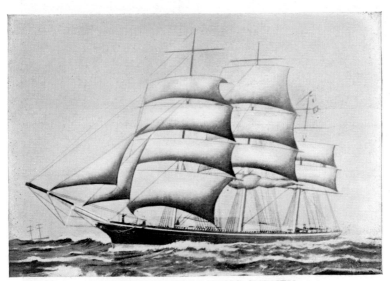

"CUTTY SARK" LEAVING SYDNEY

[*See Page* 250

ICEBERGS

Photographed from the deck of the *Cutty Sark*, by Captain Woodget,
in Lat. 62° 19′ S., Long. 155° 2′ W.

[*See Page* 253

man at the wheel, so that she came up into the wind, and for a moment or two nothing could be seen from aft but three masts sticking out of the spume and soapsuds.

On the day before Newcastle was reached the weather royal backstay carried away, with the result that the royal mast was sprung at the hounds and took an angle of 15 degrees forward.

Newcastle was reached on 5th September, 79 days from the Lizard. Here the *Cutty Sark*, after the success of her previous wool passage, was treated with great honour, whilst her apprentices were lionised everywhere, their favourite rendezvous being a pub called the "Hunter River," where the daughters of the house made them very welcome.

The *Cutty Sark* lay three months in Newcastle awaiting her wool, during which time her apprentices thoroughly enjoyed themselves, though they were badly beaten at cricket by the *Gladstone's* crowd.

Of the two ships, the *Gladstone* was the first to get away from Newcastle—on 2nd December, the *Cutty Sark* following her, with 4300 bales of wool in her hold, on the 9th. Though the *Gladstone* was a well-known wool clipper with many fine passages to her credit, she did not reach London until three weeks after the *Cutty Sark*. The latter was towed out to the Heads, where she found a nice fair wind, which compelled the tug to slip in haste to avoid being run down.

The *Cutty Sark* made a very fine run to the Horn, which was passed in about 20 days. A steady westerly gale was carried round the Horn, and the "Cutty" raced past the usual outward bounder, wearily head-reaching under lower topsails, whose crew must have looked enviously at the clipper as she surged by under whole sail to royals and crossjack.

After an uneventful run up the Atlantic, the *Cutty Sark* made the entrance to the Channel on the 77th day out. On her way up Channel a coaster named the *Tam o' Shanter* crossed her bows, whose crew on recognising Nannie, the witch, cheered her to the echo.

Off the Isle of Wight a Watkins tug spoke the clipper for a tow. Captain Moore said he would take the rope at Dungeness,

P

so away went the tug inshore out of the tide. The light fair wind then freshened, and the clipper soon caught up the tug, passed her, and on arriving off Dungeness was compelled to heave to in order to allow the steamer to catch up and pass her rope.

Cutty Sark passed through the Downs, 79 days out from New-castle, and docked next day; and of the whole wool fleet but one vessel had equalled her passage—her old rival, *Thermopylae*, which had arrived in the Thames on 24th December, 1884, also 79 days out; the only other vessels to make the passage from the Colonies in under 90 days being *Salamis, Mermerus* and *Rodney*.

The following table will show how the *Cutty Sark* overhauled all the vessels which sailed ahead of her.

Ship	Left		Docked		Days
Hawkesbury ..	Sydney	Nov. 26	Feb.	28	94
Ben Cruachan ..	Melbourne	,, 28	,,	27	91
Gladstone	Newcastle	Dec. 2	March	20	108
Mermerus	Melbourne	,, 2	Feb.	27	84
Loch Garry	Geelong	,, 5	March	30	115
Orontes	Sydney	,, 5	,,	31	116
Christiana Thompson	Sydney	,, 6	,,	27	111
Woollahra	Sydney	,, 7	,,	27	110
Cutty Sark	Newcastle	,, 9	Feb.	27	80
Cimba	Sydney	,, 12	March	27	105
Dharwar	Sydney	,, 12	,,	27	105

CHAPTER VII.

IN THE WOOL TRADE UNDER CAPTAIN WOODGET.

ON his arrival home in 1885, Captain Moore, who was only getting £200 a year in the *Cutty Sark*, was rewarded for his two fine voyages to Newcastle by being given the command of "Old White Hat's" beloved flagship *The Tweed*, whilst the famous China clipper, which had now made her name as a wool clipper, was turned over to Captain Woodget.

This was undoubtedly a very great compliment to Woodget, for he had only made one voyage in Willis's employ, having arrived home in the *Coldstream* in January; and it also shows old Jock's shrewdness and fine judgment of men, for in Woodget he had picked out the one man amongst all his captains who possessed the temperament, nerve and seamanship to get the best out of the wonderful little *Cutty Sark*.

Captain Woodget's business acumen had been proved by his handling of the old *Coldstream*, which he took out in March, 1881, and brought home in January, 1885, after a most successful voyage financially. But he not only made money with the stubborn old *Coldstream*, but he forced that 36-year old balk of teak to make passages which astonished her owner. Willis was so confident indeed in Woodget's ability, that he took the captain down to the East India Dock where the *Cutty Sark* was loading for Sydney, and pointing out the clipper with outstretched arm, said simply:—

"Captain Woodget, there is your ship. My agents in Sydney are Dangar, Geddes & Co. All you have to do is to drive her."

Woodget soon showed his owner that he knew how to drive her. He was, indeed, one of those rare men who are absolutely devoid of fear, who are as quiet and calm and collected in moments of crisis and supreme danger as other men are in their beds.

A close call to Woodget always acted like a tonic, cooling his brain and sharpening his wits. Yet he was no reckless ship driver.

211

He knew his ship and the condition of her gear to the least used rope, and he never overstepped the limit of the breaking strain though he carried on to the very last moment.

Many and many a captain has carried on until the time when "things begin to go," but no foremast hand under Woodget had need to look aloft for fear of "things clattering down upon his head."

One of his officers wrote to me:—"It was a pleasure to see the 'old man' in dirty weather. He fairly revelled in it. With one side of his moustache jammed into his mouth, and hanging on to the weather rigging, I can see him now, his sturdy figure in yellow oilskins and long leather sea boots, watching aloft and hanging on till the last minute. He gave all his crew complete confidence in him and I never remember seeing him anything but calm in dirty weather."

Another well-known commander, who served his apprenticeship in the *Cutty Sark*, wrote:—"He was a seaman of iron nerves, and drove his crew, like he drove the *Cutty Sark*: all the same not a sailor on board but admired him and agreed that he was the finest seaman he had ever sailed with."

With the self-confidence begot by experience, Woodget was a daring and enterprising navigator besides being a consummate seaman. Both his accuracy and daring are well shown in the following instance:—

When bound out to Newcastle in 1887, her noon position on 11th November was 40° 17′ S., 141° 49′ E., her distance for the previous 24 hours being 330 miles.

It was blowing hard from the south with sharp squalls. The *Cutty Sark* was reeling along under all sail to her royals, and though the last land seen was the Lizard, Woodget was so sure of his landfall that even when darkness fell he kept her going.

At 8 p.m. Cape Wickham's light was picked up, and at 10 p.m. King's Island was rounded, Woodget then set a course for the Crocodile Rock and ordered a sharp look-out to be kept. The Rock was duly picked up right ahead and the *Cutty Sark* went tearing through the passage. At 8 a.m. Wilson's Promontory was astern and the *Cutty Sark* had averaged 14 knots for the last 18 hours. That morning a Hollander was passed, making heavy weather of it under lower topsails, and the *Cutty Sark* beat her by a week into Newcastle.

This night navigation through one of the most dangerous localities in Australian waters was not an unusual but a typical specimen of Woodget's methods. It is a thousand pities that he did not command the *Cutty Sark* in her China days, for the run down the China Sea to Anjer would have just suited his skill and daring.

A tireless worker himself, Woodget got the last ounce out of his officers and men, but he told me once that he had never asked a man to do what he would not do himself. If his discipline was strict, it was also just: and he could unbend and joke with his officers and apprentices without losing his dignity. Indeed he was always full of fun and his apprentices adored him. As one of them wrote:—"He never bullied and was always 'one of us' all the time I was with him."

Yet Woodget got as much work out of his apprentices as out of his A.B.'s. A great saying of his was:—"Give me two boys and a handy-billy, and I'll rig a ship." There was probably no class of men with more independence of character than the old wind-jammer skippers, and Woodget was no exception to the rule. He was as free and independent in mind as in action.

His usual headgear was the singularly appropriate one for the master of the *Cutty Sark*—a tam-o-shanter, and this in a day when that monstrosity, the pot-hat, was the regulation covering of all self-respecting merchant skippers.

And in his beliefs and theories of life he was equally original, for he had a very active enquiring brain which delighted in conundrums, from metaphysics to dog-breeding, from photography to the secrets of exchange.

Though Captain Woodget was far from being a religious man in the generally accepted sense, in fine weather he would lie on his back for hours on deck reading his Bible. He was one of those men who thought out religion for himself and was by no means ready to accept the dogma or interpretatons of other men.

Though he was a non-drinker and a non-smoker, there was not an atom of the prig or goody-goody about him. He would probably have described himself as a philospher and a free thinker.

It is told of him with, I think, but very little truth, that he used to frighten his men into praying by his carrying on in heavy weather.

The story goes that he used to say:—"I'll make you devils pray; go down on your knees!" Then the captain would start a prayer, whilst the *Cutty Sark* was staggering along with her decks a mist of sprays. One day, in the midst of this curious prayer meeting, the "Cutty" gave an extra nasty lurch and shipped a sea which threatened to wash the devotees off their knees. Upon which one of the old men looked up in fright, whereupon the old man roared out:—"Close your damned eyes, Bill Jones, and let me finish this prayer."

At one time he had a craze for putting up texts round the cabin, yet I have a keen suspicion that he used these texts more to poke fun at certain failings of his officers and friends than from any desire to pose as a religious man.

One of the most marked characteristics of his nature was a very deep love of animals, and this love was reciprocated, for he was one of those favoured mortals for whom animals and birds had a natural affinity. Under Woodget the *Cutty Sark* became celebrated for her magnificent collies. Latterly the "old man" always had a favourite collie aboard, and very often two or three more. These collies were always prize-bred dogs, and many of them became noted afterwards for their successes in the Australian show ring.

He also bought two monkeys at Anjer on his second voyage, whose antics made them by no means too popular with the steward.

When Captain Woodget retired from the sea, he bought a farm on the Norfolk coast, and filled his farmyard with pigs, chickens, ducks, geese, turkeys, and rabbits, and it was a sight to see the old man, his snow-white hair and beard flowing in the wind, as he marched sturdily across a field followed by a trail of quacking ducks and clucking hens, and perhaps a foal and a calf and a pig or two.

It shows the sturdy breed and indomitable character of the man that at the age of 75 he should have been thrown from a colt which he was breaking in and sustained no more than a black eye.

Yet, with all his love for his farmyard, it must not be thought that his heart was ever false to the sea and ships. He still kept a boat for sailing or fishing, and showed that he could win a race in the local regattas. And the *Cutty Sark* was still his sweetheart. After his first wife's death and before he married again, when his three sons, commanding fine steamers in the East, were seldom at home, the lonely evenings of his retirement were mostly spent in reveries, in which the *Cutty Sark* was ever uppermost in his mind.

Captain Woodget's sea training had been the usual hard one of sailing ship days. He was the younger son of Richard Woodget, a farmer of Burnham Norton in Norfolk, and was born on 21st November, 1845. When 10 years of age he was sent to school at Burnham Market, where his resolute, high-spirited character soon showed itself. He was always full of fun, and this in a boy means mischief, nor would he ever give in or admit defeat, thus when his master held him down to cane him—the cane being the chief implement of education in those virile days—the boy bit his master's leg and made his escape home. He was then sent to a private school at Deepdale for a while before a second term of Burnham Market; but a boy so full of spirit could only be meant for the sea, and when he was 16 years of age his indentures were signed with Bullard, King & Co. On the 30th September, 1861, he joined the billiboy *Johns*, of 80 tons, which traded between Seaton Sluice near Blyth and London, her cargo being usually bottles. His next ship was the schooner *Peace* in the same trade. In these coasters he distinguished himself by his indomitable attitude towards the incredibly hardhearted and iron-fisted skippers and mates of those days.

No bullying could tame him, to sympathy and understanding he was a stranger, there was none in the coasting trade of the sixties, but his superb self-reliance pulled him through. The A.B.'s taught him his trade, and he soon proved himself quick and handy at all sailorising jobs.

He taught himself boat sailing, his first venture being in the West India Dock one Sunday morning. He purloined a sailing dinghy, which was hanging astern of a yacht and spent the day sailing up and down the dock. As the dinghy's rudder was missing he steered it by judiciously heeling and by working the sheets.

He was very nearly caught by the river police, but managed to return the boat and sneak aboard his ship without being seen.

On another occasion he received his first lesson in sail-making. His fellow apprentice, who was the son of a friend of the captain and thus received preferential treatment, was given a palm and needle and carefully instructed in the art, but Woodget was not to be outreached in this manner; watching his opportunity he presently pounced down on the boy Peter, seized the palm and needle and retreated to the foc's'le, where the seamen soon showed him the way of it.

This occurred on the brig *British Ensign*, which he joined in the summer of 1863, and on which he finished his time. Space will not admit of a fuller description of his early life, but a summary of his service will be found on page 217.

Captain Woodget first began to study theoretical navigation when quartermaster in the *Alexandra* under the celebrated Captain Delgarno.

One of the most interesting ships in which he sailed was the brig *Nina*, which had once been a notorious slaver. She was beautifully built of mahogany, but in Woodget's time had become so racked to pieces and loose through hard driving that she had strengthening bands all round her. Though she leaked like a bucket, she sailed like a witch.

It was Woodthorpe, the hoveller pilot, who always took Willis's and Allen's ships down Channel, who first recommended Woodget to the owner of the Cutty *Sark*.

Captain Woodget's first action on assuming command of the "Cutty" was to go over her rigging with an eye like a microscope. He was not able, of course, to put all his ideas into practice straightway, but the clipper could never have carried her royals on a Cape Horn snorter if Woodget had not been a master rigger.

The following were a few of his most important innovations:—

All braces and headsail sheets were of wire—served over so that they coiled down without a kink.

All sails were clewed up to the yardarms.

Double buntlines were rove for the courses.

The main topgallant stay was double, the sail being run up on one stay wire.

CAPTAIN WOODGET'S SEA SERVICE.

Date	Ship	Rig	Tons	Capacity	Remarks
1861	Johns ..	billiboy	80	Apprentice	Coasting Trade—Seaton Sluice and London—Cargo bottles.
1862	Peace ..	schooner	—	Apprentice	Coasting Trade.
1863	British Ensign ..	brig	196	Apprentice	Bristol to Alexandria, Limerick and London.
1864	British Ensign ..	brig	196	Apprentice	London, Trinidad, and Greenock. Sugar cargo from Trinidad.
1865	British Ensign ..	brig	196	Apprentice	Glasgow, Port Natal, London. Wool and hides from Port Natal. Indentures expired on arrival.
1865	Faith ..	billiboy	50	Only Mate	London to Newcastle.
1865	Dolphin ..	barque	346	A.B.	West Hartlepool to Baltic with coal; back with timber.
1866	Charles Lambert	barque	357	A.B.	South Shields to Lisbon and Pomeron River; back to South Shields with copper ore.
1867	Tweedside ..	brig	—	Cook and Steward	South Shields to Oporto. Discharged at Oporto and returns by steamer.
1867	Alexandra ..	ship	898	A.B. and Quartermaster	Captain Delgarno. London to Callao and Chinchas. Guano freight £5600.
1868	Princess Dagmar	barque	428	Cook	London to Mantangas, Cuba: back to Greenock.
1868	Abbotsford ..	scow	161	A.B.	Ships from Greenock to Whitby for the run. 1868 obtains only mate's certificate at South Shields.
1869	Isabel ..	brig	209	Only Mate	To Licata and back, and to Girgente and back.
1870	Caldbeck ..	ship	760	Second Mate	To San Francisco and back.
1871	Nina ..	brig	183	Mate	To West Coast of Africa and back.
1871-2	Freak ..	schooner	98	Mate	To Port Venders.
1872-3	Priscilla ..	barque	253	Mate	
1874-80	Copenhagen ..	ship	876	Mate	Three voyages to India during famine period. In coolie trade to Mauritius.
1881-5	Coldstream ..	ship	756	Captain	To Delagoa Bay, Zanzibar, Cochuin, Tuticorin; three coolie passages to Port Natal and Mauritius; back to London.
1885-95	Cutty Sark ..	ship	921	Captain	Ten voyages in Australian wool trade. Cutty Sark sold to Portuguese in 1895.
1895	Coldinghame ..	ship	1059	Captain	Australian trade.

The three barrel winches on the mainrail were used for foresheet and mainsail sheets and tacks. Without these winches there is no doubt but that more hands would have been required.

All gear was of the very best: Woodget always went aloft himself and condemned anything which showed the least sign of wear or chafe. Indifferent gear aloft has cost many lives and lost many ships. Willis never stinted the *Cutty Sark* under Woodget as he had done under Moore, probably her success in the wool trade had the effect of opening old White Hat's pocket.

Dimint stayed in the *Cutty Sark* as mate, whilst Jacques became second mate.

Captain Moore took all his boys over with him to *The Tweed*, and *The Tweed's* apprentices were turned over to the *Cutty Sark*. Woodget proved a welcome change to these high-spirited youngsters after the tyranny of Gentleman White, who affected the style of the crack Blackwall commanders and insisted on his apprentices combining the duties of a Green's midshipman with the dirty jobs of a collier's ordinary seaman.

Part of their work was to keep *The Tweed's* 'tween decks, which were painted sky-blue, as clean and spotless as a lady's boudoir. They did not object to this when the wonderful old ship was empty of cargo, for in rummaging the hold they found many interesting relics of her active service days, including a number of her cannons, which did duty as ballast.

In spite of their hard time under White, the spirit of these "young gentlemen" was by no means broken. They were great hulking lads, who fancied themselves with the boxing gloves and had little to learn in the way of devilry whether at sea or on shore. They were in fact tough nuts even for apprentices, yet they very soon became clay in the hands of "old man" Woodget. R. L. Andrewes was their leader, the others being O. Bowers, T. Dixon, A. Durrant, J. Smith, C. E. Irving and J. Weston.

There were two other characters, who joined the *Cutty Sark* with Woodget and *The Tweed's* apprentices and deserve particular mention. These were the cook and carpenter.

Tony Robson, the cook, was a Chinaman with a very romantic history. Many years before the *Cutty Sark* was launched a British ship fell in with either a small boat or raft, floating in mid-ocean. In this boat was a tiny Chinese baby. The wee mite was taken by the captain's wife and brought up like a son, and it was thus that Tony came by the English name of Robson. As soon as he was old enough, he followed his adopted father's profession, and in 1882 we find him leading seaman on *The Tweed*. A retired master mariner, who was an apprentice on *the Tweed* this voyage, gave him the following testimonial:—"He spoke English perfectly, though, of course, nothing could hide the fact that he was a Chinaman; but of all the sailors I have ever known I reckon he knew his work from A to Z better than any other man I have met." This is high praise, yet it is confirmed by all who knew Tony. On *The Tweed's* next voyage, on the cook falling ill in Australia, Tony, who was getting on in years, left the foc's'le for the galley.

When he joined the *Cutty Sark* in 1885, he is described as "a lean spare little chap with a slight stoop, as fine a seaman as ever trod a plank and absolutely English in every respect except his features."

This transforming effect which the British service has for foreign seamen, is I suppose, one of the proud signs of a ruling race, for it is rare to find its converse. The Britisher may sail for years in foreign ships, yet he is always unmistakably a British seaman. Yet I could mention many and many a case of a foreign seaman transformed into a Britisher, not only in character and speech but in his whole outlook on life.

The most notable instance is, of course, Mr. Joseph Conrad, Polish born and bred yet a British seaman, a British master mariner, and, what is still more wonderful, a British writer whose books are classics of world wide fame.

A case which is not so well known is that of Captain Enright He was an Austrian though he managed to keep the secret of his birth.*

---

* I have a letter of his, which states:—"In 1846 I took out my naturalization papers. and have so long been a genuine Englishman that I could almost forget it was ever otherwise, though in my young days I had many thrilling adventures in my determination never willingly to leave the British flag." Captain Enright passed his examination for master in 1850, and made his name as commander of the tea clipper *Chrysolite*, and later had the famous *Lightning*, which he left owing to the ill-health of his wife. After a short period in business ashore he took command.

One of the most notable cases of transformed foreigners in my own experience was that of a sailmaker, whose only name was Liverpool, his chosen home port. The hall-mark of Liverpool was not only upon his speech but upon every facet of the man. A prime deep-water sailor, he might well have been the son of a Liverpool packet rat yet he sailed from Odessa.

Another man I can remember was a sea cook who hailed from the cook's paradise, Paris, yet this French chef sailed out of the port of London and was the most perfect Cockney both in appearance and speech. It is true that he would sometimes break off from the typical Cockney ballad during a foc's'le sing-song, and give the bewildered crowd a snatch of some light Parisian ditty, but this usually fell flat and his great success as a vocalist lay in his perfect rendering of the latest London music hall song.

To return to Tony Robson, he served as cook and watchman in the *Cutty Sark* for years; and Woodget knew that he had as good as a spare bosun and a spare sailmaker washing the peas and soaking the junk in his galley. In sailing ship days the galley was usually a harbour of refuge for an old seaman, whose joints were not as lissom or his muscles as strong as they used to be.

The new carpenter of the *Cutty Sark* was a big, burly Aberdonian with a flowing beard and the features of a Greek god. And he was as handsome in character as he was in appearance. With all the sailor's generosity and camaraderie, he was a shipmate to be proud of and became a great favourite of Woodget's. Unfortunately he was rather crippled with a knee which had been badly injured in his previous voyage.

With sailmaker, steward, and 10 A.B.'s, the *Cutty Sark's* complement made up 24 all told. She left the East India Dock at 2 p.m. on 1st April and anchored off the Nore at 7.30 p.m. At 5.30 a.m. the following morning she weighed anchor and towed

---

of Dicky Green's *Highflyer* in 1861, for two voyages to Shanghai. In 1863 he was transferred to the *Childers*, which was lost towing down the river Min in charge of a pilot. Enright's next command was the auxiliary *Great Victoria*, used as a transport during the Abyssinian Expedition in 1867-8. On completion of this charter, Captain Enright finally retired from the sea and became Gracie, Beazley's overlooker at Liverpool and superintended the building of 36 vessels for various Liverpool owners. He retired from active business in 1897, when 82 years of age, and only died a year or two before the war when well over 90.

to the King's Knoll Buoy, where she cast off the tug and made sail. The mud pilot, Oats, left the ship off Deal at 8.30, and the *Cutty Sark* proceeded down Channel before a fresh N.N.E. wind. The Start was passed at noon on the 3rd, Woodthorpe, the Channel pilot, leaving off Berry Head. At 11.30 p.m. that night the Lizard lights bore N.E. by E. dipping, the *Cutty Sark* being 39 hours from Deal.

Close on her heels were the celebrated Aberdeen White Star clipper *Samuel Plimsoll* and the wool clipper *Sir Walter Raleigh*, whilst 12 hours ahead of her was the fast little City liner, *City of York*.

Besides three well-known ships, the following were also bound out to Sydney, all fast up-to-date iron ships.

Tythonus	..	.. barque	1152	tons signalled	Tuskar	March	26
River Falloch		.. ship	1586	,,	,,	,,	,, 27
Firth of Stronsa		.. barque	1251	,,	,,	,,	,, 27
Pengwern	..	.. ship	1573	,,	,,	Lizard	,, 28
Maude	..	.. barque	1077	,,	,,	Tuskar	April 4

The wind which had been favourable down Channel hauled to the S.E. about midnight on 3rd April, and for 24 hours remained light and variable with the sea making and glass falling. It was evident that dirty weather was brewing in the Bay, and the first signs of trouble came in a squall from the N.W. on 5th April in the middle watch, which split the "Cutty's" fore topgallant sail and outer jib. By noon it was blowing a fresh gale from the S.W. with heavy hail squalls and a confused nor-westerly sea. At 5.30 p.m. the main upper topsail split. The gale lasted for three days. At 8 a.m. on the 7th Cape Ortegal bore S.E. 15 miles, at 5 p.m. Cape Finisterre was on the same bearing, and the blow did not moderate till noon on the 8th when *Cutty Sark* was in 40° 43' N., 12° 29' W.

The other ships all experienced the same Biscay weather. *Samuel Plimsoll*, whilst under reefed topsails and foresail, had a man washed overboard off her foc's'le-head. With great difficulty a boat was lowered under the second officer, Charles Peters, and the man was picked up. It was a work of supreme seamanship to get the boat alongside and hooked on without being stove or capsized, but it was carried out successfully, though Captain Henderson had several ribs broken in his efforts to fend off her, being jammed against the mainrail.

All the ships except the *Firth of Stronsa* made very good runs to the line, that of the *Pengwern*, a noted fast ship, being quite remarkable.

Their times on the equator were as follows:—

Ship	Crossed equator	Days from departure
Pengwern	April 13	17
Tythonus	,, 15	20
River Falloch	,, 17	21
Cutty Sark	,, 23	20
City of York	,, 23	21
Samuel Plimsoll	,, 28	24
Sir Walter Raleigh	,, 28	24
Maude	,, 29	25
Firth of Stronsa	,, 29	33

The weather in the South Atlantic was very fine with light winds. The *Cutty Sark's* best run on the S.E. trades was 245 miles, and her best run west of the Cape was only 288 miles.

The Cape meridian was crossed in the following order:—

Ship	On Cape meridian	Days from equator	Days out
Pengwern	May 16	33	49
River Falloch ..	,, 18	33	52
Cutty Sark	,, 19	26	46
Tythonus	,, 21	36	56
Samuel Plimsoll ..	,, 21	23	47
Sir Walter Raleigh ..	,, 22	25	51
Maude	,, 23	24	50
City of York ..	,, 26	33	52
Firth of Stronsa ..	,, 26	27	60

Cutty Sark's best run in the N.E. trades was 245 miles. Captain Woodget seized the opportunity to set up his rigging, fore and aft, reeve off new lanyards, alter the slings of the main and fore-yards to his liking and square the cap at the mizen masthead: whilst he set the carpenter to work making a spare topmast and topgallant yard.

On the day after passing the Cape, Captain Woodget got his first opportunity of sending the *Cutty Sark* along.

On 20th May the wind gradually freshened from the north-east, and with her yards on the backstays and all sail set the little clipper made the following consecutive runs.

May 21—Fresh N.E. breeze and fine smooth sea. Lat. 45° 15′ S., long. 31° 18′ E. Course S. 86° E. Distance 316 miles.

May 22—Fresh N.E. breezes and fine smooth sea. Lat. 45° 36′ S., long. 38° 31′ E. Course S. 86° E. Distance 307 miles.

May 23—Moderate E.N.E. breeze and fine clear weather. Lat. 46° 05′ S. Long. 45° 38′ E. Course S. 85° E. 308 miles.

Thus the *Cutty Sark* under all plain sail on a wind ran 931 miles in 70 hours, allowing for loss of time going east.

On the afternoon of 23rd May, the wind fell light, hauled more easterly and a thick fog came up. For the next three weeks there was not a day without east in the wind, and until 3rd June the fog was generally recorded as thick.

On 4th June the breeze gradually freshened from the N.N.E., and with her yards still on the backstays the *Cutty Sark* made a run of 330 miles.

Captain Woodget went as far as 48° S. in search of strong winds, but the royals, which had been set after the blow in the Bay, did not require handling until 16th June, the day after passing the South Cape, Tasmania, when the abstract records:—

June 16—Wind N.W. to north. Moderate and squally. A large ship standing south under lower topsails. Noon, squally, the sea like a boiling pot, apparently coming from all directions.

On the whole *Cutty Sark* had very poor winds running the easting down, and practically the whole way from the Cape the yards were on the backstays. Nevertheless she rounded Tasmania a day ahead of *Pengwern*. The *City of York* was the luckiest ship on this stretch being only 23 days from the Cape.

Firth of Stronsa had dropped far behind and did not arrive in Port Jackson until 10th July.

The times the ships passed the S.W. Cape Tasmania, or Cape Otway, were as follows:—

In the run up the coast to Sydney *Sir Walter Raleigh* made the best time and *Tythonus* the worst.

Cutty Sark signalled off Cape St. George at 8 a.m. on 19th. June. At noon the wind fell light and it was almost calm at 6 p.m. when the Port Jackson light was sighted. At 8 p.m. it was quite

Ship	Passed S.W. Cape, Tas. or Otway	Days from Cape	Days from departure
Cutty Sark	June 15	27	73
Pengwern	,, 17	32	81
Samuel Plimsoll ..	,, 18	28	75
City of York	,, 18	23	76
Sir Walter Raleigh ..	,, 20	29	77
Tythonus	,, 22	32	88
River Falloch	,, 23	36	88
Maude	,, 26	34	83

calm, but an hour later Captain Woodget took steam, and towing through the Heads anchored in Watson's Bay soon after midnight 78 days from the Downs.

It will be noticed in comparing the passages that the *Cutty Sark* won on her merits, she was by no means lucky with her winds, and between points never made better than a good average run.

The final result of the race was as follows:—

Ship	Arrived Port Jackson	Days out		
Cutty Sark	June 19 midnight	**77** days from the Start		
Samuel Plimsoll ..	,, 21 1.30 p.m.	78 ,,	,,	,,
City of York	,, 21	80 ,,	,,	,,
Pengwern	,, 21 11.30 p.m.	85 ,,	,,	Lizard
Sir Walter Raleigh ..	,, 22 2.15 p.m.	79 ,,	,,	Start
River Falloch	,, 27	92 ,,	,,	Tuskar
Tythonus	,, 29	95 ,,	,,	,,
Maude	,, 29	86 ,,	,,	,,
Firth of Stronsa ..	July 10	106 ,,	,,	,,

Of the nine ships the best run to the line was made by *Pengwern* from the line to Cape by *Samuel Plimsoll*; from the Cape to Tasmania by the *City of York*; and from thence to port by the *Sir Walter Raleigh*. A passage made up of the best runs between the points would only come to 65 days, and it is rather interesting to note that *Cutty Sark*, the ship which made the best passage, would not contribute to this result at all.

"DERWENT"

[*See Page* 258

"STAR OF ITALY"

[*See Page* 258

The *Cutty Sark* discharged at Circular Quay and was towed to an anchorage in the stream on 18th July.

Most of the regular wool clippers were accustomed to lie at anchor in Port Jackson until the wool clip came down country, the wait often lasting several months.

The time was occupied by those on board in preparing the ships for the race home, and there was much rivalry as to their smart appearance amongst the different ships. As a rule the weather was delightful, but when southerly busters blew up it was sometimes very uncomfortable in these sharp-lined ships, for with only just enough ballast to keep upright they often rolled until the lower yards dipped. Once a hard blow came along when the *Cutty Sark* was lying empty alongside the wharf, and she went over until her mainyard was within an ace of going through the roof of the shed.

When everything had been done to make the waiting ships like so many perfectly kept yachts, discipline was somewhat relaxed; shore leave was given to the apprentices, and Saturday afternoon picnics were arranged in which the different ships often joined in entertaining the girls of Sydney; these picnics usually ended in 'tween deck dances.

And every evening the quiet waters rang with the dog-watch sing-songs of the waiting clippers. A ship would start a well-known sea song, perhaps a favourite capstan chanty, and then, one by one, the other ships would take up until the effect was really magnificent.

Sometimes the ships would sing the different verses in turn —the whole fleet joining in the chorus. Often there were some really skilled musicians amongst the various ship's companies, and all sorts of instruments would join in with the voices until a very fair orchestra was in full blast.

No one who has heard sailor's music across salt water but has felt his soul uplifted by its wondrous charm. Even the most scrappy of catgut instruments or the gruffest of reef topsails voices are sweetened and mellowed by the softening power of water. I am sure that there are men alive today who will never forget the windjammer sing-songs in Sydney harbour.

And as these sea gypsies were one by one hauled out to the

Q

anchorage, after discharging their outward cargoes, the sight of fine vessels and the sound of sea songs increased.

Through the months of June, July, and August in 1885 the following first class ships were lying off with yards squared, bowsprits rigged in, awnings spread and gangway ladders down, waiting to load the wool crop for the January sales in London:—*Cutty Sark, Patriarch, Samuel Plimsoll, Cimba, Woolahra* and *Sir Walter Raleigh.*

The Tweed arrived in August, after a very long passage for her of 103 days, having carried away her figure-head and jibbooms in a fierce N.W. squall in the Bay of Biscay.

Thermopylae also arrived in August. She had arrived at Port Phillip on 8th April, 78 days from the Start. After discharging at Melbourne, she had gone up to Newcastle and loaded coal for New Zealand. She left Newcastle for Lyttelton on 25th June, and made the run from land to land in five days. She left Lyttelton on 8th August, with a cargo of wheat, oats, potatoes, beans, peas, bran, sharps, cheese, hams and bacon, stiffened by old iron rails, cleared Cape Campbell on the 11th, had a hard westerly gale and high sea from 13th to 16th, and entering the Heads at 10 a.m. was towed to an anchorage below Garden Island.

The *Yallaroi* arrived from London on 11th August, 99 days out on her maiden passage.

The first ship to start loading was the *Patriarch*, but she took part of her wool at Newcastle, being followed there by the *Cimba*.

Cutty Sark was berthed at the southern side of Circular Quay on Saturday, 5th September.

It was to be Captain Woodget's first passage round the Horn in command, and the other skippers jokingly assured him that he would lose his way. He soon showed them not only that he knew the way to Cape Stiff, but that he was not afraid of going well south into the ice limits in order to make a good track.

It was probably just before the *Cutty Sark* was hauled in to load that Woodget gave his crew a glimpse into his mind, by remarking to his third mate, as he glanced up at the golden cock at the main truck of the *Thermopylae*, which was lying near by:— "I'll pull that damned bauble off her."

The *Thermopylae* berthed at Dalgety's wharf on 1st October. It was usual to stiffen wool cargoes with casks of tallow, but *Cutty Sark* and *Thermopylae* were too fine in the run to stow casks economically and never loaded tallow in Australia.

The cargoes of the two great rivals in 1885 were as follows:—

Cutty Sark.	*Thermopylae.*
4465 bales of wool.	4638 bales of wool.
2342 packages cobalt ore.	650 bags chrome ore.
1345 bags nickel ore.	1142 bags nickel ore.
29,772 horns.	15 casks milk.
122 cwt. shank bones.	1 cask sheep shears.
76 cwt. hoofs.	19 tons 19 cwt. old iron rails.
6 bales sheep skins.	
1 cwt. pith.	

Messrs. Dalgety strained every effort in order to have *Thermopylae* ready in time to sail in company with the *Cutty Sark*, and she actually cleared the Customs the day the *Cutty Sark* sailed.

The ships leaving Australia in order to catch the January wool sales sailed in the following order:—

Patriarch, 5359 bales wool, left Newcastle October 5.
Sir Walter Raleigh, 3902 bales wool, cleared Sydney Heads 8 a.m. October 11.
Loch Vennacher, 5365 bales wool, cleared Port Phillip Heads 7.30 a.m. October 15.
Cutty Sark, 4465 bales wool, cleared Sydney Heads 1 p.m. October 16.
Woolahra, 4380 bales wool, cleared Sydney Heads October 17.
Salamis, 5740 bales wool, cleared Port Phillip Heads a.m. October 18.
Thermopylae, 4638 bales wool, cleared Sydney Heads 7.25 a.m. October 18.
Samuel Plimsoll, 4888 bales wool, cleared Sydney Heads 7.30 p.m. October 24.
Cimba, 5055 bales wool, left Newcastle October 24.

Every one of these ships was a noted heeler, with many a crack passage to her credit, and Captain Woodget had a tough proposition ahead of him, yet he left Sydney with only six A.B.'s in his foc's'le, trusting to his six reliable and strong apprentices, and with a complement of only 19 made the passage of the season.

The *Cutty Sark* wasted no time getting south, and as she neared the fifties it gradually breezed up from the south-west, until by 22nd October it was blowing hard with snow and hail squalls, yet the vessel still carried her main royal and by noon had run 306 miles in the 24 hours. Captain Woodget was carrying sail with a vengeance; and that very night the famous clipper had one of the closest calls of her existence:

The bald extracts of the log read as follows:—

At 11 p.m., whilst furling the crossjack, struck by a terrific squall: ship broached to, filling whole lee side of deck, smashing skids and taking port life-boat and all the gear overboard, also smashing dinghy, shifting starboard boat, and doing other damage.

"Upper main topsail blown clean out of the rope, main top-gallant sail and main royal split to shreds, also fore topgallant sail; outer jibstay carried away, etc."

By midnight it was blowing a strong gale with very hard squalls, the "Cutty" shipping "enormous quantities of water." Capt. Woodget was no whit dismayed, and in the middle watch, when many a skipper would have been preparing to heave to, he sent up, bent and reefed the main upper topsail, the fore and mizen upper topsails being reefed as soon as the main was sheeted home.

Only those who have been to sea in sail can realise the night spent by that small crew of six A.B.'s and six apprentices—the fight aloft, the furious labour on the jumping footropes, and the more than dangerous work on the flooded main deck, puctured by the warning cries of the mates as the bigger seas raged aboard and threatened to sweep all and sundry over the topgallant rail. It was bitterly cold—the thermometer being down to 32°, a low reading in that part of the world—whilst the snow and hail squalls battered the reeling ship in rapid succession, the hail at times sounding amidst the screams of the wind and twanging hum of the rigging like bursts of machine gun fire spattering on a Hun pill-box.

The sun was, of course, obscured by the flying wrack, the reckoning by account at noon on 23rd October being lat. 54° 14′ S., long, 178° 13′ W., course S 75° E., distance 274 miles. At 6 p.m. that afternoon a very fierce squall passed over, before whose approach all hands were sent racing aloft in order to furl the mizen upper topsail.

An hour later the dreaded cry of:—"Ice on the port bow!" burst from the drenched look-out, and a large berg loomed up to leeward.

October 23 was Antipodes Day, giving an extra 24 hours. It still blew a strong gale until noon on the second day, when the wind showed signs of decreasing with longer intervals between the squalls, and the mizen upper topsail was set again.

The reckoning at noon gave:—Lat. 55° 20′ S., long. 170° 1′ W., course S. 77° E., distance 290 miles. At 5 p.m. the reefs were shaken out of the topsails, the mainsail and staysails were set, and a new main topgallant sail and main royal bent and set. By mid-night the wind had dropped light though still westerly.

October 24 was a day of repairs: a new fore topgallant sail was sent up, bent and set; a new martingale stay was fitted and the main truss fixed.

For the next week or so the *Cutty Sark* had fresh to moderate westerly breezes and made a steady average of 250 miles a day, during which the best run of the passage was made—316 miles on 2nd November, under all sail before a W.N.W. breeze.

On 6th November the *Cutty Sark* was held up by a hard gale from E.N.E. to E.S.E. and S.E., the log reading:—

4 a.m., strong N.E. wind, sleet and snow. Wore ship to the N.N.W.

8 a.m., strong E.N.E. wind and hard snow squalls.

Noon, lat. 58° 36′ S., long. 78° 07′ W. Course N. 85° E. Distance 125 miles.

4 p.m., hard S.E. gale with terrific squalls and nasty high sea. Ship taking great quantities of water on board.

By midnight, however, the wind and sea began to go down, and at 4 a.m. on the 7th Woodget set all possible sail again. At noon the wind was N.W. strong, and the *Cutty Sark* under her main royal went tearing by the barque *James Wishart* of Leith.

On 8th November, the Horn was rounded, 23 days out from Sydney, the run for the 24 hours being 278 miles. The *Cutty Sark* was only two days behind the *Patriarch* at this point, having gained nine days on the run from the Australian coast.

On Imray's 1880 chart of the South Atlantic, the track of the *Heather Bell* is pricked as being the holder of the record from the Horn to the line, which distance the little Orient liner covered in 21 days, rounding the Horn on 10th November, 1856, and crossing the equator on 1st December.

Captain Woodget in his run to the line managed to beat this record by one day, and the distances run by the two ships are worth comparing:—

Heather Bell (1856), 180 on November 11, 233,250, 268, 270, 165, 228.
Cutty Sark (1885), 262 on November. 9, 249, 271, 219, 302, 224, 134.
Heather Bell (cont.), 250, 210, 177, 180, 210, 175, 142, 135, 220.
Cutty Sark (cont.), 256, 28, 208, 135, 211, 217, 156, 161, 160.
Heather Bell (cont.), 248, 240, 238, 238, 200 on December 1.
Cutty Sark (cont.), 214, 243, 219, 246, on November 28.

The *Heather Bell* was not stopped once, but the *Cutty Sark* was held up by calms and light head winds on 17th November, which practically cost her an extra day. The latter made the best track, though the *Heather Bell* crossed the line more to the eastward, and did not find so much north and east in the wind before taking the S.E. trades.

Both ships made good time crossing the Banks; on the 12th November the *Cutty Sark* encountered a hard N.W. gale with a high sea, which constantly filled the decks fore and aft, but, as usual, Woodget kept her going and topped the 300 for the 24 hours.

Cutty Sark passed close to leeward of Fernando Noronha at 11 a.m. on 28th November, but *Heather Bell* was well to windward of the island and she also weathered St. Paul's Rocks.

Cutty Sark's record of 20 days was equalled by the *Loch Torridon* in 1892, when the latter passed the Horn on 14th May and the line on 3rd June; she had, however, spoilt her chances of making a record passage by taking 40 days from Australia to the Horn.

The *Thomas Stephens* is supposed to have made a run from the Horn to the line under 20 days, but I have not been able to verify this record. I think she made a very fine run up the Atlantic in 1882, when Captain Robertson sailed her into Carrick Roads, only 98 days from 'Frisco.

The *Cutty Sark* drew ahead of the *Patriarch* soon after passing the Horn, and, though Captain Woodget did not know it, he was leading the wool fleet home long before he reached the equator.

Woodget's best run in the N.E. trades was 252 miles. These were lost on 7th December, in 28° N., 42° 21' W., from which date to Dungeness there was hardly a day when the yards were not on the backstays, the wind hanging steadily to the northward and eastward without a slant.

Flores was passed 4 miles to leeward on 15th December in a strong northerly gale, which had been blowing with hard squalls and high sea since 12th. At 4 p.m. that afternoon the wind began to moderate and haul to the N.E., in which quarter it stuck until the *Cutty Sark* was off the Ile de Verge light, when it fell right away to a calm.

It will thus be seen that Woodget had everything against him in the last leg of the passage, yet with her wonderful powers to windward the "Cutty" made several runs of over 200 miles, though she could never lay her course. On 20th December, with a fresh and squally north wind, she kept in company all day with a steamer, and on the 21st she was in lat. 46° 29′ N., long. 12° 25′ W., having covered 251 miles against a gusty N.N.E. wind. On the 22nd she was in the Bay of Biscay, within a day's sail of the Channel, but in the dead muzzler Woodget had no chance of weathering Ushant, and was compelled to wear round to the northward. For the next two days he could make no better than N. 5° W., his distances being only 64 and 65 miles, he then tacked to the southward again.

On Christmas day the N.E. wind gradually fell away from a moderate to a gentle breeze and the *Cutty Sark*, making a S. 72° E. course, only covered 70 miles.

At 5.30 a.m. on the 26th the Ile de Verge light was sighted and at 8 a.m. Woodget again tacked to the northward and continued tacking all day in a very light head wind. On the 27th the wind dropped altogether, and from early morning to 8 p.m. a clock calm held the clipper motionless—then at last the S.W. wind began to make. St. Catherine's was passed at 5.30 a.m. on the 28th, Beachy Head at 11 a.m., the Royal Sovereign at 11.20, pilot taken on board at 1.25 p.m. and the anchor dropped in the Downs at 11.30 p.m. in a hard gale with snow and sleet from the N.N.W.

With any luck from the N.E. trades, the *Cutty Sark* would have broken the record. As it was, in spite of persistent head winds, she was off the Ushant 67 days out.

In the mouth of the Channel she took five days covering 305

miles, a distance which she exceeded in one day in 1888, when making the Channel.

It was such weather as would have held up any other ship for another week or more, and Captain Woodget had every reason to be proud of his ship and satisfied with himself. All his rivals were days astern, *Thermopylae* was still over a week below the horizon, and the *Cutty Sark* had fully proved her right to be considered the fastest ship in the wool trade, which in the eighties meant the fastest ship in the world.

It was a cold, bleak, marrow-freezing home-coming. On her arrival in dock the smart third mate showed his pride in his ship by washing the poop down and cleaning up before the mate's well-known call of "That'll do, men," and as the apprentices broomed the water along the deck it turned to thin sheet ice—a not unusual welcome home for the wool clipper which raced for the January sales.

The times of the nine ships were:—

Ship			Days		Days
Cutty Sark	Ushant	Dec. 22	67	Downs 11.30 p.m. Dec. 28	73
Salamis	Lizard	Jan. 4	79	,, Jan. 6	81
Thermopylae ..	Channel	Jan. 5	79	,, ,, 6	80
Sir Walter Raleigh ..	,,	,, 5	86	,, ,, 6	87
Loch Vennacher ..	,,	,, 6	83	,, ,, 7	84
Woolahra ..	Lizard	,, 5	80	3 p.m. Jan. 7	82
Patriarch ..	Portland	Jan. 6	93	,, ,, 8	95
Samuel Plimsoll ..	Channel	,, 21	89	,, ,, 23	91
Cimba	,,	,, 25	93	,, ,, 27	95

Captain Jock Willis was so delighted by the *Cutty Sark's* performance in making the best wool passage of the year and so handsomely beating her great rival *Thermopylae*, that he determined to give Dick Woodget a chance to lower the record from China, which had been made by *Sir Lancelot* in 1869.

Unfortunately the tea trade was now entirely in the hands of the racing steamers, and bar one or two of the old sailing fleet, who still hung on defiantly, steam bottoms took all the cargoes of Shanghai or Foochow.

Hallowe'en and *Leander* still managed to load mixed cargoes from China ports, but they had to put up with very poor freights.

Again sailing ships no longer loaded general cargo for China, this also being reserved for the interloping steamers. Thus it came about that *Cutty Sark* had either to load scrap iron or go out in ballast to Shanghai. "Old White Hat" decided to accept the scrap iron, and with this horrible deadweight cargo the poor little *Cutty Sark* was loaded down like a sand barge to a draught of 21 feet.

The ship was advertised to sail at noon on 17th February. That morning her owner appeared on board with a party of friends in order to give his ship the usual send-off. The visitors were shown over the clipper by her proud owner, and as soon as the sun was over the yardarm the whole party trooped below and refreshed themselves with wine, sandwiches and cigars.

Then, when Captain Woodget's health had been drunk and a chorus of voices had wished him a pleasant voyage, old Willis mysteriously produced a long brown paper parcel, and going to the break of the poop called for the senior apprentice.

R. L. Andrewes, the third mate, jumped aft. Whereupon Willis proceeded to unpack his brown paper parcel and presently disclosed a golden cutty sark, cleverly carved in metal and gilded, about 2 ft. 9 inches in height and with a channel for a vane right through its centre.

"Jump aloft," cried "old White Hat," "and fit this to the vane on the main truck," adding with tremendous emphasis— "Weel done, Cutty Sark."

It was a great moment. Amidst a burst of cheering, which drew all eyes in the East India Dock to the graceful form of the clipper with the Blue Peter aloft, young Andrewes sprang on to the ratlines with the golden shirt slung over his shoulders by a piece of spunyarn, and as he picturesquely expressed it—"skipped aloft as proud as Billy be damned."

Every eye aboard and on the dock side and in the neighbouring ships followed the fitting of this emblem of victory on the main truck of the *Cutty Sark*.

It did not take long for Andrewes to fit this strange metal garment over the vane, screw down the nut on top and regain the deck by means of the royal backstay, yet already the news had spread amongst the shipping, and by the time that the *Cutty Sark* had hauled out into the stream the story of the golden shirt at her main truck was being told in the Baltic.

And whilst Jock Willis stood up to a storm of chaff and congratulations, whilst the captains of the other crack wool ships discussed ways and means of lowering this proud symbol of victory, the *Cutty Sark* towed to sea and was cheered by every ship as she passed.

Before she cast off her tug, let me say a word or two about her crew this voyage.

Dimint was still mate, but Jacques had gone and the new second mate was J. Selby, a son of the manager of Bullivants, the wire rope makers.

Selby was undoubtedly the best officer Woodget ever had. He served two voyages as second mate and three voyages as mate, leaving the *Cutty Sark* in 1891 in order to take command of her old rival, *Titania*. He was, I suppose about 21 or 22 when he took the second mate's berth in 1886, but he looked older and was more of a man than his years indicated, being one of those quiet, reserved, well-controlled, self-reliant men who command the respect of those under them. Though a very strict officer, who tried to inoculate his watch with his own sense of duty, energy and tirelessness, he was popular with both men and apprentices, these last looking up to him as an example of what an officer should be. Indeed Selby was an ideal mate. He expected perfection not only in the state of the ship but in her petty officers, apprentices and crew, and he saw that he got it, malingerers finding it very difficult to exercise their talents under his regime. Yet there was no false dignity about him though he did keep those under him in their place, and he was not above showing anybody how things should be done.

He was specially good at marlinspike seamanship and a past master in the art of handling wire, splicing it and knotting it; he thought nothing of staying up in his watch below in order to finish a piece of work, such for instance as making a stopper knot in the wire main tack.

In port he invariably was out in the boat every evening when the "Cutty" was lying off, and was most particular in seeing that the masts were aligned to the last fraction of an inch and the yards dead square. Indeed the *Cutty Sark* was never more perfectly kept than when Selby was mate. Under him her bright work was always kept well cleaned and varnished, and the white paint of the iron bulwarks, panels of the deck-houses and monkeypoop was always spotless.

It was the same thing below, every voyage the skin was cleaned off and painted, the under deck swabbed and coated with pine oil, and the iron frame chipped and leaded, whilst the bilges were kept as clean as the more conspicuous parts of the ship.

Selby was also an athlete and no mean customer with his "fives." In Sydney he was often to be found boxing of an evening at Larry's. The noble art was always very popular on the *Cutty Sark*, and if her people were occasionally beaten at cricket or football, not many ships could produce a crowd more skilled with the gloves than the *Cutty Sark's* officers and apprentices.

R. L. Andrewes, *Cutty Sark's* big third mate and senior apprentice, was joined by his brother this voyage, a youth almost as big and manly as himself, who came from the *Sumatra*, a small Sunderland built barque belonging to Willis's fleet.

Of the rest Bowers and Durrant left at the end of 1885, and were replaced by Calderon, the son of the artist, and Toby Mayall.

Calderon began his apprenticeship in the little *Helen Denny*, but had cleared out in New Zealand, succumbing to the attractions of farm life. But these attractions soon faded and a day came when having fallen off the horse roller, he decided that he was more fitted for the rollers of the sea, and thus we find him on the *Cutty Sark*, which once again had a hefty lot of boys in her half-deck, namely R. L. Andrewes, W. F. Andrewes, J. Weston, C. E. Irving, P. H. Calderon, T. Dixon, J. Smith and T. Mayall.

There were only two youngsters amongst them; one of these was nicknamed "The Squeaker" by old Dimint. The Squeaker rather laid himself open to tormenters by being rather green and "rising" somewhat easily, and many a trick was played upon him until he learnt to look after himself.

One day in the second dog watch in the S.E. trades, a knowing old hand bet him that he would not run aloft to the main truck and come down again with only one boot on.

"I'll bet you $\frac{1}{4}$ lb. of baccy I will," said Squeaker, upon which the whole half deck trooped out to see the bet carried out fairly.

The Squeaker took off one boot, and up he went on the port side, over the main truck, and down the starboard side.

"There you are," said he triumphantly, "I've won."

"What about your pants and singlet," said the other, "I said only one boot on!"

It was Squeaker's great ambition to catch a booby. One second dog watch one of the hands came aft and said that there was something on the spencer gaff, which he believed to be a booby.

"By jove!" said Squeaker, "let me catch it." The spencer gaff had just been greased. The Squeaker swung out on to the heel of the gaff from the futtock shrouds, and after much slipping and swearing got out to the peak. Here he carefully steadied himself and clapped a hand over the booby, then those below heard some awful language and flop on the deck came an old sou'wester. The Squeaker came down from aloft all smothered in grease, to be jumped on by the mate for wiping the grease off the traveller of the spencer.

Even old Woodget was not above having a bit of fun with this boy.

Squeaker was notoriously difficult to turn out, and was one of those fiendish sleepers who take a quarter of an hour to wake and pass it in improving their vocabulary in the higher arts of swearing.

One morning the "old man," in turning out his cabin, succeeded in finding a nest of baby rats. He came out of the cabin companion with them just as the Squeaker had begun his one bell objection to being turned out.

Without saying a word Woodget dropped the handful of new born rats on to the face of the sleep-drugged youth. Squeaker knew nothing until the rats began to nose about for a feed, and then with a yell which fairly made the *Cutty Sark* heel over he grabbed at the rats and flung them in every direction. It was a nice awakening.

This same boy was a wonder at lifting food or drink from under the eyes of the steward, who like all stewards was rated a mean little beast and a sneak by the half-deck. However he had a good deal to contend against. Apprentices, given the opportunity, will bore a hole in a barrel of any liquid, and suck the contents by means of a stick of macaroni. And they will drop a case on its corner so as to break a bottle inside.

Of course old Willis had sufficient experience to send his maturing wine in a cask within a cask, but bottled beer in cases was a direct incentive to an apprentice's ingenuity. Squeaker had a way of abstracting bottles, which he concealed down his trouser leg, a stop tied under the knee, navvy-like, preventing the bottle from slipping out.

After a series of these petty thefts, the steward one day took rather a mean revenge.

It happened that the apprentices were scraping the monkey poop outside the steward's pantry, within reach of a barrel of raisins. Squeaker managed to get his hand in, but he could not withdraw it with his fist closed; however he managed to get a number of raisins between his fingers, transferred them to his shirt, and after work made a dandy funk and put it into the oven to bake. The suspicious steward, in going to the oven, noticed that one of the half-deck dandy funks had raisins in it. He thereupon put an open razor into his barrel of raisins. The boy, when he tried again the next day, cut his hand badly on the razor, but of course made out that he had done it with his scraper. The steward smiled; he had scored for once. One could go on yarning about half-deck escapades for ever, but space forbids.

The *Cutty Sark* anchored at 6 p.m. on 17th February below the Nore; weighed at 5 a.m. on the 18th, and was towed as far as the East Margate Buoy; at 2 p.m. Mr. Oats, the river pilot, left and sail was made to a moderate N.E. breeze. The wind gradually fell lighter and lighter; at 10 p.m. on the 19th, Mr. Chapman, the Channel pilot, left off Berry Head, and Woodget took his departure from the Start, bearing N.N.E. 6 miles at midnight.

For the next fortnight the *Cutty Sark* had to contend against light southerly breezes and did not average 100 miles a day, whilst the celebrated four-mast ship *Talavera*, which was noted for her fast passages and had passed Start Point a day ahead of the "Cutty" did not make more than one run of 100 miles in that time.

This light weather continued, there being practically no N.E. trades, and both ships made the longest passages of their careers to the line, which was crossed by the *Talavera* on 24th March, 34 days from the Start, and by the *Cutty Sark* on 28th March, 37 days from the Start. There was no wind between the trades, and the *Cutty Sark* did not pick up the S.E. trades until 3rd April, in 6° S., 22° W. Both ships took 24 days from the equator to the Greenwich meridian; but between the Greenwich meridian and the Cape meridian Willis's famous clipper managed to catch up her big rival, the two ships crossing the longitude of the Cape on the same day 24th April. The weather still continued unfavourable for passage making and the *Cutty Sark* had no chance to show her heels until she was in 50° E.

Then at last a fresh westerly breeze blew up and on 5th May the *Cutty Sark* was in 42° 12′ S., 56° 03′ E., having run 320 miles in the 24 hours.

Her best work of the whole passage was made from 9th to 11th May, when her log recorded:—

May   9—Lat. 39° 52′ S., long 75° 03′ E.   Course N. 80° E.   Distance 336 miles.
          Moderate S.W. gale, hard squalls.
      10—Lat. 40° 12′ S., long. 82° 31′ E.   Course S. 86° E.   Distance 334 miles.
          Strong S.W. wind, high sea.
      11—Lat. 39° 04′ S., long. 89° 05′ E.   Course N. 77° E.   Distance 314 miles.
          Fresh S.S.W. wind and fine.

A total of 994 miles in three days, or allowing for loss of time going east, over 1000 miles in the 72 hours, pretty good work for a ship loaded down like a sand barge.

Some good running was also made in the Indian Ocean. Java Head was made on 21st May, her week's runs being 254, 213, 230, 286, 269, 295, and 224.

At Anjer whilst the apprentices swopped white shirts and cotton singlets for bananas and ducks' eggs, Captain Woodget bought two monkeys, which, as is usual with their kind, contributed both to the amusement and annoyance of the "Cutty's" crew. Woodget kept the jenny tied up on the poop, but allowed the jack monkey to run loose. The little rascal was always up to mischief. His chief delight was to nip down to the saloon through the skylight and steal the lump sugar off the tea table, which he would bring on deck and eat, keeping just out of reach of the jenny, which would howl and "cook" most mournfully, as she watched him. Jack distinguished himself by jumping overboard at Shanghai in order to avoid a beating. He was washed away by the current, whereupon Woodget let go the painter of the "Cutty's" attendant sampan, and the sampan wallah managed to pick the monkey up.

Cutty Sark had very light winds in the China Sea, and with her very heavy deadweight cargo took close on a month to Shanghai. She passed through Gaspar Straits on 27th May, was off Swatow on 14th June, and arrived at Shanghai on 24th June, 124 days out.

With the exception of a few blue-nose and Yankee oil ships, there was not a single windjammer in Shanghai except the *Cutty Sark*, and 3½ months were spent vainly hoping for a tea charter.

The last clipper in port had been the *Wylo*, which left for London on 2nd March, with a mixed cargo. Only two other ships of the old tea fleet came out to China: these were the inseparables, *Hallowe'en* and *Leander*.

Both managed to get charters at Foochow. It was to be *Hallowe'en's* last passage. She left Foochow on 19th August under Captain Dawton, who had served his time in the ship, working his way from apprentice to master; passed Ascension on 26th November, and ran ashore at Sewer Mill Lands, Salcombe, at 7.30 p.m. on 17th January, 1887, becoming a total loss. *Leander* left Foochow on 17th September for London.

Titania had been bought by the Hudson Bay Company at the end of 1885, on her arrival home from Bimlipatam; and on 10th January, 1886, she left London under Captain Dunn on her first voyage round the Horn to Victoria, B.C. She was not the only tea clipper to beat round the Horn from the eastward, for this same year *Windhover* went out to 'Frisco from the Clyde, and *Kaisow* was already in the West Coast of South America trade. But *Titania* made no less than five voyages out round the Horn in the employ of the Hudson Bay Co. before she was sold to the Italians, and in these she showed that she could make just as good passages as the old Yankee Cape Horn clippers, as the more modern

Down Easters, and as the magnificent Liverpool and Clyde grain carriers.

Whilst in Shanghai, Woodget with a view to Saturday afternoon sailing in Sydney harbour bought an old French pinnace for 10 dollars.

It was perfectly sound, of good teak, but had been hanging from the davits at Birt's Wharf for some time, so that you could put your fingers through the seams. Woodget sent his carpenter down to caulk her up a bit, put some bags of shingle ballast in her, and fitted her with a new bamboo mainboom. He next proceeded to sail his third mate down to the Garden Wharf for the letters. Woodget luffed alongside the wharf, whilst Andrewes jumped ashore to go up to the agents for the mail. The senior apprentice came back just in time to see his skipper capsize off Soochow creek —the mainboom, with the sheet out, had dipped in the water. The pinnace immediately sank, and dragged down Woodget in the gear, but he managed to wriggle free, and grabbing his umbrella and billycock hat, which were floating on the surface, struck out for a sampan.

That afternoon Woodget left the *Cutty Sark* with his apprentices in the dinghy and the sampan, and proceeded to drag for the boat with the lead-line. This weary business produced no result until noon on Saturday, the following day, when the lead-line fouled something. A Chinese diver was then procured who went down and found that the line was foul of an old opium hulk's anchor. Woodget thereupon ceased operations. But on Sunday morning about 30 Chinks came alongside with the pinnace, which they had found drifting opposite the Hongkew Wharf, about 2 miles down stream. They, of course, all clamoured at once for a large reward: but Woodget gave them 5 dollars and cleared them out of the ship. He next fitted the boat with 10 gallon oil drums lashed under the fore and aft seats, and after testing her down to her bearings pronounced her seaworthy again.

After this, usually with the two Andrewes brothers as crew, he enjoyed many a sail in the Shanghai river.

As I have mentioned before, the *Cutty Sark's* half-deck was composed of the usual tough material in the shape of apprentices.

"CUTTY SARK" PASSING "CIMBA," AUGUST 1st, 1890

From a painting by Forster in possession of Captain Woodget.

See Page 268

"ARISTIDES"

See Page 269

It is only fair to the Seamen's Mission that I should describe how this tough material was softened and reformed by the sky pilots of Shanghai.

Cne sultry evening in August a sampan bumped against the "Cutty's" accommodation ladder, and immediately afterwards a tall figure in white ducks and solar topee stepped on to the quarter-deck. This was Mr. Newcombe, chief officer of the Hangkow river steamer, which was then lying in dry dock at the Point opposite the Hongkew Wharves.

"Can I see the captain?" he asked. Captain Woodget who was sitting in a deck chair on the monkey poop, got up and asked the visitor what he could do for him.

A short conversation followed, then Mr. Newcombe departed down the ladder, and was speedily "yo-loed" down the current to the Garden Wharf. Then the "old man" turned to his apprentices who was sitting on the quarter-hatch, just aft of their house, and said significantly:—

"There'll be a mission meeting on board tomorrow evening at 6 p.m. and you lads will have to sing up." At which glances of uneasiness and consternation were exchanged between Willis's hard bargains.

At 6 p.m. the following evening a sampan came alongside bearing three men and two ladies with a harmonium. The harmonium was hoisted up and placed on the monkey poop under the awning. The apprentices squatted down sheepishly, and the service began. After the usual prayers and two or three hymns, such as "Shall we gather at the river," "Follow, follow, I will follow Jesus," an admirable discourse was given by a young Scotsman, from one of the go-downs, on the text, "I am the Door." After the service whilst the hymn books were being collected and the harmonium lowered into the sampan, Mr. Newcombe followed the boys down on to the quarter-deck, and, picking out the brothers Andrewes, linked his arms in theirs and started to patrol the deck, asking questions the while in a friendly way.

Finally he said:—"Would you two like to come aboard my vessel from Saturday afternoon till Sunday evening?"

"If you get leave for us from the 'old man,' we'll come like

R

a shot," came the reply. Mr. Newcombe at once asked Woodget, who gave his consent.

It may here be remarked that the *Cutty Sark's* apprentices, like most of their kind, looked upon all missionaries (sky pilots or snuffle busters, they usually called them) as rather a spineless lot and only to be tolerated for what could be got out of them. And the attraction of the invitation to the Andrewes brothers consisted in the prospect of a square feed and freedom from the ship for a few hours, any idea of spiritual improvement being far from their thoughts.

But Mr. Newcombe was a tactician; he knew that the right way to tackle an apprentice was through his stomach.

The next Saturday afternoon the two boys were put aboard Mr. Newcombe's ship and immediately sat down to a repast of hot buttered toast, cakes and tea with milk and sugar.

Only a windjammer apprentice who has lived for six months on Liverpool pantiles and stewed tea water can imagine their enjoyment. The tea was followed by yarning in comfortable deck chairs under the awning on the upper deck until dinner-time. A capital dinner was done ample justice to by the brothers, then yarns and smokes lasted until it was time to turn in. The Sunday programme consisted of early morning tea and toast, a plunge into the dock basin, which had the gates open, breakfast, a service on one of the American ships lying at moorings lower down the river, back to the dry dock for dinner, smokes and a lay back till 4 o'clock, and then by sampan to the service at the Seamen's Mission Hall in the English Settlement, which was preceeded by a good tea.

About 40 seamen from various steamers and sailing ships attended the service, but there were no apprentices beyond the Andrewes brothers, as the *Cutty Sark* happened to be the only ship in Shanghai with apprentices.

After the service the boys said good-bye to Mr. Newcombe and made their way to the steamer wharves, opposite which the *Cutty Sark* was lying in mid-stream.

As neither boy had any money, a very usual state of pocket for an apprentice, they had to resort to strategy in order to get aboard.

The "three piece bamboo" was pointed out to the sampan-wallah, who was to be their victim, It was half-ebb, when a 5-knot current is running out. The sampan-wallah worked up along the shore until well above the ship and struck across diagonally, judging his distance and leeway so exactly that he just made the gangway ladder, having almost bust himself with his big oar or "yo-lo," which is worked from the stern of the sampan.

The wallah dare not stop yo-lo-ing for a moment until one of his passengers has got hold of the ladder or a rope's end from the ship.

Then the boy in the bow holding on, the Chink ships his yo-lo in order to come into the well to get his money. This is the psychological moment for the usual strategy resorted to by apprentices in Shanghai.

The boy in the well, who is searching his empty pockets for the fare, suddenly leaps forward, follows his mate on to the gangway ladder, and at the same time gives the sampan a good push off with his foot.

Before the astonished Chink can get his sampan under control again, she is probably half a mile down stream. He then resorts to loud and strong imprecations, and curses Englishmen and their ships and everything else as well, but soon gives up all ideas of working his way up stream again, and yo-los over to his moorings along the wharves.

This programme was successfully put into practice by the Andrewes brothers.

The apprentices had various other methods of getting aboard without paying. Sometimes the sampan wallah would be given a chit, but with no clue to the name of the apprentice. This was usually in the darkness of the night, and when Johnnie Chinaman appeared in daylight a day or two later in order to get his money he was rarely able to pick out his fare from the row of boys in their working kit, who were paraded before him by the skipper. At last the sampan wallahs refused to take the boys off unless they had their money first.

No doubt to the reader such tricks will sound rather low-down work, but in these days the sampan wallahs made a good living and were considered fair game by the penniless British boys; indeed the typical apprentice never paid for anything if he could possibly avoid it.

After this breaking of the ice, Mr. Newcombe had all the *Cutty Sark's* boys up to his ship and the Mission in turn, and in this way they made many friends in the port and received a good deal of hospitality.

Captain Woodget very wisely never refused leave, shrewdly surmising how beneficial this association with the Shanghai sky pilots would be to his boys. Indeed their work and behaviour steadily improved. Strong language became taboo in the half-deck, and they even began to introduce Sankey hymns into their evening sing-songs.

But the real test came one Sunday evening. The senior apprentice was walking to evening service at the Mission Hall with Mr. Newcombe, when the latter remarked casually:—"I am going to ask you to come on to the platform tonight and say a few words on the Lord's side."

Andrewes had a presentiment of something of the sort being required of him eventually—he felt that they could not go on getting so many good feeds without some kind of return. Yet with all a boy's horror of making an exhibition of himself on a public platform, he was caught flat aback and trembled at the thought. Nevertheless he felt that he could not in honour shirk it after all Newcombe's kindness, and nerved himself for the ordeal.

And when the usual invitation came at the end of the service for someone "to come out on the Lord's side," he bravely walked up on to the platform and said a few words.

Having made a declaration of this sort, he meant to do his best to stand by it. Luckily he was the senior apprentice and the rest of the half-deck backed him up most loyally. The boys were all very smart with their fists and so the forward deck-house were careful to avoid any chaffing comments on their being "saved," etc. The skipper complimented the missionaries on taming his tough lot of boys, and declared that it had made a great deal of difference to their work and behaviour—they worked very con-scientiously, rowdyism was a thing of the past, and he could absolutely trust them. Indeed it was some months before the influence of the sky pilots began to wear off.

With no prospect of a Shanghai cargo, orders were received for the *Cutty Sark* to go down to Sydney in ballast. At 5 a.m. 5th October the anchor was weighed and the *Cutty Sark* towed down to Woosung. Here a friend of Woodget's left her, four of the apprentices being detailed to row him back and land him 4 miles up the river; the boys did not catch their ship again until noon, by which time they had rowed 12 miles without any breakfast, but they were strong hefty lads. They had need to be in the old windjammer days.

Meanwhile the *Cutty Sark* had been towed on, but had not got very far down before she tailed on to a sandbank. Luckily it was not very serious, though the tug, hoping that a nice salvage job was in store, would not do her best directly it was seen that the ship was coming off. However Woodget was not the man to try these games upon, and directly his vessel was afloat again he cast off the tug and dropped down under sail in light airs and calms anchoring when the tide turned, about 7 miles down.

On 6th October, with light easterly winds and neap tides it took all day working the ship down as far as the lightship. The next day she got as far as the Inner lightship before being compelled to anchor again at 5 p.m. On 8th October, at 3.30 p.m., Gutslav bore S. by W. and the pilot left, but Woodget was again compelled to anchor at the turn of the tide. However at 10 p.m. he weighed again with the wind making from E.N.E. The next day the ship passed through the Saddle Channel and went plunging south into a strong S.E. sea, the wind being E.N.E. moderate.

Fair progress was made until 16th October, when the *Cutty Sark* was in 13° 14′ N., 112° 23′ E. at noon. All that afternoon the wind gradually breezed up, but Woodget hung on to his main royal, and during the second dog watch the *Cutty Sark* ran 33 miles, the common and patent logs agreeing. At 8 bells the "old man" took in his main royal and mizen topgallant sail, the ship having covered 78 miles in five hours.

At 3 bells in the first watch, the wind, which had been N.E., shifted in a terrific squall to the N.W. The *Cutty Sark* took it on the starboard beam.   "All hands on deck!" rang through the ship. But it was too late. The clipper heeled right over until the coaming of her main hatch was awash and half the lee mainyard arm was dragging in the water. Every rag was blown off her except the lower main topsail. Finally this went also, and she came staggering up in her usual gallant fashion. It was a close call, however—one of the closest of her existence.

All that night it blew very hard with furious squalls and torrents of rain, but at 6 a.m., on the 17th, at the first sign of the weather moderating, Woodget bent another lower main topsail and a new foresail.

There was no other incident worth recording in the run to Anjer. On 31st October the *Cutty Sark* worked through Stolzes Channel, and on 3rd November passed Anjer, 26 days out from her pilot.

She had light trades and southerly airs all the way down to the forties, but on her first day running the easting down she made 342 miles in the $23\frac{1}{2}$ hours before a strong S.S.W. wind. This was on 23rd November in 40° 8′ S., 105° 45′ E. On the following day she ran 302 miles, and her week's work from 22nd-28th November totalled 1889 miles, being just spoilt by one day of light winds.

During most of the time she had a heavy cross sea to contend against; and one day at three bells in the morning watch the mate was going round the decks sweating up before turn-to time, when she dipped her nose into the green.

The watch were heaving down on the foretack whilst old Jerry Dimint stood on the forehatch, shouting his everlasting:—"One more pawl, boys." Three times the *Cutty Sark* dived, and at the third plunge the sea swept the whole watch off the foc's'le-head. The mate jumped off the fore-hatch on to the forward deck-house and escaped scot-free, but two of the lads did not fetch up until they were banged against the break of the poop. The third mate got caught up on one of the arms of the windlass and was held there, hanging face downwards over the break of the foc's'le until the button of his long oilskin coat carried away, when he flopped on to the fore-deck, dislocating his wrist and putting his thumb out of joint. One of the hands was washed under the forward winch and had his knee cap broken, whilst another had his jaw broken, the rest escaping with minor bruises. It was a very ordinary incident during the days of sail; but in these days of hard steaming into the eye of a gale, it is even more dangerous to be caught by a sea as it generally means a smashed head or at least a broken leg.

Cutty Sark passed the Otway on 30th November, 53 days out, and after experiencing some very calm weather on the coast reached Sydney on 5th December 58 days out.

Woodget found that he was too late to get a cargo for the March wool sales, whilst the January ships had already sailed including his last years' rivals, *Thermopylae, Salamis, Patriarch* and *Loch Vennacher. Cimba, Woollahra* and *Samuel Plimsoll* had their cargoes engaged and were already loading, and the following ships were waiting to take wool in January:—*Cairnbulg, Illawarra, Port Jackson, Orontes, Smyrna, Trafalgar,* and *Dharwar*: thus *Cutty Sark* had no chance of getting a cargo until March.

In the meanwhile all the earlier ships arrived home, the best passage being that of *Mermerus,* which arrived in the Thames on 26th February, 78 days from Melbourne after beating the *Sir Walter Raleigh* by two days.

The famous Aberdeen White Star clippers, *Thermopylae, Salamis* and *Patriarch,* had a very close race, the result being:—

Ship	Left	Arrived	Days
Salamis ..	Melbourne Oct. 24	London Jan. 17	85
Thermopylae ..	Sydney Oct. 24	London Jan. 19	87
Patriarch ..	Sydney Oct. 24	London Jan. 21	89

Cutty Sark left Sydney at 2 p.m. on 26th March, 1887, with 4296 bales of wool, and was becalmed in sight of Sydney Heads most of that afternoon. The wind remained light until 30th March when it shifted to the south, and on the 31st the *Cutty Sark* made her first run of over 200 miles.

Auckland Island was sighted at noon on 2nd April, by which time the clipper was averaging a steady 250 in a strong S.W. gale with hard squalls and high sea.

The gale and mountainous sea came to its height on 8th April, when the log recorded:—

Very hard south gale and terrific squalls, blowing fore topsail clean out of the rope. Mainsail split after being hauled up. 8 a.m., ditto, wind with mountain sea. 9 a.m., passed an iceberg. Noon, lat. 54° 79' S., long. 150° 02' W. Course N. 86° E. Distance 250 miles. Hard gale and high sea. 4 p.m., decreasing gale, bent lower topsail. 8 p.m., bent the mainsail, jib and fore topgallant sail.

For the next week *Cutty Sark* was running through a maze of ice, and Captain Woodget's abstract notes:—

April 9—8 a.m., passed an iceberg about 150 ft. high.
   10—Passed 4 icebergs, one of which was about 250 ft. high, flat-topped and covered with snow, about 3 miles long.
   11—8 a.m., passed an iceberg. Passed 8 icebergs during the night.
   12—Passed 4 icebergs during the day.
   13—Noon, passed an iceberg, about 200 ft. high and a mile long. 2 p.m., passed a small berg, about 40 ft. high and 300 ft. long.
   14—Passed 4 icebergs. 4 p.m., snow and sleet.
   15—8 p.m., passed 2 icebergs, snow squalls.

On 17th April *Cutty Sark* ran 308 miles, and on the 19th rounded the Horn in a moderate N.N.W. gale with a run of 305 miles, being 24 days out.

Heavy weather continued to 30th April, when the wind fell light in 30° 34' S., 35° 06' W. During the whole of April the crew had had a pretty amphibious time of it, whilst Woodget carried sail through gales and ice with an iron nerve.

On one occasion I think on the 28th off the River Plate, when Woodget records:—"Hard gale and high sea, wind west, terrific squalls, sea one white foam"—Walter Andrewes nearly lost the number of his mess. The main royal had just been taken off her and the two brothers were coiling up the gear: Walter Andrewes was to leeward, coiling the halyards on the fife-rail, when a fierce squall struck the "Cutty" and heeled her over till the rail disappeared and her lee deck filled. Young Andrewes was swept into the scuppers with a tangle of running gear, then, as the gallant ship brought her spars to windward, he was washed overboard on the foreside of the main rigging. The next roll filled her decks again and he was washed inboard abaft the main rigging. His brother could only look on helpless, it being impossible to do anything. Andrewes was not hurt or even very wet for he had "soul and body" lashings on his oilskins.

After such an escape one is apt to register a vow never to go to sea again once one's foot is on dry land, but such vows, though common with sailors, are mostly forgotten directly the weather moderates.

The *Cutty Sark* crossed the equator on 13th May, in 31° 18′ W., only 24 days from the Horn.

The Western Isles were passed on 25th May, 60 days out. At 5 p.m. that day the *Cutty Sark* had another of her narrow shaves. The wind shifted suddenly from S.W. to N.N.E. in a squall of gale strength with torrents of rain, and catching the clipper aback, nearly ripped the sticks out of her. Luckily the canvas was none too good and blew to ribbons, thus relieving the ship.

From 28th May to 1st June, the *Cutty Sark* had to contend against head winds, then it fell calm till noon on the 3rd, when an S.E. wind blew fresh for 24 hours before it dropped light again.

The Lizard was sighted at 10.30 p.m. on 4th June, 70 days out, and the *Cutty Sark* ran up Channel before a light southerly wind in lovely summer weather.

The Start bore W.N.W. at 4 p.m. on the 5th, a pilot was picked up off Dungeness on the 6th and the ship arrived in dock just in time for the Jublilee, having once more made by far the best passage of the year from the Colonies.

The Andrewes brothers, two of the finest seamen turned out from the *Cutty Sark's* half-deck, left her at the end of her 1886-7 voyage. The elder, passing for second mate, went straight into the P. & O. service, whilst his brother with four more months to put in shipped for the run to Bombay and back in the ss. *Arabia*. It happened that the mate of the *Arabia* had been second mate of the *Cutty Sark* in the early eighties, and when he heard that Andrewes came from his old ship he made no bones about helping him into the fourth mate's berth on the liner.

None of the other apprentices left and I think the newcomers were Atkinson and Waure.

Toby Mayall, by the way, was the son of the London photographer and it was through him that old Woodget was induced to take up photography in 1887. The chief drawback to photography aboard a sailing ship from the apprentices' point of view is the constant necessity of filling up the skipper's bath tank in order to provide him with water for his developing. For this reason Woodget's photography was not entirely popular with his apprentices. It will be noticed that many of the illustrations in this book are taken from Captain Woodget's photographs.

Details	Cutty Sark	Thomas Stephens	Brilliant
Left Docks ..	August 17	—	August 24
Left Sharpness ..	—	August 19	—
Left Lizard ..	August 20	August 20	August 26
Off Madeira ..	August 30	August 30	—
Crossed Equator	Sept. 19 in 24° 30′W.	Sept. 22 in 25°W	Sept. 28 in 28° W.
Passed Gough Is.	—	—	October 14
Passed Cape mer.	Oct. 15 in 39° 40′ S.	Oct. 23 in 43° S.	—
Dismasted ..	Oct. 22 in 39° S. 45′E	—	Oct. 19 in 41° 15′ E
Passed C. Otway	November 11	November 24	—
Passed S. Cape, Tas.	—	—	November 26
Arrived Melbourne	—	November 25	—
Passed C. Howe ..	November 16	—	November 29
Passed Jarvis Bay	November 16	—	December 3
Arrived Sydney ..	—	—	December 4
Arrived Newcastle	November 17	—	—
Days out	89	97	100

In the above table *Cutty Sark's* 1887 passage to Australia is compared to those of *Thomas Stephens* and *Brilliant*. With summer weather in the North Atlantic all three vessels made long passages for such fast ships, but *Cutty Sark* and *Brilliant* both had the misfortune to be dismasted.

The only excuses that the *Thomas Stephens* had for her long passage was that she had a new master, Captain Robert Johnston, formerly of the *Abergeldie*, and was loaded very deep with salt.

For her previous three voyages she had been commanded by Captain Cross, who was a young man and a fearless carrier of sail. The *Thomas Stephens* had the reputation of being a wet ship, and Cross rigged iron stanchions above his topgallant bulwarks, to which nettings were lashed, in order to keep his ship's company inboard, whilst he let her have it.

Thomas Stephens also had an iron wheel, one which was impervious to a pooper, for she had a way of washing her helmsman over the break of the poop. Another distinctive feature, which I do not think I have mentioned before, was her figure-head, which was what would have been called in those days an elegant effigy, of Mr. Thomas Stephens, top hat and all.

There was not much incident in *Cutty Sark's* passage until she reached the roaring forties.

I noticed that in 35° S., 20° W., when almost becalmed in the doldrums, Woodget had his first essay at photography. He caught an albatross and photographed it alive, its length from wing tip to wing tip being 11 feet. This was on 7th October. Twenty four hours later a strong northerly wind sprang up, and on 11th October *Cutty Sark* crossed the Greenwich meridian, after two runs of 312 and 292 miles.

Her dismasting occurred 20 minutes after midnight on 22nd October. It was Dimint's watch, and the ship was reeling off the knots in a fresh S.S.W. wind, with the yards on the backstays, when a hard W.S.W. squall struck her. Dimint was not quick enough in his orders to the helmsman, who allowed the ship to come to. Then the chainplate eye of the fore topgallant backstay carried away, and the lanyard of the royal backstay gave, with the result that the fore topgallant mast went over the side, taking with it the fore topmast head, broken off close to the rigging eyes, the main topgallant mast and main topmasthead. The main topmast fid broke fair in the centre and the mast dropped down to the slings of the mainyard. The fore topgallant mast happened to be a cheap pitch-pine one, instead of good Oregon, and broke very short; Woodget believed that had it been Oregon it would have stayed aloft in spite of the backstays carrying away.

Luckily during the next 12 hours the wind gradually dropped away, and Woodget managed to save every bit of the wreck alongside, with the exception of the fore topmast cap which sank.

But this did not last for long, for by noon on the 25th October it was blowing a hard N.W. gale. Yet with no fore and main topgallant masts and her main topmast deck, the *Cutty Sark* never stopped, and whilst all hands were refitting the clipper made the following runs:—

October 22, 214 miles;   October 23, 228 miles;   October 24, 156 miles; October 25, 265 miles;   October 26, 280 miles.

On the 27th the wind dropped, and during the next two days Woodget managed to send aloft main topmast and topsail yards, topgallant mast and topgallant yard.

On 4th November under jury rig, the *Cutty Sark* ran 313 miles, whilst on the day she rounded King's Island, 11th November, she ran 330 miles in the 24 hours.

Brilliant's dismasting took place at 3.40 p.m. on 19th October in 40° 56′ S., 15° 20′ E.   She was under all sail to main royal when a heavy squall struck her abeam, and the fore topmast carried away close to the lower cap, taking away everything on the fore except the foreyard, of which the slings were badly strained.   The crane and standard of the lower topsail yard were broken and so that went with the rest.   The main topmast followed the fore topmast over the side, breaking off close to the hounds and taking everything above the lower topsail yard.

It was next found that the bobstay had carried away, and that the bowsprit was sprung and broken, only holding on by one plate.   The wreckage fell with a crash to port, crushing the mainrail and bulwarks, breaking off several channel plates and piercing the deck in several places.

The ship now came to and lay in the trough of the sea with the wreckage pounding and grinding alongside, and battering against her bottom.   Captain Davidson began to fear that some of the bottom plates would be stove in, so after a consultation with his officers he finally cut the whole wreck away and set to work to jury-rig his vessel.

The *Brilliant's* best run under jury-rig was 270 miles, and her performance in reaching Sydney only 100 days out was considered so good that Captain Davidson was presented with a silver tea set.   The damage was estimated at £3000.

Cutty Sark had no long wait in the Colonies this year for her wool cargo.   As the Australian papers remarked: "She was an established heeler," and as soon as her outward cargo was discharged she was put on her wool berth.

She left Newcastle at 5 p.m., on 28th December, with 4155 bales of wool.

As I have said before, Woodget was not afraid of taking the *Cutty Sark* well south in her run to the Horn. This year he went as far as 64° 50′ S., the furthest south that the clipper ever touched, and for 15 days he was south of the 60th Parallel. Ice was fallen in with in 62° 09′ S., 178° 37′ W., on 8th January, Antipodes day.

His ice log, as I might call it, records:—

Jan.   8—Lat. 62° 09′ S., long. 178° 37′ W. Course S. 29° E. Distance 252 miles. Fresh south breeze. Passed 4 icebergs.

8—Lat. 62° 25′ S., long. 172° 47′ W. S. 85° E. 166 miles. Moderate S.E. breeze. Passed 6 icebergs.

9—Lat. 62° 25′ S., long. 164° 15′ W. East 240 miles. Moderate S.E. breeze. Passed 5 icebergs.

10—Lat. 62° 19′ S., long. 155° 2′ W. N. 89° E. 250 miles. Moderate S.E. breeze. 8 a.m., passed an iceberg and photographed it. Noon, passed close by another, about 250 ft. high and 1 mile long, 4 p.m., passed close by an iceberg, about 300 ft. high, and photographed it. Passed this day 19 large icebergs, one about 3 miles long.

11—Lat. 62° 41′ S., long. 148° 05′ W. S. 85° E. 180 miles. Very light Wly. breeze, smooth sea. Up to noon passed 100 large icebergs and a great number of small. Noon, icebergs in every direction. Counted 87 from aloft, large ones besides little ones. Last night when passing between 2 large icebergs, the thermometer fell to 31°, and mist formed on the spanker boom and rails.

12—Lat. 62° 38′ S., long. 143° 32′ W. East 145 miles. Light Wly. breeze. Passed about 80 icebergs.

On the 13th the *Cutty Sark* ran clear of the ice, making 296 miles before a moderate W.N.W. wind, and on the 15th the last iceberg of the passage was passed and photographed. On the 16th *Cutty Sark* was in her highest latitude, 64° 50′ S., from which point Captain Woodget set a course for the Horn.

At 3 p.m. on 22nd January the clipper passed close to the north of Diego Ramirez, two hours later Cape Stiff was sighted, and by 8 p.m. was astern, the *Cutty Sark* being 24½ days out from Newcastle.

On 23rd January Woodget ran along the coast of Staten Island, close enough to photograph it. Favourable weather carried the *Cutty Sark* to the line without incident; the equator being crossed on 15th February, 24 days from the Horn.

The Azores were passed on 3rd March, 16 days from the line, St. Michaels being 8 miles off at 8 a.m.; then, for the first time, the *Cutty Sark* was lucky in her run to the Channel. On 7th March she was in 48° 37′ N., 9° 30′ S., having made a run of 320 miles before a fresh south breeze. The Lizard was passed that evening the "Cutty" being 69 days out. The clipper made a magnificent run up Channel. At 1 p.m. on 8th March she was off Brighton, and that afternoon, whilst she was hove to waiting for her pilot off Dungeness, the *Thyatira* came under her stern, having sailed from Newcastle on 21st November, over five weeks before the *Cutty Sark*. Other ships overhauled by the famous clipper on this splendid passage were *Romanoff*, beaten by 59 days; *Smyrna*, beaten by 51 days; *Loch Ryan*, beaten by 39 days; *Harbinger*, beaten by 32 days; *Mermerus* beaten by 30 days; *Orontes*, beaten by 32 days; *Yallaroi*, beaten by 20 days; *Trafalgar*, beaten by 19 days; *Collingwood*, beaten by 19 days; *City of Agra*, beaten by 12 days; and *Loch Garry*, beaten by 14 days. All these were well known wool clippers. It was indeed a glorious victory, and old Willis was so delighted that he proposed all sorts of extravagances, and if there had been time in London he would undoubtedly have decorated his famous clipper with a carved rope in teak along her gilt streak.

Woodget's first three wool passages constituted a record for the homeward run from Australia which has never been beaten or even approached by any other vessel. It may therefore be of interest to compare them, showing the times between points.

Date left	Days to Horn	Days to Equator	Days to Azores	Days to Channel
Sydney 9 a.m. Oct. 16 1885	23	43	59	68
Sydney 9.15 p.m. March 26 1887	24	48	60	70
Newcastle 5 p.m. Dec. 28 1887	24½	49	65	69

CHAPTER VIII.

IN THE WOOL TRADE UNDER CAPTAIN WOODGET.—*Continued.*

OLD Jerry Dimint left the *Cutty Sark* in March, 1888. I doubt if Woodget ever forgave him for being caught napping, whereby the ship was dismasted on the outward passage.

Selby took his place, and a new second mate was shipped. This man came from steam, and only lasted one voyage. He did not possess the nerve and seamanship required by Woodget in a second mate.

Of the apprentices Dixon became senior and acting third mate, the others being J. Calderon, Toby Mayall, Cooke, Yorkie Atkinson, Waure, Dick Woodget and C. M. MacDonald.

Cooke was a very smart, well set-up youngster, who had been three years in the *Dharwar*.

He would have got on well, but was washed overboard and drowned on the homeward passage. Yorkie was the son of a Yorkshire farmer. He always brought an unsmoked ham and a few other Yorkshire delicacies to sea, which were very much appreciated.

Waure was a man of over 21, having been a sugar planter in the West Indies before he came to sea. It was his third voyage, and he did the duties of lamp-trimmer.

Dick Woodget was the skipper's eldest son, a smart lad who soon learned his business. The rest of the apprentices were frankly uncomfortable at first owing to the relationship, but they soon found that young Dick was treated and behaved in every way as though it was non-existent.

Mac was a hefty lad, who at 17 years of age stood 5 ft. 10½ inches, and without an ounce of fat on his bones weighed 12 stone 7 lbs.

Though of all shapes and sizes the *Cutty Sark's* apprentices always resembled each other on one point, they were all as fit and muscular as they could well be, and all looked the picture of health and strength.

The hardness of the life in sail has always had this result **on** boys, and turned delicate shrimps into sturdy, broad-shouldered men. It is very different in steam. There was never a superfluity of food on sailing ships, to put it mildly; but the ozone breathed in supplied the place of any want of nourishment. But on the *Cutty Sark* the beef and pork were always good, and Tony Robson in the galley showed all the skill usual in his nationality. The allowance on the "Cutty" was a cask of beef and a cask of pork a fortnight.

At 5 a.m. on 17th May, 1888, the *Cutty Sark* towed away from the East India Dock, took in powder at Gravesend and anchored at the Nore at 6 p.m. The tug was cast off **at Dungeness on 18th** May, and in fine weather with a light S.E. breeze the *Cutty Sark* set off down channel in company with the *Orontes*.

Both ships landed their pilots off the Start on the 19th and continued beating against a dead muzzler, blowing fresh from W.S.W. The wind dropped right away on the night of 20th May, and all the morning of the 21st the *Cutty Sark* lay becalmed in a glassy sea in the meridian of the Lizard.

There is very little incident to record of this passage, and I shall therefore put it in form of a table, and give those of *Orontes* and *Romanoff* as a comparison to show *Cutty Sark's* superiority.

Details	*Cutty Sark*	*Orontes*	*Romanoff*
Left the Docks ..	May 17	May 16	April 27
Off the Lizard ..	May 21	May 21	—
Off Scilly ..	—	—	May 3
Crossed equator ..	June 17 in 28° 40′W.	June 27 in 26° W.	June 8 in 27° W.
„ mer. of Green'h	July 4 in 38° S.	—	—
„ mer. of Cape	July 7 in 43° S.	July 24 in 41° S.	July 3 in 43° S.
Best run (July 27)	320 in 46° S. 119° E.		
Made the Otway	Aug 1 72 days out	Aug 21 92 days out	Aug 3 92 days out
Arrived Melbourne	—	—	August 4
Arrived Sydney ..	8 a.m. Aug. 5	a.m. Aug. 25	—

On arrival in Sydney, the *Cutty Sark* was at once engaged for the January wool sales: but having made up the time lost by her futile voyage to China in 1886 by her last two rapid homeward passages, she once more had a long wait in Sydney.

"PASS OF KILLIECRANKIE"

[See Page 289

"ZEALANDIA"

See Page 282

FOUR-MAST SHIP

Taken from deck of *Cutty Sark* by Captain Woodget

"CALIFORNIA"

Photo by Captain Woodget

See Page 289

This, however, was passed pleasantly enough, and Woodget's Saturday afternoon picnics to Parsley Bay were much enjoyed, not only by his numerous friends in Sydney but by his officers and apprentices. One of these picnics nearly ended in disaster.

All deep water men were not boat sailors like the captain of the *Cutty Sark*, and the second mate, who, as Woodget contemptuously expressed it, had come out of a coffee grinder, soon showed that he had a good deal to learn in handling a sailing boat. He was steering the gig, following Woodget in the cutter down the harbour to the usual picnic rendezvous, when he gybed her all standing. His crew of apprentices were all sitting on the weather side instead of in the bottom of the boat, and over she went.

It happened that only two of the boys in the gig could swim, but they were all picked up eventually and taken back to the ship. It had been a close call, however, especially for the second mate himself and Waure, who swallowed so much salt water that when Woodget came back on the cutter to pick up his gig's crew, after they had changed into dry clothes, these two unfortunates were feeling too ill to join the party, and spent the afternoon aboard the *Cutty Sark* recovering from their ducking instead of enjoying the picnic.

Of the ships waiting in Sydney harbour for the 1888 wool clip, there were two which I have not mentioned before. The first of these was Devitt & Moore's *Derwent*, a very fine up-to-date modern ship, but more of a carrier than a clipper, yet capable of making a very fair average passage. The other was one of Corry's Irish Stars, the famous *Star of Italy*, which had deserted the Calcutta jute trade for a round the world voyage. With the exception of the *Star of Greece*, the *Star of Italy* had the finest record in Corry's fleet, and she was considered to be their fastest ship. She arrived in Sydney on 13th August with a cargo of lumber from Moodyville, Burrard's Inlet, B.C., and loaded wool for the first time.

Two familiar names will be missed from the wool fleet this year. The first is that of *Thermopylae*, which arrived very late in Australia and did not sail from Sydney until 26th March, 1889, the same date on which *Cutty Sark* had left Sydney in 1887. *Thermopylae*, however, was not able to emulate *Cutty Sark's* passage

s

and took 95 days getting home. The other ship was *Patriarch*, which took a charter for Rotterdam, and left Sydney on 18th July before the wool had come down country.

It was now becoming more and more the recognised custom in Sydney to despatch the fastest ships last so that wool could be loaded up to the last possible moment in order to catch the wool sales. And thus it is that henceforth we shall see *Cutty Sark* playing the part of last chance for the first wool sales, and leaving behind all the other ships.

In 1888 *Derwent* and *Orontes* were the slowest ships engaged in Sydney for the first of the London wool sales, and they were accordingly despatched first, the sailing dates being as follows:—

Derwent	..	..	..	left Sydney	October	10
Cimba ..	..	..	..	,, ,,	,,	18
Orontes	..	..	..	,, ,,	,,	20
Star of Italy ..	..	..	,, ,,		,,	20
Woollahra	..	..	..	,, ,,	,,	24
Salamis	..	..	..	,, Melbourne	,,	24
Cutty Sark	..	..	..	,, Sydney	,,	26
Lord Vennachar	..	..	,, Melbourne		,,	27
Mermerus	..	..	..	,, ,,	November	3

Cutty Sark, with 4496 bales of wool, sailed with a higher side than usual and Woodget soon found that he had cut his ballast rather short, so that the clipper was unable to bear sail in her usual gallant style, and in the first hard squall she frightened all hands by going over on her beam ends.

This was on 29th October, the third day out, and the log records:—

Strong S.S.W. wind and high sea. 4 a.m., decreasing, set all plain sail, moderate breeze and high S.W. sea.

Noon, lat. 40° 52′ S., long. 155° 38′ E. Course S. 30° E. Distance 172 miles. Strong wind.

At 1.45 p.m. struck by a terrific squall, throwing the ship on her beam ends and filling the decks fore and aft. Let fly everything.

4 p.m., strong and increasing wind.

8 p.m., strong gale and high sea. Decks constantly full of water, washing clean over hatches, etc.

The ship proved to be so crank that Woodget was obliged to send down his royal yards and unbend his upper staysails and return them to the sail locker. Two days later came the tragedy of the voyage, Cooke, the apprentice, being washed overboard and drowned. It is thus recorded by Captain Woodget.

Oct. 31—Lat. 46° 37' S., long. 162° E. Course S. 39° E. Distance 202 miles. Strong winds and high confused sea.

> At 3 a.m., after hauling taut the lee main brace and before the men left the lee side, the ship was struck by a sea, which caused her to lurch suddenly and fill up all the lee side of the deck. Cooke, an apprentice, was washed overboard, he held on to a rope but before anyone could reach him, he lost his hold and was no more seen. The ship being under topsails only and heavy cross sea and dark, nothing could be done to save him.

Captain Woodget, who was at the break of the poop, saw the sea coming, and told the men on the brace to jump for their lives. Cooke took a turn of the brace over the pin and hung on, but was swept overboard clinging to the end of the brace. Captain Woodget, singing out:—"Hang on, my boy, hang on," started to haul in the brace, but the *Cutty Sark* was going too fast, and the boy could not maintain his hold.

The next day at 1 p.m. the Snares were in sight, and Woodget followed his course of the previous year but the wind hung light; 60° south was reached and the first iceberg passed in 118° W. on 15th November. For the next fortnight the wind remained very light and easterly. On 23rd November *Cutty Sark* reached 64° 47' S., and the following day there was a clock calm and glassy sea, the run only totalling 27 miles.

During this time the ship was surrounded by penguins, which kept popping up all round her. And as long as the ship did not go over 6 knots, they were able to keep up, swimming alongside the vessel for hours. In addition to the penguins, the *Cutty Sark* was surrounded by sea birds of all sorts, the little blackcaps being specially numerous.

It was almost as light as night at it was during the day, and for over a fortnight there was no need to put the sidelights out.

The wind remained light and hung steadily in the N.E. right down to the Horn, which was not passed until 3rd December, 38 days from Sydney, during which time the ship had had to contend against 20 days of easterly winds.

The passage passed without further incident, the best run, 306 miles, being made on 10th December, in 45° 35′ S., 31° 21′ W.

The equator was crossed on 29th December, 26 days from the Horn. The latitude of the Azores was passed on 12th January, 14 days from the equator, and the Lizard seen from the mizen topsail yard at 1 p.m. on 18th January, bearing N. by E. ½ E., six days from the Azores. Thus the *Cutty Sark* was only 46 days from the Horn to the Lizard, and if only she had made her average run to the Horn of 25 days she would again have made the Channel in 71 days and docked in 73. However none of the other vessels did any better, though all were in time for the opening of the wool sales; their docking dates being:—

Star of Italy ..	..		.. arrived London January	14—86 days
Cimba ..	..	..	..	,,	,,	,,	15—89 ,,
Salamis	..	..	..	,,	,,	,,	17—85 ,,
Derwent	..	..	..	,,	,,	,,	17—99 ,,
Woollahra	..	..	..	,,	,,	,,	18—86 ,,
Loch Vennachar	..	..	,,	,,	,,	19—84 ,,
Cutty Sark	..	..	..	,,	,,	,,	20—86 ,,
Orontes	..	..	..	,,	,,	,,	22—94 ,,
Mermerus	..	..	..	,,	,,	,,	31—89 ,,

It may be of interest to note that *Cutty Sark's* old tea rival *Titania* arrived in dock on 19th January, only 113 days from Victoria, B.C.

The *Cutty Sark's* passage out to Sydney in 1889 was chiefly remarkable for her victory over the crack mail steamer of the P. & O. line.

The changes in her officers this year consisted of a new second mate, Walter Naylor. Of the apprentices, Dixon, Calderon and Mayall had finished their time and left. Yorkie Atkinson became senior apprentice and the new comers to the half deck were Brett, Tite, Herbert, Drew, Wallace, Wilcox, Spray, and a nipper who was nicknamed Dolly. Indeed the *Cutty Sark* was well off for apprentices this voyage, having no less than nine boys in her half-deck. Under Woodget these boys were quickly taught their work; they were always sent to the wheel as soon as possible, and Woodget was not above taking the helm himself in order to demonstrate how a ship should be steered.

Sometimes also in bad weather he would send a poor helmsman from the wheel and steer the *Cutty Sark* himself for an hour or two—and the difference to the ship would be instantly perceptible, for under his skilful touch the clipper always went along as dry as a bone, and, to use a sailor's expression, as comfortable as an old shoe.

Cutty Sark left the East India Docks on 4th May, took in powder at Gravesend, an operation which only took 3½ hours, and arrived in the Downs at 11 p.m., when it was almost calm. Very light winds were encountered in the Channel and departure from the Lizards was not taken until 9th May.

The wind remained light to moderate until 24th May when the N.E. trade was picked up in 20° N., 24° W. The trade was so light that it did not give the "Cutty" a run of 200 miles, and it was lost in 8° N. The equator was crossed on 3rd June in 26° W., the S.E. trade having been picked up on the previous day. There was a great deal of south in the S.E. trade, and the *Cutty Sark* was forced over on to the Brazil coast, where she had to tack offshore abreast of Cape St. Agostinho.

The meridian of Greenwich was crossed on 22nd June in 39° S., and that of the Cape on 27th June in 40° S. The weather continued fine with moderate to light winds as far as 50° E., but on 8th July in 42° S., 63° E. a hard N.W. gale was encountered with the usual severe squalls and high sea, which gave the *Cutty Sark* her first good run—312 miles. Her best week's work came right at the end of the passage. The Leeuwin meridian was crossed on 19th July in 41° 28′ S., and within a week the clipper lay at anchor in Port Jackson.

The details of her run up the Australian coast are truly remarkable. On 23rd July she was in 40° 45′ S., 138° 46′ E. at noon. the wind being strong at N.N.W. with clear weather.

At 5.20 a.m. on the 24th Cape Wickham light was sighted about 25 miles distant, bearing E.N.E. At 7.15 a.m. the light was 10 miles astern. At noon that day the *Cutty Sark* had made a run of 332 miles. Half an hour later Wilson's Promontory was sighted, and at 3.30 p.m. the ship hoisted her number, being 1½ miles off. At 7 p.m. that night Cleff Island was abeam. with the wind veering into the S.W., moderate and fine. At 1.30 p.m. on 25th July Gabo Island was passed, and whilst the "Cutty" was rounding Gabo Island to signal, the P. & O. *Britannia* passed inside her. The *Cutty Sark* passed and signalled Green Cape at 3.40 p.m. The wind remained moderate until 8 p.m. when it began to blow up into a southerly buster. At the change of the watch *Cutty Sark* was abreast of Montagu Island, and the *Britannia* must have been quite a distance ahead, for the wind had fallen quite light at times during the afternoon.

That night, during the second officer's watch, the *Britannia* was logging from $14\frac{1}{2}$ to 16 knots, when the *Cutty Sark* passed her going a good 17 knots. Robert Olivey, the second officer of the *Britannia*, watched the lights of the sailing ship overhauling his vessel with amazement, and he was so nonplussed that he went and called Captain Hector.

Neither of them had any idea that it could possibly be the *Cutty Sark*, which they had passed some 12 hours or more, so the following was entered in the *Britannia's* log:—"Sailing ship overhauled and passed us!"

Cutty Sark dropped her anchor inside the Heads at 9 a.m. on 26th July, 78 days from the Lizard, 48 hours from King's Island and only 17 hours from Green Cape, a distance of 220 miles.

The *Britannia* with her title of "Cock of the Walk" badly torn, entered the Heads shortly after 10 o'clock, and passed close by the *Cutty Sark*, which was lying with all sail furled except the main course, the second mate and all hands being on the main foot ropes giving the sail a harbour stow.

The passengers and crew of the *Britannia* rushed to the side to look at the gallant little clipper which had given them such a beating, and with her golden shirt glittering at the masthead the *Cutty Sark* was easily recognised. Immediately a storm of cheering burst from the steamer's deck, which was listed towards the clipper, by the crowd of people. This cheer was replied to by the men on the "Cutty's" mainyard with all the strength of their lungs. It was a great victory of sail over steam. The cock of the walk of the sailing fleet had beaten the latest thing in steam, the cock of the walk of the mail service.

Subsequently the two ships lay close to each other whilst discharging at Circular Quay, when the Sydney-siders visited the *Cutty Sark* in their hundreds. As one of the *Britannia's* officers wrote to me, there were many more visitors to the little clipper of a Sunday afternoon than to the crack mail steamer.

After the usual wait in the Bay, *Cutty Sark* was hauled alongside Circular Quay on 23rd October, to load as last chance for the first of the London wool sales.

Messrs. Talbot & Co., the well-known stevedores, screwed 4577 bales of wool into her on top of a stiffening of 4150 bags of chrome ore (about 205 tons) in nine working days. The last bale was under hatches by 11 a.m. on Saturday, 2nd November; Messrs. Dangar, Gedye & Co., cleared her at the customs the same day, and she went straight from the wharf to sea that night. Unfortunately it was blowing hard from the south with a high sea, and the *Cutty Sark* did not take her departure from the Heads until the following morning, when the wind had begun to fine away.

The following well-known clippers were ahead of the *Cutty Sark*:—

Derwent	..	..	.. left	Sydney	October	14
Cairnbulg	..	..	.. ,,	,,	,,	15
Orontes	..	..	.. ,,	,,	,,	17
Loch Vennachar	..	..	.. ,,	Melbourne	,,	21
Woollahra	..	..	.. ,,	Sydney	,,	22
Cimba ..	..	..	.. ,,	,,	,,	22
Salamis	..	..	.. ,,	Melbourne	,,	22
Sophocles	..	..	.. ,,	Sydney	,,	26
Serica ..	..	..	.. ,,	,,	,,	26
Blackadder	..	..	.. ,,	Brisbane	,,	31
Rodney	..	..	.. ,,	Sydney	,,	31

The *Cutty Sark* had raced and beaten all these vessels before, with the exception of *Serica* and *Rodney*.

Serica was an iron barque of 913 tons, Liverpool-owned and built by McMillan of Dumbarton in 1875.

Rodney was, of course, the celebrated Devitt & Moore passenger ship, which in 1887 had run from the Lizards to Sydney Heads in 67 days. She was a very fast ship indeed, and with the exception of the *Salamis* was the most formidable of all *Cutty Sark's* opponents this year

Woodget after his disastrous experience in 1888 steered a very northerly course in his run to the Horn, his furthest south being only 59° 30′. But, except for one good week's work, the weather was by no means favourable, and the *Cutty Sark* took 30 days to the pitch of the Horn.

The first ice was encountered on 16th November in 53° 53′ S., 156° W., when a flat, table-topped berg, about 300 ft., high was passed. The next day it was very misty with a strong north wind and high sea. A sharp look-out had to be kept as there was lots of ice about, and four large bergs were passed. On 18th November Captain Woodget records a hard gale at N.W. with a high cross sea and terrific squalls, the decks being constantly flooded. On the 19th it was blowing harder than ever, from the W.S.W., with the barometer down to 28.50. But Woodget kept the ship going and at noon the reckoning gave her a run of 336 miles. At 8 p.m. that evening two more bergs were passed, one of them being only 20 feet above water. At midnight the wind began to take off, and it was the last fair blow the *Cutty Sark* was to have for some time, as well as the last ice sighted.

On 29th November in 56° 48′ S., 82° 16′ W., the wind being light and unsteady from right ahead, the *Cutty Sark* began to overtake other ships. There is nothing like a head wind for bringing ships together. That evening she passed two barques and a ship.

On 30th November at 2 p.m. the barque *Chile* was spoken, 25 days out from Christchurch for Falmouth. And at 4 p.m. a four-mast ship was sighted standing to the N.W. and another vessel to the S.W.

On 1st December at noon the *Rodney* was spoken, and Captain Woodget remarks disgustedly:—"All day in company—could not get ahead of her, when the wind freshened we came up, when light, she goes ahead." That afternoon the wind began slowly to make from the S.W., and the two rivals passed a four-mast ship, steering as themselves, with the greatest ease.

On 2nd December Captain Woodget records:—

Wind moderate S.W. and puffy at times. 4 a.m., ship *Rodney* about 4 miles to leeward, about 2 points before the beam.

Noon, ditto weather. Lat. 57° 06′ S., long. 69° 18′ W. Course S. 79° E. Distance 217 miles. *Rodney* almost abreast of us. 4 p.m., moderate breeze and fine. *Rodney* on lee quarter.

"TORRIDON"

MIDSHIPHOUSE "CUTTY SARK"

[*See Page* 289

THE FAMOUS TEA-CLIPPER "FALCON"
IN HER LAST BERTH

[*See Page 293*]

"HELEN DENNY"

[*See Page 286*]

On 3rd December the Horn was rounded with the wind falling light again and working into the N.N.E. At 8 a.m. four outward bounders were passed, but *Rodney* had dropped below the horizon.

On the next two days the *Cutty Sark* went plunging into a confused cross sea with her yards on the backstays, and shipped immense quantities of water.

In spite of very indifferent weather, the *Cutty Sark* made the very fair run of 23 days from the Horn to the line. The trades only carried her to the equator, and on 28th December in the doldrums *Rodney* was fallen in with again in 3° 45′ N., 30° W. On the morning of the 29th at 7 a.m. *Rodney* was just abaft the lee beam, the weather being unsteady and squally, but at noon the N.E. trade came along fresh, and the *Rodney* fell astern rapidly and was soon out of sight.

In crossing the trades the *Cutty Sark* gave an exhibition of sailing, which could not have been equalled by any other ship afloat, her runs in the trade being:—246, 280, 283, 266 and 252.

On 4th January she was once more in the variables, and Captain Woodget records:—"A four-mast ship ahead, which we are coming up with." This ship was passed the following morning at 10 a.m., and proved to be the *Gilcruix*, 100 days out from Calcutta for London.

On 10th January, Corvo was passed, 15 days from the line and five days later at 11.30 p.m. the Lizard lights were abeam, the *Cutty Sark* being 73 days out. The *Rodney* signalled the Lizard on the 16th, both ships made good runs up Channel and docked on 17th January.

The following were the times for the January ships:—

Derwent	..	..	..	arrived London January			2	90—80 days.
Cimba ..	..	..	..	,,	,,	,,	5	,, —75 ,,
Salamis	..	..	..	,,	,,	,,	15	,, —85 ,,
Loch Vennachar	..	..	,,	,,	,,		15	,, —86 ,,
Woollahra	..	..	..	,,	,,	,,	15	,, —85 ,,
Cutty Sark	..	..	..	,,	,,	,,	17	,, —75 ,,
Rodney	..	..	..	,,	,,	,,	17	,, —78 ,,
Serica ..	..	..	..	,,	,,	,,	18	,, —84 ,,
Blackadder	..	..	..	,,	,,	,,	22	,, —83 ,,
Cairnbulg	..	..	..	,,	,,	,,	23	,, —99 ,,
Orontes	..	..	..	,,	,,	,,	24	,, —99 ,,

The little *Sophocles* was badly left behind, and did not reach London until 14th March, 139 days out.

Once again the *Titania* from distant Vancouver arrived amongst the wool fleet. This year she had a very interesting race with the *Pericles*, and gave that famous Aberdeen clipper a bad beating.

Titania left Vancouver Sept. 27, arrived London Jan. 15—110 days.
Pericles left 'Frisco Sept. 28, arrived London Jan. 18—112 days.

The *Cutty Sark* had made five passages from Australia under Captain Woodget, which showed the most extraordinary fine average in the run from the Horn to soundings; and the following times between points show that her run up the Atlantic in 1889-90, the 20th year of her age, was the best of the lot.

Date		Horn to Line	Line to Azores	Azores to Channel	Total Days
1885 Nov.-Dec.	..	20	17	7	44
1887 April-May	..	24	12	10	46
1888 Jan.-March	..	24	16	4	44
1888-9 Dec.-Jan	..	26	14	6	46
1889-90 Dec.-Jan.	..	23	15	5	43

Though 20 years old on her arrival home in 1890, the *Cutty Sark* was still as sound as a bell, and never needed pumping except occasionally after a bit of heavy running in the Southern Ocean, when she drained a little water in through her topsides and deck openings.

The only weak spot in the ship was her chainplates. These had begun to carry away with an alarming frequency. The iron eye that took the pin of the strop of the dead-eye would rust and wear thin and then snap; or the iron rod which replaced the old fashioned chain in the chainplate would sometimes snap like a carrot.

The only defect in her composite construction, due to age and electrolytic action, was that sometimes when the nuts on the inside of the hull planking were being chipped one of the nuts would fall off with the end of the bolt, and it would be found that the junction had corroded away to a white powder.

There were the usual changes in the half-deck in the spring of 1890, Yorkie left and MacDonald and Dick Woodget divided the honours of senior apprentice, their rivalry being a peaceful one owing to their always being in different watches.

Tite, who never recovered from a bad attack of influenza in Sydney, was left behind.

The newcomers were Harold Woodget, the skipper's second son, and Wallace, son of the chief coastguard at Broadstairs, making eight apprentices in the half-deck for the *Cutty's* 19th voyage.

This year the *Cutty Sark* distinguished herself by overhauling three of the fastest ships in the trade, namely *Salamis*, *Cimba* and *Aristides*. The following table clearly shows the way in which she overhauled them:—

Details	Cimba	Salamis	Aristides	Cutty Sark
Left London	May 3	May 5	May 5	May 14
Off the Start	May 6	May 7	May 7	May 16
Off the Lizard	May 8	May 9	May 9	May 19
Took N.E. trades	May 19, 24° N.	May 16, 29° 25, N.	May 25	May 31, 28° 30′ N.
Lost N.E. trades	May 18, 6° N.	May, 26, 6° N	May 28, 6° N.	June 8, 6° 52′ N.
Crossed Equator	June, 2, 24° W.	June 1, 25° 30′ W.	June 1, 24° W.	June 1, 25° W.
Took S.E. trades	June 2	May 31	May 31	June 13
Lost S.E. trades	June 12, 22° S.	—	June 21, 21° S.	June 21, 21° S.
Crossed Cape meridian	July 1, 40° S.	June 29, 39° S.	June 29, 41° S.	July 6, 44° S.
Crossed Leewin meridian	July 21	July 20	July 18	July 21
Ran easting down in	42-43°	41-42°	44°	44-45°
Best run	—	—	320	340
Cape Northumberland	July 25	July 27	—	July 29
Cape Otway	July 30	July 31	July 24	July 31
Anchored Hobson's Bay	—	Aug. 1	—	—
Off Wilson's Promontary	Aug. 1	—	July 28	Aug. 1, 10.30 a.m.
Off Gabo Island	—	—	Aug. 1, 4 p.m.	Aug. 2, 2.15 a.m.
Off Jervis Bay	—	—	Aug. 2	Aug. 2, 2.30 p.m.
Took Pilot aboard	—	—	Aug. 2, 4 p.m.	Aug. 2, 10 p.m.
Anchored Port Jackson	Aug. 3	—	Aug. 2, 8 p.m.	Aug. 2, midnight
Days out	87	84	85	75

In this passage *Cutty Sark* maintained an extraordinary high average from the Greenwich meridian to the Leeuwin. In 30 days she covered 7678 miles, a daily average of 256 miles, and from 5th July to 18th July her distance totalled 3724 miles or a rate of $286\frac{1}{2}$ miles a day. During this time she made five runs of 300 miles or over.

Like all the other ships, she had to contend against light variable winds and calms from the Leeuwin to the Otway, but from the Otway to Sydney Heads her performance was as wonderful as that of her previous passage when she beat the *Britannia*, the distance being covered in 1 day 22 hours.

On 28th July *Cutty Sark* passed the *Loch Ryan*, which vessel had left the Channel three weeks ahead of Willis's clipper. She also gave the go-by to the R.M.S. *Victoria,* which spoke to her 32 miles west of the Otway on 31st July.

Our illustration shows the *Cutty Sark* passing the *Cimba* between Wilson's Promontory and Gabo Island. It was blowing a hard south-easter and it will be noted that Captain Woodget is carrying all sail to royals whilst Fimister was reefing his topsails. The *Cutty Sark* actually beat *Cimba* by 12 hours between Wilson's Promontory and Sydney.

The *Aristides* made Sydney Heads at 4 p.m. on the 2nd, but in towing into Port Jackson she parted her hawser twice and did not get to an anchor until some time after dark. Captain Woodget, according to his usual custom, sailed in through the Heads and brought up in Watson's Bay.

Captain Spalding of the Aberdeen clipper was very disgusted at being overhauled and beaten 10 days on the passage, and he broke into print on the subject of the times the two vessels passed the different points but Woodget was easily able to reply to Spalding's discomfort.

It is curious to note also that on this passage the *Cutty Sark* made the smallest 24-hour run of her career, namely, 2 miles on 9th June in 6° N., 24' W.

The beautiful little *Salamis* made an unusually long passage for such a heeler, and she fell in with some very queer weather.

On 17th June in 38° 8' S., 7° 32' W. *Salamis* encountered tornado-like weather. After shifting from N.N.E. to S.E. with remarkable suddenness, the wind flew all round the compass, darting in furious gusts from every point in turn, whilst rain fell in torrents. This weather culminated at midnight in a squall of hurricane force from the N.N.E., which retained its strength for a whole 24 hours.

On 21st June at 4.30 p.m., whilst the *Salamis* was running before a heavy S.S.W. gale with high cross sea, a heavy dollop broke over the starboard quarter, which washed away the binnacle, sent the compass flying overboard, broke in the cabin skylight and flooded the cabin, and at the same time hurled the man at the wheel into the mizen rigging, where he hung badly injured.

On 30th June after a night of cyclonic weather with tremendous storms of thunder and lightning, the *Salamis* found herself beset by seven waterspouts, all working from east to west at extraordinary speed. At 9.30 a.m. the ship was caught aback with a squall from the southard, at the same moment a whirlwind passed close ahead with appalling force and suddenness, throwing water in monster fountains all over her. During the next few minutes the ship reeled in the grip of a wind which had the concentrated fury of a dozen ordinary squalls, whilst hail as big as pigeons' eggs mingled with torrential rain.

The clipper came through this cataclysm unscathed, but she was not to complete her passage without a tragedy. This occurred a week later in 42° S., 42° 49′ E., when a seaman fell from the main topsail yard, whilst the sail was being furled. The unfortunate man hit the deck and was killed instantly, being frightfully mangled —the bone of one arm penetrating the deck to the depth of 2 inches. Altogether it cannot be said that the passage of the *Salamis* was without incident.

The wool clippers had longer to wait for their wool than usual this year owing to the great maritime strike in Australasia, which not only blocked the bringing down of the new season's clip, but also its shipment when it did arrive.

As a Sydney paper observed:—"The consequence is that vessels which, under ordinary circumstances, would have been on their way home for the opening sales, are now in port patiently waiting their turn, while the steamships, with their higher freight rate per bale, are scooping in the bales. The only way to get the clip home in time was by means of the steamships."

After eulogising the Aberdeen White Star clippers, the writer goes on:—"There is no apology required in introducing the *Cutty Sark*, as she lies at the Circular Quay, to our readers. She is simply a picture; she is a yacht among the handsomest merchantmen, and her appearance does not belie her." After giving a short account of the *Cutty Sark's* career and her captain's record, the writer finishes: "Messrs. Dangar, Gedye have made great progress with the *Cutty Sark* during the week. (Nov. 7-15). The vessel has now 1500 bales on board and sufficient engagements have been booked to enable her to get away in a fortnight."

Cutty Sark again beat her record for a wool cargo, loading 4617 bales on top of 1576 bags of chrome ore. She sailed as last chance for the March wool sales, with only the *West Lothian*, a beautiful, modern four-mast ship, behind her.

Though it was a very unfavourable season for quick passages, there were some very good races amongst the wool fleet.

The first four ships away were the following:—

Ship			Left		Arrived		Days
Patriarch	..	..	Sydney	Oct. 27	London Jan.	18	83
Derwent	..	..	Sydney	,, 27	,, ,,	18	83
Loch Vennachar	..		Melbourne	,, 27	,, ,,	22	87
Cimba	..	..	Sydney	,, 30	,, ,,	27	89

Then *Blackadder* from Brisbane had a close race with *Loch Tay* from Geelong, their times being:—

Ship			Left		Arrived		Days
Blackadder		..	Brisbane	Nov. 27	London Feb.	26	91
Loch Tay	..	..	Geelong	,, 27	,, ,,	28	93

But the most exciting contest was that for the March sales in which *Cutty Sark* again beat all her rivals with ease, though, owing to the most unfavourable weather, it was by far the longest passage she had made up to date,

Her only serious rival was the *West Lothian*, which sailed three days behind her. This ship, however, was unfortunate enough to get on fire off the Brazil coast. She put into Pernambuco on fire on 12th February; the fire was quickly got under, but she was not able to resume her passage until 25th February. But for this she would probably have been close on the heels of the *Cutty Sark*.

The times for the March ships were as follows:—

Ship			Left		Arrived		Days
Rodney	..	..	Sydney	Dec. 6	London March	26	110
Aristides	..	..	Sydney	,, 10	,, March	27	107
Loch Lomond		..	Geelong	,, 12	,, April	6	115
Mermerus	..	..	Melbourne	,, 13	,, March	29	106
Salamis	..	..	Melbourne	,, 13	,, March	24	101
Cutty Sark	..		Sydney	,, 14	,, March	17	93
West Lothian	..		Sydney	,, 17	,, April	2	106

Cutty Sark left Sydney at 6 a.m. on 14th December, and finding a head wind outside tacked to the S.S.W. That night she ran into an electric storm, in which the peals of thunder were so terrific that they continually made the whole ship tremble.

For the next four days the *Cutty Sark* had a strong head sea to contend against, and Auckland Island was not passed until 20th January. A week later in 59° S., 155° W., Woodget was once more amongst ice, his log recording:—

Dec. 27—Fresh W.S.W. breeze and misty. Passed an iceberg about 250 ft. high and a third of a mile long. 2 p.m., passed close by another iceberg with long flat top, about 200 ft. high and a mile in length. Thermometer fell 10 degrees as we passed it. Innumerable small ice to leeward of the berg.

For the next four days it was anxious work with lots of ice about, the wind mostly ahead, a big easterly swell, and the ship shut in by thick fog.

The wind began to veer to the north, N.N.W. and N.W. on 1st January, 1891, and the weather cleared up, giving the *Cutty Sark* her only chance of travelling on this side of the Horn, her run on 2nd January being 300 miles.

Unfortunately the brave west wind soon petered out, and from 4th January right down to the Horn the ship was held up by head winds, variable airs and calms, and in a whole week she only covered 593 miles.

At noon on 15th January, with a light S.S.E. wind and fine weather, Diego Ramirez Rocks were passed, and a large four-mast ship was overhauled

It will always be found that more ships are met with in light and head winds than in more favourable weather, and on 16th January I notice that seven homeward bound and four outward bound ships were passed.

The *Cutty Sark* passed and signalled the barque *Leucadia*, from Adelaide, 41 days out, the *Myrtle Holme* from Port Augusta, 41 days out, an American ship (which did not give her name), and the four-mast ship *Tuskadale* from 'Frisco for Glasgow, 57 days out. On the following day, with the wind at W.N.W., she overhauled the ship *Annesley*, 56 days out from Lobos Island for Great Grimsby, and the Belfast ship *Kenkora*, 62 days out from Areston for

Falmouth. At 4 p.m. on the 18th a four-mast French ship was over-hauled and on the 19th the Liverpool barque *Beechdale*, 48 days out from Iquique for Falmouth.

On 22nd January the N.W. wind shifted suddenly into the S.W. and calm variable weather set in, which continued without intermission to 22° N., 26° W., where the S.E. trades were picked up. From 29th January to 6th February, the *Cutty Sark* only made 486 miles, in nine days of doldrums weather, mostly very light northerly winds.

At 10 a.m. 30th January, she passed the ship *Desdemona* of Liverpool, homeward bound from 'Frisco, and at 4 p.m. passed the *West Lothian*, which signalled that she had passed Cape Horn on 11th January in company with the *Rodney*, five days ahead of the *Cutty Sark*.

The "Cutty" added one more ship to her bag before crossing the line, the barque *Eraminta* of Greenock, 70 days out from Iquique for Falmouth. This ship was left behind on 8th February in the trades.

The line was crossed on 13th February, 29 days from the Horn, and a freshening N.E. trade was picked up the next day. This was lost on 19th February, when a head wind set in which lasted right away to the end of the passage.

As the Azores were approached the easterly wind gradually developed into a moderate gale with heavy squalls and high sea. This continued without a slant, and the *Cutty Sark* was often compelled to head-reach under lower topsails in a head sea which filled her decks.

I believe this was one of the few occasions on which the main spencer was set.

Captain Woodget declared that the sail was never of much use to him, but it was just the sail for this weather, being valued very highly by the American Cape Horn fleet when outward bound round Cape Stiff.

One or two of Woodget's apprentices declared that he some-times set this sail when running hard in the roaring forties. If the *Cutty Sark* was running dead before a heavy following sea, with the head sails not drawing except when she rolled or yawed,

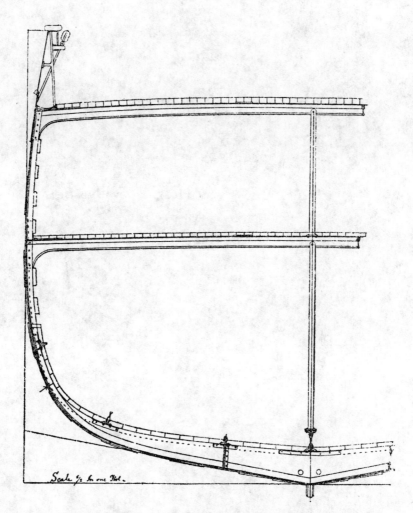

Scale ½ In one Ft.

HALF-MIDSHIP SECTION OF THE "PATRIARCH."

[*See Page* 276

it was sometimes set to ease the ship with the spanker brailed in. At other times they state that Captain Woodget would use it with reefed topsails, reefed foresail and fore topmast staysail or even with more sail such as a goose-winged mainsail, the trysail would be hauled out for a while.

It was a sail which provided unpleasant memories for the half-deck, for it was a beast to take in, being of the thickest canvas made. In addition to this, as it was generally kept bent, the apprentices had to be constantly hauling it out to dry and the subsequent refurling found out their finger-nails especially in cold weather.

After 20 weary days of hard head winds, the *Cutty Sark*, with her passage spoilt, made the Ushant light on 15th March, 91 days out. At 8 a.m. the lighthouse bore S.E. 10 miles. All that day the ship made good time with the wind at N.W. That night Woodget spent an anxious time up aloft with his telescope, picking up lights, for the *Cutty Sark* was in the dangerous neighbourhood of the Caskets. At 8.30 a.m. on the 16th St. Catherine's was in sight to the norrard; that afternoon at 4 p.m. the Tug *Woodcock* was engaged about 5 miles west of Beachy Head, and the *Cutty Sark* docked next day, having beaten the *Salamis* by over a week, the *Mermerus* and *Aristides* by a fortnight and *Rodney* by 17 days.

Though it was the *Cutty Sark's* longest passage from Australia, she had yet beaten every one of her rivals, and was the first sailing ship in for the March wool sales.

In 1890, the *Cutty Sark's* most famous rival, the *Thermopylae* was sold to Mr. Reford of Montreal, president of the Rice Milling Company, for, I believe, £5000 and she left Cardiff in June that year under a Captain Wilson, bound for Singapore. Thus her days as a wool clipper were over and for the next five years she was occupied in carrying rice from the East across the Pacific to British Columbia.

Titania arrived home from New Westminster on 24th March, 1891, 123 days out. It was Captain Dunn's fifth voyage round the Horn both ways in the beautiful ex-tea clipper, and he now decided to retire. The vacant command was obtained by Selby, who was replaced in *Cutty Sark* by the *Titania's* mate. Selby's successor was a very different man to the new captain of the *Titania*.

Instead of being eagle-eyed he was short-sighted, and the half-deck considered him very easy-going after the strict, hard-working Selby.

The *Cutty Sark* had again an interesting race out to Sydney in 1891; this time she overhauled the *Patriarch* and the *Cimba*, as shown by the following table:—

Details	Cimba	Patriarch	Cutty Sark
Left the Docks ..	April 7	April 20	April 23
Off the Start ..	April 10	April 22	April 25
Cross the equator ..	May 9	May 15	May 20
On the Cape meridian	June 2	June 13	June 13
Ran easting in ..		41°-42°	45-44°
Best 24-hour run ..		377	318
Best week's run ..		2071	1966
Made King's Island ..	July 5	July 8	July 10
Made Wilson's Prom.			July 11 (noon)
Made Gabo Island ..	July 12		July 12, 8 p.m.
Anchored Port Jackson	July 12, 11 p.m.	July 13	July 13
Days out	93 days	82 days	79 days

The *Cimba*, which left the Channel 15 days before the *Cutty Sark*, lost most of the days, which the latter caught on her, off the Australian coast.

When up with King's Island she ran out of a westerly gale into an electric storm, which covered her mastheads and yardarms with corposants. This brought up a hard northerly wind, against which she had to contend through Bass Straits and all the way up the coast.

It was Captain Mark Breach's first voyage in command of the *Patriarch*. He drove her for all she was worth and actually gained three days on the *Cutty Sark* between the Cape and King's Island. The *Patriarch* took 20 days running from the Cape meridian to the Leeuwin, whilst the *Cutty Sark*, 3 degrees further south, took 21 days. Both vessels had a hard westerly gale on the meridian of the Leeuwin; the *Patriarch* had her decks swept and some damage done, but the *Cutty Sark* came through it unscathed with a run of 290 miles.

Captain Mark Breach brought out a number of prize pigeons in safety. It is extraordinary to note the way in which clippers brought all kinds of livestock through the roaring forties without casualties.

With regard to Woodget's prize collies, he never allowed them off the poop when at sea for fear of their being washed overboard, and he would allow no one to attend to them but himself—thus he never lost a dog overboard, which would certainly have been the case if they had been allowed to roam about the maindeck.

There are only two or three incidents to note about *Cutty Sark's* passage.

She made a good run down Channel, being 24 hours from Dover to Portland, where she landed her pilot, and another 12 hours to the Eddystone.

On 18th May in a smart squall the fore topgallant mast went over the side, another defective chainplate giving way.

On 28th June in a W.N.W. gale she rode over what was probably the biggest sea encountered in her whole existence.

Captain Woodget in his log gives the following account of it:—

8 a.m., hard gale and terrific squalls with hail and very high sea. Noon, ditto weather. 5 p.m., ditto weather. An immense sea rolled up right aft. When I looked at it, towering up so steep, in fact, like a cliff, it looked as if it was about to drop down over our stern and completely bury the ship: but her stern rose without much water being pooped, but as it rolled along to the main rigging it dropped on board both sides with tremendous force; smashing in the doors of the fore and after houses, it rushed aft covering the poop. The water was up to my waist whilst I was hanging on the rail: you could see nothing but the boats and the masts—the whole ship was completely submerged, a great quantity of water rushing down into the cabin, stern rooms, etc.

There had been a very heavy sea all day, in fact the glass had begun to rise.

During the 31 years that I have been sailing the seas, I never saw anything approaching it in size and steepness. The apprentices' house was filled up to the top bunks, soaking almost everything they had—beds, pillows, and bedclothes.

The A.B.'s house was not quite so bad, only filling the lower bunks.

Wind W.N.W. throughout. 8 p.m., the squalls less severe, sea going down. Midnight, moderate gale, hard squalls with hail. Lat. 45° 24′ S., long. 87° 34′ E. Course east. Distance 300 miles.

When this huge sea reared up astern, the second mate was standing forward by the carpenter's shop, and, as he looked aft, he saw the white crest of the wave showing over the top of the crossjack yard. Feeling sure that the "Cutty" and all on board were doomed, he jumped into the carpenter's shop and slammed both doors to.

Then for some uneasy moments whilst the wave roared aboard amidships and covered up the portholes of the house, both he and the carpenter thought they were well on the way to Davy Jones' locker.

Captain Woodget told me that the ship ran down the advancing wall of water with her stern cocked up at an angle of 45, whilst her bows split the side of the monstrous wave with a roaring hiss; the *Cutty Sark* was running under a main topgallant, and she probably never went faster in her life than she did on that sea. She ran dead straight without any attempt to broach to—then as soon as her bow began to lift, the water, which had filled the main deck so that neither rail could be seen, poured aft and out over her stern. Dick Woodget and an A.B. were at the wheel, and if they had not been lashed they would most certainly have been washed overboard.

Luckily no one on deck except the skipper and the helmsmen remained to face that mountain of water, the others made a dash for the houses when they saw it coming, and but for their discretion several would undoubtedly have been swept overboard.

Of all the many desperate situations of her long career, the *Cutty Sark* was never in greater danger. Not a man that saw the sea but believed that his last moment had come. Even Woodget could not believe that the little beauty would be able to lift her stern to such a steep hill of water—yet she came through it un-scathed except for a few broken doors.

This year the *Cutty Sark* had the usual mail boat to try her out. The *Ballarat* left Port Phillip just 24 hours after the *Cutty Sark* had passed the Heads, but she could not make anything on the clipper and did not arrive at Sydney Heads until 12.20 p.m. on 14th July, still 24 hours behind the sailing ship.

The *Patriarch* took her tug off Broken Bay at 3.15 p.m. and made fast to the Orient buoy in Neutral Bay. The *Cutty Sark* passed *Jervis Bay* at 6 p.m., slipped through the Heads under sail and brought up in Watson's Bay.

The next morning Mark Breach, on arriving at the agents, gave loud expression to his delight when he found that nothing had been heard of that terror to Australian traders, the *Cutty Sark*. He had hardly finished speaking before old Woodget poked his head in at the door with a broad smile on his face, having listened to Breach's remarks with much amusement.

In the autumn of 1891 *Cutty Sark* again loaded as last chance for the January wool sales. She did not start loading until 27th October, but in eight working days she had 4638 bales screwed into her hold and was down to 19 ft. 8 inches of draught. Once again the cargo was the largest amount of wool ever stowed in the *Cutty Sark*, and the time taken to put it aboard was claimed to be the shortest on record.

The usual ships sailed ahead of her—*Loch Vennachar, Derwent, Cimba, Aristides, Patriarch, Salamis,* and *Loch Ryan*.

Cutty Sark towed away from Circular Quay at 6 a.m. on 5th November, six days behind *Salamis* and *Loch Ryan*. Finding a strong southerly breeze outside, Captain Woodget headed to go north of New Zealand, and in four days had rounded the North Cape with runs of 324, 310, 284 and 247. On 10th November at 6 p.m., East Cape bore S.W. 10 miles. Antipodes Day was on 11th November, just under a week from Sydney, and the wind did not falter until *Cutty Sark* was in 40° S., 172° W. Though the course that Captain Woodget steered this year was not his usual great circle to the Horn, being over 1000 miles further than those of his first three passages, the *Cutty Sark* made some fairly steady running and averaged 208 miles a day against the 220 of Woodget's first and best run to the Horn from Australia.

The *Cutty Sark* passed 6 miles to the northward of the Diego Ramirez Rocks at 4 a.m. on 23rd December. *Salamis* rounded the Horn on 28th November, having taken one day longer than her rival.

On the 5th in a gentle E.S.E. breeze the *Cutty Sark* overhauled and passed two nitrate traders, the *Artemis* and *Queen of Cambria*, 42 and 39 days respectively from Iquique.

On 12th December with a fresh N.W. breeze on the beam, the little clipper ran 304 miles. Six days later in a N.N.W. squall the fore topgallant mast went over the side for the second time in the voyage.

On 14th December light head winds had set in and these lasted for over three weeks, during the whole of which time the *Cutty Sark* only averaged 104 miles a day.

On 31st December the head wind gave way to the S.E. trade in 9° S., 27° W., and the equator was crossed on 3rd January, 31 days from the Horn.

After poor N.E. trades the *Cutty Sark* had easterly winds all the way to the Western Isles, which were passed on 22nd January, 19 days from the line.

On 13th January the clipper overhauled and signalled the four-mast barque *Eudora*, 120 days out from 'Frisco to the Channel. The *Eudora* was a crack ship, which afterwards made some very smart passages in the 'Frisco trade, such as 99 days from Lundy to 'Frisco in 1894, 105 days from 'Frisco to the Lizard in 1895; one of her best being 57 days 12 hours from Deal to Coquimbo. It shows how unfavourable the season was in the Atlantic this year when we find such a noted ship taking 152 days from 'Frisco to Plymouth, where she arrived on 12th February, having dropped a fortnight behind the *Cutty Sark*.

I have often received letters from masters of these modern four-masters, declaring that their ships could overpower and outrun the toylike tea clippers, as they called them, and only admitted the superiority of the latter in light winds, but I can find no instance of the *Cutty Sark* ever having any difficulty in passing iron or steel ships, especially in strong winds.

On this same passage, just two days before she overhauled the *Eudora*, she had run past the ship *Qimara*, 113 days out from 'Frisco to the Channel. This vessel arrived Galway on 11th February 145 days from California, another good scalp for the little *Cutty Sark*. The *Eudora* rounded the Horn on 16th November, thus between the Horn and the United Kingdom the *Cutty Sark* actually gained 31 days on the smart modern four-poster, and very nearly sailed two feet to her one.

Cutty Sark made good time from the Western Isles; she sighted the Lizard lights on 27th January, five days from Corvo, and engaged a tug at 2 p.m. the next day, after signalling St. Catherine's at noon. It was a good finish to a rather unfavourable passage, as she ran from 46° N., 21° W., to the Wight in exactly 72 hours, which was all but as good as her run up Channel in March, 1887.

The following were the times of the January ships:—

Ship.	Port left	Made Channel	Arrived London	Days out
Loch Vennachar ..	Melbourne Oct. 23		Feb. 1	101
Blackadder	Brisbane „ 24		Jan. 28	96
Cimba	Sydney „ 24	Lizard Jan. 15	„ 18	87
Derwent	„ „ 24	Lizard „ 28	„ 30	98
Patriarch	„ „ 29	Eddystone „ 20	„ 23	86
Aristides	„ „ 29		„ 28	91
Salamis	Geelong „ 30	Lizard „ 18	„ 20	82
Loch Ryan	Melbourne „ 30		Feb. 2	95
Cutty Sark	Sydney Nov. 5	Lizard „ 27	Jan. 29	85

In the spring of 1892 *Cutty Sark* was over six months in port, before loading a general cargo for Newcastle, N.S.W., and this delay made her too late to load at Sydney or Newcastle for either the January or March wool sales. She left the South West India Dock on 12th August, and after a beat down Channel took her departure from the Lizard on 16th August.

The passage was without any outstanding incident. The line was crossed on 10th September, 25 days out, and the meridian of Greenwich on 3rd October, 23 days from the equator. Up to this point it had been a fine weather passage, but on the afternoon of the 9th it began to breeze up from the west, and by noon on the 10th the *Cutty Sark* had run 312 miles in the 24 hours.

This was the commencement of some fine steady work, which may be best shown by the following data:—

Cape to Leeuwin—8th October-24th October—4060 miles in 16 days.
Cape to King's Island—8th October-2nd November—5448 miles in 25 days.
Best 24-hour runs—324, 312, 310.

From the 21st October to King's Island the wind was mostly light from ahead, the "Cutty" being braced sharp up.

At 1.40 a.m. on 2nd November the King's Island light was sighted, and at 7 a.m. the *Cutty Sark* passed west of the Harbinger Rocks. The clipper had to tack up the coast against very light head winds and a strong southerly current, and did not moor in Hunter's River until 7th November, being 78 days from the Lizard to King's Island and 83 from the Lizard to Newcastle.

After discharging at Newcastle, Captain Woodget went down

to Sydney in hopes of a wool cargo, but he found that the tonnage had already been engaged for the London market, and he was forced to content himself with a cargo for Antwerp. However he made up for missing the London sales by cramming 4723 bales of wool into the ship, being 87 bales more than her previous record cargo and 434 more than her first wool cargo.

The *Cutty Sark* towed to sea on 7th January, 1893. After two days of fair winds, light head winds set in, and the ship had her yards on the backstays all the way to 54° S., 178° E., on which day, 21st January, she made her first respectable run, 290 miles.

This passage is chiefly interesting for the *Cutty Sark's* encounter with a vast icefield. The first ice was seen on 23rd January, when two large bergs were passed in lat. 59° 07′ S., long. 160° 35′ W., the weather being misty, the wind moderate at S.W. and the run for the day 290 miles. On the next day the weather was very foggy with the wind round to north, and it was a case of sharp eyes on the look-out, for nine icebergs were passed.

I will now quote the captain's log:—

Jan. 25—Fresh north breeze, sleet and snow. Noon, moderate, N.W. breeze and cloudy. Bar. 28.30. Lat. 60° 53′ S., long. 150° 23′ W. Course S. 85° E. Distance 160 miles. During this day there has been a constant line of icebergs on both sides, as many as 30 in sight at one time.

Jan. 26—Moderate N.W. breeze and cloudy. Noon, moderate W.N.W. and misty. Lat. 60° 53′ S., long. 143° 31′ W. Course east. Distance 200 miles. Numbers of icebergs on both sides, sea striking the weather sides of bergs, 250 or 300 feet high; and sprays of sea and foam going up far above the top of the ice. Some of the bergs had holes underneath and the sea spouting up on the lee side in immense columns. One berg passed today was all streaked with what appeared to be earth. I counted 30 lines about one foot thick, of earth, and then one of ice, and so on right through the mass, I passed within half a mile of it. 8 p.m., fresh wind. Midnight, strong wind and high sea.

On 27th January, with the wind strong at W.N.W. and a high sea, the *Cutty Sark* made a run of 340 miles, covering 12° 16′ of longitude, which, if one allows difference of time 48 minutes equal 11 miles, brings the distance covered in the 24 hours to 351 miles.

For the next few days only an occasional iceberg was seen. On 1st February, with the wind fresh from the south, *Cutty Sark*

"CUTTY SARK" LYING OFF
MOSAMEDES

See Page 298

"CUTTY SARK" IN MID-OCEAN
ALMOST BECALMED

"THERMOPYLAE" UNDER CANADIAN ENSIGN

"CUTTY SARK" IN TABLE BAY
Re-rigged as a Barquentine, 1918

See Page 302

ran 306 miles; on 5th February the Horn was rounded, 29 days out, and on the next day the run was 308 miles.

On 8th February, in 50° S., 46° 40′ W., Captain Woodget once more found himself beset by ice and his log records:—

Gentle S.W. breeze and fine. 6 a.m., foggy. 6.30 a.m. fog lifted and we found ourselves surrounded with icebergs. 8 a.m., ditto breeze, and foggy again. Found ice ahead, in fact, there was ice all round—as soon as we cleared one another would be reported on either side. You could hear the sea roaring on them and through them, the ice cracking sometimes like thunder, at other times like cannon, and often like a sharp rifle report, and yet could not see them.

At 1 p.m. the top of an iceberg was seen, which one could hardly believe was ice, it looked like a streak of dark cloud. Then we could see the ice a few feet down, but we could not see the bottom. It was up at an angle of 45 degrees, we were only about 1000 feet off, so it would be 1000 feet high. It had a circular top but we could not see the ends.

A few minutes later another was under the bows, we only cleared it by a few feet. It was about 100 feet high and flat-topped. Just as we were passing the corner there was a sharp report that made you jump, as if it was breaking in two.

Found another on the other side quite close, and a few minutes later saw the long ridge of ice almost ahead. Kept off, and then another came in sight on the other bow. We were too near it to keep away, but I felt sure it was no part of the big one—as we were passing this the point of the big one came in sight, the fog cleared and we passed in between them, there being not more than 400 feet between them.

When we had cleared the big one I saw its north end and took bearings. After sailing 8 miles I took other bearings and found that the east side was 19 miles long; and we could not see the end of the side we sailed along. We sailed about 6 miles alongside of it, water now quite smooth. Before noon the water was quite lumpy from all ways. After we had cleared the passage by about 3 or 4 miles, it cleared up astern, and what a sight it was! Nothing but icebergs through the passage and on the south side of the passage (for the south berg was only about ⅓ mile long north and south, same height as the big berg. I expect it had not long broken off.) There was nothing but a sea of ice astern, and another large flat-topped iceberg, which, as far as you could see, extended like land, it must have been 20 miles long or more.

After we were through there was nothing but small ice, from small pieces to bergs 100 feet long. Also there was one about a mile long covered with what looked like pumice stone or lumps of tallow. I did not see it till it was abeam or I should have gone close to it—there was ice on either side of it. Ice now cleared.

On the 9th only three bergs were seen, and it was evident that the *Cutty Sark* had run clear of this icefield, as with a fresh N.W. wind she proceeded to put 300 miles between the danger and herself.

This ice was encountered by every ship bound round the Horn in 1892 and 1893, and extended from 44° to 55° S., and from 25° to 52° W. Evidently a huge continent of Antarctic ice had broken adrift during the summer weather, and was in the grip of the current slowly working north.

The *Cutty Sark* crossed the equator on 2nd March, 25 days from the Horn, for 11 of which the yards were braced sharp up.

After contending against a succession of light easterly winds, the *Cutty Sark* made Flores at 8 a.m. on 23rd March, 21 days from the equator. The wind continued very light from right ahead until the end of the month. On 28th March, at 2 p.m., the *Cutty Sark* sailed close by the *Zealandia*, which was 100 days out from Napier. *Zealandia* did not arrive in the Thames until five days after the *Cutty Sark* had docked at Antwerp.

The former reported speaking the *Blackadder* in 43° S. on 31st January. *Blackadder* had left Brisbane on 20th December, and docked in London on 30th March, 100 days out.

On the day that the "Cutty" passed the *Zealandia* her run was only 13 miles, but by midnight the wind began to make from the N.W., but speedily swung into the N.N.E. On 2nd April with the wind freshening from ahead and a nasty cross sea, a sad catastrophe happened. The *Cutty Sark* was going close-hauled under a main royal. Woodget, as usual, was carrying sail, for a four-mast barque was in company, running south under lower topsails. At 2 p.m. the "old man" gave the order for the royal to be taken in and the outer jib to be hauled down. Whilst two men were on the jibboom footropes making fast the jib, the ship gave a plunge and washed them both away, but let me give the occurrence in the captain's own words:—

April 2—Strong N.N.E. wind and clear dry weather, nasty cross sea. Noon, lat. 47° 04′ N., long. 8° 52′ W. Course N. 80° E. Distance 197 miles.

At 2.30 p.m. John Doyle and John Clifton, whilst making fast the outer jib, were washed from the boom and drowned. Everything was done that could be done considering the state of the weather. I heard crying from forward and thought someone was hurt. I looked to leeward and could see nothing, but when I went to the weather side of the poop, I saw the two men struggling in the sea about 40 or 50 feet to windward abreast of the mizen rigging. I ordered the helm to be put down and at once threw a life-buoy, but it was some distance to leeward of them. I saw Doyle sink and rise to the surface again, and then I could see him struggling under water. Clifton did not appear to me to make any effort to reach the buoy, he was going round and I saw him no more.

There was too much sea to lower a boat. I wore ship and hovered about to see if I could see either of them, but we could see neither and at 4 p.m. I wore ship again.

Up to 2.15 p.m. the ship was going along so nice and dry. I was forward helping to haul down the jib and had no oilskins on, but the two men that were drowned put theirs on after the jib was down. On the wheel being relieved, no sooner had the man Lewis got to the wheel, than he ran the ship off to east by S. $\frac{1}{2}$ S., wind almost abeam, which of course increased her speed from about 7 to 11 knots: he then brought her up to east $\frac{1}{2}$ N. and almost head to sea.

I told him that he would wash someone from the foc's'le head overboard, and no sooner had I spoken than she gave a plunge and put the boom under.

I had no idea that the boom went under till I saw the men struggling in the sea. I thought that they had come in and were on the foc's'le-head, but I found that the jib was not made fast, so they must have been on the boom.

Fancy, only a minute before they were on the boom laughing to see the sprays come over the bows and the others getting wet, whilst they were dry on the boom; but, one more minute, and things were changed; poor fellows, they were struggling in the waves. Doyle could not swim, so he sank to rise no more. Oh, what a gloom it cast over the ship! Two young men gone to Eternity, and only a few minutes before they were in high spirits and the best of health. During the seven years that I had commanded the *Cutty Sark* I never knew her to put the boom under before.

By the afternoon of 3rd April, the wind had dropped, what little there was of it being east, a dead muzzler, and by midnight it was almost calm. For the next three days the most usual entry in the log was constant calm, and on 6th April the *Cutty Sark* only covered 12 miles in the 24 hours. The Bishop Rock light was sighted at 6 p.m. on the 7th, the wind being light to gentle at N.E. with patches of fog. That night the wind breezed up from east and Woodget tacked to the S.E. Next morning he stood in close to St. Michael's where a tug came alongside and took his report ashore.

The *Cutty Sark* had to beat the whole way up Channel against fresh easterly winds and a nasty head sea. Plymouth was abeam on the 9th, Portland on the 10th and St. Catherine's on the 11th, the Antwerp pilot being picked up off the Wight. With never a slant it was tack and tack all the way to Antwerp where the *Cutty Sark* was docked on 15th April, having taken 15 days from the Western Isles to the Bishop, and 8 days from the Bishop to Antwerp.

The *Cutty Sark* left Antwerp for Sydney on 1st August, 1893. After towing down the river, Captain Woodget anchored off Flushing in order to wait for a slant. On 4th August, as the wind hung steadily in the west, Captain Woodget decided to proceed, and worked his way down between the Flemish Banks.

It was a dead beat down Channel; the *Cutty Sark* passed a Loch liner, bound for Melbourne, off the Wight, and passed the Otway 27 days ahead of her.

Off Berry Head the *Cromdale* was encountered; and she also was left far behind on the passage out, as she did not reach Sydney until 24 days after the *Cutty Sark*.

Captain Woodget took his departure off the Lizard on 9th August. The clipper had the usual light August and September weather down to the line, which was not crossed until 9th September, 31 days out. Trinidad was sighted on the 16th, on which day the *Pericles*, homeward bound from Sydney was spoken.

From 17th to 19th September good progress was made before a fresh W.S.W. breeze, the runs being 279, 300 and 280. On 21st September the wind shifted from S.E. to E.N.E. and finally freshened into a moderate gale at east, which held the ship up for three days.

At 2 p.m. on 23rd September, Tristan d'Acunha bore S. 15 miles.

On 26th September, with the wind freshening from E.N.E., the *Cutty Sark* made one of the best three days runs of her existence, crossing the Greenwich meridian on 27th September, 17 days from the equator, and the Cape meridian on the 30th. Her log records:—

Sept. 27—Strong E.N.E. wind and cloudy. Noon, lat. 39° 32′ S., long. 1° 38′ E. Course S. 65° E. Distance 306 miles. 10 p.m., sighted an iceberg right ahead. 11 p.m., passed another iceberg.

28—Strong E.N.E. wind and constant rain. Lat. 41° 42′ S., long. 7° 48′ E. Course S. 65° E. Distance 308 miles. Passed 10 icebergs from 40 to 250 feet.

29—Fresh N.E. breeze and fine weather. Lat. 44° 42′ S., long. 14° 43′ E. Course S. 60° E. Distance 350 miles.

In three days the *Cutty Sark* had made 964 miles; if we allow 17 miles for the one hour and 16 minutes necessary to make up the 72 hours, the total distance run comes to 981 miles.

The distance from the Cape to the Leeuwin was covered in 18 days from 30th September to 18th October.

From 14th October to 20th October the *Cutty Sark* made a week's total of 2142 miles her distances being 305, 353, 291, 280, 310, 316, and 287. The 353 miles on 15th October was the biggest run she ever made under Woodget.

The best eleven days during the passage came to 3457 miles.

At 8 a.m. on 23rd October, the Black Pyramid was abeam, the *Cutty Sark* being 75 days out from the Lizard. That afternoon the wind dropped light, and for the next three days nothing but variable airs and calms were experienced; then on 27th October the N.N.E. wind which had started up during the night, suddenly shifted into the south-west and *Cutty Sark* reached her port on 28th October, 80 days out.

The *Cutty Sark* was again too late to load for the January wool sales, but managed to obtain a good charter to Hull. Whilst Woodget had been away from Sydney, Messrs. Dangar, Gedye, the agents, and Messrs. Tablot & Co., the stevedores, had put their heads together with the intention of getting so many bales into the *Cutty Sark* as to dumbfounder Woodget, who believed that he had already seen the limit that she would hold, screwed into her. The result of the plot was startling. No less than 5010 bales of wool were got in place. As each bale is supposed to weigh 400 lbs., the cargo worked out at over 2,000,000 lbs., and was roughly worth £100,000.

The rate of freight paid was one halfpenny per lb. for washed wool, and three-eighths of a penny for greasy, so that the freight amounted to about £4000, from which must be deducted the cost of putting the wool on board, which exceeded £800.

The *Cutty Sark* left Sydney on Christmas Eve, and Captain Woodget little thought, as he said goodbye to the pilot at noon, that it was the famous clipper's last wool cargo from Sydney.

For the first 12 days of the passage the *Cutty Sark* had to contend against very light head winds all the way down to the

Snares, but after rounding New Zealand the westerlies sent her romping along to the Horn, which was rounded on 21st January, only 15 days from the meridian of the South Cape, Stewart Island.

The west wind held steady to 41° W., which was crossed on the 26th; from 8th to 26th January the *Cutty Sark* had made the following runs:—262, 302, 272, 266, 157, 302, 280, 228, 220, 290, 250, 221, 299, 255, 258, 208, 162, 203, 304, and 280, giving a total of 5019 miles in 20 days, an average of 250 miles a day.

On 5th February, close-hauled against a very light head wind, the *Cutty Sark* weathered the little *Helen Denny*, which was 60 days out from New Zealand so that the former had sailed over 2 feet to her one.

The equator was crossed on 16th February, 26 days from the Horn. The *Cutty Sark* passed inside the Western Isles on 12th March, and sighted the Scillies on 21st March, 87 days out. As usual at this time of the year, she had found nothing but light head winds from the line to soundings, and once more she had to beat up Channel against a fresh easterly breeze, which delayed her arrival in Hull until 27th March.

For the time of year this passage was a long way above the average. Although the *Cutty Sark* was 25 years old, she had lost none of her speed; and, though her pumps had not been touched throughout the passage, the cargo came out without a stain upon the bales.

She aroused great interest in Hull, and the local newspapers devoted columns to her history.

We now come to the *Cutty Sark's* last voyage under the British flag. For the last two or three years old Willis had been complaining that she was losing money, though, as a matter of fact, this was not quite true, As Woodget explained, she was not losing money, but owing to the severe competition of the modern large carriers and the drop in freights, she was not making as much money as she used to do in the eighties. Also in both 1892 and 1893, Willis had laid her up for six months in London and Antwerp, and thus lost his chance for the season's wool clip. I fear also that Willis had begun to neglect her again and cut down her upkeep, for on her last voyage her copper was in very bad shape and her gear was constantly carying away.

For the past half-dozen years or more the *Blackadder* had been paying a steady dividend in the Brisbane trade, and in 1894 old Jock determined to see if Woodget could not do likewise, and he therefore put the *Cutty Sark* on the berth for Brisbane.

The *Cutty Sark* left the East India Dock on 25th June, 1894, took in gunpowder at Gravesend, and anchored off Deal at midnight. On the next day sail was made to a light N.E. wind, Mr. Woodthorpe, who had taken the "Cutty" down Channel so often, was landed off Portland at 10 a.m. on 27th June, and the Lizard left astern on the morning of the 28th. With light summer winds all the way to the line, the *Cutty Sark* did not cross the equator until 26th June, 28 days from the Lizard.

Better speed was made in the South Atlantic, and the meridian of Greenwich was crossed on 13th August, 18 days from the line, and that of the Cape on 16th August. The main royal did not require handing until 24th August, on which day the *Cutty Sark* ran 280 miles in a hard N.W. gale. That night a heavy sea washed her fore and aft, smashing the cabin doors and looting the cabins and store rooms, whilst Woodget carried sail in his usual fearless manner, through squalls, which he noted in his log as "terrific."

The westerlies continued to pipe up strong and the ship made fine progress, though if her copper had been in better condition her daily runs would have been from 20 to 30 miles longer. It required nerve to carry on with the gear in the state it was, but everything held until 31st August when, in 43° 30' S., 98° 24' E., in a smart squall at 2 a.m. the martingale stay broke and the fore topgallant mast went over the side, breaking off the port yardarm of the upper fore topsail.

On the next day the wind moderated sufficiently to allow Woodget to get the broken yard on deck. The yard was sent down at 8 a.m., fished and sent aloft again at 4 p.m., when the sail was bent and set.

On 5th September, with the wind fresh at N.N.W., the *Cutty Sark* ran 320 miles in the 24 hours. Two days later there was again trouble with the unlucky fore upper topsail yard, the tie carried away this time, and the lifts took both yardarms off. On the following day, 8th September, three of the defective chainplates broke, but by smart handling Woodget saved the spars.

At 10.15 p.m. on 9th September the Black Pyramid was sighted, and an hour later it was abeam. The *Cutty Sark* had covered 7107 miles between Tristan d'Acunha and the Black Pyramid in 30 days, an average of 233 miles a day. She had run from the Cape to the Leeuwin in 19 days, from the Cape to the Black Pyramid in 24 days, and from the Lizard to the Black Pyramid in 73 days.

Sydney light was passed at 5 a.m. on 13th September, 77 days from the Lizard, and the *Cutty Sark* anchored in Moreton Bay on the 15th, 79 days from the Lizard. Thus, her last outward passage to Australia in spite of ragged copper and worn out rigging, was quite up to the standard which she set in her prime.

Cutty Sark found *Blackadder* loading at Brisbane: the latter sailed on 20th October and reached London on 20th February, 123 days out, a very poor passage for such a clipper hull, but *Blackadder* was feeling the effects of old age and want of upkeep as much if not more than the *Cutty Sark*.

The latter left the wharf at Brisbane on her last passage under the British flag at 9 a.m. on 9th December, and towed down to the Pile lighthouse, where she anchored at 12.45, as it was blowing hard from the south-west. On the next day at 9.30 a.m. the anchor was weighed, the tug let go off Cape Moreton at 2.45 p.m. and sail was made to a gentle easterly air. After two days of light airs and calms, the wind came out of the S.E., very squally, with thunder, lightning and torrents of rain, Sydney was passed on 2nd January. New Zealand was doubled on 7th January, 8 days out; and on 10th January in a fresh S.W. breeze and high sea the *Cutty Sark* passed and signalled the *Torridon*, which had left Sydney on the same day that the *Cutty Sark* had left Brisbane.

The run from Brisbane to the Horn was made in 27 days, the best 24 hours of which totalled 308 miles.

On 26th January the high land of the southern point of America was close aboard, all covered with snow with which the surf of the heavy Cape Horn swell seemed to mingle. There was next to no wind, one of those short breathing spells for which the latitude of Cape Stiff is notorious. However that evening the westerlies

"CUTTY SARK" IN SURREY COMMERCIAL DOCK, 1922

See Page 304

"CUTTY SARK" IN DRY DOCK, 1922

[See Page 305

set in again, and the *Cutty Sark* speedily ran an American four-mast barque out of sight, after having been in company with her since the previous day. The westerlies held until 6th February, 33° 57′ S., 28° 01′ W., when the wind set in very light from the E.N.E. This head wind spoilt the passage, for it lasted almost without a slant until the line was crossed on 28th February, 33 days from the Horn. As usual with a long spell of head wind, the homeward bound ships began to bunch up.

On 7th February *Cutty Sark* spoke the barque *Lady Wolseley*, 53 days out from Taltal to Hamburg.

On 13th February she spoke the barque *Pass of Killiecrankie* from Pisagua for Falmouth, 73 days out. This ship had rounded the Horn on 12th January, a fortnight before the *Cutty Sark*.

On 15th February the latter spoke the ship *Flintshire*, 90 days out from 'Frisco to Cork; the *Knight of St. Michaels* homeward bound from Iquique and 39 days out, and a German barque from Rio Negro for Havre. On the next day the ship *Dawpool* of Liverpool from Pisagua for Georgetown, 57 days out, was spoken, whilst on the equator the *Cutty Sark* passed and spoke the fine four-mast barque *California*, which had left 'Frisco for Liverpool on 18th November.

All these ships were both out-footed and out-pointed by the *Cutty Sark*, though she was badly handicapped by the state of her copper.

On 13th March in 29° 47′ N., 42° 49′ W., with a gentle southerly air just rippling the water, the *Cutty Sark* spoke the *Torridon* again; under these conditions the *Torridon* actually gained 6 miles on the *Cutty Sark* in six hours, which Woodget attributed to his ragged copper—certainly under ordinary conditions the *Torridon* was no match for the "Cutty" and had been outsailed by her over and over again.

The *Cutty Sark* passed the Western Isles on 18th March, 18 days from the line, and then had a nice fair wind to soundings. On 23rd March in 49° 13′ N., 10° 50′ W., the little clipper passed the big four-mast ship *Earl of Dalhousie*, and the next day she picked up the Start. With a fine S.W. breeze she went roaring up Channel, and docked in London on 26th March, being 84 days

U

from Brisbane to the Start and 81 days from the latitude of Sydney. The *Torridon* managed to dock on the same day, having made the best passage of her career and hung on to the "Cutty" from 51° S., 177° E., though in contrasting the passages from the latitude of Sydney the latter beat her by three days.

Of the other ships encountered during the passage:—

Lady Wolseley arrived Dungeness on 18th April, beaten 24 days by the *Cutty Sark* from 32° S., 28° W.

The *Pass of Killiecrankie* arrived Falmouth 24th April, beaten 31 days from 24° S., 29° W.

The *Flintshire* arrived Queenstown 18th April, beaten 25 days from 22° 34′ S., 27° 30′ W.

The *Knight of St. Michaels* arrived 26th April, beaten 31 days from 22° 34′ S., 27° 30′ W.

The *Dawpool* arrived New York on 10th April, 15 days after the *Cutty Sark* arrived London, another severe beating, from 21° 38′ S., 29° 43′ W.

The *California* arrived Liverpool on 28th March, the only one of these modern sailing ships which had made a race at all against the old tea clipper. Her time from 'Frisco to Liverpool was 130 days, and from the line 28 days, a good performance under the circumstances.

The *Earl of Dalhousie* arrived Antwerp on 30th March, being badly left by the "Cutty" in the Channel.

I have given these figures as they are an eloquent proof of the superior speed of the old clipper over that of the finest modern steel ships.

To his infinite disgust Captain Woodget learnt on arrival that Willis intended to sell the famous clipper, and in fact was already in negotiation with the Portuguese.

Old Jock gave his celebrated skipper command of the steady going *Coldinghame*, and when Captain Woodget left the Docks for Brisbane on 26th July, 1895, he bid goodbye to his old ship with a heavy heart, knowing that henceforth her flag would be Portuguese and her identity hidden under the name *Ferreira*.

CHAPTER IX.

UNDER THE PORTUGUESE.

DURING the last ten years of the nineteenth century, the economical steam tramp slowly drove the older windjammers out of existence, and even proved a severe rival to the big four-posters, which, though built by the yard of steel and manned by crews which would not have been considered sufficient for 500-ton ships in the sixties, found an ever greater difficulty in gaining profitable charters.

It is, therefore, not surprising to find owners, looking upon such vessels as 25-year old clipper ships, with their growing repair bills, heavy insurance rates and poor freight capacity, as certain money losers.

And thus we find old John Willis selling his favourite ship to Ferreira & Co., of Lisbon, in July, 1895, for the paltry sum of £2100.

At the beginning of August, 1895, the famous name of *Cutty Sark* appeared for the last time in Lloyd's *Shipping Index*, but starred with the note "see *Ferreira*"—for thus the Portuguese had renamed their new purchase, though they usually spoke of her as —"El Pequina Camisola."

On 5th September she left Gravesend, disguised under the name of *Ferreira*, arrived at Oporto 15th September and Lisbon 28th October, from which date she straightway disappeared into oblivion.

The memory of the zenith years of the sailing ship is now becoming dim. Forty years ago the era of sail was still too close, too much a part of sea life for there to be any sentiment or enthusiasm for "has-beens," nor had the general public begun to look upon the sailing ship as one of the most romantic products of the past.

Though undoubtedly a number of officers and men in the Merchant Service still maintained their affection for the old favourite, no one went so far as bothering to follow her movements under the Portuguese flag. She was in truth forgotten in the present though remembered in the past; and when in her shabby, threadbare loneliness she was seen tucked away alongside some obscure wharf in some South African or South American dago port, it was seldom that more than a casual glance was expended upon her, with the usual comment—"Poor old-timer!"

If we cannot help deprecating the British lack of sentiment in the business-like sale to the foreigners of our old sailing ships, we can at any rate give the dagoes credit for a keen eye where ships are concerned. In the nineties the Portuguese picked up many a wonderful bargain besides the *Cutty Sark* from our shipowners, who could only think of steam and steel.

In 1896 the Portuguese Government bought both *Thermopylae* and *Thomas Stephens* and converted them into training ships, the former being given the name of *Pedro Nunez* and the latter that of *Pero d'Alemquer*.

Thermopylae after being sold by the Aberdeen White Star Line had had five years in the cross-Pacific trade between British Columbia and Hongkong, during which time she managed to break the record of the Pacific. She left Port Blakely on 29th June, 1895, and after a long passage arrived at Leith on 17th December. This was her last passage under the Red Ensign.

The last voyage of *Thomas Stephens* under the British flag was a disastrous one. On 27th December, 1894, she left Barry under Captain Belding for Esquimalt; off the Horn she was partially dismasted and put back to the Falklands, where she arrived on 28th February, 1895. Here Captain Belding refused the extortionate demands of the Stanley shipwrights, preferring instead to sail under jury-rig for Capetown, where he arrived on 14th May. Leaving Capetown on 22nd June, the *Thomas Stephens* at length reached Esquimalt by the Eastern route on 24th September. The homeward passage was without incident, but on arrival Captain Belding was informed that the ship was sold to the Portuguese, with the request that he would deliver her in the Tagus. This trip proved sufficiently exciting, for the ship caught fire, and it was only by Captain Belding's splendid leadership and resource that the blaze was got under and the ship saved. Indeed, the Portuguese Government were so impressed that they not only gave Captain Belding an order and a service of plate, but asked him to continue in the command of the ship and in fact to become a trainer of their Navy.

In 1896, out of the famous tea fleet, there were only three other clippers besides *Cutty Sark* and *Thermopylae* which were still afloat. These were *Titania*, *Lothair* and *Blackadder*. Both *Sir Lancelot* and *Leander* had foundered in Indian Ocean cyclones in 1895, after many years as country ships.

Our illustration shows *Falcon* in her last berth. *Windhover* was wrecked on the Australian coast 1888, and *Kaisow* abandoned on her beam ends, 60 miles W.S.W. of Valparaiso in November, 1890. Of the rest, with the exception of *Wylo*, *Maitland* and *Belted Will*, of whose fate I am ignorant, not one reached the nineties.

Titania, after six voyages in the Hudson Bay Company's employ from London to Vancouver Island and back, during which time she had made the wonderful average of less than 115 days a passage, was sold to the Italians in 1893. Her new owners were P. Pollio & Co., and her new master, Captain Pollio.

On her first voyage, under the new flag, she left London on 1st June, Penarth on 2nd July and arrived Table Bay 27th August. She left Table Bay on 19th September and arrived Port Augusta on 20th October. In the run round the coast from Port Augusta to Sydney she collided with the S.S. *Connowarru*, off Green Cape on 15th April, 1894, her second officer being found to blame. From Sydney she ran to Suva, Fiji, in 8 days 10 hours; and leaving Levuka on 5th December, reached Marseilles on 27th June, 1895.

For the next fifteen years *Titania* traded from Marseilles, either to Reunion and Mauritius, or else to Rio and other South American ports. Her distinguished career came to an end in March, 1910, when she was broken up at Marseilles.

Blackadder remained almost continually in the Brisbane trade until the death of John Willis, when she was sold. She came to her end at Bahia on the 9th April, 1905.

The only other tea clipper, which is still afloat, is the *Lothair*.

She was first of all sold to the Genoese and then to the **Peruvians**. For some years she was employed in carrying Chinese coolies from Hongkong to the West Coast of South America. Just before the late war (1914-1918) it was reported that she was lost on the coast of Peru; but if she stranded she was refloated and continued trading, being then owned by F. G. Piaggio of Callao.

Whilst *Thermopylae* and *Thomas Stephens* swung comfortably to their Government moorings in the Tagus, *Cutty Sark* tramped to and fro between that port and the Portuguese colonies. The once crack clipper of London, Shanghai and Sydney now became known as a regular visitor to Rio, New Orleans, Delagoa Bay and St. Paul de Loanda. Forlorn and forgotten, she lay listlessly alongside obscure sugar and timber wharfs instead of lording it at Circular Quay; or else she rolled her dead-eyes under it in some West or East African roadstead, waiting wearily for palm oil or elephants teeth, tobacco or whalebone. In the twentieth century she gradually settled down to a leisurely yearly round of Oporto, Rio, New Orleans, and Lisbon.

Occasionally a short paragraph in a shipping paper drew one's attention to her neglected old age. Her Portuguese officers declared that she was still good for 16 knots. Of her passages the following are a good sample.

Lisbon to New Orleans	..	..	..	..	25 days.
Lisbon to Rio	..	..	..	..	36 „
Lisbon to St. Paul de Loanda	..	..	..	31 „
Lisbon to Delagoa Bay	..	..	..	..	53 „
New Orleans to Lisbon	..	..	..	..	29 „

Neither her new name, her want of paint, nor her obscure wanderings could hide the halo of romance which surrounded the *Cutty Sark*.

In 1905 she suddenly turned up in Cardiff with images of saints stuck up all round her decks; and straightway she became the one topic of conversation in that busy port. Yarns of her records and adventures, mostly incorrect or highly coloured, spread through South Wales shipping circles. Then she sailed for Portuguese waters and once more disappeared into oblivion.

Five years before this date her designer had died at Bervie

in Kincardineshire, the family home. Soon after the launch of the *Cutty Sark*, Hercules Linton went to Dundee, where he became manager of a shipbuilding firm. He was next heard of at Southampton and Woolston, and it is probable that he may have had some influence on the designs of the many famous sailing ships of the Oswald and Mordaunt regime.

Whilst he was at Woolston, the death of an aged uncle enabled him to retire to Bervie, where he lived quietly until his death in May, 1900.

In 1914 I gave a description in *The China Clippers* of the famous old clipper, as seen lying alongside the Wharf at New Orleans the year before. This at once brought me letters declaring that my informant must be mistaken, as she had been wrecked in a West Indian hurricane several years back.

However I had scarcely taken up my pen to reply before the *Cutty Sark* answered the letters herself by turning up in the Mersey in June, 1914, with a cargo of whalebone and oil from Mossamedes. It is true that she did get ashore during a West Indian hurricane and narrowly escaped destruction; she was refloated, however, with the loss of her rudder, a new one being fitted at Key West.

During those fateful months of the summer of 1914, thousands of people read of the fame of the *Cutty Sark* in the columns of the newspapers, whilst photographers snapped her, tourists wandered round her decks, curio hunters sought opportunity to ransack her for mementos, so that the after-bell, the smaller of her two bells, had to be hidden below, and seamen in every British port told fanciful yarns of her career.

From that date her passages have been followed and reported on by crowds of enthusuasts. Owing to the account of her in my *China Clippers*, I have been bombarded with letters from these enthusiasts: schoolboys wrote that they were making models of her and required the dimensions of her houses and hatches: sailormen wrote, proud of having been passed by her at sea: her many Portuguese admirers wrote from Lisbon: and even soldiers in the thick of the Great War wrote giving me any information they had or asking for the latest news.

From every part of the world came these letters from *Cutty*

Sark enthusiasts, from the tropics and the trenches, from the Arctic and the South Seas, from rest camps and hospital ships. Forwarded on by my publishers, they formed a comforting relaxation from the stress of war. During the first year of the war letters from Australia, from South Africa and from the Americas tracked me down in the Punjaub, followed me to the North-West Frontier, and even came by runner to Himalayan camps, 8000 to 12,000 feet above the sea level.

Later on they caught me in Egypt, and for the first time I saw the stamp "Damaged by salt water" crossing envelopes, upon which the addresses and readdresses were almost washed out. Finally they were read and re-read amidst the mud and shell holes of the Ypres salient, in gun-line dugouts along the crest of Vimy Ridge and in the shattered mining villages round Lens. One man, a mining engineer of Johannesburg, wrote from a London hospital sending me a photograph of the old "Cutty" lying off Mossamedes. A curt postcript informed me that he was slowly recovering from a dozen shell wounds.

Quite a number of letters reached me from a driver in a New Zealand battery, which was only in the next division to my own. Then about the middle of the war letters began to pour in with South African postmarks. I think the first of these came from a steward in a Castle liner; it was quickly followed by long screeds from the captain of a cable layer and a Captain of Marines; others followed containing clippings from newspapers and snapshots of an almost unrecognisable "Cutty".

About this time pretty nearly every British and Colonial newspaper rushed into print with lengthy columns describing the past life and war adventures of the great little ship. The fact was that, though she had escaped the submarines, she had been dismasted and nearly lost off the Cape.

But I must hark back to the Birkenhead Dock, where she was discharging a cargo of whalebone and oil shortly before the outbreak of war. During July, 1914, she loaded a cargo of coal and bricks, coal in the hold and bricks in the 'tween decks, also a number of empty oil drums, and sailed for Mossamedes at a moment when the whole world was ringing with the news of a war which was to change the face of Europe.

Braving mines, submarines and inquisitive cruisers the old tea clipper safely reached the exposed roadstead off the West African coast. The anchorage off Mossamedes is not a pleasant spot for a steamer to lie, and still less for a sailing ship. The holding ground is doubtful and exposed to the full force of the Atlantic; often a mountainous swell runs in which shatters itself with a tremendous roar upon the beach. At such times cables are veered to the limit and windjammers get ready to slip at a moment's notice.

The *Cutty Sark* managed to load another cargo of whalebone and oil without mishap, but hardly were the hatches on before unmistakable signs told of coming bad weather. The Portuguese captain was both an experienced and prudent man. Without a moment's hesitation he slipped his anchors and put to sea, preferring to sacrifice his ground tackle rather than be caught on such a terrible lee shore. The one awkward part about knocking his shackles out was that he had no spare anchor with both bowers gone.

Fifty-nine days later, in February, 1915, the "Cutty" arrived off Port Lynas. Here, after the usual bargaining, she was taken in tow by the *William Joliffe*; the skipper of the tugboat being sublimely ignorant of the fact that his tow was without any means of bringing up. His bargain was to tow her into the Sloyne, and as soon as he was abreast of the Liverpool Landing Stage, he sang out to the ship to get her anchor ready, being no doubt somewhat surprised that preparations to get an anchor over had not already been made.

The reply which came back in the laconic language of a foreigner with little English at his command must have dumfoundered the crew of the *William Jolliffe*.

"Got no anchor," the Portuguese skipper called out calmly

We can well imagine the amazed ejaculations aboard the tugboat.

"She aint got no anchor! For the Lord's sake s'elp me, but she aint got no blommin' killick."

The tide was out and there was no hope of getting the windjammer inside the dock gates, so that there was nothing the tugboat could do but hang on to the forlorn *Ferreira* until the flood made. But the skipper of the *William Joliffe* was not slow to realise that this was a case of salvage, not towage. The sailing ship was helpless without her anchors and with her sails stowed, and ranked as a vessel not under control.

The tugboatman thereupon blew five blasts on his whistle for another tug to come and help him hold his prize. The *Canada* appeared in answer to his summons, and between them they hung on to the famous clipper until the tide made.

The "Cutty's" second appearance in Liverpool within a year was the signal for a further show of enthusiasm on the part of all local ship lovers. And besides her dramatic entry into port, there was a further interest in her arrival, for had she not safely navigated through the most perilous waters of the world—through the densest part of the war zone and come through unscathed.

Once more the old clipper, in spite of her great yellow *Ferriera* name-boards, her broad white strakes instead of gilt lines, her painted bright work and slovenly, threadbare rigging, lorded it over every other ship in the basin and submitted to the stream of visitors with what seemed to be a truly regal air of indifference.

This time she cleared for Lisbon, where she arrived without unusual incident. She left Lisbon for Mossamedes on 15th June, 1915; on a voyage which was to be as full of adventure, of evil fortune and narrow escape from destruction as her tenth.

The first attack from the malevolent goddess of fortune came when she was ten days out—her third rudder, the American-built one, was carried away, but once more her commander proved equal to the occasion. Captain Frederick V. Sousa was the resourceful man, and he managed to make Mossamedes under a makeshift of some sort, which served its purpose, though not in the same class as Moodie's famous jury-rudder.

At Mossamedes the *Ferreira* was obliged to wait four months for a new rudder, eventually sailing for Delagoa Bay in October, 1915. At Delagoa Bay Captain Sousa experienced his second piece of ill fortune. Whilst the ship was at sea Portugal had declared war on Germany, and the anchor was barely on the ground before every man-jack forward was called to the colours. It is more than likely that Portugal's entry into the war had a good deal to do with the old *Cutty Sark's* subsequent misfortunes.

No doubt her cargo of coal was loaded carelessly, with everyone's thoughts on the war; and it is far from likely that the scratch crew she picked up in Delagoa Bay were as good as her old hands.

She left Delagoa Bay on 23rd April, 1916, and the following extracts, translated from her log, give a very clear account of her dismasting and narrow escape from destruction.

April 23—Left Delagoa Bay for Mossamedes with a cargo of 1142 tons. of coal.

April 30—Heavy seas damaged the rigging and carried some poultry overboard.

May 1—Bad weather continued, and owing to the heavy rolling of the ship, the cargo began to shift, and the ship took a list to port. The seas were so heavy that it was impossible to lift the hatches in order to retrim the coal.

2—At 8 p.m. the hatches were opened and a start was made a shifting the coal, so as to bring the ship on an even keel.

3—The wind increased almost to a cyclone, and fears were entertained for the safety of the masts. The cargo again shifted.

4—The wind changed to the south-west, heavy seas sweeping the decks.

5—Owing to the extensive rolling the cargo once more shifted, and the port bulwarks were almost under water. The wind dropped at midnight.

6—Heavy seas prevented the hatches being opened, and so threatening was the outlook that it was feared that the vessel would have to be abandoned. The tops of the main and foremasts* were cut off in the hopes of steadying the ship.

7—The mainmast, which was of iron, bent to such an extent as to almost submerge the ship. All hands were employed in cutting away the rigging and sawing through the main mast, which in its fall carried away the mizen topmast. (This was in lat. 36° 47' S., long. 24° 28' E.)

8—At 4 p.m. the work of clearing away the rigging and mainmast was completed.

9—Weather improved slightly, and by 6 a.m. the ship was once more in navigable order. A ship was sighted at midnight.

10—At 1 a.m. was spoken by the Shaw, Savill and Albion liner, *Kia-Ora*, bound from Cape Town to Australia. Captain Sousa went on board the *Kia-Ora*, which offered to carry him and his crew to Australia, but the offer was declined so the *Kia-Ora* sent a wireless message to the Cape, asking that assistance be sent to the *Ferreira*.

11—Fair winds, but very heavy seas. A steamer was sighted at 10 a.m., but communication was not able to be established.

12—Very strong winds were experienced and heavy seas breaking inboard made it almost impossible for the crew to work the few remaining sails. At this time the *Ferreira* was only 30 miles from the shore.

---

* Main and fore topgallant masts.—B.L.

[1]0—Met the Blue Funnel chartered steamer *Indraghiri*, bound from Durban to Capetown, which offered to tow the *Ferreira* to port. As the latter was in dangerous proximity to the land it was deemed advisable to accept the offer.

14—Arrived in Table Bay at 11 a.m.

Although most of the space in every news sheet was taken up by war news, the dismasting of the old champion and her narrow escape from destruction produced a veritable crop of articles and letters dealing with her mishap and giving a resume of her many feats of sailing.

In this way the *Cutty Sark* was once more forced into the limelight, and every seaman who touched at the Cape made it his first duty to visit the crippled veteran. Thus the crew of the famous clipper suddenly found themselves in a position which is more natural to museum guides than to seamen. But Captain Sousa, his young mate and five Portuguese apprentices, were very proud of their ship and submitted to the business of showing round visitors with the utmost good humour; though when a steamship officer was caught trying to walk off with one of the bells they realised that it was necessary to keep a sharp lookout in order to prevent the ship from being looted. The bells seemed to be the main attraction to curio and memento hunters, and eventually the smaller of the two did find its way aboard a British steamer, which was commanded by a man who had once been an apprentice in the *Cutty Sark*. However, I am glad to say that this bell was returned to the ship when she once more came under the old Red Ensign.

The most interesting curio of all, the short shirt of bright metal which had stood for so many years on the pin at the main-truck, was unfortunately lost when the mainmast went over the side. Many visitors cast envious eyes at the extended right arm which screwed on to the figure-head; but, as a matter of fact, this was not of much interest, for neither was it the original arm nor was it in proportion to the rest of the figurehead, the hand being much too large.

The presence of the *Ferreira* in Capetown docks roused the old contention between sailing ship men as to the sailing merits of the *Cutty Sark* compared to those of her life-long rival, *Thermopylae*.

The crew of the former naturally supported the claims of their own ship. Her complement, which numbered 20 all told, consisted mostly of coloured men, and the story goes that one of her foremast hands enforced his argument with a stiletto.

The *Ferreira* was inspected at Capetown on behalf of the underwriters by Captain H. B. McKeown, late of Iredale Porter's Liverpool ship *Ainsdale*. The old clipper was only insured for £1800, and the cost of repairs was estimated at £2500. The hull was hardly damaged at all. The mainmast in its fall had smashed in about 20 feet of the port rail and broken the cathead, but beyond this the crashing masts and spars seemed to have done very little harm.

How the masts had stood up for 47 years, during the last twenty of which they had evidently been badly neglected, was certainly a cause for wonder. The main-mast had been cut off close to the deck, but what remained of it proved to be deeply pitted and, in places, as thin as paper, whilst one of the yards, which lay across the deck, broken at the slings, was rotten more than halfway through.

The difficulty, of course, was to procure new masts and yards, for the *Ferreira* had been brought into Dock with only her fore lower masts and topmast and mizen lowermast still standing, the latter being broken off just above the top. The only yards aloft were the foreyard, the fore lower topsail yard and the crossjack, which was cockbilled and without a sail bent. The bowsprit and jibboom were intact, but the spanker gaff and boom were both gone.

In spite of the condition of her masts and gear, bad loading was undoubtedly the cause of her dismasting. They had filled the hold full of coal, but there was no cargo of any sort in the 'tween decks. It was soon realised that, owing to the war, a complete outfit of new spars would cost a small fortune, and thus it was decided to convert the grand old full-rig ship into a barquentine.

Steel lower masts for main and mizen were made locally, the new mainmast being 96 feet long from heel to cap, which gave a 50 to 60 ft. hoist for the fore and aft mainsail; the mainboom was 50 feet long. Only a stump topgallant mast was sent aloft on the fore, which did not admit of a royal yard being crossed.

The jibboom, also, was shortened so much that the bowsprit looked out of all proportion in comparison; and with this shortened jibboom the flying-jib was given up, and the poor old ship had in future to rest content with three head sails.

The repairs to the hull did not take long, the ship-wright who had the job declaring that the vessel was as sound as ever. But the masts took a long time to make, and I have photographs of the ship lying at anchor in Table Bay, looking for all the world like a typical British coaster, brigantine rigged, with new mainmast and topmast on end but no mizen mast.

The whole refit took 18 months, which passed peaceably enough at Capetown, though the world war was at its height. Ships, whose adventures had never been paralleled in the past, came and went. War veterans, clad both in khaki and in blue, visited the old "has-been" between spells of the hardest active service ever known, whilst hospital cases, slowly recovering from every kind of wound and war sickness, spent many hours lounging about her decks.

At last a day came when all the repairs were finished, and the metamorphosed clipper was advertised to sail for the familiar port of Mossamedes. At once the evil demon which had so often followed in her wake was aroused to fresh mischief.

The skipper gave a great farewell party aboard, in which I believe, many corks were pulled. Then, as the guests were leaving the ship, a motor-car must needs run over the edge of the dock and fall into the water, by which means three or four people were drowned, who but a short while before were making merry in the *Ferreira's* saloon. If this was not sufficient for the day, some blundering whilst the ship was being towed out of dock caused her to collide with the quayside doing considerable damage to the stem and smashing the figure-head to pieces.

This second accident effectually stopped her departure on the advertised date, and she once more hauled alongside whilst the shipwright was called for. However, repairs were speedily effected the famous figure-head being carefully pieced and bolted together, most people being under the impression that it was her original figure-head. At last on the 10th January, 1918, the barquentine-rigged clipper got safely to sea, and it was soon found that even with such severely clipped wings as she now spread she was capable of a good 12 to 13 knots under favourable conditions.

From 10th January, 1918, to 4th June, 1919, the famous clipper was once more lost to sight by the large British public who were now keenly interested in her career. But again letters from seafaring enthusiasts gave me glimpses of her wanderings.

She arrived at Mossamedes on 21st January, from whence apparently she went round the Cape to Mozambique. In June, 1918, I was told that she was at St. Thome, and in September loading cocoa beans at Accra.

On 16th January, 1919, she arrived at Ponta Delgada, St. Michaels, with her captain ill. Here she lay idly at anchor for over two months, apparently awaiting the recovery of her commander. At last, in April, 1919, the old ship was once more got underweigh, her destination being Havre, where she arrived on 12th May. Three weeks later, to the delight of her many admirers, she was reported to be on her way to London. She arrived in the Thames on 4th June, and had scarcely made fast in dock before *Cutty Sark* enthusiasts, newspaper reporters and press photographers began to clamber about her decks. But many an old seaman, who knew her in her prime, came away from his visit in sorrow and anger after seeing her thread-bare condition, her worn decks and neglected bright work, not to speak of her contemptible coasters' rig, with its shortened jibboom, stumpy masts and baby sails. Yet some slight comfort was gained by the assurance of her Portuguese officers that she was still as dry as the proverbial bone and was capable of a good 12 knots in spite of the barquentine rig.

The old ship was only a month in London. Her master wished to dry-dock her, but no dry dock happened to be available, so on 2nd July she left for Swansea. The *Ferreira* did not leave Swansea until 28th September, and 13 days later, on 11th October, once more anchored in the Tagus. In 1920 she made a trip to Newcastle, returning to Lisbon with a cargo of coals in August.

Messrs. Ferreira had seen no profits from their celebrated ship for some years and they now reluctantly decided to sell her. The first news of her being sold came to me in a laconic letter, which said:—"*Cutty Sark* sold to a Rock Scorpion."

The change of ownership caused a much needed survey and overhaul. The old ship was first of all drydocked and her copper stripped off. Her planking was then carefully examined and, with the exception of one or two planks which were replaced, was found to be as sound as the day she was launched. She was thereupon resheathed. The iron frames were chipped, scraped and painted with two heavy dressings of red lead, and the cables were ranged on deck and similarly treated.

The repairs were carefully done and took nearly a year of leisurely post-war work. It was therefore not surprising that they cost a great deal of money, much more indeed than the new owner expected, but he had at least the satisfaction of knowing that the old ship was as sound as ever with no signs of decay anywhere.

After this thorough overhaul, the *Ferreira* sailed from Lisbon for the Gulf port of Pensacola, where she loaded pitchpine in short lengths for parquet flooring. In November, 1921, her many devoted admirers were electrified by short paragraphs in their morning papers which announced that the famous vessel had arrived in the Thames, 50 days out from Pensacola, and she was scarcely berthed before the police at the Surrey Commercial Dock gates were busily at work inspecting passes to view her.

To the horror of the *Cutty Sark* enthusiasts, the sides of the famous clipper now showed a dull grey with painted ports, nevertheless the false line of ports could not disguise the shapely beauty of her hull.

The skipper, a careful old Portuguese, who was evidently very fond of his ship, told me that they had not had to touch the pumps the whole voyage, though she had experienced some very bad weather, which had done a little damage to her port quarter and smashed a spoke or two in the aged wheel.

Apparently the freight from the Gulf did not nearly pay her running expenses, and the agents soon let it be known that the *Cutty Sark* was once more for sale; but when a small syndicate of her admirers made an offer from a purely sentimental point of view, without any idea of trying to make good business out of her, a prohibitive price was asked, and this killed the hope of many of us that the *Cutty Sark* might once more be restored to her old

See Page 305

"CUTTY SARK" IN FALMOUTH HARBOUR, 1923

FIGURE-HEAD OF "CUTTY SARK," 1922

[*See Page* 306

flag. Indeed, when Denny Bros. showed a desire for one of the bells of the ship they had had a hand in building, the Portuguese owners estimated the sentimental value of the bell at £500!

However, though we were disappointed in our hope of buying the old ship, we were able to console ourselves by exploring her from end to end, and by photographing her from every point of vantage. Whilst the *Ferreira* was discharging, the largest sailing ship in the world, the *France*, was berthed on the other side of the dock, and the difference between the ancient thoroughbred and the modern carrier was very interesting.

Even when the cargo was out and only a sufficiency of stiffening in her hold, the "Cutty" retained her good looks from whatever vantage point one chose to view her, but the *France* required both distance and a low side to give her any beauty at all.

The huge five-master sailed away to her doom, but the dainty clipper, over half a century old, after going into dry dock for a scrub, left London with a new lease of life in store. Some ships, like some men, have a destiny which not even the severest attacks of the fates and furies are able to affect.

The *Ferreira* cleared for Lisbon in January, 1922, and straightway ran into a Channel gale, which split her canvas and put a kink in her mizen boom; in vain the angry wind and sea tried their best to overwhelm her, but the stout-hearted veteran once again proved her right to be called "Queen of the Seas." And the old Portuguese skipper, when the westerly gale had done its worst, quietly put his helm up and ran back to the safe waters of Falmouth harbour, where, without calling in the local experts, he repaired the damage to his ship and mended his torn sails. As usual with the *Cutty Sark*, what at first seemed to be a misfortune turned out in the end to be the very best of luck, for the direct result of her forced detention in Carrick Roads was her return to her old flag.

It happened that a retired windjammer skipper had lately settled at Trevissome, near Falmouth. This man, Captain Dowman, had served his time in the Dale Line and latterly commanded the cadet ship *Fort Garry*. At Falmouth he still kept up his interest in the training of seamen by maintaining, at his own expense, the

v

brigantine *Lady of Avenel*. Both he and his wife belonged to that large section of the British race which is still devoted to sail, its special seamanship and its glorious memories. Captain Dowman's devotion to the *Cutty Sark* dated back to his apprenticeship days in the *Hawksdale*.

When homeward bound from Sydney in 1894 the latter was passed at sea by the *Cutty Sark* in a manner which could not fail to impress itself upon the inmates of the *Hawksdale's* half-deck, and Captain Dowman had always retained a vivid memory of this encounter.

But there is no doubt that this visit of the old ship to Falmouth had a wonderfully stimulating effect upon Captain Dowman's interest in her, and put the idea of buying her back from the Portuguese into his head. Rumour states that Mrs. Dowman was equally enthusiastic and declared that if her husband did not buy the "Cutty," she would.

The *Ferreira* duly sailed from Falmouth and reached Lisbon without further mishap.

In June, 1922, I heard that she had been sold in Lisbon to a new Portuguese owner, who had changed her name to *Maria di Amparo*, and was loading her with scrap iron for the Hamburg market. But three months later came the great piece of news. A short paragraph appeared in most of the shipping and daily papers, which announced that the Falmouth tug *Triton* was on her way to Lisbon in order to fetch back the *Cutty Sark*, which had been recently bought by Captain Dowman.

So Captain Dowman succeeded in restoring the *Cutty Sark* to her old flag in spite of the rapacious Portuguese, who not only made him pay £3750 for the old ship, but compelled him to allow her to be brought over by a Portuguese crew, who insisted on being sent back at his expense in the second class of a mail boat.

Thus the *Cutty Sark*, after an interval of 28 years, once more appeared in British waters with the Red Ensign at her peak.

The *Cutty Sark* has been re-rigged according to her original sail and spar plan, and Captain Dowman dreamed of the "Cutty" once more topping the 300 miles running her easting down and making the famous Heads of Port Jackson in under the 70 days, but alas!

In 1938 the famous clipper was presented to the Thames Nautical Training College by Mrs. Dowman, widow of the late owner of the vessel. The *Cutty Sark* is now moored abreast of the *Worcester* of Greenhithe, and forms a valuable addition to the space available in the ship.

In my *China Clippers* I ended up with a lament over the lack of sentiment showed by the Britisher where his ships are concerned.

In the light of such happenings, as the buying of the *Cutty Sark*, the preservation and restoration of the *Victory* and the growing interest displayed in old models and shipping prints, I am glad to be able to retract that lament and to rejoice in the knowledge that the British Empire is interested in its ships which, besides being an ever present necessity to its existence, were undoubtedly the prime cause of its being.

APPENDIX

APPENDIX I.

The Scantlings of "Cutty Sark" and "Thermopylae."

Scantlings.	Cutty Sark	Thermopylae
Upper deck—Fore and aft and diagonal tie plates on beams	$13\frac{1}{2} \times \frac{11}{16}$	$13 \times \frac{11}{16}$
Stringer plate..	$30\frac{1}{2} \times \frac{11}{16}$	$34 \times \frac{11}{16}$
Angle	$5 \times 4 \times \frac{9}{16}$	$5 \times 4 \times \frac{9}{16}$
Wood deck	E.I. teak $3\frac{1}{2}$ in. thick	Yellow pine 4 in. thick.
Beams bulb plate	$9 \times \frac{10}{16}$	$8\frac{1}{2} \times \frac{9}{16}$
Angles	$3\frac{1}{2} \times 3\frac{1}{2} \times \frac{7}{16}$	$3 \times 3 \times \frac{8}{16}$
Upper deck waterway	—	teak 14×10
Lower deck—Fore and aft tie plates on beams	$15 \times \frac{11}{16}$	$13\frac{1}{2} \times \frac{11}{16}$
Stringer plate..	$22\frac{1}{2} \times \frac{11}{16}$	$23 \times \frac{11}{16}$
Angles	$5 \times 4 \times \frac{9}{16}$	$5 \times 4 \times \frac{9}{16}$
'Tween deck	Pine 3" thick	No deck laid
Beams bulb plate	$10 \times \frac{11}{16}$	$9 \times \frac{5}{8}$
Angles	$4 \times 3\frac{1}{2} \times \frac{8}{16}$	$3\frac{1}{2} \times 3 \times \frac{9}{16}$
Hold pillars—diameters	lower $3\frac{3}{4}$ upper $2\frac{5}{8}$	$3\frac{1}{2}$
Frames (spaced 18")..	$4\frac{1}{2} \times 3\frac{3}{4} \times \frac{9}{16}$	$4\frac{1}{2} \times 3\frac{1}{2} \times \frac{5}{8}$
Reverse frames	$3 \times 3 \times \frac{7}{16}$	$3\frac{1}{2} \times 3 \times \frac{8}{16}$
Floors	$24 \times \frac{9}{16}$ to $9\frac{1}{8} \times \frac{9}{16}$ at bilge keelson	$24 \times \frac{5}{8}$ to 7" at bilge keelson
Centre keelson single plate	—	$16 \times \frac{3}{4}$
Angles	—	$5 \times 4 \times \frac{9}{16}$
Foundation plate	$18\frac{1}{4} \times \frac{11}{16}$	$14 \times \frac{1}{2}$
Top plate	—	$\frac{9}{16}$
Side keelson—bulb plate	$10 \times \frac{11}{16}$	$9 \times \frac{5}{8}$
Intercostal plate	$14 \times \frac{10}{16}$	$9 \times \frac{5}{8}$
Bilge keelson—bulb plate	$10 \times \frac{10}{16}$	$8\frac{1}{2} \times \frac{5}{8}$
Side stringer in hold—angles ..	$5 \times 4 \times \frac{9}{16}$	$5 \times 4 \times \frac{9}{16}$
Ceiling in hold	—	3"
Iron sheer strake	$35 \times \frac{10}{16}$	$34 \times \frac{11}{16}$
Iron bilge plate	$23\frac{1}{2} \times \frac{10}{16}$	$18 \times \frac{10}{16}$
Diagonal plates on frames	$9 \times \frac{10}{16}$	$9 \times \frac{10}{16}$
Keel	$15\frac{1}{2} \times 17$ rock elm	$15\frac{1}{2} \times 21$ American oak and English elm
	—	
Iron keel plate	$31 \times \frac{11}{16}$	$31 \times \frac{3}{4}$
Garboard strake (rock elm) ..	—	12"
Outside planking rock elm from keel to topside planking. East India teak gradually diminished from topside planking at sheer strake..	$\frac{3}{8}$ depth of hold 6" — 6" to $4\frac{3}{4}$" $4\frac{3}{4}$" thick	$\frac{3}{8}$ depth of hold 6" — $5\frac{1}{2}$" to $4\frac{3}{4}$" $4\frac{3}{4}$" thick

APPENDIX II.

List of Best-known Ships built in 1869.

Ship's Name	Material	Reg. Tonn.	Length	Breadth	Depth	Builder	Date Launched	Owner	Trade Built for
Deerhound	C.	573	157.1	31	18.5	Pile	January	J. R. Kelso	China
City of Lucknow	I.	1195	231.1	35.5	22.2	Barclay	March	Smith	Indian
Doune Castle	C.	887	197.1	34	19.8	Elder	"	Skinner	China
Centurion	C.	965	208.1	35	21	Hood	April	Thompson	Australian
Wylo	C.	799	192.9	32.1	20.2	Steele	"	Killick	China
Loch Awe	I.	1053	217.7	34.5	21	Barclay	"	Wilson	Australian
Oberon	C.	1194	241.1	36.2	21	Inglis	May	Shaw	China
Ambassador	C.	692	176	31.3	19.1	Walker	"	Lund	China
Hoghton Tower	I.	1538	247	40.1	23.7	Clover	"	Ismay	Australian
Golden Fleece	I.	1257	229.3	36.8	22.3	Barclay	June	Carmichael	General
Zealandia	I.	1116	215.6	35.1	20.3	Connell	"	Shaw, Savill	New Zealand
City of Hankow	I. & W.	1195	223	35.2	22.3	Stephen	"	Smith	China
Normancourt	C.	834	197.4	33	20	Inglis	July	Baring	Australian
Thomas Stephens	I.	1507	263	38.2	23.1	Potter	"	Stephens	New Zealand
Otago	C.	993	207.3	34.5	20.1	Duncan	"	Albion	China
Osaka	C.	527	165	30.1	17.2	Pile	"	Killick	Australian
Berean	C.	526	160.5	30.2	17.2	Pile	August	Walker	Australian
Loch Katrine	I.	1200	226	35.8	21.5	Lawrie	"	Aitken,Lilburn	China.
Caliph	C.	914	213.3	36.1	20.4	Hall	Sept.	Hector	Indian
City of York	I.	1195	222.7	35.8	21.7	Elder	"	Smith	Australian
Patriarch	I.	1339	222.1	38.1	22.3	Hood	"	Thompson	Australian
Loch Ness	I.	1194	225.5	35.6	21.6	Barclay	"	Aitken,Lilburn	China
Duke of Abercorn	C.	1050	212	35.1	20.5	Connell	October	Montgomerie	Australian
Loch Tay	I.	1191	225.4	35.5	21.6	Barclay	"	Aitken,Lilburn	Australian
Otago	I.	348	147	26	14	Stephen	"	Grierson	Australian
Eme	C.	774	199.7	32.6	19	Connell	Nov.	J. Wade	China
Cutty Sark	C.	921	212.5	36	21	Scott & L	"	Willis	China
Blackadder	I.	918	216.6	35.2	20.5	Maudslay	Feb. '70	Willis	China

APPENDIX III.

Spar Plans of "Ariel," "Titania," "Spindrift," "Normancourt," "Cutty Sark" and "Hallowe'en."

Spars	*Ariel*	*Titania*	*Spindrift*	*Normancourt*	*Cutty Sark*	*Hallowe'en*
	Ft.	Ft.	Ft.	Ft.	Ft.	Ft.
Bowsprit—Jibboom outside cap ..	38	$38\frac{1}{2}$	42	44	40	41.7
Bowsprit and jibboom, extreme	—	—	—	—	—	—
length	62	63	$68\frac{1}{2}$	$68.4\frac{1}{2}$	60	63.7
Foremast—Extreme length (deck to	—	—	—	—	—	—
truck)	128	128	$126\frac{1}{4}$	131.9	129.9	124.9
Lower mast (deck to cap)	61	$61\frac{1}{2}$	$61\frac{1}{2}$	58	$61\frac{3}{4}$	61
Lower mast (doublings)	13	14	$13\frac{1}{2}$	$13\frac{1}{4}$	14	15
Topmast	44	$43\frac{1}{2}$	45	43	48	47.3
Topmast (doublings)	7	7	7	$7\frac{1}{2}$	9	9
Topgallant mast	—	—	25	25	26	26.6
Topmast (doublings)	44	44	—	—	—	—
Royal Mast	—	—	16	26.6	$17\frac{1}{2}$	15
Foreyard	70	71	76	71	78	78
Lower topsail yard	60	62	62	61	68	68
Upper	56	57	60	56	64	61
Topgallant yard	$43\frac{1}{2}$	44	46	41	48	47.4
Royal yard	$33\frac{1}{2}$	$33\frac{1}{2}$	33	32	38	38
Mainmast—Extreme length (deck to	—	—	—	—	—	—
truck)	143	146	147.9	$141\frac{1}{2}$	145.9	140.9
Lower mast (deck to cap)	65	66	66	$61\frac{1}{2}$	64.9	64
Lower mast (doublings)	$14\frac{1}{2}$	$14\frac{1}{2}$	15	$13\frac{1}{2}$	14	15
Topmast	44	$46\frac{1}{2}$	48	$46\frac{1}{2}$	48	47.3
Topmast (doublings)	7	7	8.3	$7\frac{1}{2}$	9	9

Topgallant mast	55	—	27	26	26	26.6
Topgallant (doublings)	—	56	—	—	—	—
Royal mast	—	—	17	16	15	15
Skysail mast	—	—	12	12	14½	12
Mainyard	73	76½	84	74	78	78
Lower topsail yard	64	67	67	65	68	68
Upper topsail yard	59½	62½	65	60	64	61
Topgallant yard	46	48	48	44	48	47.4
Mainmast—Royal yard	35	36	34	32	38	38
Skysail yard	27	28	26	24	34	30
Mizen Mast—Extreme length (deck truck)	113	114	109	107¾	108.9	107.9
Lowermast (deck to cap)	58	59	57	50¼	55.9	56
Lowermast (doublings)	11½	12	11	10	11	12
Topmast	36½	37	36½	33	38	37.6
Topmast (doublings)	5¾	6	6	5½	7	6
Topgallant mast	36	36	18½	18	19½	19.3
Topgallant (doublings)	—	—	—	—	—	—
Royal mast	—	—	13½	21	13½	13
Crossjack yard	59½	61	65	60½	60	57
Lower topsail yard	51	52	single topsail	50	54	40.4
Upper topsail yard	47	48	50	44	48	46
Topgallant yard	34½	35½	38	32.4	39	38
Royal yard	26	26½	26	24	33	29
Spanker gaff	35	36	39	31	34	30.3
Spanker boom	47	49	50	48	52	47.6
Outer end of flying jibboom to end of spanker boom	267	274	292	256	280	—
Dolphin striker	11	10½	12	11½	8	—

APPENDIX IV.

Rigging of the "Cutty Sark"—Sizes.

Wire Standing Rigging—	
Fore and main shrouds and stays	5 inch.
Mizen " " "	4 "
Fore and main topmast rigging	$2\frac{3}{4}$ "
Mizen " " "	$2\frac{1}{2}$ "
Fore, main and mizen topgallant rigging	2 "
(stays, backstays, jib-stays and guy in proportion)	
Fore and main lifts "	$3\frac{1}{4}$ "
(other lifts in proportion)	
Running Gear—	
Fore and main sheets	5 "
Fore and main braces	$3\frac{1}{2}$ "
Fore and main clew garnets	$3\frac{1}{4}$ "
Fore bowlines	$3\frac{1}{4}$ "
Crossjack and topsail braces	3 "
Studding-Sail Gear—	
Lower studding sail—halliards	$3\frac{1}{2}$ "
sheet	$3\frac{1}{2}$ "
inner halliards	3 "
tack	$2\frac{3}{4}$ "
whip	$2\frac{1}{2}$ "
downhaul	$2\frac{1}{4}$ "
Skysail studding sail—halliards	2 "
sheets	2 "
tacks	24 thread

Footropes were of 4-strand cordage.

APPENDIX V.

Abstract Log of "Thermopylae."

December 27, 1870. Left London.
   ,,   29 Left the Downs.
January   1, 1871. Dropped pilot off the Lizard. Wind S.W. At noon. Lat 49°
10′ N., long. 9° 20′ W. Distance 160 miles.

		Lat.	Long.	Wind.	Distance.
,,	2	44° 35′ N.	12° 40′ W.	N.W.	320 miles.
,,	3	41° 10′	15° 20′	N.W. by W.	238 ,,
,,	4	37° 16′	18° 26′	N.W. by W.	275 ,,
,,	5	33° 46′	20° 45′	N.E.	220 ,,
,,	6	30° 25′	23° 31′	N.E.	260 .,
,,	7	25° 35′	25° 25′	E.N.E.	310 ,,
,,	8	20° 26′	25° 51′	E by S.	310 ,,
,,	9	15° 18′	25° 46′	East	312 ,,
,,	10	11° 0′	24° 44′	East	263 ,,
,,	11	7° 12′	23° 54′	East	238 ,,
,,	12	3° 58′	22° 52′	S.E.	200 ,,
,,	13	3° 50′	23° 17′	Variable	27 ,,
,,	14	3° 40′	22° 54′	Variable	20 ,,
,,	15	3° 8′	23° 30′	S. by E.	50 ,,
,,	16	2° 29′	25° 35′	S. by E.	131 .,
,,	17	1° 23′ N.	27° 1′	S.E. by S.	124 ,,
,,	18	1° 5′ S.	29° 55′	S.S.E.	180 ,,
,,	19	3° 38′	32°	S.S.E.	190 ,,
,,	20	6° 54′	32° 54′	S.E.	200 ,,
,,	21	10° 36′	32° 56′	E.S.E.	222 ,,
,,	22	14° 58′	32° 20′	E. by S.	265 ,,
,,	23	19° 28′	31° 30′	E. by S.	276 ,,
,,	24	23° 16′	31° 1′	E.S.E.	231 ,,
,,	25	26° 41′	29° 49′	E.N.E.	216 ,,
,,	26	28° 52′	28° 41′	North	146 ,,
,,	27	29° 58′	28° 1′	S.E.	74 ,,
,,	28	32° 5′	27° 57′	E.S.E.	128 ,,
,,	29	34° 13′	26° 50′	East	138 ,,
,,	30	35° 38′	25° 50′	E.N.E.	100 ,,
,,	31	37° 25′	23° 25′	N.E.	150 ,,
February	1	39° 52′ S.	19° 0′ W.	N.E.	260 miles.
,,	2	42° 6′	13° 22′	W.S.W.	290 ,,
,,	3	43° 8′	7° 46′	S.W.	250 ,,
,,	4	44° 17′	2° 33′ W.	S.S.W.	235 ,,
,,	5	45° 21′	2° 46′ E.	N.W.	244 ,,
,,	6	45° 49′	10° 22′	N.N.W.	320 ,,
,,	7	46° 13′	15° 26′	N.W.	215 ,,
,,	8	46°	20° 42′	W.N.W.	222 ,,

Abstract Log of "Thermopylae,"—Cont.

		Lat.	Long.	Wind.	Distance.	
,,	9	45° 41'	25° 55'	West	220	,,
,,	10	45° 30'	32° 4'	S.S.W.	255	,,
,,	11	45° 33'	36° 32'	N.W.	191	,,
,,	12	45° 42'	42° 27'	North	253	,,
,,	13	45° 54'	49° 29'	N. by E.	302	,,
,,	14	45° 54'	55° 3'	N.N.E.	235	,,
,,	15	46°	59° 23'	N.W.	180	,,
,,	16	46°	62°	S.W.	120	,,
,,	17	46°	67° 21'	N.N.E.	224	,,
,,	18	46°	75° 21'	N.N.W.	333	,,
,,	19	46° 6'	81° 21'	S.W.	255	,,
,,	20	46° 7'	88° 18'	S.W.	292	,,
,,	21	45° 53'	94° 46'	N.W.	265	,,
,,	22	45° 10'	102° 20'	West	327	,,
,,	23	45° 18'	108° 31'	W.S.W.	264	,,
,,	24	45° 3'	112° 36'	W.S.W. & N.	177	,,
,,	25	45° 5'	117° 32'	N.E. to E.N.E.	210	,,
,,	26	44° 1'	123° 40'	N.N.W.	267	,,
,,	27	42°	129° 54'	West	296	,,
,,	28	40°	135° E.	West to S.	270	,,
March	1	39° 54' S.	139 15' E.	W.N.W.	195	,,
,,	2					

5 a.m., Cape Otway distant 25 miles.

11 a.m., hoisted ship's name off signal station.

6 p.m., entered Port Phillip Heads.

10.15 p.m., anchored Hobson's Bay.

13,000 miles, average 219 miles a day, which was 9 knots.

APPENDIX VI.

Abstract Log of "Cutty Sark."

LONDON TO SHANGHAI, 1870-1.

Nov. 8—1 p.m. left E.I. Dock in tow of *MacGregor*. Ship drawing 19 ft. 3 ins. and 19 ft. 8 ins.; 6.30 p.m., anchored off Nore light.

9—6 a.m. weighed; 1 p.m., anchored off North Foreland.

10, 1870—3 a.m., passed through the Downs, wind north, moderate, 6 a.m., off Dungeness, 9 a.m. off Beachy Head. Noon, Owers N.W. by N., 1 mile. 2 p.m., signalled St. Catherines. 9 p.m., Start Point North 8 miles, from which departure taken. Set topgallant sails.

Lat. 47° 57′ N., long. 7° 6′ W. Course S.47° W. Distance 277 miles. Winds N.N.E. to west, strong, hard squalls, heavy hail showers.

12—Lat. 44° 46′ long. 9° 36′. Course S. 29° W. Distance 218 miles. Winds west to N.N.W. and north. Squally, rain and hail. Split inner jib.

13—Lat. 41° 21′., long. 12° 41′. Course $33\frac{1}{2}$° W. Distance 234 miles. Winds north to N.N.E. and variable. Begins strong gales, hard squalls, heavy rain and hail. At 4 more moderate. A ship in sight to west steering S.W. Midnight, calm.

14—Lat. 40° 6′, long. 12° 58′. Course S. 10° W. Distance 76 (D.R.) Winds variable and calms, dry but cloudy. Signalled brig *Emilia*. Crossed royal yards.

15—Lat. 38° 21′ long. 13° 59′. Course S. 24° W. Distance 115 miles. Winds variable N.N.E. to N.E. Begins light variable airs and calms. Noon, moderate breeze from N.N.E. Set stunsails. Rove fore topmast stunsail gear.

16—Lat. 35° 20′, long. 15° 49′. Course S. 26° W. Distance 201. Winds N.E. and variable. Moderate breeze, cloudy but fine. P.M., wind variable and light. Sent main topgallant and royal stunsail booms aloft. Crossed skysail yard.

17—Lat. 32° 30′, long. 17° 40′. Course S. 29° W. Distance 194. Winds N.W. to North. Begins light variable and fine; squally. In all stunsails. 6 a.m., saw Madeira, S. by E. 9 a.m., West Point S.S.E., 12 miles.

Nov. 18—Lat. 28° 21′, long. 20° 8′. Course S. 27° W. Distance 280. Winds north and N.N.E. A stiff breeze, squally at times. All starboard studding sails set. P.M., wind moderate.

19—Lat. 24° 42′, long. 22° 32′. Course S. 30° W. Distance 255. Winds N.N.E. to N.E. A moderate breeze and fine. Set port stunsails. Passed several brigs and barques. P.M., wind light.

Nov. 20—Lat. 21° 37'. long. 24° 28.. Course S. 30° W. Distance 214. Winds N.E. to east and variable. A moderate breeze and passing showers. 8 a.m., signalled barque *Mary Ann Holman*, Cardiff to Valparaiso, 17 days out.

21, 1870—Lat. 18° 11' N., long. 25° 59' W. Course S. 23° W. Distance 224. Winds N.N.E., east, E.S.E. Very unsettled, wind flying from N.N.E. to E.S.E. 4.30 a.m., lost fore topmast stunsail boom. In all stunsails. Noon wind more steady from east. P.M., saw St. Antonio. 4 p.m., west end bore S.E. about 18 miles. Stiff breeze and clear.

22—Lat. 13° 57', long. 25° 43'. Course S. 3° E. Distance 255. Wind, east, a stiff breeze and clear. A.M., signalled barque *Batavia*, Amsterdam to Macassar, 17 days out.

23—Lat. 9° 39', long. 24° 32'. Course S. 15° E. Distance 267. Wind E. by S., S.E., calm. Begins stiff breeze and cloudy. Noon, moderate and clear. 8 p.m., shifted to S.E. with black ugly appearance. Midnight rain and calm.

24—Lat. 8° 7', long. 24° 16'. Course S. 10° E. Distance 94 (D.R.). Faint airs and calms with rain. Wind, round the compass. 8.p.m., wind flew to southward in a squall.

25—Lat. 6° 56' long. 23° 32'. Course S. 30° E. Distance 83. Baffling airs and calms with torrents of rain. Noon, dry light breeze from east.

26—Lat. 4° 49', long. 23° 37'. Course S. 10° E. Distance 129. A light breeze from eastward, dry but cloudy.

27—Lat. 3° 15', long. 22° 37'. Course S. 19° E. Distance 100. Faint airs and clear sultry weather. Three ships in sight to eastward.

28—Lat. 2° 49', long. 23° 31'. Course S. 64° W. Distance 60. Mostly calm. Midnight, light breeze from S.E.

29—Lat. 0° 23' N., long. 25° 16'. Course S. 29° W. Distance 181. A moderate breeze from S.E.rd. Shifted upper main topsail and outer jib.

30—Lat. 3° 19' S., long. 27° 10'. Course S. 27° W. Distance 250. Wind S.E. by S., a stiff breeze and fine. Overhauling footropes.

Dec. 1—Lat. 7° 15', long. 28° 56'. Course S. 24° W. Distance 258. Wind, S.E. by S. to S.E. by E., a stiff breeze and fine.

2—Lat. 11° 5', long. 29° 35'. Course S. 9° W. Distance 234. Wind, S.E. by E., moderate and fine. P.M., wind light.

3—Lat. 14° 3'., long. 30° 13'. Course S. 12° W. Distance 182. Very light E.S.E. wind and fine. P.M., variable airs, nearly calm.

4—Lat. 16° 42', long. 29° 40'. Course S. 11° E. Distance 162. Winds, East and S.E. Begins light variable winds. Noon, squally, long swell from southward. P.M., moderate wind and squally.

5—Lat. 20° 38', long. 28° 24'. Course S. 17° E. Distance 247. Winds, E.S.E. and east. Moderate, cloudy with passing squalls. 9.30 a.m., Martin Vaz Rocks, W. by S., 25 miles.

6—Lat. 24° 16', long. 27° 6'. Course S. 18° E. Distance 229. E.S.E. winds to east and E.N.E. P.M., light sometimes, nearly calm. Scraping and cleaning iron bulwarks.

Dec. 7—Lat. 26° 31', long. 25° 41'. Course S. 28½° E. Distance 154. Light, variable and east winds and very unsettled.

8—Lat. 28° 32', long. 24° 16'. Course S. 32° E. Distance 143. Begins light breeze from eastward. Noon, faint airs and calms.

9—Lat. 29° 33', long. 23° 39'. Course S. 24° E. Distance 67. Faint airs and calms.

10—Lat. 29° 54' S., long. 22° 49' W. Course S. 64° E. Distance 48. Faint airs and calms. Sent down mizen topgallant mast and sent up another P.M., light breeze from northward.

11—Lat. 32° 4' S., long. 21° 16'. Course S. 31° E. Distance 152. Light N.N.W. breeze and fine.

12—Lat. 34° 6', long. 19° 24'. Course S. 37½° E. Distance 155. Light wind and variable. Noon, baffling airs and calms. P.M., a most unaccountable sea got up and suddenly from the S.E. Midnight, calm. Ship pitching and rolling; thick fog. S.E.

13—Lat. 35°, long. 18° 20'. Course S. 44° E. Distance 75. Begins faint airs and calms and heavy confused sea. Noon, light breeze from norrard. P.M., moderate breeze.

14—Lat. 37° 54', long. 15° 46'. Course S. 35½° E. Distance 214. Moderate north breeze and fog thick. P.M., wind light and hauled to S.S.W.

15—Lat. 39° 27', long. 13° 53'. Course S. 57° E. Distance 174. Winds, S.W. to north, very light and dull cloudy weather, high westerly swell.

16—Lat. 40° 44', long. 8° 24'. Course S. by E. Distance 125. Fresh, Nly. wind and clear. 4 a.m., saw Gough's Island S.S.E. 6 a.m., passed north end 2 miles offshore.

17—Lat. 41° 42'. long. 3° 26' W. Course S. 78° E. Distance 229. Winds, N. by W., north N.N.E. Moderate breeze, thick fog. Cleaning main deck beams.

18—Lat. 42° 17' S., long. 3° E. Course. S. 83° E. Distance 289. Winds, north, N.N.E. Strong breeze and thick foggy disagreeable weather. In all stunsails.

19—Lat. 42° 16', long. 10° 16' E. Course east. Distance 324. Winds, north strong and thick fog. Noon, fog, cleared away. P.M., wind light.

20—Lat. 42° 27', long. 15° 57'. Course S. 88° E. Distance 258 miles. Winds, N.N.E., N.E., E.N.E., and east. Moderate and fine, heavy swell from W.S.W. Noon, very light. P.M., round to east with thick fog.

21—Lat. 43° 50', long. 19° 3'. Course S. 57° E. 161 miles. Ugly threatening weather. Wind hauled from east to E.S.E., very unsettled, sometimes thick fog, sometimes clear, wind at times blowing a gale then nearly calm. Midnight, wind veered to N.W.

22—Lat. 44° 10', long. 23° 30'. Course S. 84° E. Distance 139. Winds, N.W. by N. to W.S.W. and S.W. Moderate breeze and clear. Midnight, strong breeze. 2 a.m., wind hauled to W.S.W. in a thin misty rain.

23—Lat. 43° 35', long. 30° 45'. Course N. 84° E. Distance 318. Strong breeze and dry weather, S.W., high sea. Shipping much water on deck. P.M., wind fell light and hauled to westward.

Dec. 24—Lat. 43° 30′ S., long. 35° 42′ E. Course east. Distance 216 miles. Winds S.W., N.W., light and fine, high westerly sea, rolling heavily. P.M., showery and fresh breeze.

25—Lat. 43° 29′, long. 41° 45′. Course east. Distance 263. Fresh N.W. breeze and fine, high westerly swell.

26—Lat. 43° 25′, long. 46° 53′. Course east. Distance 225. Begins fresh N.W. breeze and rain. 6 a.m., wind hauled to west. P.M., faint airs and calms from eastward.

27—Lat. 43° 53′, long. 49° 48′. Course S. 29° E. Distance 129. Light and variable airs, thick fog. Noon, fog cleared away.

28—Lat. 43° 32′, long. 56° 19′. Course N. 86° E. Distance 283 miles. Begins fresh Nly. wind. 4 a.m., rain cleared and wind fell light. Noon, dry but cloudy. P.M., wind very light.

29—Lat. 43° 43′, long. 60° 41′. Course S. 87° E. Distance 190. Very light Wly. winds and fine. Noon, calm. Midnight, strong N.E.

30—Lat. 43° 22′, long. 66° 4′. Course N. 85° E. Distance 238. A strong breeze from N.E. Sea very discoloured.

31—Lat. 42° 51′, long. 73° 30′. Course N. 84½° E. Distance 326. Strong N.E. to N.N.E. breeze and dry. All plain sail set. P.M., slight rain, wind hauled to westward.

Jan.   1, 1871—Lat. 42° 37′, long. 79° 20′. Course N. 87° E. Distance 257. Light W.N.W. wind. Pleasant weather. High westerly swell.

2—Lat. 42° 22′, long. 84°. Course N. 86° E. Distance 211. Light W.N.W. wind throughout. Rain at times.

3—Lat. 41° 49′, long. 88° 46′. Course N. 81° E. Distance 215. Light W.N.W. winds with drizzling rain at intervals.

4—Lat. 40° 59′ long. 93° 43′. Course N. 77° E. Distance 229. Winds W. by N., W.N.W. Light winds and fine dry weather.

5—Lat. 39° 31′, long. 99° 15′. Course N. 71° E. Distance 269. Winds W.N.W. to north. A fresh breeze and fine. Noon, drizzling showers. P.M., wind variable and light.

6—Lat. 37° 41′ S., long. 102° 56′ E. Course N. 57° E. Distance 207. Winds N.E., light, unsteady. P.M., calm. In all stunsails.

7—Lat. 36° 44′ S., long. 103° 55′ E. Course N. 40° E. Distance 89. Calm with heavy rain. Noon, light unsteady breeze S.S.W.

8—Lat. 34° 10′, long. 105° 50′. Course N. 51° E. Distance 180. Light variable winds and showery. P.M., fresh breeze S.S.W.

9—Lat. 30° 45′ long. 108° 3′. Course N. 28° E. Distance 237. Wind S.S.W., a fresh breeze and squally.

10—Lat. 27° 38′ long. 109° 19′. Course N. 20° E. Distance 199. Light unsteady winds varying from south to S.E. High S.W. swell.

11—Lat. 23° 59′, long. 110° 16′. Course N. 13° E. Distance 225. A moderate south breeze and fine. Painting bulwarks, etc.

12—Lat. 20° 15′, long. 112° 12′. Course N. 26° E. Distance 250. A pleasant south breeze and fine. P.M., wind very light indeed.

13—Lat. 18° 12′, long. 113° 49′. Course N. 37° E. Distance 154. Very light south wind with clear scorching weather. P.M., calm.

Jan. 14—Lat. 16° 52', long. 114° 44'. Course N. 33° E. Distance 95. Winds N.N.E. east, N.E. Faint variable airs and calms. Noon, wind fresh from E.S.E. P.M., strong squalls from N.E.

15—Lat. 14° 33', long. 115° 56'. Course N 20° E. Distance 149. Moderate winds from east and N.E. This is our S.W. monsoon, supposed to blow here at this season. P.M., calms and squalls.

16—Lat. 13° 34', long. 115° 50'. Course N. 21° E. Distance 63. Light variable airs and calms. Squalls always catching us aback no matter what tack we are on. Wind generally from N.E.

17—Lat. 13° 20', long. 116° 41'. Course N. 73° E. Distance 48. Light variable airs and calms, sultry. P.M., light Sly. breeze.

18—Lat. 11° 48', long. 118° 19'. Course N. 46° E. Distance 133. A light breeze from southward with clear hot weather. Midnight, thunder and much lightning with heavy squalls from N.E.

19—Lat. 11° 14' S., long. 119° 32'. Course N. 74° E. Distance 84. Faint airs S.E., sultry weather. P.M., continuous thunder and lightning and torrents of rain.

20—Lat. 10° 39', long. 120° 16'. Course N. 52° E. Distance 56. Faint airs, calms, thunder, lightning and rain. 5 a.m., saw Sandalwood Island N.E. by N. Noon, Fly Islands N. by W. 19 miles. Burning hot wind round the compass.

21—Lat. 10° 20', long. 121° 17'. Course N. 73° E. Distance 64. Calms. 5 a.m., a squall came right in our teeth. Noon, Savu Island S.E. by E. ¼ E., 22 miles (true).

22—Lat. 9° 35', long. 122° 59'. Course N. 60° E. Distance 112. A fresh breeze from N. by W. to N.N.E. 6 a.m., Keopang (Timor), north end bore S.E. Noon, light winds and squally—squalls mostly from north.

23—Lat. 9° 4', long. 123° 35'. Course N 37° E. Distance 66. Light variable airs, mostly from N.N.E. Found current to set S. by W. 22 miles in the 24 hours.

24—Lat. 8° 32', long. 125° 5'. Course N, 71° E. Distance 95. A light breeze from westward. Steering towards the Ombay Passage between Timor and Ombay Islands. Two ships in sight, which proved to be *Titania* and *Sir Harry Parks*, former from London to Shanghai, latter London to Hongkong. Another ship coming up astern which proves to be *Taeping*, from London for Shanghai. This ship left London 17 days before us, we took her berth after she was loaded. Noon, calms and baffling airs. East end of Ombay bears N.E. 13 miles. Current S. by W. ½ W. 11 miles.

25—Lat. 8° 30' S., long. 125° 17' E. Course N. 82° E. Distance 12. Baffling airs and calms. Ship *Taeping* in company. *Titania* and *Sir Harry Parks* just on sight to westward. Strong currents S. by W. 58 miles. Noon, east end of Ombay N. by W. ½ 10 miles. 2 p.m., got out of the Strait. 4 p.m., strong wind, heavy squalls, wind west and W.N.W.

26—Lat. 5° 1' S., long. 126° 15' E. Course N. 15° E. Distance 218. Begins with strong breeze from W.N.W. with violent squalls, Noon, wind light and very unsteady. P.M., wind from northward steering for Manipa Strait.

w

Jan. 27—Lat. 3° 56', long. 127° 26'. Course N. 47° E. Distance 96. Baffling airs and calms. 4 a.m., heavy squall, Noon, light air from north. A barque in sight to northward. 4 p.m., west end of Boeroe N.N.W. ½ W. 45 miles.

28—Lat. 3° 22' S., long. 127° 22' E. Course N. 6° E. Distance 34. A moderate north breeze right down the Manipa Strait. At 4 a.m. a heavy thunder squall when just in the narrowest of the Strait. Night pitchy dark and with the darkness and lightning it was impossible to see anything. Hove ship to until daylight. At 6 p.m. *Taeping* in sight and American ship *Surprise*, New York to Shanghai, 95 days. Noon, *Titania* came through the Strait with a fair wind while we lay becalmed outside. 1 p.m., breeze from west. 6 p.m., baffling airs. Midnight, calm.

29—Lat. 2° 17' S., long. 127° 45' E. Course N. 19° E. 69 miles. Faint airs and calms, E.N.E. *Titania* and *Taeping* in company to leeward. *Surprise* out of sight astern. P.M., strong breeze from west with rain. 6 p.m., passed Gasses Island, 2 miles off. Midnight, calm.

30—Lat. 0° 58' S., long. 128° 46' E. Course N. 38° E. Distance 100. Faint airs and calms. *Titania* and *Taeping* in company close at hand. Just after noon went on board *Titania*, at 1.30 p.m. returned with Captain Dowdy. 3.30, Captain Dowdy returned to his ship. 7 p.m., a squall from westward with heavy rain.

31—Lat. 0° 18' N., long. 129° 30' E. Course N. 30° E. Distance 88. 4 a.m., light breeze from westward. 7 a.m., passed Geby Island, Gillolo Pass. Noon, faint airs, strong swell from N. and W. *Titania* and *Taeping* a few miles off. Signalled barque *Capiolana* from Cardiff, 130 days out·

Feb. 1—Lat. 0° 55' N., long. 129° 42' E. Course N. 29° E. Distance 42. Not a breath of wind up to noon. *Taeping, Titania* and *Surprise* in company. P.M., a breeze from the N.W.

2—Lat. 1° 40' N., long. 130° 36' E. Course N. 45° E. Distance 78. Begins with a light breeze. 4 a.m., showery and calm. Noon, calm. Current S.E. by S. 14 miles. Only ship in sight is *Surprise*, the *Taeping* and *Titania* having gone out of sight astern yesterday afternoon. P.M., not a breath of wind.

3—Lat. 1° 57' N., long. 130° 51' E. Course N. 42° E. 23 miles. A clock calm. Noon, faint air. *Surprise* in sight. P.M., squall from S.W. with torrents of rain. Current S. by E. 28 miles.

4—Lat. 3° 3' N., long. 130° 56' E. Course N. 5° E. Distance 66. Day-light, calm. Saw Lord North's Island bearing E. by N. 9 miles. Noon, faint airs. Lord North's Island E. ½ S. 10 miles. About 10 a.m. canoes came off with from 6 to 12 men in each. Brought only a few cocoanuts and small shells. They eagerly sought for iron of any description, knives and old clothing. P.M., fresh breeze from N.E.

5—Lat. 4° 31', long. 130° 42'. Course N. 9° W. Distance 89. Fresh from N.E. At 8 a.m., squalls and torrent of rain. Noon, squally, wind flying about from N.E. to S.W. P.M., hard squalls.

Feb. 6—Lat. 7° 2′ Long. 130° 30′. Course N. 4½° W. Distance 152. Begins moderate from N.E. At 8, calm, torrents of rain. Noon. baffling N.E. to S.W. Very confused sea. Midnight, light from N.E.

7—Lat. 9° 16′, long. 130° 38′. Course, N. 4° E. Distance 134. A moderate breeze and dry N.E. to east. P.M., light baffling wind and confused sea.

8—Lat. 11° 13′ N., long. 130° 39′. Course north. Distance 113. Baffling winds and calms, showery. Midnight, fresh from N.E.

9—Lat. 14° 15′ N., long. 129° 52′. Course N.14° W. Distance 188. Very unsettled, sometimes fresh, sometimes nearly calm, with frequent sharp squalls. Ships pitching heavily in a most unaccountably, confused sea and tumbling about but making no progress through the water.

10—Lat. 17° 5′, long. 129° 4′. Course N. 15° W. Distance 176. Winds, north to east. Strong breeze and heavy confused sea.

11—Lat. 20° 10′, long. 128° 14′. Course N. 14½° W. Distance 191. Strong breeze N.E., and E.N.E. Noon, more moderate and much less sea than yesterday. P.M., stiff breeze, fine and clear.

12—Lat. 24° 39′, long. 127° 55′. Course N. 4° W. Distance 270. Strong breeze E.N.E. to east and E.S.E. and clear. 2 a.m., a most unaccountable sharp sea from northward. Ship plunging heavily at times. P.M., squally.

13—Lat. 27° 26′, long. 125° 46′. Course N. 34½° W. Distance 203. Dull and cloudy with rain and fresh breeze from south. 10 a.m., squalls and rain from S.W. Noon, dry, fore topsail tie broke which broke the cap on lower masthead. P.M., light variable winds.

14—Lat. 29° 43′, long. 124° 25′. Course N. 27° W. Distance 154. Got soundings 37 fathoms, dark sand. Light variable wind north, N.E., and N.W. Noon, drizzling rain, no sights, soundings corresponded with dead reckoning. P.M., strong gale from N.W.

15—Lat. 30° 24′, long. 123° 10′. Strong gale with sharp short sea. Wind north. At 9 a.m., tacked close to southward of Leaconna Hummocks. Split main topmast staysail, main topsail tie broke. P.M., more moderate but still blowing hard with a little snow at times.

16—Lat. 31° 32′ N., long. 122° 16′ E. Course N. 33° W. Distance 81. Strong north winds and cloudy with frequent showers of snow. 8 a.m., North Saddle bore W.S.W. 15 miles. Noon, N. Saddle bore south 20 miles. Wind moderate from N.N.E. 4 p.m., got a pilot. 6.30, passed the light vessel. 9.30, anchored in the river.

17—11 a.m., anchored off Shanghai.

W*

APPENDIX VII.

CENTRAL CRIMINAL COURT.

(BEFORE MR. JUSTICE STEPHEN.)

CHARGE OF MURDER ON THE HIGH SEAS.

John Anderson, alias Sydney Smith, 31, described as a seaman, was yesterday charged with the wilful murder of John Francis on May 11 (*sic*) 1880.

Mr. Poland and Mr. Montagu Williams prosecuted on behalf of the Public Prosecutor; the prisoner was defended by Mr. Edward Clarke, Q.C., and Mr. Besley.

The alleged murder. it appeared, was committed two years ago, and under the following circumstances. The prisoner was chief mate of an English vessel, called the *Cutty Sark*, which sailed from London in May, 1880, on a foreign voyage. The deceased, who was a black man, joined the vessel at Cardiff as an able seaman, but after the vessel had been at sea a few days it was discovered that he was unable to perform the duty, and this led to a great deal of unpleasantness on board, and the deceased was not at all on good terms with the crew.

The prisoner was on several occasions very angry with the deceased and used violence to him, but there did not appear to be any doubt that the deceased was very insolent to the prisoner, and had been heard to threaten that he would use a capstan bar to protect himself.

The occurrence in question took place at eleven o'clock (*sic*) on the night of July 11 (*sic*) and the case for the prosecution was that on this night the deceased failed to obey some order that was given to him and the prisoner struck him on the head with a capstan bar and inflicted an injury which caused his death.

When the vessel arrived at a Dutch port the prisoner ran away and found another vessel, and the captain, who was alleged to have assisted the prisoner to make his escape, while the *Cutty Sark* was at sea, committed suicide by jumping overboard, and the prisoner was not heard of until recently when he arrived in London on board another vessel, and he was taken into custody upon the present charge.

Evidence was given in support of the statement of the learned counsel, and it was admitted by them that the deceased was an object of almost general dislike on board the ship on account of his not being able to perform the duties of an able seaman, and it was stated that the prisoner frequently called the deceased an imposter and asked him to jump overboard, as he was of no use on board the vessel. It was admitted that the deceased had been very insolent to the prisoner at the time the assault was committed, and that he had told the prisoner that he had got a capstan bar ready for him if he came near him.

The prisoner upon this, it appeared, went towards the deceased and at the same instant the capstan bar was raised and the fatal blow was inflicted upon the deceased.

The prisoner appeared to have stated at the time that the deceased had, in the first instance, raised the capstan bar to strike him, and he afterwards said that the nigger would not raise any more capstan bars against him. It appeared that when the captain was informed what had occurred he said it served the deceased right.

In cross-examination it was elicited that the witness had given a very different account of the transaction in the official log of the vessel.

Mr. Justice Stephen, after hearing the facts, expressed his opinion that the evidence was hardly sufficient to support a charge of wilful murder, although it was abundant to support the minor charge of manslaughter.

Mr. Clarke said he could not resist a conviction upon that charge. The jury consequently found the prisoner guilty of manslaughter.

Mr. Clarke urged in mitigation of punishment the previous good character of the prisoner, and also that at the time of the occurrence he was placed in a position of great difficulty and danger, and that he was responsible at the moment for the safety of the vessel and the crew, which were endangered by the conduct of the deceased. Several respectable witnesses, many of whom had known the prisoner nearly all his life, were called to speak to his character, and they described him as a most humane and kind man.

Mr. Justice Stephen, in passing sentence, said that the case was a very painful one, and while giving full effect to the good character the prisoner had received, and also taking into consideration the fact that the deceased had behaved very ill and had given him a great deal of provocation on several occasions, still he felt it his duty to pass a sentence of considerable severity, and it was with great pain that he ordered him to be kept in penal servitude for seven years.

One of the witnesses as to character was John Willis, who did what he could to help his officer. I believe that the mate would have been let off with a much lighter sentence if he had not declared that he would do the same thing again given the same circumstances.

The mate spent his time in prison at work on the Dover breakwater, of which he used to say he knew every stone. On coming out of prison he went straight to John Willis, who managed to get him a billet as bosun acting second mate on a vessel bound out to Australia.

He had all his way to make again for his ticket and certificates had, of course, been taken from him when he was sentenced. On arrival in Australia he went up for his second mate's ticket. In gaining this, he was very lucky: it so happened that both he and his examiner were Bluecoat boys, and as soon as the latter found this out and was told the reason why such an old man was applying for a second mate's ticket, he did his best to help the unfortunate Smith, with the result that although he had forgotten a great deal of his navigation whilst in prison, the ex-mate passed his examination.

Sidney Smith had plenty of grit and slowly worked his way up to a command, his last ship being that oil-tank the *Navahoe*, which with her attendant tow-boat, was nicknamed "the horse and cart of the Atlantic."

As a skipper he was spoken of as a "regular hard old case," with that flavour of the bluff story-book mariner, whose type is now practically extinct. Smith retired from the sea on a pension from the Anglo-American Oil Company.

In February, 1922, when 73 years of age, he was operated upon for cancer, and did not survive the operation.

He died facing fate with the old Bucko spirit which feared neither man nor devil.—AUTHOR.

APPENDIX VIII.

Cargoes Loaded by the "Cutty Sark" 1870-1895.

OUTWARD CARGOES.

19 General—(18 from London, 1 from Antwerp) 3 to Shanghai, 3 to Newcastle, N.S.W., 1 to Melbourne, 1 to Brisbane, 11 to Sydney.
1 Case Oil—26816 cases from New York to Samarang.
1 Scrap Iron—from London to Shanghai.
1 Coal—from Penarth for Yokohama, discharged at Singapore.

HOMEWARD CARGOES.

8 Tea—4 from Shanghai, 4 from Hankow, all to London.
2 Jute—1 from Manila, 1 from Zebu, both for New York.
1 Joggery
  Myrabolams } from Madras, Bimlipatam and Coconada to London.
  Horns.
12 Wool—3 from Newcastle, N.S.W., 1 from Brisbane, 8 from Sydney; 10 to London, 1 to Antwerp, 1 to Hull.

INTERMEDIATE CARGOES.

8 Coal—from Sydney to Shanghai.
1 Coal—from Nagasaki to Shanghai.
1 Tea—from Calcutta to Melbourne.
1 Rice—from Bangkok to Hongkong.
1 General—from New York to London.

DETAILS OF CHINA TEA CARGOES.

Loaded June 1870—1,305,812 lbs. at Shanghai.
  ,,   Sept. 1871—1,315,100 ,,   ,,
  ,,   June 1872—1,303,000 ,,   ,,
  ,,   July 1873—1,353,072 ,,   ,,
  ,,   June 1874—1,270,651 ,,   Hankow.
  ,,   June 1875—1,347,699 ,,   ,,
  ,,   July 1876—1,375,364 ,,   ,,
  ,,   June 1877—1,334,000 ,,   ,,

DETAILS OF AUSTRALIAN WOOL CARGOES.

Loaded December 1883—4289 bales at Newcastle, N.S.W.
  ,,   December 1884—4300 ,,   ,,
  ,,   October   1885—4465 ,,   Sydney.
  ,,   March   1887—4296 ,,   ,,
  ,,   December 1887—4515 ,,   Newcastle, **N.S.W.**
  ,,   October   1888—4496 ,,   Sydney
  ,,   November 1889—4577 ,,   ,,
  ,,   December 1890—4617 ,,   ,,
  ,,   November 1891—4636 ,,   ,,
  ,,   January   1893—4723 ,,   ,,
  ,,   December 1893—5010 ,,   ,,
  ,,   December 1894—5304* ,,   Brisbane.

* Concerning the stowage of this record cargo, F. T. Brown, the stevedore, wrote to the press, as follows:—

"Captain Woodget had a book containing the number of bales in every half longer in the ship as stowed in Sydney and was constantly referring to it as the work went on here; at the time the average weight of bales shipped in Brisbane was greater than those he had been used to in Sydney, and as the work proceeded it became doubtful whether the ship would be able to load herself full; there was very little scoured wool offering, so the agents secured undumped wool at higher rates. Some of these went up to 600 pounds weight. Finally when the ship was finished, Plimsoll was about two inches under water. In the whole of my forty years' experience I have never known any other ship to go down to her load-line with a full cargo of wool.

"The skipper reminded me occasionally that the ship was not being half screwed, but towards the finish I got level with him by remarking that I would have to go easy with the screws as the shipping inspector would probably stop the loading before she was full. For once in his life he was beaten, and wore a worried look for a day or two, fearing that I would get a little more out of the ship by slack screwing. However, she was screwed hard from start to finish."

INDEX

:02

CUTTY SARK

GREENWI

NatWest STREAMLINE

437432   T17305103

04-96   14.95 14:23

3 X

MASTERCARD

5300000441968

R2880

C/BARK SALE

£66.45

NatWest STREAMLINE

CODE:028944

SE RETAIN RECEIPT

NK YOU

NatWest